ON THE IMPORTANCE
OF BEING AN INDIVIDUAL
IN RENAISSANCE
ITALY

HANEY FOUNDATION SERIES

A volume in the Haney Foundation Series, established in 1961
with the generous support of Dr. John Louis Haney

ON THE
IMPORTANCE
OF BEING AN INDIVIDUAL
IN RENAISSANCE
ITALY

Men, Their Professions,
and Their Beards

DOUGLAS BIOW

PENN

University of Pennsylvania Press
Philadelphia

Published by
University of Pennsylvania Press
Philadelphia, Pennsylvania 19104-4112
www.upenn.edu/pennpress

Printed in the United States of America on acid-free paper

1 3 5 7 9 10 8 6 4 2

A Cataloging-in-Publication record is available from the Library of Congress
ISBN 978-0-8122-4671-1

To
Simone, Erica, and Giulia,
because I promised them I'd dedicate
my next book to them,

To
Annabelle and Annamaria,
because they came into my life
while I completed this book,

&

To
David,
because he would probably
be somewhat miffed
if he weren't in the dedication

Why, look you now, how unworthy a thing you make of me! You would play upon me. You would seem to know my stops. You would pluck out the heart of my mystery. You would sound me from my lowest note to the top of my compass. And there is much music, excellent voice, in this little organ, yet cannot you make it speak? 'Sblood, do you think I am easier to be played on than a pipe? Call me what instrument you will, though you can fret me, yet you cannot play upon me.

—William Shakespeare, *Hamlet*

Reflection shows us that our image of happiness is thoroughly colored by the time to which the course of our existence has assigned us.

—Walter Benjamin, *Thesis on the Philosophy of History*

Brian *(shouting to his followers)*: Look, you've got it all wrong. You don't need to follow me. You don't need to follow anyone. You've got to think for yourselves. You're all individuals.

Followers *(shouting back in unison)*: Yes. We're all individuals.

Brian: You're all different.

Followers: Yes. We are all different.

A male follower: I'm not.

Another follower *(hushing him)*: Shh, shh, shh.

—Monty Python, *Life of Brian*

CONTENTS

❧

PREFACE

❧

THIS BOOK REFLECTS ON THE IMPORTANCE OF THE NOTION OF THE INDIVIDUAL in the Italian Renaissance, with an "individual" understood as someone with a mysterious, inimitable quality, a signature style, and/or a particular, identifying mode of addressing the world. More specifically, it examines how the notion of the individual was important for a variety of men in the Italian Renaissance, both men who belonged to the elite and those who aspired to be part of it, as a way of understanding, characterizing, and representing themselves and others, both "real" and "fictional" others. At the same time, this book explores the individual in light of the new patronage systems, educational programs, and work opportunities that had come into place and in the context of an increased investment in professionalization, the changing status of artisans and artists, shifting attitudes about the ideology of work, technological advances, the collecting habits of people with significant disposable incomes, new dominant fashions among men, an increased concern for etiquette, and the eventual rise of court culture in the sixteenth century. Moreover, scholars, beginning with the cultural historian Jacob Burckhardt in his foundational essay *The Civilization of the Renaissance in Italy*, have not—this book shows—always adequately appreciated how complex and sometimes deliberately mystifying the notion of the individual in the period actually was. Nor have they always sufficiently recognized how that notion permeated simultaneously so many different areas of expertise, from the visual arts to the medical arts to the intellectual arts of the humanists, and how it pervaded so many different visual and verbal forms, from works of imaginative literature to treatises to paintings to fashion.

The overriding concern of this book, then, has been not to resuscitate in any form or manner a Burckhardtian view of the Renaissance individual. Rather, it has been to reconsider how valuable the notion of the individual was for some men who lived and worked in Renaissance Italy and, at the same time, to reassess the value of thinking about the notion of the individual in the period generally. This notion, it is important to emphasize from the outset, has largely, if not at times completely, fallen out of favor when we talk about identities in the period. And it has come under serious attack over the past few decades. A good deal of that attack has come from the so-called New Historicists, primarily literary-trained scholars associated with Stephen Greenblatt and his project of "cultural poetics," which is deeply invested in a variety of anthropological, Marxist, and postmodern critical theories but principally those that locate identity as a cultural product endlessly constructed and performed in light of a person's historically determined subject position. However, some of the reason that the notion of the individual has fallen out of favor over the past decades has to do, in part at least, with the work of scholars engaged in social history. Social history itself, which is still for every good reason a significant force in the academy even with the formidable rise of cultural history, does not per se call into question the importance of the individual or deny the existence of individuals in periods. Indeed, one key, vital aim of social history, which is dedicated to examining and tracing macro structures, has been to comprehend better the limits within which individual agency may or may not occur, for many social historians—of various liberation movements, for example—actually see agency as a crucial category at the individual as well as collective level. And yet as social historians have labored hard to explain large-scale trends and developments, drawing on the insights and methodologies of sociologists, they have also nevertheless offered generalizations at the macro level that tend to break down at the individual level. As a result, the individual has virtually disappeared from their narratives and consequently, in time, faded from view. This is even true, up to a point, with respect to microhistory, which focuses on the individual less as an individual, and certainly not as a means for investigating the notion of the individual itself, and more as a vehicle for understanding different sorts of interwoven intellectual, cultural, legal, and social trends that macrohistorians have neglected, shown little interest in, or traditionally had difficulty accessing in their studies.

As this book works to rehabilitate the notion of the individual, it also seeks to provide an historical explanation for why certain things took place in the period, in particular why certain momentous changes concerning the individual took place when and where they did, especially as these matters are addressed in the first chapter of this book, which is by far the lengthiest of them all. Yet the historian's task, it is also fair to say, is not always to explain *why* something took place in the past, although that is always a desirable and ultimate goal. A good deal of the historian's task is to just try to document *that* something had taken place, to disclose its complexities, unveiling them as deftly as possible for the reader, and to make a case for its overall importance. Surely scholars of the Italian Renaissance have to face that sort of issue over and over again. For a host of strong explanatory models that historians have put forth to try to account for why the Renaissance itself emerged in Italy when it did, in roughly the mid-1300s, have fallen to the wayside over the years or have been found wanting in one way or another. Scholars, to be sure, will continue to debate and debunk each other's explanatory models. Yet scholars of the Italian Renaissance still persist in documenting and arguing that there was in fact a Renaissance in Italy and that it differed from "renaissances" elsewhere, both before and after, even though to this day it remains such a vexing issue for scholars to try to explain convincingly why the Italian Renaissance happened when and where it did in Europe. So, mutatis mutandis, it is with this book: the notion of the individual did indeed have cultural force in the period for many men, it did matter to them, and it did manifest itself in extremely complex and often novel ways. To that end, if this book has successfully documented that fact as indeed a fact (despite the claims of many historians—as well as literary scholars—to the contrary), then *On the Importance of Being an Individual in Renaissance Italy* has done its main job, even if it cannot always provide a satisfactory, strong explanatory model to account for all historical changes.

Finally, to adopt a much more personal mode of address, I feel compelled to say something in this preface about the book's focus strictly on men—an issue significant enough to warrant frank discussion here. For a host of scholarly studies dedicated in great measure to the notion of the individual in the Italian Renaissance, much less the European Renaissance, were written principally by men about men. And those books were written often enough, as in the case of Burckhardt's key essay, with the presumed, and somewhat anachronistic, identification of male authors with their male subjects. Consequently, for some readers, those books inevitably shaped a view that the notion of the individual in the Renaissance was and should be associated strictly with men. For the record, I do not share this view. There were, as I see it, male *and* female individuals in the period, each operating within a variety of gendered and institutional constraints and power relations that determined and conditioned agency. Were I looking at primarily or uniquely women in this book, for instance, I'd be forced to engage in a serious manner the history of domesticity along with, among other areas, the history of letter writing and the like. However, even if I do not endorse a male-inflected view of the notion of the individual, I may well seem to do so just by writing this book because its focus is exclusively on men. And that is an objection to this book that no position statement placed in a preface can ever preemptively forestall, even as it exercises self-conscious critical detachment about matters of gender and authorial identification. In any event, if this book achieves anything, it demonstrates that we should not shy away from embracing the notion of the individual when it comes to looking at either men *or* women in the Italian Renaissance. More important, it shows that if we dismiss the notion of the individual from our narratives of the European Renaissance in general, as so many scholars have done over the past few decades, we do so at the peril of significantly impoverishing our understanding of the past.

∽

Introduction

I BEGIN WITH A REFLECTION, AND A DECIDEDLY PERSONAL ONE AT THAT. Some time ago, in the late 1970s, long before I embarked on a career in the humanities or even ventured to imagine doing so, when a host of fascinating topics of highly specialized scholarly interest were not even remotely on my mind or, for that matter, in some cases even circulating as topics of widespread interest in the academy, I began working my way through Bach's solo violin sonatas and partitas in bucolic Bennington, Vermont, doing the best I could on my own with those complex pieces of music. One day, thinking I had sufficiently mastered the opening adagio of the first sonata, I performed it as a surprise for my teacher, a remarkable and generous violist—the late Jacob Glick—who sat in his office with his oversized hands drooping over the ends of his armchair, as if he were wearing worn, leathery baseball mitts that didn't quite fit. No sooner had I finished playing than he rose, shaking his head, and told me in so many words that it was a mess. I could play the notes well enough, which was no small achievement given that there were a lot of challenging chords to try to master, but I was not keeping time. Worse, my refusal (or inability) to adhere to what was written on the score, to play metrically what Bach wanted and not what I somehow felt should rhythmically be played, bothered him to no end. It was then that he asked me a question, arguably more aptly framed by a social scientist than a classical musician, as he walked over to the piano and put on the metronome. "What," he inquired, "is your definition of freedom?"

His question went to the heart of the matter of not just classical music but, it dawned on me, much of life itself, for we all ultimately have to deal with the various constraints that bind us and constitute us, whether we are always entirely aware of this fact or not. And as I dutifully redoubled my efforts to work my way through the challenging notes yet again, with the ticktock, ticktock of the metronome now beating out time in precise, equal measure and the prison bars of the musical score oppressively facing me, it occurred to me—years before I had ever learned about the sociological concepts of "structure," "agency," and "habitus"—that what we do within the limits of those constraints in our everyday lives and practices directly speaks to how we are able to locate some measure of freedom and find the means to express and explore our own "individuality"; exhibit our personal mode of phrasing given our deeply ingrained, acculturated dispositions; and experience and enact in our bodies our peculiar habit of addressing the world through whatever instruments we possess. Then, a few months later, when I was about to graduate from college and the same teacher was encouraging me to think, with generous but misplaced optimism, of pursuing a career as a classical musician, he said something else that seemed particularly relevant. He insisted that if I ever joined an orchestra that I should play at least one hour a day on my own so that, as he put it, I would continue to hear my own individual voice—or at least the distinctive voice of my violin—and not lose it in the all-encompassing and seductive mass of orchestral sound.

Both these observations strike me as noteworthy, particularly in a period in which we have made some serious scholarly investment within the humanities in dismantling the notion that we each have a core, individual identity, some essential, distinctive character and personal style that make us who we are, often enough taking grim delight in the intellectual thrill of sawing through the branch, as David Lodge once wryly put it, on which we sit.[1] In large measure—according to this somewhat dire vision—selfhood was, is, and always will be purely a dynamic cultural and discursive construct that we must constantly and endlessly deconstruct in all our blindness and insight precisely because it was, is, and always will be just that: a construct. But my former teacher's observations also seem to me germane to some of the concerns covered in this book as we turn back the clock to the Italian Renaissance in six chapters, leaving as best we can the (post)modern world for the largely early modern one and laboring to understand that distinct and distant world on its own terms, although occasionally pausing to gauge in the process how the past relates to, yet still dramatically differs from, the present.

For this book is in part (and I should reiterate that it is only in part) about the mystery that lies at the heart of individual identity, a mystery that remains steadfastly and resiliently "there" even when, or precisely when, we think as Rosencrantz and Guildenstern presumptuously did that we can securely pluck out someone's mystery, play people as if they were mere empty wooden pipes with apparently simple stops to them, as if they possessed no intrinsically distinctive, individual quality—a special tone or timber all their own, as it were—that makes them at times unfathomable and impossible to pin down by even the most inquisitive and perspicacious minds. Because if I am not altogether mistaken in reflecting on my own life experiences, this really isn't the case about people once we take into consideration the many and varied constraints within which we all operate and that shape us in a host of extremely complex ways. For there is, I contend, something mysterious that makes people who they are, both now, in twenty-first-century America, and back then, in the period covered in this book, when a host of entirely different historically determined constraints fashioned people and enabled some of them to try to figure out who they and others—both in practice and in essence—were.

Hence this book, the broad aim of which is to examine through the disciplines of art, literary, intellectual, medical, and cultural history how male identities were conceptualized in Renaissance Italy, where the European Renaissance is conventionally thought to have begun. This is by no means a new topic in contemporary Renaissance studies generally. Both Stephen Greenblatt and John Jeffries Martin, for instance, have vigorously revised Jacob Burckhardt's famous, although justly contested, notion that a free, untrammeled, "individual" self emerged in Renaissance Italy in contradistinction to the constrained, collective, "corporate" self of the Middle Ages. Albeit in strikingly different ways, both Greenblatt and Martin have construed identity—for the most part a distinctly male identity—as a dialectic between, on the one hand, a self formed by historically determined cultural constraints and, on the other hand, a self formed in reaction against those powerful cultural forces (forces, to be sure, that both enable it to come into being and always condition it). The interests of both scholars have been largely on the first side of the dialectic. They have thus tended to focus on the cultural factors that shaped the self, such as institutions, rituals, and sodalities, even though Greenblatt has discussed at length the period's growing interest in the values of self-reflection, wonder, and privacy, while Martin has explored in detail such things as the values of sincerity, emotional transparency, and interiority, along with varying notions of intimacy and inner character in ways that resonate felicitously with my own manner of thinking.[2]

To some extent, then, my book is a polemic, taking issue with Greenblatt and (to a far lesser degree) Martin, as well as with a variety of scholars, by examining the other, oppositional side of the dialectic without denying the centrality of Renaissance culture in both shaping and constraining individual male identities.[3] More specifically, I want to look at (1) how certain men emphasized that a special mysterious quality—an "I don't know what" (*nescio quid*)—defined extraordinary male individuals and underwrote their ability to succeed brilliantly as professionals applying an art (*ars/arte*) as a form of highly specialized knowledge; (2) how they asserted themselves as individuals through an intensely aggressive, personalized voice and/or signature style in the practical and productive arts; and (3) how they highlighted the particularity with which they or others performed their identities as individuals in the context of a broad cultural fashion. In distinctly different ways, then, this book explores the significance of the notion of the individual for an understanding of the Italian Renaissance conception of male identity without, however, subscribing to Burckhardt's widely discredited (and for him, as it turns out, deeply pessimistic) view that the individual in the period was an autonomous agent operating freely in the world, much less Burckhardt's equally discredited argument that the modern individual emerged for the first time more or less in fourteenth-century Italy as a radically new phenomenon.[4] At the same time, in focusing on men and male identities, my aim in this book is not to gainsay the fact that women offered both impressive and often novel ways of expressing their identities within collectivities in the Italian Renaissance, as the studies of a number of literary and cultural historians have increasingly and amply demonstrated in the past few decades.[5] Quite the contrary, my aim, as announced in the preface, is to enhance our understanding of how male identities were conceived, and could be conceived, with the hope that some of my observations may be of use to scholars working more exclusively on women, along with the hope that perhaps some of those observations may indirectly contribute to our understanding of how the notion of the individual itself in the period was gendered in complex ways.

To examine these issues, I have divided this book into three parts, each of which contains two chapters centered on a single topic that is explored from different, yet complementary, angles. My focus in these parts has been principally on the sixteenth century because during that period, for reasons that will become evident as the book unfolds, we witness in Italy a marked increase in the investment in the individual among men in a broad array of activities—an investment that will flower in the seventeenth century in the visual arts, for instance, in the cult of the individual. Moreover, as we move from one part to another of this book, we should bear in mind the following: Although the word "individuo" was broadly understood in the Italian Renaissance to mean "indivisible," as it is defined in the *Vocabolario degli Accademici della Crusca* (*Lexicon of the Academy of the Crusca*, 1612) in light of standard usages of the word as a "dialectical term" in, say, theological argumentation,[6] during the same period the word "individuo" also began to acquire the more familiar modern meaning, which first gained currency in England in the mid- to late 1600s, of "distinguished from others by attributes of its own," "marked by a peculiar and striking character," and "pertaining or peculiar to a single person or thing or some one member of a class" (*Oxford English Dictionary*). In this regard, it is worth noting that the word "individuo" is also furnished with the meaning of "cosa particolare" ("a particular/specific/identifying thing") in the *Vocabolario della*

Crusca and eventually provided with apposite examples from the sixteenth century in later editions,[7] all of which suggests that sometime in the late Renaissance the word "individuo" in Italy began to acquire the meaning we might roughly associate with it today, at least in a very generic way.[8] In any event, it is hardly necessary for a word to have been actively and pervasively used in a period in order for it to serve as a placeholder for scholars talking about a concept that otherwise possessed meaning in some measure for people in the past. We customarily employ the words "selfhood," "agency," "interiority," and "subjectivity," for instance, to talk about matters related to identity in the European Renaissance generally, even though those particular words were hardly current in the period either, at least as we are accustomed to conceptualizing them today. That said, one of the principal burdens of this book is to demonstrate that some men in Renaissance Italy thought in terms of the concept of the "individual," that it was a concept that thus had significant cultural force in the period, and that a number of men expressed themselves as individuals through the verbal and visual means that they had at their disposal. It is *not* a burden of this book to argue for the notion that the concept of the individual in the Enlightenment, Romantic, or post-Romantic sense of the term as it has been explored in the modern disciplines of philosophy and sociology emerged for the first time in Renaissance Italy, a period that runs, I take it, from roughly 1350 to 1600. Nor is it a burden of this book to trace a genealogy of the concept of the individual from the Italian Renaissance to the modern era, however much it occasionally draws comparisons between the present and the past in an effort to articulate salient convergences and differences.

Part I focuses on a topic of broad cultural interest of the period: professionalism. It shows how a few men primarily in the sixteenth century deliberately mystified the success of masterful individuals in a profession—a profession that was, to be sure, collectively defined by, as, and for a male group. In Chapter 1, "Professionally Speaking: The Value of *Ars* and *Arte* in Renaissance Italy—Reflections on the Historical Reach of *Techne*," I examine both Baldassare Castiglione's landmark *Il cortegiano* (*The Courtier*) and Benvenuto Cellini's *Due trattati di oreficeria e scultura* (*Two Treatises on Goldsmithing and Sculpture*) as complex discourses written by practitioners who appear to invite everyone interested in the profession to participate in it by openly disclosing the rules of their arts. At the same time, however, Castiglione and Cellini reveal that only a privileged group of unique men, a select few who already somehow possess a certain mysterious, innate quality (effectively a *nescio quid*), can successfully master the art of the profession in question so that they emerge as not just exemplary individuals but inimitable ones worthy of admiration and wonder. In Chapter 2, "Reflections on Professions and Humanism in Renaissance Italy and the Humanities Today," I examine principally Ermolao Barbaro's *De officio legati* (*On the Duty of the Ambassador*), Niccolò Machiavelli's *Il principe* (*The Prince*), Francesco Guicciardini's *Ricordi* (*Maxims and Reflections*), Torquato Tasso's *Il secretario* (*The Secretary*), and, once more, albeit briefly, Castiglione's *Il cortegiano*. My aim here is to demonstrate how five different men who were either humanists or greatly indebted to humanism engaged the topic of professional identity in their writings. They did so, I argue, to reveal how certain individuals, thanks in large measure to that enigmatic *nescio quid*, manage to succeed in a profession while others prove only moderately adept at it or else fail miserably in it. In this way the authors here examined mystify the very process by which a person can acquire the skills necessary to achieve professional mastery through the diligent application of an art.

Part II focuses on the topic of "mavericks" in the context of issues related to professional self-definition, concentrating more exclusively on test cases of individuals in the paired chapters: one test case focuses on a doctor working in the practical arts, the other a painter working in the productive arts. Specifically, this part of the book examines how two men—the surgeon/physician Leonardo Fioravanti and the painter Jacopo Tintoretto—embedded themselves in Venetian culture and owed their identities in great measure to their strong associations with the institutions, customs, and sodalities of that city while, at the same time, they worked hard to stand out from it as individuals in their chosen professions. In the process, they often challenged the professional or local cultures in which they labored and to which they were indebted for their sense of themselves as individuals. Fioravanti did so in the process of fashioning an aggressive and highly personalized voice in print, Tintoretto in the process of fashioning an aggressive and highly personalized style in painting. In Chapter 3, the first chapter of the two in this part, "Constructing a Maverick Physician in Print: Reflections on the Peculiar Case of Leonardo Fioravanti's Writings," I examine how a radical empiric openly challenges the institutionalized practices of medicine and its elite, bookish, Latin-based culture. Fioravanti does so by taking advantage of the thriving book industry of Venice and aggressively presenting himself through the medium of print culture and in the popularizing language of the vernacular as a unique—indeed, a rather defiant and iconoclastic—individual operating within his chosen profession of medicine. In Chapter 4, "Visualizing Cleanliness, Visualizing Washerwomen in Venice and Renaissance Italy: Reflections on the Peculiar Case of Jacopo Tintoretto's *Jews in the Desert*," I turn to a male painter who incorporates into a large religious canvas the prominent image of washerwomen as gendered symbols of Venetian refinement, purity, and piety. At the same time, he aggressively asserts his individuality in the unique manner in which he renders those washerwomen by placing them conspicuously in the center of his canvas. In this way, they function not only as symbols of the myth of Venice (that is, of the uniqueness of Venice as a harmonious republic in which the individual is ideally suppressed in favor of an all-embracing social and religious collectivity) but also as symbols of the uniqueness of Tintoretto himself—a uniqueness that defines him within Venetian culture as a maverick artist who stands out from the collectivity and feels free to assert his individuality through a signature style, in particular by focusing on the lower classes in a novel way.

In the first two parts we move from a matter of broad cultural concern for a variety of men ("professionalism") to specific, individual cases of two male professionals in the practical and productive arts (the "mavericks" Fioravanti and Tintoretto). In the third and final part we concentrate more narrowly on a single distinguishing physical sign associated strictly with men as we also move from matters that are primarily intellective in nature (humanism and theories of knowledge underpinning the arts, for instance, in Part I) to those that have to do more conspicuously with the body (anatomical dissections and the physical work of a painter, for instance, in Part II). To this end, Part III focuses on the topic of "beards" in order to explore the performative practices of certain individuals as they both assert and define themselves within collectivities by claiming to have specific identities unequivocally rooted in the male body. In particular, Part III focuses on the dominant, widespread fashion among elite men in sixteenth-century Italy of wearing beards, examining how that particular fashion took hold and was coded in a variety of imaginative works, both visual and verbal. That encoding, I argue, allowed men a way of bodily marking through their self-presentations not just their group identities but also individual ones. In Chapter 5, the first chapter of Part III, "Facing the Day: Reflections on a Sudden Change in Fashion and the Magisterial Beard," I examine a series of portrait paintings, including those by Agnolo Bronzino of Duke Cosimo I de' Medici, to demonstrate how certain elite men yearned to conform to *and* distinguish themselves from collectivities as they fashioned their beards on their faces, choosing from and manipulating a dazzling array of designs and shapes. Through beard design, in other words, they asserted their own particularity as individuals, in carefully crafted, public self-presentations, within the context of a fashion that was widely accepted by collectivities and that aligned them with them. In Chapter 6, "Manly Matters: Reflections on Giordano Bruno's *Candelaio*, and the Theatrical and Social Function of Beards in Sixteenth-Century Italy," I turn to a bawdy comic play to examine how the numerous beards worn in it reinforce male collective identity, particularly as the male characters act out stock roles in the very moment that they adopt a fashion that marks them bodily as men. At the same time, the appropriation of someone else's identifying beard as a form of disguise by one male character within the play only serves to remind us that at least one man has—or, more important, *feels* he has—a specific identity that separates him from everyone else and is rooted in his particular, individual body—a distinctly singular corporeal identity that is nevertheless always at risk of being stolen and then counterfeited in a highly social public performance.

Now if a primary focus of this book is to explore the importance of being an individual in the Italian Renaissance, another focus—a less dominant yet still prevalent one rendered evident in the book's subtitle—is to reflect on male identities in the period. To do so, I examine writings and works of visual art produced by and for men who belonged to the cultural elite or aspired to be part of it. To this end, two general guiding presuppositions underlie this book when it comes to thinking about masculinity in Renaissance Italy.[9]

> ∾ First, although maleness was conventionally associated with such things as war, dominance, politics, reason, order, form, testicular fertility, heat, stability, and restraint, whereas femininity, conversely, was associated with such things as love, submissiveness, domesticity, emotions, excess, matter, vaginal receptivity, cold, instability, and intemperance, both male writers and visual artists of the period consciously toyed with these and other logical oppositions as they explored issues of gender. Visual and verbal art in this way not only reflected male identities but also gave shape to them as part of an ongoing process of definition and redefinition in a world that was, for all intents and purposes, economically, socially, politically, and ideologically male dominated and male centered. As a result, we witness throughout the Italian Renaissance a wide range of codifications of what constituted maleness in visual and verbal forms, thereby offering men a variety of ways of responding to the tacit injunction that a man should indeed behave as a man.
>
> ∾ Second, as represented within the context of a variety of verbal and visual forms, men were performing their maleness not only for women but also for each other. Sometimes they did so to coerce one another into behaving in a certain way, sometimes to redefine the norms of masculinity, sometimes to forge a group identity as men, and sometimes to stand out as individuals among men. To this end, women could function as enablers in a variety of verbal and visual forms, effectively allowing men through their presence to be men and act as men, to engage one another as men, and, last but not least, to distinguish themselves from one another as men and as different sorts of men—as

well as, to be sure, from women. In this regard, the calculated presence
of women in visual and verbal forms at times allowed men to exhibit
the origins of their own originality through a process not just of group
male identification but also of heightened self-individuation. Furthermore, if in visual and verbal forms it was often imagined that maleness
had to be actually manifested (by wearing armor, say, or by producing
hairs/heirs, by engaging in duels, or, for that matter, by ejaculating the
generative fluid of semen), it was also imagined that maleness was
something that inhered in the person's character and could be
construed as something that did not, in fact, always need to find
continuous material expression. Men, that is, could be men just by
refusing to reveal what they thought, by remaining silent, by dissimulating, by being, in a sense, surreptitious, duplicitous, and coy.

These two presuppositions are certainly not intended to embrace everything
that has to do with male identity in the Italian Renaissance, and they are neither
uniformly nor systematically examined in this book. But they do inform it, and
they surface with differing degrees of emphasis in the chapters that follow. Both
these presuppositions, moreover, address a fundamental concept that underpins
this book in various ways as we think about masculinities as a plurality as
opposed to a tightly bracketed, singular concept of masculinity: maleness in the
Italian Renaissance existed across a broad spectrum of possibilities. Maleness
was thus understood to be a fluid and dynamic concept, as well as something
that could be conceived at times as elusive.

There are, in addition, a variety of other issues that structurally and themati-
cally hold this book together and collectively enrich it as the three parts unfold.
They include such issues as how rhetoric, imitation, and exemplarity played a
key role in identity formation; how certain human body parts were shaped and
adjusted as a matter of self-fashioning; how decorum in the Italian Renaissance
was aggressively codified yet repeatedly and purposely breached; how rivalries
in the arts played themselves out in a variety of ways and powerfully shaped
identities; how social mobility was realized and fantasized about; how marveling
and wonder pervaded Italian Renaissance culture; how the concept of *politia*
(politeness, cleanliness, elegance, polish) functioned in defining personal and
communal boundaries; how terribly vulnerable elite men felt in court culture;
and how sexual desire was routinely performed. But the core issues outlined
earlier, particularly in the paragraphs providing a breakdown of the three parts,
are for the most part the crucial ones that constitute the overriding argument
of the book, which is largely about the importance of being an individual in
light of the period's conceptualizing of male identities, as well as the importance

of thinking about the value of the term "individual" in literary and historical studies generally.

Finally, a word about men, or rather how I refer to them in this book. Often enough I refer to them, not surprisingly, as "men," pure and simple. But more often than not I refer to them as "writers," "painters," "goldsmiths," "practitioners," "artists," "artisans," "scholars," "physicians," "surgeons," "anatomists," "humanists," "professionals," "functionaries," "lawyers," "secretaries," "ambassadors," "architects, "engineers," "cooks," "barbers," "soldiers," "the cultural elite," "entrepreneurs," "leaders," "charlatans," "quacks," or, for that matter, just "people," without necessarily employing the defining modifier "male" to identify them as strictly men. My aim in doing so is not to reduce everyone tout court in the Italian Renaissance, however they are identified or labeled, to a single gender category. Rather, my aim was to avoid belaboring a fact abundantly clear to anyone reading this book, which, not to put too fine a point on it, is all about men and male identities in an unquestionably male-dominated and paternalistic culture and society. Moreover, it seems to me that to emphasize over and over again through various mechanisms that men and male identities are indeed the focus of this book would only potentially undercut the ways in which we can all be drawn to envision through identification how the past occasionally relates to the present and thus obliquely touches our own lives, as both men and women. For the concept of the individual, even if centered on men in this book, still matters to us today. And by extension the Italian Renaissance treatment of that concept as it pertains to men still raises issues important to us in our own time and place, whether we happen to be male *or* female "people" curious about how others in the past thought about and experienced their identities in light of the varied constraints within which they operated.

I close with a reflection, but this time not a personal one.

The year is 1510. Paolo Cortesi's *De cardinalatu* (*On Being a Cardinal*) appeared in print, shortly after the author's death, in a still incomplete state. Roughly three years later Machiavelli composed *Il principe*, and then, in 1521, he published his less well-known but still seminal *L'arte della guerra* (*The Art of War*), the only book he wrote that ever appeared in print in his own lifetime.[10] Broadly speaking, these three books, so different in outlook, rhetorical strategies, and style, addressed two key areas of interest in the Italian Renaissance that this study does not examine in any detail but that we would do well to consider briefly before turning to matters related to *techne*, *ars*, and *arte* in Part I. For two extremely important ways that men made themselves into conspicuous individuals in the period while also participating in male group identities that they sought to exceed was by rising in the church hierarchy and being great military leaders. Cardinals, to be sure, sought to enrich themselves, acquire honor, and assist the papacy in creating the state—in this instance the church—as a major temporal power that would endure in time, while condottieri sought to excel in the art of military affairs, which was one of the great master arts of the Italian Renaissance and certainly a foundational art that Machiavelli deemed absolutely necessary for the prince to master in order to succeed.[11] Visual artists, of course, were routinely employed to highlight not only the corporate but also the individual achievements of great cardinals and military men. They pictured these men in a manner that revealed how their accomplishments, honor, status, wealth, and power depended upon their affiliations with all sorts of activities that men typically and collectively engaged in. But they also characterized them as lone, sometimes heroic individuals, even as we are made cognizant of their indebtedness to various communities, customs, and sodalities.

Now no one in the Italian Renaissance—not the most adept man of arms adhering to Machiavelli's strategy of innovation in military matters or the most adept cardinal pursuing Cortesi's strategy of self-promotion in religious matters—should or could be construed as possessing an absolutely "pure, unfettered subjectivity," in Greenblatt's memorable phrase.[12] I take this as a given, a "finding," to borrow and adapt from the language of the social sciences, that we can consider "robust" in that it holds up to scrutiny whatever prior variables we seem to introduce into our discussions. Hence even when the condottiere Bartolomeo Colleoni in Andrea del Verrocchio's bronze sculpture of him (figs. 1 and 2) is presented in heroic isolation, we can readily recognize that Colleoni—his manliness emphasized through the motif of testicles incorporated into the statue in light of his family name (Colleoni/"Coglioni")—wears an armor that links him not only to military activities generally but also to culturally normed conceptions of how armor functioned in shaping and representing male identities. In addition, Colleoni is singled out and glorified because he putatively led his soldiers to protect and serve a community, just as he owes his ascent to the Venetian senate (or so we are led to believe), which collectively approved of the sculpture and inscribed itself onto the pedestal with the initials "s.c." (senatus consulto; by decree of the senate). Furthermore, with his fierce, bronze face fashioned to recall the Emperor Galba, Colleoni is meant to serve, in a distinctly classical mode, as an inspiration for other like-minded leaders to take up the Venetian cause, just as other statues of military leaders were expected to serve as such honorific, exemplary monuments. And, to be sure, he fits into a traditional type of the ancient equestrian figure, such as the most famous extant one of Marcus Aurelius on the Campidoglio in Rome (fig. 3), even as Verrocchio deviates from that foundational classical model by putting

FIGURE 1. Andrea del Verrocchio (1436–1388), *Condottiere Bartolomeo Colleoni*, ca. 1479–1492. Campo dei Santi Giovanni and Paolo, Venice. Reproduced by permission of Alinari/Art Resource, NY. Detail of Colleoni's highly delineated and particularized face in profile.

the horse much more conspicuously than ever before into a twisting, energetic motion.[13] Similarly, even when the cardinal Pietro Bembo is pictured sitting in pensive isolation in Titian's portrait of him (fig. 4), we can readily recognize that the scarlet *biretta* and *mozzetta* Bembo wears tie him to religious activities generally and the community of cardinals in particular. Likewise, his beard signals, as beards were wont to do, his manliness in a profession so blatantly defined by and for men, while the book he holds, regardless of what he happens to be reading, inevitably alludes to his role as a sophisticated and famous humanist within the broader community of a *res publica litterarum* (republic of letters). Finally, the pose he strikes, including the decorous gestures he adopts, presents him with culturally approved modes of comportment for the male

FIGURE 2. Andrea del Verrocchio (1436–1388), *Condottiere Bartolomeo Colleoni*, ca. 1479–1492. Campo dei Santi Giovanni and Paolo, Venice. Reproduced by permission of Mauro Magliani. Alinari/Art Resource, NY. Colleoni statue seen from below.

FIGURE 3. *Equestrian Statue of Marcus Aurelius*, erected 176 CE. Campidoglio, Rome. Reproduced by permission of Alinari/Art Resource, NY.

elite.[14] These men have "attributes," in other words, that signal who they are within a broad set of group classifications, much as saints bear attributes identifying them as specifically who they are, while linking them all along to the broader community of the blessed of which they are always a part. Moreover, the images themselves were fashioned not by artists operating freely and independently, crafting works on spec in an impersonal, wide-open market, but within a workshop, guild, and patronage system in which consumers dictated how things should appear and works of art were contractually and collaboratively produced.

FIGURE 4. Titian (Tiziano Vecellio, ca. 1488–1576), *Cardinal Pietro Bembo*, 1545. Museo Nazionale di Capodimonte, Naples. Reproduced by permission of Erich Lessing/Art Resource, NY.

All this, I take it, is true. Yet however much Verrocchio has idealized him as an equestrian hero with facial figures resembling those of the Emperor Galba, and however much Colleoni is represented as a stalwart, rugged figure whom we are implicitly meant to measure over and against an imperial classical type (as well as over and against modern, competitive revisions of that very same classical type brilliantly designed, for instance, by Donatello in his sculpture of Gattamelata in nearby Padua, fig. 5), we are also no doubt meant to recognize

FIGURE 5. Donatello (ca. 1386–1477), *Equestrian Statue of Gattamelata*, 1453. Piazza del Santo, Padua. Reproduced by permission of Cameraphoto Arte, Venice/Art Resource, NY.

Colleoni as a distinctive and singular condottiere who is celebrated because he protected and preserved Venice, leading his soldiers to victory in military affairs. Similarly, however idealized the portrait of Bembo may be as Titian has captured a stern yet "sublime" vision of him, and however much we are meant to situate the imperious and slightly frowning Bembo within a set of broad classifications that define him and make him who he is as a model figure commanding profound respect for anyone gazing at his portrait, we are also no doubt meant to recognize Bembo as specifically Bembo, as that distinctive and singular humanist patrician within the church who proved to be such a seminal figure of religious affairs.

Needless to say, I have no hard evidence to back up these assertions. I possess no letter from Bembo indicating that he wanted to appear as distinctly and singularly him and no one else when it came to fashioning an accurate, up-to-date likeness of him that would somatically register his own peculiar, individual "motions of the mind."[15] Similarly, I can find no injunction from Colleoni insisting in his last will and testament that the statue crafted with the money appropriated by the state should capture him as specifically and individually him and no one else, although Colleoni did indeed request that the statue be placed in Piazza San Marco, which in fact it was not, precisely because the Venetian senate deemed it to be too bold and individualistic a gesture to erect it in such a uniquely privileged spot (fig. 6). Nevertheless, as we reflect on the various forces that shaped men and male identities in the Italian Renaissance, from economic forces to social, cultural, and artistic ones, it seems to me that we need to be far more attuned to the importance of the individual in the period—not the Burckhardtian individual that anticipates modernity with a free, untrammeled, and socially untethered self but the individual as someone "distinguished from others by attributes of its own," "marked by a peculiar and striking character," and "pertaining or peculiar to a single person or thing or some one member of a class." It is to this end, then, that this book examines how some men in the Italian Renaissance possessed—or were represented as possessing—a mysterious quality that rendered them inimitable within the context of professional life; an aggressive, personalized voice and/or signature style in the practical and productive arts; or a particular mode of addressing the world through the performative staging of something so seemingly insignificant, and physically superficial, as the distinctive, identifying beard. And it is in this context that the concept of the individual matters and is explored in this book, both in terms of how a variety of men advocated that something "else" accounted for singular, masterful success and in terms of how they took concrete steps to be at once like and unlike others, as they exercised their agency and searched for a particular mode of distinguishing themselves by strategically manipulating roles, styles, cultural scripts, and widespread fashions.

FIGURE 6. Andrea del Verrocchio (1436–1388), *Condottiere Bartolomeo Colleoni*, ca. 1479–1492. Campo dei Santi Giovanni and Paolo, Venice. Reproduced by permission of Erich Lessing/Art Resource, NY. Colleoni's commemorative statue was finally placed directly in front of the Dominican basilica, where the funeral services celebrating doges took place and so many illustrious doges were buried—not Piazza San Marco but still a prominent position, to be sure.

PART I

❧

PROFESSIONALISM

Professionally Speaking: The Value of *Ars* and *Arte* in Renaissance Italy—Reflections on the Historical Reach of *Techne*

LET ME BEGIN A REFLECTION ON THE ROLE OF ARS AND ARTE IN RENAISSANCE Italy, the first such reflection of this book, by sketching out the history of the concept of techne in classical antiquity. By doing so, we will be in a position to see how the Italian Renaissance treatment of it rehearses as well as revises elements that were originally embedded in the classical notion of techne itself. To this end, I examine in the first section of this chapter the general significance of the term "techne" (pl. "technai") in ancient Greece and then how that term changed, and in many respects did not change, as it evolved into ars from ancient Rome through the European Middle Ages. Readers not particularly interested in the complex evolution of the concept of techne over almost two thousand years, which I try to compress into as few pages as reasonably possible, may jump directly to the second section, where I provide an overview of the role and value of ars and arte as forms of knowledge in Renaissance Italy, exemplifying some of the issues explored in my discussion by examining briefly the writings of three very different sixteenth-century practitioners of arts: Leonardo Fioravanti, Vannoccio Biringuccio, and Giorgio Vasari. In the third section, having furnished a broad context for an understanding of the concepts of techne, ars, and arte from classical antiquity to the sixteenth century (devoting in the process special attention to the Italian Renaissance), I offer a more focused and extended reading of two very different treatises written at roughly the same time by two very different practitioners versed in two very different arts: Baldassare Castiglione's treatise on the art of the courtier and Benvenuto Cellini's on the art of the goldsmith. In the fourth and final section, I explore what I take to be both significant and new about the Italian Renaissance treatment of the arts and then investigate some salient aspects of Jacob Burckhardt's famous claim that the very concept of art (in his terms "Kunst") lay at the heart of what defined the Italian Renaissance—a claim that still resonates in scholarly literature today and undergirds discussions about Renaissance self-fashioning, although in a manner that elicits serious qualifications on the part of a variety of literary, intellectual, art, and cultural historians when it comes to thinking about the notion of the individual, be it a male or female individual, in the period.

Before turning to these matters, however, I should clarify a few points about terminology. Because the term "techne" evolves not only conceptually but also linguistically as we move from ancient Greece to ancient Rome (when the term "ars" is used) to the European Middle Ages (when both the terms "ars" and "arte," among others, are used) to finally sixteenth-century Italy (when, again, both ars and arte are used), I typically employ the three terms selectively in the context of the period examined at any given point in my discussion. It seemed to me perverse and historically inaccurate to do otherwise, to use the term "techne," for instance, when speaking of the Italian Renaissance or, inversely, to speak about ars or arte when talking about ancient Greece. Moreover, when talking about guilds, which were, of course, "arts" (*artes/arti*), I refer to them directly as guilds so as to avoid, I hope, confusion in terminology. Furthermore, where it seems to me clear from the general discussion that I do not need to employ the terms "techne," "ars," and "arte" over and over again to make it evident to readers that the terms were used in specific periods and places, I have adopted the English "art" and "arts," with the understanding throughout my discussion, however, that I am not referring to the fine arts or visual arts, which is how we conventionally tend to think of the word "art" today, but all the practical and productive arts generally. Finally, I distinguish from time to time between the practical arts (defined here broadly as arts directed at doing something) and the productive arts (defined here broadly as arts directed at making something) where it seemed to me necessary and appropriate to do so, but the distinction between the two should always be borne in mind as a significant and durable one during the *longue durée* covered in this chapter, even when the distinction is not always fully articulated in my discussion, and even when the distinction itself changed over time and can be perceived as blurry in the periods themselves.[1]

The ancient Greek term "techne" ranged widely in meaning.[2] As a matter of epistemological concern, techne could evoke the notion of shrewdness and trickery, thus making it conceptually akin to *metis* (cunning intelligence) and its clever ruses. On some occasions it could be used interchangeably with *episteme* (a body of ideas deemed to be intellectually certain) and consequently taken as a model for the type of superior knowledge toward which the philosopher aspired. More typically, techne meant productive or practical, rather than theoretical or speculative, knowledge. For the most part it was conceived as the authoritative but not always absolutely dependable knowledge required to make or do something limited, precise, and clearly defined with acknowledged expertise. Along these lines, the term "techne" was used as a synonym for the special know-how of some skill. It could be a basic manual skill: house building and carpentry, for instance—the sort of routine, lower-order, banausic (vulgar) skill that Plato repeatedly holds up to prefigure, by way of analogy, the clear, purposive, and goal-oriented knowledge that deals with abstractions and speculative philosophy.[3] It could also be a complex demanding skill: rhetoric, medicine, military strategy, and statecraft, for instance—the sort of higher-order, open-ended, and refined skill that Aristotle identifies both with the practical knowledge of *phronesis* (prudence) and with the act of "doing," *praxis*, rather than "making," *poiesis*.[4] Furthermore, while on the one hand techne is often associated with hard-and-fast rules and handbooks, on the other hand it could also demand an acumen for improvisation, require an exquisite sensitivity to the contingency of opportunity, assume an ability to apply general principles to the particulars of an occasion, and presume a talent receptive to extensive training and professional development. Additionally, there are some fundamental assumptions about a techne worth emphasizing from the outset. A techne as a form of specialized knowledge linked the particular to the universal, whereas the knowledge garnered from only experience dealt just with particulars. A techne served as a means to an end rather than as an end in itself. It was never used, say, for its own sake or appreciated as such. A techne was process- and goal-oriented in a manner that was conceived as organic, ordered, and purposive. For this reason it was sometimes likened to the workings of Nature in the very moment that it allowed people to acquire some control over Nature and independence from it, as well as, ideally, from the gods and fate. And the persons possessing a techne could provide a rational account of the techne itself. Those very persons, that is, could cogently explain the techne's subject matter, its causes and ends, the nature of the knowledge associated with it, and why certain decisions were made to achieve predetermined results by adhering to a correct, calculated course of action.

There were two dominant but related strands of thought about techne operating in ancient Greece, although both strands developed and found expression at different times as they evolved, and the distinction between the two depended primarily on the nature of the techne in question. According to one strand of thought, someone with a techne possessed for the most part completely dependable knowledge about something very specific. He or she could therefore produce whatever was made or done and reliably guarantee that it would be effective and the same over time. A builder, whose craft was associated with the concept of techne from the outset (a view still captured in the notion of the "architect" as an "arch-technician"),[5] could confidently construct a house that would not fall down, barring accidents of nature or unanticipated acts of human destruction, and the house could be readily duplicated, assuming the materials and geographies of the locations remained the same or similar in nature. According to another strand of thought, someone with a conjectural (*stochastic*) techne, as opposed to an "exact" one such as that involved in building houses, did not possess infallible knowledge but relied on educated yet still precarious guesswork—rules of thumb that allowed for flexibility, openness, and an ability to adapt to the nuances of the materials employed and the unpredictability of coping with particulars in a world of constant flux.[6] He or she therefore could not absolutely guarantee that the result of applying a techne would always be effective or the same over time, even if the body of knowledge associated with the techne was viewed as complete and certain with respect to the assigned task. A physician could prescribe drugs for patients with the same diagnosed illness, but in no way could the physician assure all of them that they would survive, much less guarantee that patients with life-threatening ailments would be cured. Similarly, a general could never absolutely guarantee that his strategy for a military campaign would always succeed, any more than a rhetor could promise that he would always persuade and move the audience toward an anticipated and desired goal by appealing simultaneously to people's occasionally unreceptive hearts and minds. Either way, whether we are talking about a techne conceived as an "exact" or "stochastic" form of knowledge, which is to say as one that is presumed to be completely or just dependably reliable, possessing a techne for the ancient Greeks allowed them to have a significant measure of control over chance (*tuche*) through the conscious application of reason in a precise manner to a determinate subject matter.

Since the body of knowledge of a techne had to be realized in some form or manner, a techne was associated with accomplished performance (actually playing Bach well over and over again, say) rather than just imagined competence (thinking one can always play Bach well but consistently failing to keep time). It had to be put into action, its potentiality made manifest so that it could be verified as effective applied knowledge. Additionally, what made a techne a techne—whether the outcome of exercising it was viewed as absolutely reliable or not—is that the form of knowledge associated with it was communicable. A techne was therefore teachable in a rational, but not necessarily always systematic, way: sometimes through rules and precepts, sometimes through examples or experience, sometimes through a process of imitation, sometimes in a direct, intimate, and highly personal manner. Furthermore, the persons who possessed a techne needed to be viewed as authoritative and masterful. In sociological terms, they enjoyed a jurisdictional claim over a clear, distinct, and conceptually circumscribed field of knowledge. Thus the persons who possessed a techne potentially held a privileged position in society, particularly within the city-states of ancient Greece, because they could explain the rational content of a techne and actualize it as only an expert dependably could. People possessing a techne in this respect were "professors" insofar as they could "profess" credible knowledge that was publicly valued, that ostensibly fulfilled a social need through the reliable and reproducible services performed, that they could take some pride in as they made use of their acknowledged expertise as a form of worthy work, and that functioned in a practical way as an "invitation for work."[7]

There are also some noticeable limitations associated with the concept of techne, and they raise important issues about ancient Greek thought and life generally. A techne as a form of specialized knowledge was viewed as useful and beneficial to society, but more often than not it was taken to be neither moral nor immoral but *a*moral. In a phrase, it was ethically limited in that it was morally ambiguous. It all depended on not only the nature of the techne in question but also how the techne was used and thus on the underlying, predetermined character of the person applying it. Additionally, some people putting into practice a techne ineluctably found themselves in a precarious position within the polis. Even in the most favorable of times, some remained vulnerable to attacks of quackery since in many instances there were no formal schools for accrediting them and thus no socially accepted mechanisms either for policing the jurisdictional boundaries of what they claimed they knew how to do or for assuring institutional longevity and support for what they did.[8] Furthermore, discussions as to whether some activities were or were not technai, such as those dedicated to medicine and rhetoric, only served to highlight the inherent risks involved in attempting to do anything with real confidence in an uncertain, vulnerable world governed by chance and fate, even as those discussions sought to assert some control over the contingency of occasion through the mastery afforded by possessing a techne. What is more, discussions about techne also revealed much about the limits of educability—issues that will reappear, as we shall see, in various guises in the Italian Renaissance. Can all people possess a techne? What are the prerequisites? Should it be inculcated through precepts, through imitation, through examples, through handbooks, abstractly, intimately? How much of the knowledge pertaining to a techne was determined by hard-and-fast rules, how much was derived from improvisational learning, how much was instead the product of intuition, how much was just somehow passed on from parent to child? Did someone, in point of fact, need some kind of primary ur-knowledge—a sort of innate shrewdness or acumen—to recognize instinctively how to adapt the acquired knowledge associated with a specific techne to the particulars of the moment and the unpredictability of occasion?

Lastly, there is an underlying sociopolitical dimension to the classical Greek notion of techne. On the one hand, we can detect significant expressions of democratic unease at the claims of sophists to have access to an art of political virtue and rhetoric—an art that could be taught for vast sums of money and therefore challenged the egalitarian claim that the poor majority can have as much civic virtue and knowledge as the wealthy. On the other hand, and in critical terms more important for this present study, people possessing and applying a techne could be viewed in ancient Greece as dangerous to the prevailing aristocratic social order. An alluring yet threatening aspect to the possessor of a techne was that the persons making use of it could potentially challenge persons of higher social position through applied specialized knowledge. In this context, persons putting into practice a techne might be deemed ambitious social climbers seeking to advance themselves through their "careers," potential Promethean upstarts who could adopt outsized ideas about themselves through their position as experts in a society that had a keen demand for what they dependably offered through their skills.[9] Because they possessed a knowledge that serviced real social needs within the polis (and because they exercised skills that at times were much admired and held in prestige within city-states, as in fifth-century Athens), they could potentially exercise that knowledge for self-aggrandizing change. Because they had managed to lift themselves up through education and transform themselves by acquiring authority and legitimacy through their techne, they necessarily undercut, by virtue of that specialized knowledge that allowed them to become acknowledged masters, the aristocratic presumption that nature, rather than nurture, defined who one already always was and that one only had to cultivate a character inescapably ascribed to someone from birth through family line. Therein lay the menace of techne, its edgy rebellious side in ancient Greek thought. A techne held out the possibility of "unregulated mobility" in an aristocratic social world, with the people applying a techne taking advantage of and thriving on change, and it could thus "compensate," as Serafina Cuomo has succinctly put it, "for the lack of noble birth by producing honor via alternative routes."[10] In this respect, much as the definition of techne ranged widely in ancient Greece, so too did the sociopolitical value of techne, not least when framed within the broader context of the history of work.[11] Mastering a techne in the end represented potentially possessing not just a form of productive and practical knowledge but also a threatening form of sociopolitical power. And this shifty and shifting aspect of techne, which reconfigured such knowledge as a sociopolitical strength, could be viewed as a boon or a bane, depending on where you stood within the polis and depending on what sorts of work you were engaged in.

The Greek concept of techne remained largely identical in ancient Rome, reflecting the same broad range of meanings as it was translated into Latin as ars, even if there were significant differences governing the social structures within which practitioners exercised their skills.[12] Like Greek writers thinking about techne, Roman writers, or at least those aligned with what we can call, following Cuomo, an "aristocratic" approach to the issue of techne and ars, were interested in activities associated with arts that developed character and thus activities that made men virtuous as leaders, such as agriculture and military strategy. A general did not win a war, for example, because he had better fighting equipment or technical virtuosity but because he possessed superior moral qualities needed for ruling and leadership, such as courage, temperance, fortitude, loyalty, persistence, reasonableness, moderation, piety, and the like. A techne/ars, by contrast, undercut the aristocratic ethos and made men weak, morally lacking, or uninvested in civic virtue. A techne made men soft, as Xenophon had earlier put it, rendering them lax from laboring indoors, although his denigration of such arts, we should bear in mind, occurs in a highly rhetorical and didactic speech by Socrates arguing with some comic—and characteristically ironic—exaggeration for the superiority of husbandry in an attempt to make the ne'er-do-well son of Crito take more seriously his household duties as a landowner and, consequently, exert himself through toil, with toil here understood as a stylized form of labor that legitimated aristocratic virtue and defined elite status.[13] Still, by and large, the aristocratic concept of techne had far more openly negative than positive associations attached to it, not just in Greek but also in Roman thought generally. An ars debased men, Cicero avers, if it is manual, banausic, servile, the product of the workshop or in any way deemed remunerative.[14] It was not uniformly taken as a badge of honor, for instance, that Gaius Fabius, who was given the cognomen Pictor for painting the temple of Salus (Health) in about 304 BCE, was in fact a painter: for Cicero, unlike for Pliny, it degraded his dignity within an illustrious line.[15] For this reason, arguably, when Cicero and Quintilian talked about whether or not rhetoric was an art, they were quick to moralize it *and* socially enhance it, thereby ensuring that a rhetor was truly a rhetor if, and only if, he was a "good man" (*vir bonus*), meaning not just a morally upright man but also a citizen of elevated social standing, an optimate.[16]

In Greek and Roman antiquity, then, certain arts as forms of specialized knowledge were or could be viewed as edifying and character enhancing in nature, depending on who said what about whom and where and under what circumstances. Architecture, husbandry, rhetoric, and medicine were key in this regard. And they could be elevated to the level of "liberal arts" (*artes liberales*)— arts pursued by free men to liberate the spirit, without any aim for personal gain and without any concern that the person involved in the art would be engaged in physical, sensuous pleasures or was occupationally dependent on others. Those liberating arts could thus be cast as building virtues and character, the very virtues and character that certain freemen within the aristocratic social order already necessarily possessed from birth and merely needed to enhance and perfect through training.[17] Moreover, when it came to the banausic crafts, the user, rather than the producer, of the durable material good was privileged: the aristocratic wearer of the shoe rather than the shoemaker himself was of far greater cultural interest and, naturally enough, enduring social value. Additionally, one typically appreciated the material produced (the art on the Parthenon, the sculpture on a frieze) and not, albeit with the exceptions of such men as Phidias, Apelles, and Lysippus, the producer (the artist who sometimes toiled in the vulgar grime of his sweat), a point synthetically captured by Plutarch when he pithily observed in his *Lives* that "while we delight in the work, we despise the workman."[18] Finally, for those arts that belonged to or were elevated to the level of being considered one of the liberal arts or placed in a sort of limbo category of semiliberal arts, a general precondition for ensuring that they continued to be viewed in that manner was that they not be practiced for remuneration or pursued strictly for pleasure.

In this way, much as a good deal of ambivalence lay at the heart of the classical concept of work itself as various people articulated the merits and demerits of different forms of labor in a period that "abounded" in a "polyphony" of voices on the subject,[19] so, too, a deep ambivalence lay at the heart of the classical concept of the arts themselves. And this is especially true with regard to the productive arts. On the one hand, Greeks and Romans valued the productive arts and took great pride and pleasure in their notable advancements achieved through them. The lasting monuments from antiquity bear witness to this fact and often broadcast it, perhaps most famously in Trajan's magnificent column, which both represents and enacts the civilizing process and glories of the productive arts as a form of valued, specialized knowledge. Rome can not only build a spectacular pontoon bridge across the Danube to enable the emperor Trajan and his troops to succeed in their military campaign, as is evident in the panels as they unfold from the bottom and spiral upward. Rome can also construct an innovative, freestanding, intricately designed, and hollowed-out column with slender vertical windows and a narrow winding staircase incorporated into it, carving out an entire hillside to accomplish the

FIGURE 7. *Trajan's Column*, 106–113 CE. Rome. Reproduced by permission of Gianni dagli Orti/The Art Archive at Art Resource, NY. Detail with reliefs showing victorious Dacian campaigns, including detail of soldiers crossing the impressive pontoon bridge.

extraordinary architectural feat, while placing Greek and Latin libraries on either side of the richly adorned column as lasting symbols of the complete appropriation and assimilation of *all* knowledge (both techne- and non-techne-oriented knowledge) on the part of imperial Rome (fig. 7).[20] Some philosophical positions, such as Stoicism and Cynicism, scholars have pointed out, also viewed the productive arts somewhat positively by recognizing the social value of paid banausic occupations, although certainly not, it bears stressing, typically the practitioners of those occupations themselves.[21] Or as Harry W. Pleket encapsulated the issue some time ago, "there is a good deal of evidence that some Greeks"—and indeed some Romans, it is safe to say—"were by no means hostile to techne."[22]

On the other hand, as much as ancient Greeks and Romans took seriously the knowledge associated with certain productive arts and valued their sometimes sublime achievements, they also recognized the threat that the possessors of such knowledge theoretically posed to the aristocratic social order and its ethos of entrenched privilege as people involved in those arts potentially asserted themselves, acquired social power, and thrived on, as well as brought

FIGURE 8. *Tomb of the Baker Marcus Vergilius Eurysaces*, late first century CE. Rome. Reproduced by permission of Scala/Art Resource, NY.

about through their activities, change. In the end, as much as they could and did serve the polis, and as much as they tangibly expressed pride in their work and how it sustained themselves and others (perhaps most memorably in Marcus Vergilius Eurysaces' remarkable, still largely extant, funerary monument dedicated to his profession as a baker), people involved in the productive arts were typically viewed as bound to, or ineluctably associated with, physical matter and/or material gain (fig. 8).[23] To paraphrase Plutarch, one can admire the product and still despise the producer, even though the producer can be credited with benefiting society in manifold ways and, by the same token, can feel entitled to recognition and, at least in some cases, win esteem, such as the visual artists praised by Pliny the Elder.[24] Some of this ambivalence, at least with regard to specifically the productive arts, is perhaps captured mythopoeically in the figure of the Olympian god Hephaestus (the Roman Vulcan): his status among the gods may be deemed decidedly ambiguous insofar as he is an ugly, cuckolded cripple, but the banausic arts, insofar as they are divinized through him as a master craftsman capable of shaping such magnificent objects as Achilles' shield, are not unambiguously demoted. In a similar vein, we are no doubt meant to ascribe a positive ideological and moral value to the exertion of Hercules' virtuous and onerous labors, some of which, such as his cleansing the Augean stables of an enormous quantity of dung, were certainly intended to be viewed as base, degrading, and menial in nature.[25]

The loss in some instances of a thoroughgoing understanding of classical thought proved to contribute to a more positive appraisal of the arts generally in the Middle Ages, although it is important to stress that we should not overstate the magnitude of the historical change. As the content of much classical thought became inaccessible or unintelligible in the early Middle Ages, even though the organizing principles and underlying social and moral hierarchies of antiquity remained largely in place, writers occasionally responded in a pragmatic manner to the concept of the arts and revealed in the process some enthusiasm for them. In thinking about the arts, these writers responded often enough not to philosophical interests but practical needs and hence, in their putative ignorance of the content of classical culture, were somewhat liberated from prior prejudices and could alter classifications in an unfettered manner.[26] In other instances, as classical thought became increasingly accessible in the later Middle Ages and as more and more thinkers appreciated it and adopted both its content and categories, the profound ambivalence of classical culture toward the arts as a concept—its "flexible and ambiguous" treatment of it, as Elspeth Whitney has astutely put it— allowed for a "creative, positive revision and development by medieval writers."[27] As a result, even the productive arts—or, more precisely, the "mechanical arts" (a term only adopted in the ninth century in John the Scot's commentary to Martianus Capella's *De Nuptiis Philologiae et Mercurii* [*On the Marriage of Philology and Mercury*])—became more extensively examined and cast in a somewhat more positive light than they had been in the classical period. Nevertheless, we still need to recognize that when it comes to evaluating the concept of the arts over the long run, we can ultimately trace as much continuity as change between periods as we move from Greek and Roman antiquity to the Middle Ages. Overall, as Birgit Van Den Hoven has cogently cautioned, much remained the same regarding basic attitudes about the arts as the concept fit into moral and social hierarchies within the broad and sometimes elaborate classifications of knowledge crafted during those periods.[28]

To be sure, we find many of the old ambivalences about the arts intact throughout the Middle Ages, albeit infused with matters of religious concern. For the key church father Augustine of Hippo, "ars" in the *De civitate Dei* (*City of God*) constitutes a mark of the superiority of humankind because it revealed our "natural genius" to transform the environment. And Augustine does indeed wax eloquent about this fact in a long, inspiring, and influential passage praising the arts, much as he does in a number of his writings when he talks about all sorts of honorable forms of work. Yet in the very same passage from the *De civitate Dei*, Augustine also deems "ars" to be "superfluous, perilous, and pernicious," presumably because it potentially binds us to worldly matters rather than automatically directing us on an upward and uplifting path toward spiritual enlightenment and thus toward God.[29] In the Augustinian framework familiar to many modern readers of medieval literature, particularly those indoctrinated into his seminal *De doctrina christiana* (*On Christian Teaching*), the arts needed to be used (*uti*), we can say, not enjoyed (*frui*)—a notion certainly not lost on Dante's edified wayfarer as he journeys through the otherworld. Other medieval thinkers, including those indebted to Augustine, approached the productive arts in particular with more hostility, perpetuating the longstanding hierarchies that privileged intellectual work (the so-called liberal arts, whose features could change in antiquity) over physical labors (the *artes sordidae*, *vulgares*, and *illiberales*). And yet gradually thinkers in medieval culture worked to soften some aspects of the harshness of much of classical culture toward the productive arts in particular, especially in and after the Carolingian renaissance, when philosophers and theologians developed new and more positively inflected categories for thinking about crafts and manual labor. And by the twelfth century, especially with the writings of Domingo Gundisalvo, Hugh of St. Victor, Albertus Magnus, Vincent of Beauvais, and Robert Kilwardby, we seem to witness, if only haltingly at times, a more comprehensive exploration of the virtues of the productive arts generally, even if we cannot always attribute to this period a completely innovative recalibration of the value of them as a full-fledged expression of the dignity of man or, for that matter, attribute to the period a radical reconfiguration, much less social upscaling, of certain forms of work and the arts underpinning them.[30]

In the end, then, by the thirteenth century, thinkers in the Middle Ages had at one time or another reconceptualized the arts generally in more positive terms. They had validated the productive arts in particular as expressions of reason and as valuable forms of knowledge. They had justified them as integral parts of elaborate and comprehensive systems of thought. They had awarded them prominence within their systems of thought, thus partly breaking down the ancient classical opposition between, on the one hand, unworthy productive and practical arts that served the body, financial gain, and pleasure and, on the other hand, worthy intellectual arts that nourished the soul and enhanced virtue. They had legitimated them as vehicles contributing to salvation, while still placing a number of them, such as the productive arts, at the bottom of a conceptual ladder on an ascending hierarchy that elevated humans step by step from matter to spirit. They had, in keeping with many from the classical period, designated some of them as occupying a middle ground between illiberal and liberal arts (such "semiliberal" arts as medicine, husbandry, architecture, navigation, painting, sculpture, gymnastics, and the like). They had assigned them a positive moral value by envisioning them as part of God's plan for humankind to both recapture a prelapsarian state through applied specialized knowledge and take advantage of an opportunity for humans to perfect nature and care for themselves through their ingenuity. They had deemed them conducive to the virtuous life in a variety of ways, much as they embraced them as part of an overall theology of work. They had secularized them by lauding their utilitarian and exploitative value for humankind generally insofar as they furnished humans with the means to use available natural resources for positive practical ends. And, finally, they had articulated a model for them to be integrated into, and viewed as interdependent with, the theoretical sciences.

A number of contributing socioeconomic and religious factors, it has been argued, led to this treatment of the arts—especially the productive arts—in the Middle Ages. Monasticism, and more broadly a variety of institutionalized Christian religious practices, proved influential—a number of scholars have contended—by exploring and configuring work as crucial for spiritual development, perhaps most vigorously beginning in the eleventh century with the seminal writings of Peter Damian.[31] Serious scholarly pressure, however, has nevertheless been applied to crediting the culture of cenobitism with fundamentally redefining the perceived value of work generally and thus with reevaluating the various forms of knowledge underpinning different manifestations of specialized work. Certainly there is little evidence that monasticism constituted the seedbed for the eventual growth of capitalism in the West.[32] Another important factor, scholars have also maintained, was the increased mechanization of Europe in the Middle Ages and thus the concomitant value placed on technology as people invested in and modified all sorts of inventions, from watermills to windmills, and in the process innovated technologically in order to find better and more efficient ways to exploit their environment and existing natural resources. However, technological innovations, we should bear in mind, did not in and of themselves lead philosophers or theologians in the Middle Ages to alter how they ranked, in their sometimes elaborate classificatory systems, the productive arts that in fact led to such innovations. Yet another key factor, it is generally assumed, was the intensified reurbanization of Europe in the high Middle Ages, the accompanying positive value placed on the accumulation of wealth in a money and credit economy during the commercial revolution, the positive value placed on urban professions in a period of greater social mobility, and the shifting perceptions about the ideology and meaning of work itself. Significantly, however, thinkers in the Middle Ages do not seem to have ever revealed in their writings an intimate, hands-on knowledge of the nature of the work involved in the varied productive and practical arts they so freely classified, although at times they did explore the arts, as Jacques Le Goff has argued, in the context of economic and social changes taking place, particularly in the twelfth century. And, as Le Goff further maintains, they did indeed expand the purview of the arts to incorporate into their writings and classifications a number of those technological changes.[33]

All things considered, then, it is supremely difficult to gauge precisely what socioeconomic factors can be said to account for the change in sensibilities about the arts as a form of specialized knowledge as we move from the classical period to the Middle Ages, just as it is extremely difficult in many instances to determine if indeed there was historically much of a significant change in overall sensibilities. For while many thinkers had managed in one way or another to frame the arts as "an essential kind of knowledge which shared in the ultimate aims of natural philosophy or theology,"[34] and while many had come to think of them as essential, morally valuable, and conducive to the good life within an overall "theology of work,"[35] social hierarchies still largely mapped themselves onto the classificatory rankings of the arts, much as they did in the earlier classical period.[36] Certainly a number of forms of work long associated with specific denigrated arts came to be viewed as inherently sinful, or else, almost as bad, they rendered the practitioner all the more susceptible to sin.[37] Consequently, in the Middle Ages as in antiquity, it was impossible to dispel entirely the pejorative connections linking social place with certain arts, particularly those that required manual labor and were thus perceived as demanding physical effort that dulled the senses as opposed to the mental effort that nurtured the soul, even if, to be sure, monastic culture, as well as the mendicant orders of the thirteenth century, profoundly elevated the value of all honest labor generally, even the most menial labor, as an important vehicle for serving the glory of God in an overall theology of work.

This, then, was the broad intellectual and cultural framework within which Italian Renaissance authors wrote about both the productive and the practical arts and considered issues related to work and professional identity.

∞ ∞ ∞

As we move from the late Middle Ages to the Renaissance in Italy, something quite extraordinary seems to take place outside the ambit of the intellectual elite who produced commentaries on, for instance, Vitruvius's first-century BCE book on architecture and who, in the process of generating these and other writings, raised various issues about the arts.[38] For, strikingly, practitioners *themselves* started composing discourses about arts in significant numbers, beginning in the fifteenth century but with a veritable outpouring of them in the sixteenth century.[39] These discourses ranged widely in nature and quality, and they appeared in print and manuscript form. They constituted what the historian of science Pamela O. Long has aptly dubbed, borrowing from the Aristotelian categories dominant from antiquity to the Renaissance, discourses about "praxis" and discourses about "techne," which is to say, discourses dedicated to inculcating the practice of *doing* something, along with the knowledge required to build the moral character prepared to fulfill the practice in question, and discourses dedicated to inculcating the craft of *making* something, along with the knowledge required to fulfill the specific skill in question.[40] These discourses about arts—which for the purposes of this study constitute *both* of Long's categories of praxis and techne, since the terms "ars" and "arte" encompassed both categories in the Italian Renaissance—also varied substantially in formal and conceptual complexity. At one end of the spectrum, we find sophisticated, "dialogic," humanist treatises written in Latin or in a polished volgare, with models of imitation and emulation calculatingly underpinning them and a host of erudite allusions enriching the rhythmic, periodic prose. At the other end of the spectrum, we find practical, unembellished, "monologic" manuals that are fundamentally instructional in nature. Either way, the fact that a substantial number of practitioners with extremely different backgrounds and levels of schooling turned to authorship and wrote so many discourses about the productive and practical arts covering so many different fields in just under two centuries is indeed new. And it speaks to a large-scale cultural shift in attitudes taking place in Renaissance Italy regarding the value of the arts specifically, the value of professional life more generally, and, as some historians have argued even more expansively in the context of early modern Europe, the ideological and moral value of work itself.

Practitioners of specific arts who turned to authorship in Renaissance Italy wrote these discourses in a period when political leaders recognized the need to make use of the productive and practical arts in order to legitimate themselves and succeed as rulers.[41] It was not enough to have character, build character, train character, and possess virtue in order to govern, as was traditionally believed to be the case in the classical period when an aristocratic ethos of social privilege prevailed and virtue and superior character were viewed as largely the distinct right of birth and family lineage. To succeed in governance, one also needed—leaders in the Italian Renaissance soon came to understand—the most skilled artisans capable of creating advanced weaponry and defense systems so that the state could remain secure and potentially grow (the most up-to-date and effective guns, cannons, forts, and the like), as well as the best-trained functionaries capable of engaging their skills so that the state could run as smoothly as possible (the best secretaries, ambassadors, courtiers, and the like). Not surprisingly, in writing these discourses about arts, practitioners turning to authorship sought to take advantage of manifold opportunities potentially available to them, from bureaucratic to artisanal ones. In this respect, a host of what we might call broadly "professional" reasons can be said to account historically for why a significant number of practitioners became authors of discourses about their arts.

Some practitioners turning to authorship were undoubtedly seeking to enhance the art underpinning their profession, endowing it with prestige and making a spirited claim for its cultural value as sophisticated and teachable with a determinate, rational, rule-bound, communicable, and reliable knowledge underlying it. In the process these practitioners were promoting themselves and seeking to elevate their own position, readily inviting readers to acknowledge their achievements and, in some instances, those of like-minded professionals in the author's own field. In rhetorical terms they were establishing their exemplary "ethos," or character, in the context of their expertise as professionals and, to be sure, as men worthy of recognition. They thus presented themselves as authorities who could legitimately hold forth about an art *and*, at the same time, reliably and masterfully apply the art in question to achieve a clearly defined and purposive end. We certainly find these strategies of professional self-definition employed in a broad variety of discourses about arts, from those dedicated to the art of being a secretary to those that concentrate on multiple sectors of the economy devoted to the visual arts.

Within the productive arts, one particularly interesting example of a technical treatise devoted to mechanics that addresses such issues is Vannoccio Biringuccio's *De la pirotechnia* (*The Pirotechnia*, 1540).[42] This early exoteric treatise on metallurgy, composed in a period when Europe experienced a growth in exploitative capitalist enterprises in general and a mining boom in particular, not only serves the important economic and social function of providing potential wealthy investors and established practitioners in Italy with the means to imitate the Germans and make a substantial profit (fig. 9). Biringuccio's *Pirotechnia* also serves to expand the opportunities of the author himself, who has labored in the profession and is taking advantage of a thriving market for minerals and metals in the sixteenth century by positioning himself as an authority

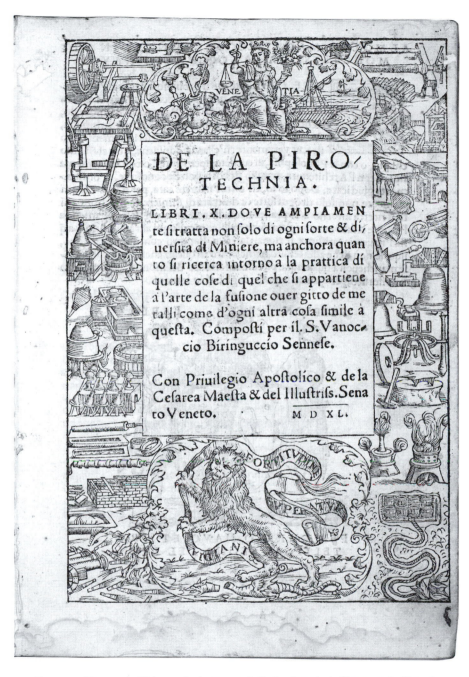

FIGURE 9. Vannoccio Biringuccio (1480–1539), *De la pirotechnia* (Stampata in Venetia per Venturino Roffinello. Ad instantia di Curtio Navo. & fratelli, 1540). Reproduced by permission of the Harry Ransom Center, The University of Texas at Austin. Frontispiece.

on the art in question and, above all, by championing the social and cultural value of the art he professes to teach. As a form of specialized knowledge, the art of metallurgy—Biringuccio asserts from the outset—investigates the life-blood of minerals coursing through the veins of the earth (13). Accordingly, it yields up to a well-trained and experienced eye such as Biringuccio's—which is thoroughly versed in the art of reading manifold surface signs spread out across creeks, ditches, riverbeds, valleys, hills, plains, and mountains—where all the longed-for riches lie hidden deep within, ready for eager entrepreneurial spoil (14–15). In professional terms, then, Biringuccio, like so many other practitioners writing about their arts, takes up authorship to present himself with a highly specialized expertise and thus as a "professor," in essence, professing knowledge. His art, like the art of other practitioners making a case publicly for themselves, is worthy of esteem and therefore should be culturally, socially, and economically valued.

Along with defining their own exemplary professional status as they sought to enhance, and in many instances socially elevate, the value of their art, some practitioner authors were attempting to pass on or expand a critical vocabulary related to their art and engage in competitive rivalries, debating the pros of their art and its specialized knowledge in relation to the cons of others, as well as making all sorts of jurisdictional claims within—to borrow the terms of the sociologist Andrew Abbott—a "system of professions."[43] In doing so, they were also occasionally engaging in more personal rivalries and advocating for certain traditions of making or doing things in the productive and practical arts. Biringuccio does something of this sort when he provides an extensive vocabulary to understand every aspect of mining and repeatedly takes on alchemists, defining that particular, well-established esoteric art, which he finds to be suspect, fanciful, obscure, and charlatan-like, over and against the reliable, open, and highly useful art of the metallurgists, which he contends consistently yields positive results for the avid and patient investor. Similarly, the maverick surgeon/physician Leonardo Fioravanti, often considered something of a charlatan himself, takes on entrenched members of the medical community in a number of his writings, competing with them for a jurisdictional claim within a highly stratified, hierarchical profession.[44] Nor is it difficult to imagine why Fioravanti, whose writings we will examine at length in Chapter 3, would have attacked the established university-based medical community so vigorously. Who, after all, possessed the "secrets" of Nature and understood so profoundly its language? Surely it had to be the traveling surgeon Fioravanti, the radical empiric who went out into the world and, turning his back on arcane bookish learning, accumulated those secrets of medicine from common folk in order to cure people. *He*, Fioravanti would have us know, discovered this coveted and useful

information, not the established doctors who relied on institutionally transferred knowledge.[45] In this light, Fioravanti's hostility toward much of the medical profession arose over a competition within the medical community
regarding who in fact had access to and possessed hidden knowledge, the mysteries of the medical *misterium*, with the term "misterium" here understood to
signify a craft, occupation, trade, or calling—in a word, an "art."[46] For Fioravanti surely felt that tracking down and learning medical secrets was *his* job
and the province of expertise of *his* art. Collecting, testing, and then eventually
divulgating through print those medical secrets in a language accessible to all
was indeed a principal way Fioravanti aimed to make his mark in the medical
community, following in the path of not only the classical empirics of the
ancient world but also the peripatetic Don Alessio Piemontese, the fictional
author of the best-selling *Secreti* (*Secrets*, 1555).[47]

As a number of practitioners advocated the virtues of one art over another,
engaging in a competitive system of professions, they were also—in a far more
mundane manner—simply trying to make a profit during a period that witnessed an increased interest in professions and professionalization in the
intensely urban world of the Italian Renaissance—an interest that found expression in a number of cultural forms, as George McClure has demonstrated, and
culminated in Tomaso Garzoni's massive and often quirky encyclopedic *La
piazza universale di tutte le professioni del mondo* (*The Universal Piazza of All the
Professions in the World*, 1585/1587). In the process these practitioner authors
were capitalizing as best they could on a widespread demand for their expertise
in the "market" and court culture.[48] In crudely materialistic terms, they were
trying to "cash in." Hence some practitioner authors, such as once again Fioravanti and Biringuccio, wrote in some measure to advertise their skills and/or
products so as to capture a broad-based consumer demand. Biringuccio, for
instance, enthusiastically urges investors to take advantage of his expertise so
that they can reap rich rewards from the mining boom of mid-sixteenth-century
Europe. His book, which guarantees wealth for the bold and adventurous entre-
preneur, is in one sense an invitation for work as he implores Italians in particular to turn away from the untold risks and endless drudgery of mercantile labor
and encourages them to invest their energies and capital in looking for such
rare yet valuable minerals as gold in, oddly enough, Italy (34–35)—not, to be
sure, a geographically resource-rich region of Europe. Far more bluntly, Fioravanti, who was always keen on selling himself and his services, even provides
readers in a few of his discourses with the addresses of selected apothecaries in
Venice where the products of his labor can be readily purchased by mail order.[49]
Other practitioners, including those discussing the art of being a secretary,
courtier, painter, sculptor, architect, or goldsmith, wrote to win over members

of a cultural elite that needed assistance in governing and had developed a passion to possess durable objects of all kinds and sizes as a way of fashionably expressing their own social position and distinction but also as a way of creatively constructing culture and distinction itself.[50] In sum, functionaries and artists had services and products to sell, and practitioners eagerly sought to sell them and themselves as they turned to authorship through the writing of discourses about their arts.

Additionally, a number of practitioners wrote discourses about arts to puzzle over problems related to their particular skill and explore avenues for expanding their own understanding of the art in question, both as a practice and as a form of knowledge. These discourses can be seen as functioning as a cognitive act. A few of them even unfold as essays in the root sense of the word, as the staging of an attempt to come to terms with a serious intellectual problem through an ongoing process of reflection. Leonardo da Vinci's remarkable writings about the art of painting, for example, which never finally cohered into a formal printed treatise during his lifetime, would fall into this particular category. His surviving writings on painting in manuscript form, accompanied by his dazzling sketches about ideal proportions and the like (fig. 10), do more than engage us in a characteristically Renaissance *paragone* (competition) about the relative value of the art in question within a system of professions defined by established hierarchies of the arts (painters, of course, belong to the loftier major guild, "arte," of apothecaries in Florence, for instance, whereas sculptors belong to the minor guild of stonemasons). Nor do Leonardo's scattered remaining writings on the art of painting only serve to pass on information about the language of painting or, for that matter, only seek to elevate socially the art of painting by characterizing the painter as a distinguished, clean, and elegant gentleman leisurely applying his skill in his well-ventilated, dust-free studio with musicians all the while fashionably entertaining him. Leonardo's writings about painting also function as ongoing explorations into the nature of the world and the human form, linking the work of the painter to the insights of the natural philosopher, the particulars of the experience of applying the art in question with the episteme of mathematical principles, optics, and universal harmony. Painting and examining the world closely as a unified—indeed fused—coordinated practice in Leonardo's writings consequently engage him in epistemological inquiry, making the art of the painter a veritable science that is creative and fundamentally divine in nature.[51]

More broadly, a distinctive feature about a number of these sorts of writings—writings by practitioners, that is, in which the arts are viewed as having an important cognitive function—is that for the first time since the classical period we witness a sustained, full-fledged theorizing about the practices in question in

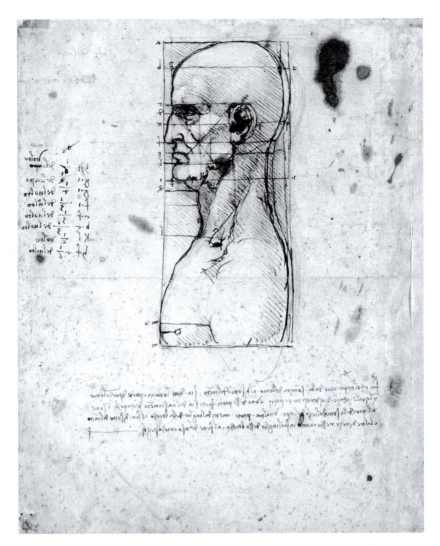

FIGURE 10. Leonardo da Vinci (1452–1519), *Head of a Man with Scheme of Its Proportions*. Accademia, Venice. Reproduced by permission of Scala/Art Resource, NY. Leonardo's examinations into the perfect proportions of the human body, here developed in the context of an examination of a head, dovetail with Piero della Francesca's and Albrecht Dürer's similar mathematically grounded reflections on such matters, also conceived as a science, an "art."

significant discursive form. This process of theorizing takes place not only in writings that remained inchoate in manuscript form, such as Leonardo's on painting, but also in those that were fully fleshed out and appeared in print, such as Leon Battista Alberti's on architecture and painting and Biringuccio's on metallurgy. As Paolo Rossi long ago observed in his seminal *Philosophy, Technology, and the Arts*, "the medieval technical writings gave ample and detailed instructions on the way 'to work.' They offered themselves as a compilation of rules, recipes, and precepts. They were completely devoid of 'theory' understood as an attempt to derive the precepts from general principles and then to base them on a totality of verifiable facts." Moreover, even if we apply some pressure to Rossi's all-embracing assertion that medieval technical writings were absolutely devoid of theory, this strategy of theorizing about the arts by practitioners certainly seems to have found its greatest impetus and most sustained development discursively in the postclassical period in the Italian Renaissance, where "for perhaps the first time a fusion had been effected between technical and scientific activities, and manual labor and theory."[52] As a result, the workshop in which visual artists were apprenticed became in Renaissance Italy not just a place for the construction of objects but also a space of reflection—a laboratory of sorts, in which the particulars of experience were linked to the universals of broader fields of knowledge, such as geometry, anatomy, optics, and perspective (fig. 11).[53] In this way the Italian Renaissance resuscitated the classical concept of techne as not just the specialized knowledge of *how* to make or do something with expertise but also the specialized knowledge *about* the making or doing of something with expertise. This theoretical knowledge in its turn allowed the experts in question to understand in depth why something was done or made in a particular way and thus, by extension, allowed those experts to be in a position to explain in their varied discourses the underlying causes that made the art possible in the first place. Furthermore, these discourses became viewed as learned subjects and the province of interest of patrons curious about different aspects of the world, above all in a period "fueled by a growing appreciation for novelty and new inventions," revitalized by the conspicuous consumption of large- and small-scale objects by the cultural elite, and increasingly invested in the relationship between philosophical inquiry and the arts.[54]

As practitioners turned to authorship, some of these discourses about arts can also be construed as ego documents, it is important to stress. This appears to be a somewhat new phenomenon as well in the Italian Renaissance, a period when there is a notable rise not just in autobiographical modes of writing but of artisanal autobiographies themselves—a rise that continues well into the early modern period in Europe.[55] These discourses about a particular art ranged from full-fledged "lives," which draw on classical models and eventually figure into the development of the genre of biography and autobiography in the early modern period, to treatises that purport to inform us about specific skills but end up effectively functioning equally well as ego documents, at times offering up examples of some of the most egregious forms of aggressive self-fashioning of the entire European Renaissance. In the first group we could readily place such

FIGURE 11. Agostino dei Musi (Agostino Veneziano, ca. 1490–ca. 1540), *The Academy of Baccio Bandinelli*, 1531. Biblioteca Marucelliana, Florence. Reproduced by permission of © DeA Picture Library/Art Resource, NY. Baccio Bandinelli's academy, in some ways a forerunner of the Accademia del Disegno, here represents the artist's workshop established not only as a place of training but also as a space of intellectual inquiry in the teaching of disegno.

works as Giorgio Vasari's monumental *Le vite de' più eccellenti pittori, scultori, ed architettori* (*The Lives of the Most Excellent Painters, Sculptors, and Architects*, both the 1550 Torrentiniana and 1568 Giuntina editions), as well as Castiglione's masterpiece *Il cortegiano* (printed in 1528 but certainly in circulation, and therefore "published," earlier), even if Castiglione purports not to be representing himself in the process of fashioning the perfect courtier and deliberately absents himself from the conversations that putatively took place over four days in spring 1507 in the ducal palace of Urbino. In the second group we would place everything from Benvenuto Cellini's treatises on goldsmithing and sculpting (1568) to a number of Fioravanti's varied treatises on medicine, such as his *Il tesoro della vita humana* (*The Treasury of Human Life*, 1570), published while he worked in the ambit of the combative, industrious, and financially strapped writers closely associated with the print industry in Venice, the so-called *poli-grafi* (polygraphs).[56] There is a notable range, then, to the sorts of discourses that practitioners composed that are dedicated to their arts and, at the same time, function in one form or another as ego documents.

The authors of these discourses about arts that function as ego documents are performing a number of important cultural functions. What is perhaps most significant is that they are often seeking to elevate their art in some measure as a form of specialized knowledge built on rational rules rather than just experience, as well as rational rules derived from extensive experience, in the very moment that they promote themselves and seek status, occasionally with the aim of securing work and patronage. Put differently, if in the classical and medieval periods, to paraphrase Plutarch once again, we are meant to admire the product but not the producer, in the Italian Renaissance the authors of many of these discourses about particular arts would have us admire not only the knowledge associated with the specialized work they do with such evident expertise but also *themselves* as masterful practitioners who have defined, assimilated, communicated, and, at times, surpassed through their practices those very same rules discussed in their writings.[57] In this context a key operative word or concept underpinning some of these discourses about arts that function as ego documents is "admire," along with its variants in the vernacular (*ammirazione, meraviglia, ammirare*) derived from the Latin "miror," with its concomitant emphasis on gazing and the privileging of vision as a vehicle for understanding the world. Indeed, often enough there is a language of marveling associated not only with the work produced or performed but also the workers themselves, whether we are talking about Cellini's and Fioravanti's over-the-top, self-aggrandizing representations of themselves as near miracle makers in their stupefying ability to accomplish certain feats of labor with dazzling skill or, inversely, Vasari's and Castiglione's far more tempered self-presentations as they showcase their complete command of their art as indeed admirable yet still, in keeping with the dominant behavioral codes of the cultural elite in the period, subtly represent their achievements with the appropriate decorum and restraint.[58]

Moreover, in the course of writing about themselves as they write about a specific art, these practitioners who turned to authorship in the Italian Renaissance are often redefining the value of work and by extension the cultural value of an art itself as a form of specialized knowledge as it is embodied in their own spectacular achievements or the achievements of other remarkable practitioners. Bear in mind that from classical antiquity to the medieval period, work was not deemed in discourse to be done for one's own personal self-development, reward, and growth, although some practitioners did indeed occasionally express exceptional pride in their accomplishments achieved through work. Modern historians examining the ideology and meaning of work have driven home this point in a variety of ways, perhaps none more effectively than Catharina Lis and Hugo Soly in their comprehensive historical survey *Worthy Efforts: Attitudes Toward Work and Workers in Pre-Industrial Europe*. In classical Greece and Rome, work, to be sure, could sometimes be conceived unfavorably, as the negation of a privileged, productive *otium* (leisure), as *neg*(not)-otium. In the intervals when one was temporarily and mercifully freed from the tedium and tyranny of work, the very work that could render one captive to either one's own or someone else's ongoing bodily needs and desires, one could exercise and enhance one's powers, nourish oneself spiritually, dedicate oneself intellectually, say, to the liberal arts or, for that matter, the semiliberal arts through a certain rarefied *otium cum dignitate* (leisure with dignity). More generally, however, work was immensely valued in a period that "abounded in [a] polyphony" of voices on the matter.[59] For some thinkers advocating its distinct moral and social benefits, work made life more tolerable for individuals and families: most people needed to work to survive much less thrive. At the same time, and perhaps most important of all, work itself served to reinforce social hierarchies, inculcate discipline, and serve the community. It was certainly preferred to idleness, the dark side of otium as a form of slothful "inertia." And it could enhance virtuous behavior, particularly such work as husbandry in antiquity but also, for Cicero and other elite classical authors, such essential activities as statecraft and public service broadly conceived. Work also generally made life more tolerable for others in the community. Some people through work, such as physicians, demonstrably improved the lot of those around them, while others, such as large-scale merchants engaged in socially accepted forms of legitimately acquiring wealth through commerce, could benefit society by being charitable, by proving themselves magnanimous, and by ensuring that goods flowed freely from one place to another. And, of course, work inevitably served in so many occasions as a palliative to life's uncertainties and onslaughts. Some treated work, we might say to borrow from the pervasive language of modern therapy, as a coping mechanism.

Even in the monastic environment where work was codified and championed both as a necessary part of cenobitic life and as a virtuous activity that commanded respect (beginning with the earliest formative rules of Basil, Augustine, Pachomius, and Benedict),[60] the specialized knowledge associated with any given particular art served not as an end unto itself. One did not go to Heaven, that is, because one possessed an art or was an expert in any one specific art. Rather, the specialized knowledge associated with any given art served to ward off the sluggishness of *accidia* (spiritual apathy and desperation), to eschew sloth, to suppress the appetite of carnal desire and chasten the body, to provide for a self-sufficient monastic community by taking care of what was necessary for everyone involved to survive in a mutually reinforcing collectivity, to prepare oneself spiritually and eschatologically for the Second Coming, to engage in penitence, to inculcate obedience, to be one with the sacred, to bear witness in word and deed to the Truth, to practice more efficiently asceticism, to adhere more rigorously to the *vita apostolica* (apostolic life), to promote charity, to ensure that idle hands do not become the devil's workshop, to make oneself useful socially, to discourage evil thoughts and encourage patience and obedience, to aid in prayer and transform work into prayer, to practice humility, to take personal responsibility for caring for the world, to develop the spiritual self through useful endeavors, to do God's work by participating in creation, to exalt God, even to produce material sweat itself as a divine offering.[61] Hence, as James R. Farr summarily puts it, "work was, in short, a spiritual discipline. Medieval theologians . . . did not think about work in terms of the economic calculation or the material value of production, that effort would somehow create wealth and better one's position in life. Instead, they conceived of work in moral terms, a distinctly premodern notion."[62] What mattered, in brief, was social utility, not modern notions of economic productivity, when it came to thinking about the value of work.

There is some reason to believe, however, that during the Italian Renaissance—beginning in the mid-fifteenth century but intensifying above all in the sixteenth century—professional identity associated with the knowledge of a certain art mattered also as an end unto itself, at least as the work associated with that art was defined and configured in discourse outside the context of the monastic environment. Consequently, having a profession and applying the art underpinning it in the form of work was seen not just as a means of acquiring recognition and even honor in a status-conscious, hierarchical society bound by an ideology of discipline, utility, service, and obedience but, as McClure has argued, as a source of personal, nonspiritually determined happiness and fulfillment. Or, to frame the matter in terms more congenial to this study, in the Italian Renaissance the happiness and self-satisfaction derived from work, as it is voiced in a number of discourses about arts written by practitioners, seems to grow increasingly out of the sorts of direct, personal, self-serving—in Marxist terms, "unalienated"—connections that practitioners made with the product created or the act done. In such discourses one could actually revel in, and indeed feel good about reveling in, the "self-indulgence of personal labor" in a manner that we do not at all find typically expressed in the literature of the classical period, in the elaborate classifications of the arts composed in the Middle Ages, or, for that matter, within the confines of writings connected to or emerging out of monasticism and the mendicant orders.[63] As "polyphonic" as the notion of work was in classical Greece and Rome and the European Middle Ages, work was principally valued because it served some end goal larger than the individual person exerting "worthy effort": something such as the family, a secular or ecclesiastical community, the state, the social and political order conceptualized according to the presumed hierarchical functions of the individual parts of the human body, corporatism, or the divine.[64] Put differently, if, as Lis and Soly have emphasized, from classical antiquity through the preindustrial period in Europe "the standard universal command was that one must exert oneself," a notion of exertion that the Greeks captured "with the term *ponos*" understood as a form of "tireless activity, work," one was still always expected to toil in a virtuous way for something larger than the individual self.[65]

We do, however, find powerful expressions about the intense, personal, self-serving rewards of labor voiced in the writings of the above-mentioned Cellini and Fioravanti, for example, although other practitioners who turned to authorship from the period could be adduced in support of this claim.[66] In Cellini's exuberant autobiography, which is not a discourse strictly about an art but nevertheless details exhaustively the habits and attitudes of an artisan and his extensive, onerous labors, we are presented with a glorified image of the artist so passionately absorbed in his work that he simply cannot find the time to write down the story of his life and must therefore dictate it to an assistant while keeping his hands busy with all sorts of taxing projects and competitive commissions. And the intense self-satisfaction Cellini feels in the process of "doing" (*il fare*) as opposed to just "talking" (*il dire*), to use terms from his treatises on goldsmithing and sculpting, can transform Cellini within his narrative into a demonic demiurge with a brazenly outsized sense of his place as a professional in society. As he transforms objects, shaping them with his hands so that they become works of arresting beauty, so, too, Cellini transforms himself into a wondrous figure for all to admire. Emblematic of this self-transformation is the key moment when Cellini boasts with characteristic fustian bravado how he masterfully crafted a large, multifigured statue of Perseus and Medusa in bronze in a single casting, thereby achieving (even though he did not in fact achieve it) something through his art never done before in the ancient or modern era. In this highly dramatic self-portrayal, Cellini presents himself as a heroic Perseus figure who can grant life and defy death through his creative energies, while he also emerges as a terrifying Medusa figure petrifying others who gaze, transfixed with astonishment in the public square, at the extraordinary expertise embodied in his monumental sculpture. Cellini's heroic and demonic efforts as a maker are one, we are invited to believe, with the statue he daringly crafts and puts on display for all to see and appreciate with

FIGURE 12. Benvenuto Cellini (1500–1571), *Perseus with the Head of Medusa*, 1545–1553. Loggia dei Lanzi, Florence. Reproduced by permission of Alinari/Art Resource, NY. Side view with Michelangelo's *David* and Bandinelli's *Hercules and Cacus* in the background, both conceptually "petrified" from the Medusa's gorgonizing gaze.

such amazement, while the severed Medusa head held aloft and designed with such astonishing artistry transfixes with her transmogrifying gaze the surrounding statues in the square—according to a play of allusions within the context of Cellini's paragone as a goldsmith turned sculptor—by petrifying those very hardened lapidary statues, the famous works of art of Cellini's Florentine rivals with whom he vies, into so many isolated pieces of stone (figs. 12 and 13).[67]

Similarly, fantasies about self-satisfaction derived from work, as well as the self-importance and honor associated with work, abound in Fioravanti's writings, so much so that he characterizes himself over and over again as a wonder with a sort of thaumaturgic touch to him, stunning others in his highly theatrical performances and gradually acquiring—thanks to his complete command over his art—status, recognition, honor, wealth, and, last but not least, a title of knight that he is only too happy to flaunt. Not entirely unlike the charlatans of his time, Fioravanti was something of a spectacle wherever he went, a sort of curiosity figure in an age that possessed an insatiable appetite for exhibiting and collecting curiosities.[68] His ability to appear as a marvel to so many people

FIGURE 13. Benvenuto Cellini (1500–1571), *Perseus with the Head of Medusa*, 1545–1553. Loggia dei Lanzi, Florence. Reproduced by permission of Archive Timothy McCarthy/Art Resource, NY. Detail of the head of Medusa, with blood spewing from the severed neck.

perhaps explains in some measure the enmity he aroused from some in the medical community, the persecution he felt he endured in Rome, Venice, Milan, and Madrid.[69] A number of physicians no doubt felt threatened by his success in putting on such a good show and, perhaps, competing with them all too successfully for coveted clients. In this regard, Fioravanti may have been something of an irritating and obnoxious gadfly within the medical community of the period, especially as he overtly challenged and rebuked well-ensconced authorities, but he was a popular gadfly, he emphasizes, and one, as we shall see in detail in Chapter 3, who took great satisfaction in his accomplishments, his social advancement, and his mastery over his art as a highly specialized and rewarding form of knowledge. Time and again, Fioravanti's sense of identity, like Cellini's and that of so many other practitioners of arts who turned to authorship, was intimately bound up in the specialized knowledge that underpinned his art and in the final realized products of his labor. Professional identity, then, mattered. And it mattered because it allowed such exemplary practitioners as Cellini and Fioravanti to feel not only socially enhanced in relation to others but also positively about themselves and their relationship to their art as self-proclaimed and acknowledged professionals.

Given the deep personal investment that practitioner authors sometimes made in their work, at least as they characterized themselves and their relationship with their work in their writings, as well as the associations often assumed in the period between the personalities of people (Raphael, for instance, is deemed by Vasari to be full of grace) and the products of their labor (Raphael's paintings are likewise deemed by Vasari to be full of grace), some of the discourses by practitioners inevitably find themselves tied to more broad-based cultural issues related to creativity, character, and conduct. This is particularly true in the sixteenth century, when Italians exhibited an intensified interest in etiquette and a keen concern for how men should behave with one another in a variety of homosocial situations, as well as how they should and should not behave in relation to a variety of social superiors, both men and women.[70] On the one hand, in the sixteenth century anyone applying an art who aspired to be accepted by the cultural elite should behave in some measure, we are often led to believe, with decorum, exercising prudence, control, caution, and discretion at every turn. To this end, some of the practitioners who have taken up the role of authorship as they write about their art as a form of specialized knowledge occasionally spend time trying to indoctrinate others, who might well aim to put into practice the art they write about in their discourses, into the pleasantries of polite social conventions. Don't be a slob, Vasari is repeatedly teaching visual artists through edifying examples, if you aim to succeed in a career as an artist in a society increasingly dominated by court culture and complicated patronage relationships. Please, he seems to plead when writing about such people as the bizarre Piero di Cosimo, try not to eat only boiled eggs cooked all at once, as well as by the dozens, in a filthy bucket, if you want to be taken seriously by the cultural elite and be invited to interact with them on an ongoing, if not even intimate, basis. Don't be abrasive, obnoxious, difficult, offensive, obsessive, recalcitrant, spacey, vulgar, dirty, overly taciturn, eccentric, uncouth, or even, in the case of the otherwise perfectly apt Raphael, excessively libidinous.[71] Castiglione similarly reprimands courtiers for engaging in all sorts of boorish habits, from bragging too much to acting out brashly like impudent schoolchildren.

On the other hand, in the sixteenth century in Italy, the self-importance some practitioners of an art arrogated unto themselves within their discourses allowed them at times to reject all the accepted pleasantries of polite comportment and pose alternative modes of interacting with the cultural elite—modes that fly directly in the face of everything espoused by such men of distinction as Monsignor Giovanni della Casa in his influential etiquette treatise *Il Galateo overo de' costumi* (*The Galateo or a Book on Comportment*, 1558), much less

Stefano Guazzo in his equally influential book of manners designed for gentle-men of the court, *La civil conversazione* (*Civil Conversation*, 1574). Both Cellini and Fioravanti are emblematic of the more aggressive, assertive, and at times even uncouth practitioner who emerges in sixteenth-century Italy. This sort of abrasive practitioner presents himself occasionally exercising his art with such dazzling mastery that he feels, by virtue of his talents that render him one of a kind, that he can get away with behaving in all sorts of indecorous ways, at times even egregiously transgressing the norms of polite behavior, particularly when it comes to interacting with social superiors. Cellini, for instance, even goes so far as to tell us in his life story how he snubbed his patron the king of France—an ill-advised move, Vasari would have surely declared. Fioravanti casts himself in the role of the upstart upsetting social conventions with superi-ors within the medical community wherever he went, both up and down the peninsula as well as from Italy to Spain.

At one level, these distinctly opposing yet still related strategies of behavior explored by practitioner authors in their discourses about the arts can be seen to disclose competing conceptions of manhood emerging above all in sixteenth-century Italy, a period that featured some exceedingly powerful, larger-than-life male rulers of both decorous *and* indecorous comportment.[72] On the one hand, one conception of manhood in the period required a person to be deferential, prudent, and highly rational. It owed much to classical rhetorical and contem-porary poetic strategies. And it can be seen as having appropriated what were then perceived in gendered terms as distinctly male strategies of self-discipline and self-control over the emotions. On the other hand, another conception of manhood in the period entitled one to be abrasive, imprudent, and occasionally highly irrational. It owed much to longstanding codes of chivalric honor and patterns of aggressive, violent behavior long associated with feudal aristocratic privilege. And it can be seen as having appropriated what were perceived in gendered terms as distinctly male habits of responding to people and events with forcefulness, aggression, and assertiveness as a way of both defending and affirming collective and individual honor. Either way, some of the male prac-titioners in question who turned to authorship clearly wanted to level out the social playing field in their discourses and envision themselves through their varied modes of temperate or intemperate comportment as near equals in a highly stratified world of extremely competitive men, precisely when their rela-tionship with their (typically, but not exclusively, male) superiors was, and always would remain, hierarchically arranged rather than laterally configured in society. To this end, they occasionally pictured themselves in a primarily male-dominated professional world collaborating with their social superiors in the spirit of mutually reinforcing processes of exchange. So configured, they occasionally idealized their relationships with their male superiors as reciprocal, perhaps most blatantly in Filarete's (Antonio Averlino's) treatise on architecture, which, as Long has thoughtfully posited, establishes a sort of conceptual "trading zone" where ideas could be fruitfully exchanged in a manner that perhaps looks ahead to the sorts of interactions that formally took place within the scientific communities of the seventeenth century.[73]

Along with teaching and thinking about character and conduct, as well as instructing us on how to interact with the cultural elite in the context of applying an art as a form of specialized knowledge, some of these discourses are both reflective and instructive of burgeoning aesthetic values and address what we might broadly call, partly in Pierre Bourdieu's terms, "taste." Consider in this context Vasari's monumental *Le vite*, which offers us not only a host of exemplary biographies of visual artists, replete with colorful tales about their sometimes fascinating personalities, along with abundant information—both accurate and erroneous—about the products of their labors, but also a lengthy introductory section, expanded in the second edition, on highly technical matters related to the three principal arts of architecture, painting, and sculpture. As a result, when we come to *Le vite* we readily presume, on the one hand, that many of the rules that define the art of the painter, sculptor, and architect—the very same rules that define a knowledge about and rational ability to represent a variety of concepts, such as grace, harmony, sweetness, and urbanity—spoke to desirable qualities that constituted part of the shared vocabulary aimed at describing and evaluating visual art in the period. Hence Vasari's *Le vite* can be taken, as it so often is, as a document that reflects a broad-based horizon of expectations. In part it provides us retrospectively with an understanding of what constituted the period eye of the Italian Renaissance.[74] Consequently, as scholars we regularly consult *Le vite* to get an historicized understanding of how some people collectively viewed visual art at the time and thereby learn some of the critical terms they applied to it as the product of a supremely rational techne.

On the other hand, when we come to Vasari's *Le vite*, we can also envision it as a book of instruction that taught readers of the period how to appreciate visual art so that they might better know what they, as nonpractitioners, should value when they looked at visual art, unpacked its formal construction, and situated artifacts in a broader historical development. In this regard, Vasari was not just defining accepted rules of a certain community related to a particular art as a form of specialized knowledge worthy of respect. He was also consciously fashioning how we, as potential viewers and consumers, are expected to make careful distinctions, thereby teaching us what to look for in assessing whether a painter, sculptor, or architect is indeed "excellent" in his art—if he knows the rules of the art, if he adheres to them too slavishly, or if he transcends them by liberating himself from those very same rules through years of rigorous training. In this respect, *Le vite* is an edifying book about the very discipline of looking at visual art. It not only trains readers to understand how art is made in the introductory section, thereby reminding us all the more emphatically that the author is indeed a broadly trained artisan fully qualified to talk about the matters at hand—that he has, in rhetorical terms, ethos in the context of his profession and the art underpinning it as a form of specialized knowledge. Vasari's *Le vite* also trains its readers to value certain kinds of visual art and, what is more, certain trends in art. And in this respect *Le vite* taught its readers and potential consumers in the sixteenth century—and thus teaches us today— "taste." Read Vasari, for instance, and you are led to privilege Florentine and Tuscan art over other "regional" forms of art, as well as, of course, "disegno" ("design" understood as primarily an intellectual practice realized through diligent preparatory drawing before actually applying paint, while demonstrating a predilection for hard, defined edges) over "colorito" ("design" understood as more of an intuitive practice realized through coloring as a way of creating forms in the act of applying paint, while demonstrating a predilection for soft, blurry edges). Those visual distinctions mattered to Vasari, presumably they mattered to his readers in search of marking themselves with distinction and in search of understanding visual art, and they still matter to us now—or at least the "us" that makes up an ever-dwindling community of readers still interested in Vasari and the Italian Renaissance.[75]

Moreover, within the context of thinking about *Le vite* as a book that edifies by performing for its readers a discipline of looking, *Le vite* offers us—and offered its readers over four centuries ago—two very different but still interrelated master narratives about the development of visual art in the context of the arts themselves as forms of specialized knowledge.[76] One narrative—the narrative we have all grown most accustomed to over the years—is fundamentally heroic in nature. It is grounded in the achievements of primarily exceptional Florentine and Tuscan artists over time, from Cimabue to Giotto to Masaccio to Leonardo and the like. These heroic individuals within Vasari's discourse gradually uncover, disclose, and make use of the universal rules underpinning the knowledge that makes up their art. That core master narrative, familiar to anyone who has read through even an anthologized version of *Le vite*, has its ultimate flowering in Michelangelo, particularly in the first Torrentiniana edition of 1550 but also still very much so in the enlarged Giuntina edition of 1568. In this regard, it is crucial that Michelangelo, the telos of this heroic narrative and providential process of artistic awakening, is viewed as inimitable so that his achievements are not readily transferable and always remain historically specific to his hand, his particular, individual, awe-inspiring *terribilità*, most divine nature, and enviable talent.[77] Another core narrative, by contrast, is fundamentally institutional in spirit. It is grounded, as Marco Ruffini has perceptively observed, in a corporate structure of artistic production that goes all the way back to the medieval guild system, finds expression in such exemplary artists as Ghirlandaio, Verrocchio, and Raphael with their extensive workshops, and has its great flowering in the Accademia del Disegno (Academy of Design), of which Vasari was such a vital and inspirational participant. The climax of one master narrative of historical artistic development—the heroic life work of the individual Michelangelo at the service of single patrons—in fact prepares for the upswing of the other—the rise of institutional visual art produced by an impersonal collectivity at the service of a bureaucratic "state."[78] Hence Michelangelo becomes an even more exceptional figure for Vasari within *Le vite* as these two master narratives—one valuing and privileging individuals, the other valuing and privileging collectivities—strategically dovetail at the end. Accordingly, Michelangelo is viewed not only as the heroic master of the three major visual arts of painting, sculpture, and architecture, as Vasari makes plain, but also as the mythical foundational hero whose providential and timely death, mourned in an elaborate funeral staged by the Accademia, makes possible the new professionalizing corporate structure of visual art of Vasari's time—an impersonal, discipline-bound, transhistorical, and rigorously rule-governed art that will be fashioned by and through an academy, so much so that it will become, as Ruffini has elegantly phrased it, "an art without an author."

Read this way, *Le vite* is not just about promoting rules for a certain type of visual art based on a form of specialized knowledge that Vasari values and seeks to elevate socially as an accomplished practitioner. Nor is it just about promoting a discipline of looking at works of visual art and understanding how they are skillfully made. Nor is it just about promoting a particular group of exemplary artists, or about promoting primarily Florentine and Tuscan artists. Nor is it just about promoting the author as a learned practitioner with a thorough command of his art within a book that ineluctably comes off as a self-reflexive ego document in the very moment that it talks primarily about other people's lives. Nor is it just a book about promoting a heroic conception of the development of visual art with individual artists contributing to the punctuated evolution of the artist's craft presented as possessing a form of specialized knowledge. Nor even, as I have argued elsewhere, is it just a book about promoting rules of behavior for artists (and allowing for exceptions to those rules for exceptional artists) in a period so feverishly committed to codifying conduct and civility yet so clearly peopled by larger-than-life, aggressive male personalities from Cesare Borgia to Julius II. *Le vite*, as Ruffini has brilliantly demonstrated, is also very much about promoting an institutional approach to an art and, as a result, a certain institutionalizing of taste as a marker of distinction. This strategy of shaping what we would probably call today a sort of "corporate taste" within a discourse about an art by a practitioner writing about the art in question is new, and it finds its first forceful and most seminal expression in the Italian Renaissance in Vasari's *Le vite*.[79]

Finally, many of these discourses composed by practitioners about their arts address matters connected to issues of educability and the possibility (or fantasy) of social mobility. Framed in terms of our contemporary belief systems, knowledge creates opportunities for both employment and social access, and a key way of acquiring knowledge, we readily assume (and we are invited to assume today by publishers and educators alike through all sorts of pedagogical hype), is through books (or electronic versions of books on an ever-changing array of inventive platforms). Want to be a goldsmith? Learn the lessons in Cellini's treatise.[80] Want to be an architect? Learn from Leon Battista Alberti, Sebastiano Serlio, Filarete, Francesco di Giorgio Martini, or Andrea Palladio.[81] Want to be a metallurgist to meet a demand for the exploration and exploitation of minerals for a variety of commercial and productive ends, including the fabrication of armaments and the minting of coins? Read Biringuccio's *Pirotechnia*, which displays multiple designs of how that art can be profitably put into practice, beginning with the very border of the frontispiece (fig. 9). Want to be a builder of forts, an inventor of war machines and armaments, a military leader, a soldier? There are a host of informative printed books to enjoy on the topic, too many to even begin to list, but they are certainly there to edify you.[82] Want to be a visual artist? Learn from Cennino Cennini, Piero della Francesca, Leonardo da Vinci, Benvenuto Cellini, Giorgio Vasari, and, up to a point, Gian Paolo Lomazzo.[83] Want to be a courtier, a surgeon, a secretary, an ambassador—even a cook or steward? Learn from Baldassare Castiglione, Leonardo Fioravanti, Andrea Nati, Giulio Cesare Capaccio, Angelo Ingegneri, Giambattista Guarini, Bartolomeo Zucchi, Tomaso Costo, Benedetto Pucci, Ermolao Barbaro, and Cristoforo Messisbugo, among others.[84] An art as a form of specialized knowledge was repeatedly explored in the Italian Renaissance through an unprecedented flourishing of discourses written by practitioners invested in a variety of professions. What is more, a host of nonpractitioners— not to be outdone—contributed to the outpouring of discourses about arts in Renaissance Italy, from a mere handful of authors who remain well-known in academia (Niccolò Machiavelli writing on princes and the work of military leaders, Leon Battista Alberti writing on painters, and Torquato Tasso writing on secretaries and ambassadors),[85] to those who are reasonably well-known by specialists within subdisciplines (Francesco Sansovino writing on secretaries, Roberto Valturio writing on military science, and Paolo Cortesi writing on cardinals),[86] to those who remain obscure even for academics occasionally toiling away in what Herman Melville would have no doubt called sub-sub-sub-disciplines (Gabriele Zinano, for instance, writing on secretaries, Ottaviano Maggi writing on ambassadors, and a plethora of authors writing about soldiery and related military tasks).[87]

Collectively and individually, these discourses serve to edify, and at face value the knowledge purveyed in them about a particular art is presented not secretively but openly, offering up information in the spirit of full disclosure.[88] People eager to pursue or perfect a career as a painter, architect, medic, surgeon, ambassador, sculptor, engineer, goldsmith, soldier, ambassador, or secretary—even, to be sure, as a new prince terrorizing his subjects in order to secure his position and state or a worldly cardinal climbing the social food chain by building and running the household of a magnificent palace in Rome—can, it would seem, begin at the very least by reading these edifying discourses, which often enough reveal how one can go about trying to succeed in a particular profession grounded in an art with its distinct knowledge. In the Italian Renaissance, mastery of an art as a form of specialized knowledge was repeatedly presented in these discourses as something to be desired, in which the ability to transform objects or people's minds and abilities symbolized the artists'—understood as the makers' or doers'—protean capacity to potentially change themselves in society by becoming acknowledged, exemplary masters through discipline and self-control as well as, at times, masters over others by giving shape to other people's lives and by directing them toward purposive ends. Moreover, acquiring mastery over an art can be viewed as the source of no small self-satisfaction on the part of practitioners who have actively pursued professional life and can take personal pleasure in it and the specialized knowledge necessary to succeed in it.

And yet the crucial, underlying issue about how to go about actually acquiring the specialized knowledge of an art and then apply it masterfully, thereby becoming through some calculated process of inculcation and training a first-rate practitioner, can turn out to be exceedingly complex in some of these discourses—far more complex than it may at least at first glance seem to be. As these books divulge information openly about an art as it is configured as necessary for success in a profession, they often lay claim to the value of a particular profession so that people will want to enter it and admire it, and they make the profession and the art underpinning it appear accessible by presenting the knowledge related to it as eminently learnable. But in at least a few cases, the authors of these books adopt a strategy of enticing and openly edifying readers only—in truth—to close off access to the profession they want everyone to admire and learn about by mystifying the very process by which one can actually acquire the ability to become a true acknowledged master over the art in question. It is therefore essential that some of these discourses function as ego documents. We must admire the practitioners and their mastery over the specialized knowledge of their art so that we will want to be like them, laboring to imitate them through exemplarity in good Renaissance fashion. And in our admiration we must trust that we can be taught by them, likewise disclosing in good Renaissance fashion our faith in our own educability and consequently our sustaining belief, in Erasmus's terms, that humans are "made," not "born," at least when it comes to the belief that we are made, and not born, to make or do certain defined things in life.[89] It is equally essential that some of these discourses frame the work or knowledge of the authors themselves as something that is to be admired or wondered at within the text itself. For these remarkable practitioners who have turned to authorship, we are led to believe, have the capacity to edify us, so that by following them we, too, can learn, succeed, and be admired, even if, as I shall argue in the following section, some of the practitioners who turned to authorship lay claim to a position that is decidedly at odds with what the discourse in practice actually does. Put differently, the writers of these discourses may indicate that the art they teach as a form of knowledge requisite for a profession is learnable through the diligent application of rules, thereby rendering the art accessible to professional aspirants as they disclose its specialized knowledge. But in truth they surreptitiously reveal that the art itself can only be applied with real success by a precious few who somehow possess the "right stuff," thereby effectively closing off access to the profession in question for many while rendering the practitioner authors themselves all the more exquisitely exceptional in light of their obvious, yet still mystifying, achievements as professionals who have so brilliantly mastered their art as a form of useful specialized knowledge that benefits the community at large.

Consider in this context Castiglione's *Il cortegiano* as a discourse that brilliantly deploys a strategy of simultaneously disclosing and withholding information necessary to succeed in applying a specific art—in this particular case a practical, as opposed to productive, art.[90] First of all, we should bear in mind that Castiglione (fig. 14) in *Il cortegiano* characterizes courtiership as indeed an art, with

FIGURE 14. Raphael (Raffaello Sanzio, 1483–1520), *Portrait of Baldassare Castiglione*, 1514–1515. Louvre, Paris. Reproduced by permission of Scala/Art Resource, NY.

it possessing all the characteristics of a techne in classical antiquity. The knowledge associated with it, Castiglione underscores, is determinate, it has an end, it is teachable, it allows us to move from the particular to the universal, it has rules (even if Castiglione is quick to point out that he is not writing a typical catechistic-style, rule-bound manual),[91] it is communicable, it is reliable (or so he contends, even if it is certainly far more stochastic than exact in nature), it is performative (one must put courtiership into action so that it can be verified as an art), and it is supremely rational. It is not, for instance, the product of a knack but of calculated reasoning and practice honed through extensive training. Or so we are told with some insistence.

Moreover, Castiglione would have us believe, at least at first glance, that we are made into courtiers, not born into being them. Hence the "grazia" (grace) that is required of all of us to be a courtier—the "grazia" that not only renders us full of grace in our comportment but also wins the gratitude of the prince as we ingratiate ourselves to him as dutiful and delightful courtiers—is not the sort of grace that is divinely bestowed upon someone from on high, any more than it can be conceived in Alexander Pope's terms as a sort of transcendent "grace beyond the reach of art."[92] Quite the contrary, Castiglione is concerned with a grace that is well within our reach if we just put our minds to it: it is secular in nature, learnable, practical, purposive, and decidedly explicable. It is also a grace that can be readily acquired through rules—or, above all, by heeding one all-encompassing, universalizing rule: we must avoid "affettazione" (affectation) and practice in everything we say and do a certain "sprezzatura" (a crucial term that for the moment we shall leave undefined). There are, to be sure, other rules to courtiership that we learn along the way, most of them fairly obvious to modern habits of etiquette: don't throw food around the dining table, for instance, and don't be a bore, braggart, or brute. But the general rule that we must act with sprezzatura in all that we say and do is undeniably the most important one within *Il cortegiano*. Without sprezzatura we will not have the grace needed to "season" all that we say and do ("che mettiate per un condimento d'ogni cosa, senza il quale tutte le altre proprietà e bone condicioni sian di poco valore" [that you require this in everything as that seasoning without which all the other properties and good qualities will be of little worth], 1.24). And without grace we will fail in our ultimate professional goal, which is to please the prince so that we may gain access to him, counsel him regarding what course to take from day to day as a ruler, and thus strategically work our way into having influence over the course of events. We need to follow this rule of sprezzatura, then, not only for our own benefit (the courtier, realistically, is always looking out for his own hide as he strives to advance in a profession and seek honor and recognition in the process) but also for all those people who have anything at all to do with the princedom in general and its harmonious workings in a truly complex and dangerous world fraught with tensions and widespread conflicts (the courtier, not unlike cheerful Miss America competitors, is idealistically supposed to be interested in such niceties as "universal peace").

Now the key term "sprezzatura" coined by Castiglione and drawn from the verb "disprezzare" (to scorn, diminish, disdain, reduce in value) suggests that at any given moment, if you have difficulty locating the exact mean between extremes as you seek that perfect Horatian *aurea mediocritas* (golden mean) in all that you say or do, you should always offer up less rather than more, particularly since the mind for Castiglione is quick to draw a complete picture from the part. What is more, this overarching rule holds true about a whole range of matters. It dictates how much time one should dedicate to fixing up one's hair: don't spend too much time on it lest you appear a fop. It suggests how one should speak with friends at court and in public ceremonies: understatement, the privileged strategy of the ironist, is preferred to overstatement, it would seem, so one should theoretically employ litotes rather than hyperbole as a figure of speech and thought. It dictates how much specialized knowledge one needs to possess on any given subject: one should know just enough to convince everyone that you do indeed know what you calculatingly hint at knowing even if you lack, and are expected to lack, any real studied expertise in the subject so that your measured, decorous performance masks at best an amateurish ability and at worst a true underlying incompetence. And, to be sure, it even identifies how physically tall the ideal courtier should be: a bit shorter is always better than a bit taller if it is tough locating the perfect mean in a given culture where you happen to be seeking employment as a courtier (1.20).

At the same time, the term "sprezzatura" by its very nature suggests something about the ideal emotional state of the courtier, if we can be allowed for the purposes of this argument to gauge his temperament in terms of literally temperature. For the ideal mean between someone who is hotheaded (someone, that is, who is easily inflamed and overemotional and perhaps just a bit too effusively sympathetic) and someone who is cold-hearted (someone who is unemotional, indifferent, excessively detached, insensitive, or unsympathetic) is presumably someone who is "warm" or "warm-hearted." And yet, because it is so very difficult in practice to know exactly what constitutes "warm" for everyone we meet as we interact with a variety of people in a wide array of social circumstances on a daily basis and are forced to behave differently according to the ravages of occasion in different settings and contexts, we should shave off a bit—scorn and thus diminish the potential excess—and act just a bit colder if we are ever in doubt as to what constitutes the perfect degree of emotional "warmth" warranted in our behavior in all that we say and do. Or, rather, to adopt the language of the 1950s still current today, we should "be cool." But then again, we must be careful never to be *too* cool. If you're "too cool for words," to be prosaic about the matter yet again, you're still affected. And if you're affected, you've simply made a horrible mess of it and will never prove to be a good, much less perfect, courtier.

Ideally, then, the courtier who has mastered the "virtue" of sprezzatura can espouse convincingly the specialized knowledge associated with a whole host of arts, even if he knows only a smattering of any one of them and is consequently clueless as to the real rational, communicable, determinate, and reliable knowledge underpinning the very arts he pretends to know so well as he seeks to impress everyone—and in particular the prince—with his grace. Anyone who stands in admiration of the courtier's ability, who thinks the courtier as a practiced dilettante can in fact do or know all these things with some credible mastery (dance, sing, paint, and the like), is clearly not part of the professional club. That person as an onlooker has sadly mistaken the appearance for the reality and has thus failed to realize that the courtier's performance is completely studied and mannered, even as it comes off as supremely natural and the product of real, rather than feigned, expertise. The truly accomplished courtier has worked hard, with all due "labor, industry, and care [*fatica, industria e studio*]" (1.24), at appearing not to work at all, in convincing people that the part can stand in for the whole. For there is labor involved in dancing and singing, as well as even just standing about the court with a seemingly natural pose in elegant choice apparel, yet that labor is artfully—as in cleverly—hidden.

In professional terms, then, sprezzatura functions within the court as a "signaling device." All the courtiers looking on with the requisite sprezzatura know that the person is merely acting, that it is a performance that dupes others, and that the courtier, at best sometimes an informed amateur, is clueless about the specific arts in question in a manner that would render him a master in so many things he only hints at being able to do with some reliable and credible expertise. What the exemplary courtiers collectively observing the performance in the know discreetly admire, however, is instead the illusion created, the courtier's calculated ability to act with a like-minded sleight of hand. They astutely and instinctively grasp the trick of the trade as an essential part of their own collective profession of courtiership and commend him for what the Greeks would have no doubt called his metis. In this respect, they admire his professionalism and they recognize him as one of their own. He's "in." He's an "insider." He's one of "them." He is part of the select closed circle of the group with its finely tuned strategies for success. And he is decidedly secretive about it. Or, rather, what he conveys is an "open secret" whose core truth—that the courtier doesn't know as an expert does the various arts in question as he seeks to apply them in his clever, studied performances—is available only to those initiated into the specialized form of knowledge underpinning the profession of courtiership and, needless to say, to all those courtiers who apply that specific art in practice with seemingly perfect aplomb.[93]

But this only begs the question. How exactly can one really go about acquiring sprezzatura in order to become part of this "new profession," as it is so defined in the first, but then eventually discarded, preface to *Il cortegiano*,[94] so that one's mastery of sprezzatura in all that one says or does can indeed function as a substitute for a mastery over the forms of specialized knowledge of a host of *other* arts that the courtier feigns to know in some measure and that are the province of expertise of *other* professionals, from musicians to painters to dancers, who likewise periodically sought to attach themselves to courts? We know, to be sure, that we must work hard in order to appear to do so many different things without any work whatsoever—something that would no doubt have pleased the cultural elite in classical antiquity since the very concept of work often carried with it the lingering odor of vulgarity. But what exactly are we supposed to do by way of preparatory "labor, industry, and care" so that we may acquire sprezzatura and thus perform in a manner that conceals all work and, at the same time, convinces people that we possess the requisite knowledge associated with those different things that we appear to be, but indeed are *not*, masterful practitioners of when all is said and done? How, moreover, do we practice acquiring sprezzatura, since there is no school of courtiership that can show us how to develop and refine this strategy of locating the perfect mean in all that we say and do? Or at least there is no formal institutionalized adult school that can train us in these matters, since the humanist classroom did to varying degrees of success inculcate poetry, grammar, rhetoric, history, and moral philosophy and was ideally intended to prepare the cultural elite for success in leadership but certainly had no specific professional bent to it and, of course, served to educate boys rather than full-grown men. Nor is there a formalized guild system—a system, that is to say, of "artes"—whose primary function was to serve as "a device designed to organize and order society" but through which one could also be indoctrinated into the practices of the profession of courtiership and the art underpinning the very mysteries of that particular misterium.[95] Nor, directly related to this, is there an extensive workshop structure that would-be courtiers can take advantage of as visual artists can when they link themselves to a master, such as Ghirlandaio, Verrocchio, or Raphael, and are apprenticed to him until such time as they have thoroughly absorbed all the lessons of the art and can then ideally emerge at the end, after years of diligent practice and hard "labor, industry, and care," as an adult master on their own within the chosen profession, if indeed they choose to pay the dues and enter and belong to the guild as a recognized master.[96] Nor, of course, does the university system prepare anyone for courtiership.

Surely, moreover, it is not enough to borrow from accepted poetic practice, as Castiglione indirectly insists we should, and tell would-be courtiers to rely simply on their "bon giudicio" (good judgment), go out into the world, choose the best qualities of courtiers who exhibit grace, and then, after deftly mixing all those admirable qualities together in one's own behavior, somehow, magically, become a figure of grace for others to imitate, so that the process of inculcation productively repeats itself in an endless, regenerative feedback loop.[97] For how do we acquire good judgment in the first place unless we are born with it? Castiglione never tells us how to acquire this requisite ur-knowledge of good judgment, which indeed remains something of a puzzle in a book that sets out to provide an underlying rational basis to account for success in all sorts of behaviors and skills related to this "new profession" of courtiership. Worse, how do we put into practice the process of imitation itself? Surely it is one thing for a poet to sit in a room as the laureate Francesco Petrarca did and scribble away with ponderous classical models in mind, then cross out some of his writings that did not satisfy him, then rewrite them, then return to them hours, days, or years later and revise it all over yet again with increased critical detachment until it is just right, so that the power of the classical allusion underpinning the writing and lending it authority and gravitas is not too obtrusive and has been thoroughly absorbed into a signature style after much "labor, industry, and care."[98] But it is really quite a different matter altogether, for a host of practical reasons, for an eager aspirant to try to adopt the same strategy of poetic imitation and continuous revision as he seeks to become a courtier with the requisite grace that will win him the desired favor of the prince. For, unlike being a poet, being a courtier means you are involved in a constantly interactive, often spontaneous, improvisation-based, and oratory-bound profession. And that means you are consequently engaged in an essentially theatrical, relational, and conversational activity that you just cannot simply put into practice in solitude or revise in private through an act of calculated withdrawal and reflection.[99] At any given time, you—as a dutiful functionary whose job is to serve—stand on the stage before others and you must act, come what may. You are out there, vulnerable and visible. And when you are called upon to talk or act, which for Castiglione a courtier is constantly called upon to do on a daily basis, and if, alas, you happen to fail at talking or acting properly at any given moment, you potentially fail in a shame culture in which, we can readily glean from *Il cortegiano* itself, a variety of people took great pleasure in seizing upon the slightest blemish of rivals to discredit them. Being a courtier, in sum, was extremely risky business in a culture so thoroughly steeped in the widespread trafficking of gossip.[100]

Now, at first glance it would seem that if Castiglione fails to tell us how to exert all that preparatory "labor, industry, and care," much less show us how to do so, it would be because the universal rule that one must flee affectation and in all things practice sprezzatura is teachable as a rule but only as a rule. That is to say, it would appear that Castiglione cannot provide us with clear-cut mechanisms for learning sprezzatura and thus for systematically acquiring grace. He can name what we need: we need to act and be full of grace and possess good judgment. He can shrewdly, and with some performative nonchalance of his own, invent words to name what we need to do: we need to act, as he suavely puts it through an interlocutor in a casual, offhand manner, with sprezzatura. He can draw on standard rhetorical and poetic practice to suggest how we acquire grace: we need to be like a bee—Seneca's bee, Petrarca's bee, any fine, roaming, clever, industrious bee[101]—gathering the best nectar of courtiership from the choice flowers of the finest courtiers whom we can ever hope to meet and then busily mix all that precious courtly nectar together to come up with our own exemplary signature style of graceful comportment. Castiglione can also rely on classical rhetoric—particularly Cicero's *De oratore*, which is the most obvious classical model underlying *Il cortegiano*—to articulate an overall strategy for success: we need to be persuasive in all that we say and do by choosing our words carefully, by being apt, by understanding the role of wit, by learning all the figures of speech and thought, and the like. Castiglione may even presume that the *studia humanitatis*, with its focus on grammar, poetry, rhetoric, moral philosophy, and history, will inculcate good judgment and grace, although there is some question that it ever achieved such a goal, much less aimed at inculcating it. Finally, Castiglione can show us what the finished product of all that preparatory "labor, industry, and care" might well look like by nostalgically presenting a group portrait of accomplished courtiers interacting in a conversational mode in Urbino and by assuming that the examples presented will adequately instruct us all on how to become accomplished courtiers. But Castiglione cannot really systematically teach us how to go about acquiring this grace and sprezzatura, much less go about learning how to possess good judgment, through preparatory "labor, industry, and care." Or at least, more important, *he doesn't do so*.

Nor, for that matter, does Castiglione point to some other edifying book that he wrote that would teach us about all the preparatory work we need to do in order to succeed in the profession of courtiership, some sort of companion volume that lays it all out practically and methodically as a basic training manual for professional success and the art underpinning it. Nor does Castiglione tell us what informative books we should read to become at least moderately adept in a host of productive or practical arts that we may need to be versed in as courtiers, or tell us where and how we may hope to get the requisite preparatory training in those arts, so that we can in fact apply ourselves with "labor, industry, and care" to any particular task at hand that is required of us when the occasion arises for us to do so in this "new profession" of the courtier. If Cicero, for instance, the classical author whose works most obviously influenced the shape of *Il cortegiano*, does not furnish us with *all* the rules of what it means to be an orator in his "surprising" and "innovative" *De oratore* (although he does indeed provide us with so many of those rules, particularly in the second and third books), we can at least look to one or two of his other rhetorical treatises—his (youthful, by his own admission) *De inventione* (*On Invention*), for instance.[102] Some of Cicero's books, including the influential first-century BCE textbook *Rhetorica ad Herennium*, which was taken by some to be genuinely Ciceronian in Castiglione's time and was typically paired with *De inventione* in printed editions, do indeed rather meticulously and systematically provide us with some of the ins and outs of rhetoric, so that we can practice our oratorical skills and learn how to become accomplished public speakers through dutiful preparation in the process of consulting and working through these more technical, prescriptive, manual-structured books.[103] But nothing of the sort exists in Castiglione's dialogue, which, far from being catechistic, instead leaves us high and dry, with no formal method of practical training to adopt and methodically follow. In sum, *Il cortegiano* tells us *that* we must work at being a courtier, but it does not systematically show us at all *how* to work at it.

In this sense *Il cortegiano* functions as a discourse that appears to be open as it purports to tell us what we need to do to succeed in learning a specific art as a form of specialized knowledge but is indeed secretive and mystifying in providing us with the real, viable means for success in the profession of courtiership. Read this book and you are edified about what it means to be an exemplary courtier but not so much about how to actually become such a courtier by acquiring the art underpinning the profession through careful preparation and training. The artfulness of *Il cortegiano*, in the sense of its strategic cleverness as cunning intelligence (metis), is to make people reading it believe from the outset that there is in fact an art underpinning the profession of courtiership—that courtiership possesses a distinct techne in the classical sense of the term as a rational, communicable, rule-bound, and reliable form of highly specialized, determinate knowledge that one can learn through some sort of training, as Cicero would seek to offer us, for instance, in his likewise dialogue-structured *De oratore*. But in truth, Castiglione does not systematically teach us how to acquire that specialized knowledge, and he does not tell us how to acquire the requisite training to develop into a masterful courtier. Or rather, to frame the matter slightly differently, Castiglione's book overtly says that grace can be acquired, but then Castiglione's contention conveyed as an assertion turns out to be, at least upon closer examination, somewhat at odds with what the book actually does insofar as Castiglione never teaches us really how to acquire grace through preparatory training, either by instructing us systematically within his book itself how to do so, by pointing to some other book he wrote that will show us how to do so, or by pointing to other people's books that will authoritatively show us how to do so. We may therefore initially be willing, at least at first glance, to concede that grace—as Castiglione envisions it—is not beyond the reach of art, that it is indeed something that can be acquired through "labor, industry, and care," and that it is therefore something that is not enigmatic or transcendent in form, a sort of ineffable *nescio quid*. But upon further reflection as we progress through the book we may also legitimately wonder, since we are never actually indoctrinated into a practical method of training to acquire grace, if people are not in fact "born" rather than "made" to be courtiers—if, in the end, contrary to what we were led to expect from the outset of *Il cortegiano*, there is simply a mysterious quality bestowed on people that allows one person to succeed in the profession of courtiership while another is condemned to fail at it no matter how hard that individual person works at it with "industry, labor, and care" and no matter how much that person seems, for all intents and purposes, to possess a natural inclination to succeed as a courtier and thus seems to have precisely the right stuff to become an exemplary one.[104]

In the most obvious sense, this "ruse," as I see it, of inviting everyone to admire those who can play the game of courtiership successfully allows Castiglione to persuade the ruling elite that courtiership itself is a socially valuable profession with a specialized knowledge underpinning it as an art. After reading this book with its sweeping nostalgia, its elegant, periodic prose suavely expressed in the vernacular, its classicizing models so thoroughly absorbed into a signature style, and its colorful cast of (for the most part) delightful male characters populating it, what eager, ambitious man aspiring to be part of the cultural elite in sixteenth-century Italy wouldn't have wanted to become a courtier, value courtiership, and hang out in a court exercising sprezzatura all day long? Who wouldn't have wanted to applaud these courtiers who charm each other, as well as the delightful elegant ladies of the court, for so many hours of the day? Who wouldn't have wanted to learn how to be like them by trying to follow their examples (or those of other praiseworthy courtiers) and then in turn be conceptually applauded by others when one finally becomes after years of practice an esteemed courtier too? Who wouldn't, to borrow the still persistent language of the 1950s in our own culture, have wanted to be so damn cool? But at the same time, this ruse of inviting everyone to admire those who can play the game of courtiership successfully permits those very same professionals who somehow already mysteriously possess sprezzatura to close ranks and actually control social mobility, *not* enhance it, by effectively winking at one another from across the room as they recognize who belongs, who doesn't, who is a boor, who isn't, who is "cool," who isn't. What is more, this ruse of inviting everyone to admire those who can play the game of courtiership successfully allows Castiglione to define taste for the prince, much as Vasari teaches taste for potential collectors and consumers of visual art as he clarifies what to look for when viewing "excellent" painting, sculpture, and architecture. In this way, Castiglione's book serves once more as a signaling device, defining who is "in," who is "out." He, like Vasari, is articulating "excellence," both as an aesthetic quality and as a marker of social and cultural distinction.

Put differently, if in the classical period the ruling elite might potentially fear the Promethean upstarts seeking to advance themselves through the acquisition of a techne as a form of specialized knowledge, thus opening up fantasies of "unregulated mobility" in the minds of those who occupied a secure, privileged station in society, here it is the professionals *themselves* who are fearing upstarts within their ranks, the very upstarts Castiglione seems to invite into his ranks as he reveals so openly the putative rules by which one can become a courtier in the spirit of full disclosure yet effectively excludes from the ranks of courtiership by making it virtually impossible, at least through a reading of *Il cortegiano*, for those aspiring newcomers who lack grace and good judgment from the outset to acquire the reliable mechanisms to prepare them to become, through "labor, industry, and care," just like all those admired and exemplary courtiers portrayed together in Urbino as they ever so fashionably entertain each other for four festive evenings in a row. Castiglione's book in this way functions less to inculcate a precise art that allows for access to his "new profession"—it can hardly be construed in this respect as a full-fledged prescriptive how-to book or primer for social mobility[105]—and more to establish "taste" by informing a prince what behavioral qualities he should look for in a courtier when he recognizes at any given moment in his lifespan as an autocratic ruler that he needs to surround himself with distinctive, qualified, professional functionaries in order to more efficiently run the ever-growing and increasingly complicated bureaucracy of his expanding princedom. Needless to say, the prince, we are told, should look for someone who possesses grace and all the delightful, ingratiating attributes associated with people who have grace. Or, not to put too fine a point on it, the enlightened prince should look for someone just like Castiglione and his exemplary humanist friends, all of whom can write and speak beautifully but were largely clueless about the one thing a courtier—whose declared primary "profession," after all, was that of "arms"— was expected to do in Castiglione's treatise as a hangover from a defunct feudal period in northern Italy: fight in a war, defeat enemies in battle, and prove victorious in combat. Truth be told, the best most of these fashionable, well-dressed, witty, and garrulous men gathered together in Urbino could possibly do when it came to war, I'd wager, was talk their opponents to death—or at least charm them all the way through the night until sunrise. In the final analysis what most of Castiglione's characters possess—and this is fairly obvious but nevertheless still warrants being stressed—is rhetorical, not military, prowess. Elegant talking, not heroic military fighting, was their principal "manly" activity, which in the context of *Il cortegiano* becomes the source of no small anxiety on the part of some of the men who find themselves engaged in activities that risk making them appear effeminate in the eyes of others, from caring about how much time they should or should not dedicate to dancing before the prince to how much time they should or should not devote to coiffing their hair and beards.[106]

How, we might therefore ask, does Castiglione's strategy as a practitioner author compare to that of Cicero's, whose *De oratore* serves as the dominant classical model of a discourse about an art underpinning *Il cortegiano*? In the middle of the first century BCE, two significant pressures were arguably being exerted against oratory at the time Cicero was writing, each coming from different directions.[107] On the one hand, the rise of the First Triumvirate and the silencing and censoring of Cicero in the period certainly made his own position as orator vulnerable in the face of generals, and so he presumably felt that oratory by and large was threatened, although it does not appear to be quite so endangered in the *De oratore* as in his late works, notably the *Brutus*, where the end of oratory seems to haunt the scene and where the notion of the orator is significantly expanded to stand in for some broader category like "statesman" or even, perhaps, "citizen." On the other hand, the core members of the aristocracy, of which Cicero was indeed not a part, always directed significant hostility toward oratory itself insofar as they preferred to appeal more directly to naturalized forms of entitled authority instead of having to labor to persuade on every occasion. In any event, while Cicero unquestionably needed to defend both "oratory" and "rhetoric" in his writings (indeed, rhetoric was always in need of some sort of defense ever since Plato leveled a series of savage charges against it),[108] in his *De oratore* he was not particularly concerned with fundamentally redefining the nature of the art of rhetoric he was discussing as he fashioned a perfect orator in dialogue form, even if, all things considered, he certainly did moralize it and thus, like Quintilian, helped transform it in a number of significant and lasting ways.[109] By contrast, Castiglione instead very much aimed to do precisely that—namely *fundamentally* redefine the art he was investigating in his treatise—as he transformed the courtier from being a boorish soldier of the feudal past versed in accomplished equestrian fighting tactics to a cultured classicist of the humanist schoolroom versed in being stunningly eloquent, from someone who performs in a belligerent manner that is conventionally taken as embodying a male virtue of swashbuckling epic force (of engaging in violent tournaments or heroically thrusting a sword into someone's gut and taking great personal pleasure in watching the victim squirm) to one who performs in a stylized way that risks being construed as effeminate in light of lavishing undue attention on ephemera (of thinking about hairdos, dancing, table manners, choice apparel, and, more generally, how to please the prince and everyone else associated with the court—especially taciturn, elegant women in the evening—with colorful talk, wry humor, biting gossip, and playful language games).

Unlike Cicero, then, Castiglione, who was precisely one of those well-trained and well-mannered humanists with primarily linguistic rather than military skills to offer a prince through service, composed his discourse about the art underpinning courtiership in a period when interest in professionalization was keen and intensifying for a variety of social and political reasons, not the least being the development of a host of competitive courts in need of male functionaries to service their complex daily workings. Moreover, unlike Cicero, Castiglione was speaking to a cultural elite that was in need of validating its profession with an art as a specialized form of knowledge as it staked out its jurisdictional claim in competition with other rising professions for men within the growing bureaucracies of sixteenth-century Italian courts, such as the profession of the secretary and the specialized art underpinning secretaryship. Rulers, to be sure, always needed letter writers within their chanceries, whereas it was arguably questionable whether they really needed these courtiers attending to them all day long if all they were good for (at least until we get to the fourth book of *Il cortegiano*) was to look great, talk well, crack good jokes, play coy games, and charmingly entertain each other and some elegant ladies in a sort of fashionable evening salon.[110] Furthermore, within this competitive system of professions, Castiglione was speaking to a cultural elite that was in need of making a case for the value of courtiership as an essential profession that the prince must be coaxed into believing he wants to make use of in order to succeed as a ruler. And, finally, Castiglione was speaking to a cultural elite that appreciated the threat posed by the social mobility of upstarts potentially infiltrating their ranks and displacing entrenched members who may have viewed their position as secure when indeed it was not. The value of the courtier in sixteenth-century Italy was not, in sum, a given, any more than the value of the orator was in Cicero's time. Indeed, the courtier's position, somewhat like Cicero's orator, was not secure. It was, instead, decidedly vulnerable.

Consequently, Castiglione adopts a rather convoluted strategy to validate courtiership as a critical profession worthy of respect and, at the same time, to close off access to the "new profession" of courtiership while securing a position for some of its entrenched members, such as himself. First and foremost, he makes courtiership appear so endearing as an exemplary profession that everyone reading the book would ineluctably want to practice it and admire it. Hence he adopts the language of marveling throughout the book, rendering the courtier something of a wonder worthy of intense, discriminating admiration (*admiratio*). At the same time, he initially makes courtiership appear to be so accessible that all those aspiring individuals seduced into the profession will believe they can indeed be part of a group identity by following some "apparently"—and I use the adverb advisedly—straightforward rules. To this end, in the course of assuring his readers that the profession of courtiership has an art to it and is therefore something they can readily acquire through instruction and training, Castiglione proceeds to provide his readers with a seemingly foolproof set of reliable rules by which they can learn how to be a courtier, above all the universal rule they should act with sprezzatura and seek the mean between extremes (or just a bit less than the exact mean between extremes) in all that they say and do, as well as the general rule that they should learn through example by imitating masterful courtiers. Along with this, Castiglione makes courtiership appear to be so very necessary for the prince that the ruler will want to employ these people so that he might be surrounded by them, benefit from their advice, and, indeed, be charmed by them in the very moment that he is instructed by them and counseled to be a good ruler. Accordingly, if at first glance these courtiers seem to have a purely ornamental function as decorative and decorous window dressing (much as the late fifteenth-century courtiers appear in Andrea Mantegna's *The Family and Court of Ludovico III Gonzaga*, fig. 15), finally, in the fourth book, Castiglione's courtiers are at long last given a goal-oriented political and ethical function as teachers of wisdom to the prince and counselors of good policies. Indeed, without these courtiers as counselors, we are led to believe, things will lamentably fall into ruin both in the prince's state and in the world at large. Hence Castiglione configures courtiership as a profession that ultimately has a necessary and exemplary ethical and political service to offer the prince within the court (the courtier in his service can give sound advice that will allow the prince to rule well and with dignity), and he holds courtiership up as a model profession that will please the prince and everyone else within the court (the courtier as an educated functionary confers distinction upon the prince and his court through his fine manners and elegant, fashionable, humanist-style talk). Finally, Castiglione makes courtiership appear to be so very simple to learn—read this book and you're off and running—but in truth he makes it so difficult to practice in reality that in the end the vast majority of all those competitive would-be courtiers, even as they are openly instructed into the art underpinning the profession as a form of specialized knowledge, will

FIGURE 15. Andrea Mantegna (1431–1506), *The Family and Court of Ludovico III Gonzaga*, 1465–1474. Camera degli Sposi, Palazzo Ducale, Mantua. Reproduced by permission of Scala/Art Resource, NY. The theatrically poised and stylish courtiers make up virtually half of the "famiglia"—to the right of the Gonzaga family—within the decoratively framed "window" of Mantegna's ingeniously frescoed image.

inevitably fail at it because they will lack what it takes—the good judgment, the sprezzatura, the grace—to guide them properly in all that they say and do. Hence Castiglione may seem to prescribe how to become a courtier as he provides us with apparently infallible rules, but in fact he only describes how to be a courtier and, in the final analysis, never shows us how to become a masterful one through a rigorous program of preparatory training.[111]

There is no mistaking it. *Il cortegiano*, one of the great prose masterpieces of the Italian Renaissance and the European Renaissance generally, was—and remains—an especially sophisticated text written by a smart and gifted humanist who could readily draw on a variety of erudite sources to build a nuanced argument as he strategically engaged in a rivalry with classical culture, particularly Cicero's *De oratore*. In doing so, he constructed a profession for his own time, cognizant of the distance that historically separated his world from Cicero's, his profession of the courtier from that of the classical Roman orator, his art underpinning courtiership from the art of rhetoric espoused in Cicero's varied treatises, his "new" profession of the courtier, who is an expert in polite comportment and advice giving in a "stylish style,"[112] from the long-established but (for Castiglione) now no longer desirable profession of the courtier in sixteenth-century Italy who was an expert in fighting and could be viewed as something of an aggressive, swaggering bore/boor. We should hardly be surprised, then, that *Il cortegiano*, written by such a talented practitioner and discriminating humanist writer, is more complex in structure than any other discourse about arts composed in the Italian Renaissance as practitioners turned to authorship and sought to define the art underpinning a profession. Nevertheless, some aspects of the overall complex strategy Castiglione shrewdly employs to legitimate the "new profession" of the courtier and the art underpinning it—in particular of presenting the specialized knowledge underlying courtiership openly yet mystifying the very process by which one can truly succeed as a master in acquiring and applying the art in question—can also be found to varying degrees in some other writings composed by practitioners as they talked about arts in sixteenth-century Italy, including discourses about the productive, as opposed to the practical, arts.

A case in point is Cellini's treatise on goldsmithing, the work of a near contemporary who lived and labored just a generation after Castiglione.[113] Like Castiglione, Cellini (fig. 16) aims to impart a knowledge that is determinate, rule-bound, rational, reliable, and communicable. Since Cellini is writing this discourse with the aim of instructing us about what goes on in the finest possible goldsmithing workshops (fig. 17), we can only assume that Cellini presumes his knowledge is teachable. In a word, he is inculcating an "art" in the classical sense of it as a "techne," much as Cennino Cennini emphatically did before him when writing about painting in the visual arts.[114] And Cellini is transparently open about what he will teach us, undertaking, as he puts it in the preface, "to write about those loveliest secrets and wondrous methods of the great art [*arte*] of goldsmithing" (1). This is patently the case. If you happen to wake up one morning with a hankering to know everything about goldsmithing in the Italian Renaissance, from how to do complicated filigree work to how to tint a diamond, Cellini is your man. He is open to a fault in providing us with details about his art as a specialized form of knowledge, carrying on for thirty-seven chapters (some fairly long, some quite short) so that in the end we can have a full and informed grasp of the technical ins and outs of goldsmithing. Moreover, if any of the information he is conveying can at all be considered secretive, either because it is the sort of information that might be viewed as constituting the intellectual property of a closed group of highly specialized artisans or because it can be construed as the sort of information that appeared in so many self-styled books of secrets containing the mysteries of a misterium, Cellini in his treatise is repeatedly letting the cat out of the bag as he unveils the "secrets"

FIGURE 16. Francesco Ferrucci del Tadda (1497–1585), *Portrait of Benvenuto Cellini*, ca. 1555–1570 (probably after a design by Cellini). Museo Nazionale del Bargello, Florence. By concession of the Ministero per i Beni e delle Attività Culturali e del Turismo. Photo courtesy of Louis A. Waldman.

of his craft. Or at least he is divulging a good portion of those secrets, having, he tells us in the context of talking about just the art of niello alone, "not even said half of what is needed" (9) in order to understand and appreciate fully the nature of that particular branch of goldsmithing as a form of darkened engraving. And as Cellini talks about these matters so openly, he seems to be having a good time of it, taking pleasure in broadcasting so much of what he knows and has learned over his fifty-three years as an exemplary goldsmith, from the year he entered into apprenticeship (1515) to the year the book appeared in print (1568). Yet again like so many practitioners who turned to authorship before

FIGURE 17. Alessandro Fei (1543–1592), *The Goldsmith's Workshop*, ca. 1570. Studiolo of Francesco I, Palazzo Vecchio, Florence, Italy. Reproduced by permission of Scala/ Art Resource, NY.

him, Cellini is here establishing in rhetorical terms his ethos, his character as an expert within the context of his profession and the form of specialized knowledge of the art underpinning it.

Along with this, Cellini takes great pleasure in tracing the development of goldsmithing as a productive art within the broader context of the visual arts, with its own process of revival punctuated by the achievements of remarkable individuals. At the outset he roots the greatness of the visual arts even more resolutely than does Vasari in Florence (Vasari has something of a bias toward Florence, to be sure, but he casts his net much more widely), and he then proceeds to list the major players in the profession of goldsmithing, pausing briefly to acknowledge that some of the greatest visual artists of the recent past not only were Florentines but also began their careers as goldsmiths, just as Cellini did. Like Vasari, then, Cellini is articulating an uplifting history of a particular sector of a profession within the visual arts: learn how to become a goldsmith and you may even emerge as another Lorenzo Ghiberti, he suggests, as he outlines the trajectory of the development of the art underpinning it, hinting at wonderful career opportunities open to you, a path leading to success and glory and, if we can judge from Cellini's egregious vaunting about himself, a strong sense of professional self-worth. Moreover, like Vasari, Cellini is teaching taste in the visual arts, so anyone reading the book will not only learn what is quality but also feel supremely confident that Cellini is the person who can define quality. In Vasarian terms he can identify true "excellence." Accordingly, Cellini builds our faith in him as a dependable guide in a variety of ways, most evidently by just overwhelming the reader with his strong opinions about who is a good goldsmith and what constitutes excellence in the art as a form of specialized knowledge underpinning the profession of goldsmithing. He certainly does not suffer fools. He can distinguish the specialist from the bungler precisely because, we can only surmise, he is the former and not the latter. And as someone with a rare ability to be a specialist in so many branches of goldsmithing (he may claim, adopting the false modesty topos, that he does not know much about filigree work, for instance, but then concedes that he has produced breathtakingly beautiful examples of it),[115] Cellini repeatedly regales us with his observations about what constitutes "good" and "bad" professional work grounded in his broad and deep knowledge of the art underpinning goldsmithing.

More to the point, Cellini dramatizes within his treatise how men of significant power, authority, and social standing, such as the king of France himself, turn to him to discern the quality of objects of goldsmithing. Perplexed, they actively seek out Cellini's opinion, thus affirming through a corroborating eyewitness community within his discourse that he has the requisite expertise to instruct us about all these matters since he seems to know everything related to goldsmithing. Even more important, these men of power, authority, and elevated social standing want to learn from Cellini how the very things he defines as works of quality are in fact *made*, something only a true master in the profession would know how to do, since only a true master of such a complex productive art could dismantle mentally an object and then painstakingly put it back together again so minutely, piece by piece. Consider in this light the following passage, which I cite at length (and I beg the reader's patience for doing so) precisely because it evolves eventually into a detailed discussion of technical matters related to the profession of goldsmithing and its art as a particular form of expert knowledge. "One day, a solemn feast day," Cellini tells us as he adopts the infectious storytelling mode that comes so naturally to him before he shifts his focus and launches into a lengthy discussion of highly specialized technical matters related to the topic at hand:

> the King went at Vespers to his Sainte-Chapelle in Paris. He sent word to me that I was to be at Vespers too, as he had some beautiful things [*belle cose*] to show me. When Vespers were over the King called me to him [*mi fe' chiamare*] through the Constable, who sometimes represents the King himself. This gentleman came to call me, took me by the hand, and led me before the King, who with great kindness and grace [*grazia*] began to show me the most beautiful jewels, not many, nor even did he ask me about them at too great length [*né anco mi domandò troppo a lungo*]. After these he showed me several ancient cameos bigger than the palm of a large hand, and asked me many things about them, on which I gave him my opinion [*alle quali io dissi il mio parere*]. They had stood me in the middle of all of them—there was the King, and the King of Navarre his brother-in-law, and the queen of Navarre, and all the first flower of the nobility, and of those that came nearest to the crown [*più appresso a sua corona*], and so [before all of them] his majesty showed me many beautiful and most expensive things, about which we talked for a long time to his great pleasure [*sopra le quali si ragionò molto a lungo, e con suo molto gran piacere*]. After these most expensive things, he showed me a bowl without a foot and of a reasonable size, wrought in filigree with the choicest spray-work [*fogliamenti*], upon which much other ornamental detail was admirably applied. Now listen to me well [*Ora intendetemi bene*]: in among the spray-work and interstices of filigree were settings of the most beautiful enamel of various colors; and when you held the bowl to the light [*all'aria*] these enamel fillings gleamed—indeed it seemed impossible that one could ever do such an

impossible thing [*essere cosa impossibile da potersi fare*]. Thus at least thought the King, and he asked me [*mi dimandò*] very pleasantly, since I had highly praised the bowl, could I possibly imagine how it was done [*se io potessi immaginare in che modo quella fussi fatta*]. Now to his question I said: "Sacred Majesty, I will tell you exactly how it is done [*io vi dirò in che modo l'è fatta appunto*], even so much so that you, being the man of rare ingenuity [*raro ingenio*] that you are, shall know how exactly as the master himself that made it knew [*il detto modo voi ne saprete tanto quanto il proprio maestro che la fece*], but I cannot teach you in a short span of time [*con tanta brevità*] how that beautiful design of the aforementioned work was made." At these words of mine all the remaining noble assembly that waited on his Majesty thronged around me [*mi si ristrinse addosso tutto quel restante di quella gran nobiltà che ivi era con sua maestà*], the King said he had never seen work so wondrous [*maraviglioso*] of a kind, which I so readily promised to teach him. Then I said: "If you want to make a bowl like this, you must begin by making one of thin sheet iron, about the thickness of knife back larger than the one you want ultimately to produce in filigree. Then with a brush you paint it inside with a solution of fine clay, cloth shearings and Tripoli clay finely ground; then you take finely drawn gold wire of such a thickness as your wise-minded master may wish that of his bowl to be. This thread should be so thick that if you beat it out flat with a hammer on your clean little cup, it bends more readily in the width than otherwise, in such a way that it may then be flattened out to a ribbon shape, two knife-blades broad, and as thin as a sheet of paper. You must be careful to stretch your thread out very evenly, and have it tempered soft, because it will then be easier to twist with your pliers. Then with your fine design before you, you commence to compose your stretched thread inside the iron bowl, first the principal members, according to their way of arrangement, piece by piece painting them over with solution of gum tragacanth, so that they adhere to the clay solution with which you pasted the inside. Then when your craftsman has set all his principal members and larger outlines, he must put in the spray-work, each piece in its place, just as the design guides him, setting it spray by spray, bit by bit in the way I have told you. And then when all this is in proper order, he must have ready his enamels of all colors, well ground and well washed. It is true you might do the soldering first before you put in the enamel, and the soldering of filigree work, but it's as good one way as the other, soldered or not soldered. And when all the preliminary work is carefully done, and all the interstices nicely filled with the colored enamels, you put the whole thing in the furnace, in order to make the enamel glow. To begin with you must only subject it to a slight heat, after which when you have filled up any little openings with a second coat of enamel you may put it in again under a rather bigger fire, and if it appears after this that there are still crannies to be filled up, you put it to as strong a fire as the craft allows and as your enamels will bear. When all this is done you remove it from the iron bowl, which will be easy by reason of the paste of clay to which the actual work and the enamels are attached. Then with a particular kind of stone called frasinelle, and with fresh water, you begin the process of smoothing it down, and you must go on with this so long till the enamel is polished down to an equal thickness throughout and as may seem good to you. And when you have got as far as the frasinelle can take you, you may continue your polishing with still finer stones, and lastly with a piece of reed and Tripoli clay (as I explained it in niello work), then the surface of your enamel will be very smooth and beautiful." When the admirable King Francis heard this manner [of working], he declared that they who knew so well how to explain doubtless knew still better how to do [*operare*], and that I had so well spoken [*ben detto*] about the whole process of a work that he had thought impossible, that now, owing to my words [*e che per le mie parole*], he really thought he could do it himself [*e' gli saria bastato la vista di farla a lui medesimo*], and I grew so much in his favor as one can possibly imagine in the world [*e mi crebbe di tanta benivolenzia quanto mai immaginare si possa al mondo*]. (13–14, 983–84)

As we read here about all the ins and outs of goldsmithing, and as—or, better yet, *if*—we display interest in all this information presented at length, admiring and appreciating Cellini for his professional acumen and his thorough command of the productive art presented in such exhaustive and exhausting detail, we are behaving, it would appear, like the king himself, who finds it all so very fascinating. For a brief moment, as we take a keen interest in such technical matters, we, too, share the king's passion for understanding what it actually takes to make something extraordinary in the art underpinning goldsmithing, and like the king, we appreciate goldsmithing as a profession that possesses an art, a veritable and valuable "techne." If we are bored, we reveal our ignorance and lack of distinction. We reveal, in a sense, that we lack a refined sensibility, a certain royal curiosity and finesse. Go back and reread the extremely long passage and see if your mind doesn't wander and your eyes don't glaze over the words. Treat it as a test: how much of an enlightened Renaissance king and royal patron could you really have been? At what point, if ever, would you have dozed off or have swiftly dismissed Cellini from your presence as a smug, loquacious, social-climbing practitioner far too patently taken with himself to warrant anyone's extended attention?

More to the point, if we read Cellini's treatise with this key passage in mind as an interpretive model for the kind of reader we should be, we can view Cellini's entire treatise itself not just as a potential guidebook for specialists or even as a manual for the would-be specialist wishing to learn about the art that underpins goldsmithing. Specialists, after all, would or should presumably know all the ins and outs of the art of goldsmithing if they are well trained and not just the bunglers whom Cellini derides. Similarly, aspiring goldsmiths would—in theory—not need this book since they would enter into apprenticeship, precisely as Cellini did in an appropriate manner in his "fifteenth year,"[116] and through the workshop experience be indoctrinated into every aspect of the art as specialized knowledge, until they ideally developed into exemplary masters themselves, exactly as Cellini did. Nor, as a practical matter, would apprentices probably have possessed the financial resources, one can only imagine, to purchase Cellini's book. Rather, this book, Cellini seems to suggest, was written in many ways for the eager and inquisitive consumer, someone just like the king of France, who yearns to understand how something exquisite is made so that he can appreciate more fully and intimately the precise nature of the art that makes for a work of exceptional quality, even to the point where he can feel, with his imagination fired up upon hearing Cellini speak about such technical matters so minutely, *as if he could make the object himself.* Think of Cellini's treatise in this context as a sort of elaborate and exacting training manual for connoisseurship and collecting, which goes on and on about technical matters in a manner that would bring about the collective clunk of heads on the table in a classroom if ever read out loud to students today but that we are invited to imagine as electrifyingly interesting for the king and his royal entourage.[117]

To be sure, visual artists were routinely asked to attest to the quality and value of objects, not only in courts but also in legal proceedings, so there was in fact a long tradition of them offering their technical expertise in a controlled public forum both before and during the Italian Renaissance. Artists such as Cellini were customarily retained in some measure for that very purpose, much as they were hired to track down and purchase quality goods: the *laudum* (*laudo* in Italian), for instance, is a contract in which (theoretically) neutral artists functioning as arbiters (often described as *amici communes*) arrive at a financial settlement, and the document in which such arbiters are appointed is generally called a *compromissum/compromesso/compromisso.*[118] Furthermore, every now and then an artist such as Leonardo, Vasari informs us, could be deemed of "such wondrous reasonings" that an enlightened and curious patron would want to consult him and engage him in extended conversations.[119] In the context of working on the *Last Supper*, for instance, Leonardo deliberately chose to unburden his mind at length, we are told, and "reasoned much with the duke [Ludovico Sforza] about the art of painting [*gli ragionò assai de l'arte*]" (562, 1.632), shunning the foolish prior who had actually commissioned the fresco in the first place and who kept urging Leonardo to hurry up, not realizing that profound invention always requires extended deliberation and, above all, the requisite time to meditate on how best to convey the underlying idea. Diligent thought and forethought are more important than swift action, Vasari leads us to believe. And yet in his heady exchanges with the duke, Leonardo—at least as Vasari tells the fanciful story—did not go into highly specific technical details about matters at hand related to the "arte" in question. As far as we know, he did not talk with the duke about how to prepare the refectory wall, properly mix colors so that the frescoed images would endure over time (something Leonardo failed to do as he experimented with the medium of paint), or handle the brushes on the wet plaster. Rather, Leonardo consciously remained in his conversation with the duke at the level of conception and "invention," highlighting the intellectual as opposed to mechanical and technical side of the art of painting by explaining that "men of lofty genius sometimes accomplish most when they work the least, seeking out inventions with the mind, and forming those perfect ideas which the hands afterwards express and reproduce from the images already conceived in the brain [*gl'ingegni elevati, talor che manco lavorano, più adoperano, cercando con la mente l'invenzioni e formandosi quelle perfette idee, che poi esprimono e ritraggono le mani da quelle già concepute ne l'intelletto*]" (562, 1.632). What the duke is most interested in, the courtly Vasari is only too happy to emphasize in his life of Leonardo, is the idea, not the execution, the use of the mind ("la mente"), not the hands ("le mani"). As such, from a Vasarian point of view, one may reasonably wonder if Cellini was ever even invited to talk about all those highly specific technical matters at such length or in such detail or, for that matter, if anyone ever bothered to listen to him with anything but thinly veiled or grudging boredom.

Beyond that, given Cellini's well-known proclivity to inflate everything about himself in his *Vita*, we may legitimately wonder if there is not in fact a great deal of extensive mythmaking going on in Cellini's posturing in his treatise on goldsmithing as he trumpets himself as not only a thinker in the manner of Leonardo but also an indefatigable maker of things with such extraordinary command over the most minute mechanical aspects of his art. In the same way, we may reasonably wonder, given Vasari's yearning to elevate through mythmaking the status of the visual artist as a person exercising an intellectual rather than mechanical art, whether Leonardo indeed engaged in such lengthy,

involved, cerebral conversations with the duke of Milan about the art of painting and the underlying problems of conceptual "invention," as opposed to
manual execution, related to the making of the *Last Supper*.[120] Either way, whatever the truth of the matter, like the spectators of Velázquez's remarkable *Las
meninas*, we are ultimately invited to look into Cellini's discourse about the art
of goldsmithing and find ourselves reflected back within the enchanted realm
of the imaginary as appreciative royalty if we find that what Cellini has to say is
at all compelling. For this, evidently, is the sort of stuff that the king, as an avid
consumer and collector of valuable artifacts, finds deliriously enjoyable to listen
to, so enjoyable that he showers Cellini with commissions in all his excitement,
lavishing attention on him. And so, too, we are led to believe, did the royal
entourage surrounding the king, who found it all to be so very interesting as
they marveled at Cellini's specialized knowledge and warmly commended him
for it.

But Cellini doesn't stop there. He is not content in his treatise on goldsmithing to tell us just how something is done so that he can position himself as
an exemplary master with a complete command of the specialized knowledge
underpinning his profession. No, Cellini must go one step further and make an
absolute spectacle of himself, presenting himself over and over again as someone who has exceeded expectations in every way, just as he does in his unfinished autobiography. He must be viewed as the one unsurpassed and
irrepressibly inventive, individual goldsmith who exists in the superlative and
whom even the divine Michelangelo appreciates as exceptional for all the marvelous works he indefatigably produces. And therein lies Cellini's great poker-
faced challenge as an inveterate and aggressive self-promoter, his delightful version of Renaissance chutzpah. For Castiglione, as we have seen, describes how
to *be* a courtier but does not actually detail in a systematic way how we should
go about practicing to *become* one with due "labor, industry, and care." And
Castiglione arguably fails to provide us with all those techne-training details for
any number of reasons: (1) because he simply refuses to convey that information
in the spirit of exercising the virtue of sprezzatura that privileges offering less
rather than more; (2) because Castiglione cannot convey that information, since
he just does not know how to lay out a practical and rigorous courtier-training
program; (3) because Castiglione deliberately chooses not to lay out a systematic
program of training to become a courtier because as a humanist he prefers to
teach indirectly by example; and/or (4) because Castiglione deliberately wants
to conceal all the putative secrets of the art underpinning courtiership and thus
prefers to hold all his precious trump cards close to his scheming chest as a
cunning, dissimulating expert might well be expected to do. By contrast, Cellini
openly provides us with all the information he can pack into a slim treatise that

indeed teaches us systematically how to do one thing after another if what we really want to do is understand in depth all the rather mundane technical details related to the art in question as a specialized form of knowledge.

But in the end—and this is the key point—even with all that information at our disposal, even when we are openly told how to do this and do that in such mind-numbing detail, it is really quite inexplicable how Cellini gets from the actual page of professional and technical talk, in which his manifest competence in his art as a form of specialized knowledge is displayed and passed on to readers in bookish form, to the actual performative stage of physical artistic production within the workshop, in which Cellini's labor as an individual master craftsman leads to wondrous material designs and constructions that amaze the king and inspire praise from even the divine Michelangelo. And that is the enduring mystery, the taunting secret that lies at the heart of the apparent openness and exhibitionist-like transparency of Cellini's treatise on the art underpinning the profession of goldsmithing. How does the wonder-working Cellini do it? How does he make these exquisite objects that repeatedly elicit "meraviglia"? Or rather, how can we explain his unparalleled ability as an exemplary professional who can elicit such wonder over and over again if we do not pass it off as raw talent, the indelible, magical, one-of-a-kind ingenium that defies explanation, the mysterious, inimitable "something"—*nescio quid*—that transcends the rules and training of an art as a form of specialized knowledge and allows one individual to succeed so brilliantly where another fails so miserably? For, yes, the king may be inspired by Cellini's talk about technical matters to feel vicariously that he, too, can make an exquisite object himself. But the king also knows full well that were he ever to try to do so, he would botch the job altogether, just as we know full well that we, too, would make a mess of it if we ever dared put our hand to the task of trying to make something even remotely similar to the objects that evoke such wonder from nonpractitioners and practitioners alike.

We are now in a position, I believe, to pull some of the strands of this extended reflection together and assess the broad significance of the Italian Renaissance treatment of the arts, having sketched out a history of the concept of techne as it evolved into ars and arte in the first section of this chapter, contextualized the Italian Renaissance treatment of it in the second section, and then, in the third section, examined against this intellectual and cultural background two very different test cases of impressive sixteenth-century practitioners writing about the arts in complex and often mystifying ways. Before pulling these strands together, however, we should take stock of, and momentarily apply some pressure to, the longstanding historiographic emphasis on newness whenever the two words "Italian" and "Renaissance" are conjoined. Indeed, the Italian Renaissance—we typically read—introduced new diplomatic practices with the creation of the new resident ambassador, new technologies, new educational programs, new styles of living, new artistic trends, new consumption patterns, new collecting strategies, new emphases on empirical explorations in the "sciences," new approaches to understanding and possessing the past and to writing history, new ways of systematically and mathematically organizing pictorial space, new treatments of rhetoric, new methods for determining the authenticity of a text and arriving at a critical edition, new standards of hygiene, new linguistic capabilities and ranges, new habits of comportment, new social spaces for interaction, new approaches to the classical past and appreciation for antiquities, new authorial voices for women, and new opportunities for social mobility (principally for men). This rather copious, Rabelaisian list can go on and on, admittedly ad nauseam, but the underlying idea remains essentially the same. The Italian Renaissance, one hears time and again, is all about newness—a concept that ordinarily makes the Renaissance scholar smile and the medievalist cringe but needs to be treated gingerly however we approach it. And, of course, as we turn to writings from the Renaissance, and as we hear a great deal of self-aggrandizing and exhilarating talk about newness in some of those writings themselves, we need to distinguish between assertions and reality. For a host of extremely self-conscious writers of the period repeatedly staked out a claim of absolute newness—it was a fairly standard rhetorical trope—when, to be sure, they were patently standing on the shoulders of others. Perhaps the most famous claim of this sort in a work of imaginative literature of the Italian Renaissance remains Ludovico Ariosto's bold insistence that he was creating something absolutely never before done in rhyme or prose in the *Orlando furioso* in the very moment that he was conspicuously picking up the thread of the plot from Matteo Maria Boiardo's unfinished *Orlando innamorato* and, as Pio Rajna rather pedantically sought to show, relied so heavily on every possible literary model under the sun in crafting his brilliant, classicizing masterpiece that virtually few of the actual storytelling inventions contained within his otherwise novel and original poem were ever even his own.[121] Hence, as we listen to writers from the period, we need to be careful about reproducing in our own narratives of the past their enthusiastic claims about newness voiced from the past.

Certainly in the case of the arts, we need to remind ourselves that much was not in fact radically new, for the Renaissance inherited and reproduced both medieval and classical approaches to the arts. Time and again, Italian Renaissance writers, including practitioners who turned to authorship, forged nuanced revisions of established positions within a longstanding tradition of thinking about the arts that extends back through the Middle Ages to classical Rome and, to be sure, ancient Greece, where the concept of the arts as technai has, as we have seen, its roots in European thought. When Castiglione therefore claims in the early discarded preface of *Il cortegiano*, for instance, that he was writing about a "new profession" with a new art underpinning it, he surely did not mean to say that there were no courtiers before the Renaissance and that the profession he describes sprang up out of nowhere, any more than he meant to suggest that periods before his own had no need for courtiers—a suggestion that would be patently absurd. Castiglione, who in an exaggerated classicizing gesture has one of the interlocutors in his book ludicrously equate the courtier in his own time with Plato and Aristotle in antiquity (4.47), was well aware of a long tradition of courtiers in the period directly preceding his own and their professional roles as dutiful functionaries, both in Italy and elsewhere in Europe. Presumably when he wrote about the newness of the profession of the courtier he had in mind a reconceptualization of it as being associated with letters rather than arms and consequently a redefinition of a set of activities along with the appropriate skill sets and male behavioral strategies that traditionally went with those activities. He also probably had in mind what was not universally the case regarding comportment and strategies for success in his time but what he would have liked to have seen uniformly applied as a standard of selection as he looked around the courts of Italy and Europe and witnessed all sorts of brash, ill-mannered people (particularly the French, it seems) passing themselves off competitively as distinguished courtiers in a profession he valued for entirely different reasons. That there were courtiers who acted like boors and brutes was evident to him, he makes plain in his book, just as there were courtiers whose only real profession was arms and whose notion of diplomacy perhaps lay in slicing off someone's nose without a moment's thought at the slightest provocation. Arguably, the very fact that Castiglione periodically feels compelled to tell courtiers through the interlocutors gathered together at Urbino how they should comport themselves constitutes indirect evidence that, for him at least, there were those who behaved to the contrary, much as the fact that della Casa needs to tell people not to show off the gray-green globs of snot they have blown into their handkerchief, passing off all that slimy ooze as a prized personal collection of jewels worthy of everyone else's rapt attention, reasonably suggests that people occasionally did something akin to that in polite company and indeed, one can only guess, worse.[122]

But having said that, much does seem strikingly new when we look at the Italian Renaissance treatment of the arts, not least that a wide variety of practitioners from different backgrounds turned to authorship in significant numbers. As those practitioners took on that role, they also broadened the purview of what constituted an art and, by extension, professionalism itself. They argued that what they did as professionals legitimately required an art as a form of specialized knowledge, thus making a case publicly for their profession and its overall social and cultural value in a way that had not been done either ever before or in so thorough a fashion—or, to be sure, in many cases at such extraordinary length. Courtiers, secretaries, ambassadors, architects, metallurgists, painters, goldsmiths, sculptors, and cooks—in sum, a variety of people engaged in both the practical and the productive arts—now had their enthusiastic contemporary champions who vigorously argued for the exemplary value of the art underpinning their professions, occasionally in the context of (imagined) social mobility. At the same time, many of these practitioners as authors sought to advance their own social standing as people with a valuable skill to offer society in general and, often enough, patrons in particular through their work. They used these discourses to tell highly selective aspects of the stories of their lives and of others, thus contributing to the growth of autobiography and biography in the early modern era. They defined new tastes and patterns of behavior and edified others about those tastes and behavioral norms. They defined the arts they possessed over and against those of the classical past. They articulated boundaries for professional self-definition and a communal identity defined by an art as a specialized form of knowledge. They opened up avenues for professional self-advancement for those engaged in both the productive and practical arts and, at the same time, ingeniously worked on occasion to impede others from entering into the profession defined by an art. They fashioned a vision of mutually reinforcing collaboration between the person possessing the art (the maker or the doer) and the persons doing the hiring (the consumers), sometimes configuring that collaboration as a dialogue of equals in a highly stratified society where the maker or doer occupied a social position inferior to the consumer. They characterized the tradition that makes up their art as a specialized form of knowledge and charted its historical development, occasionally casting their explorations into the nature of the art as a matter of philosophical concern, as indeed a cognitive act. They promoted a vision of the person possessing an art as someone who finds inherent value in professional experience itself as a form of self-fulfillment and personal satisfaction in the very moment that that person served others in the community. And they forged links between the person possessing the art and the results of that very same person's labor, thus bringing together issues related to character, creativity, and conduct in the context of professional life and the art underpinning it.

Above all, one key feature that I have sought to stress in the previous section has to do with what we might call the desire for inimitability within the broader context of the Italian Renaissance investment in professionalization. On the one hand, there was a profound, widespread, and persistent belief in the Italian Renaissance, which only intensified in the sixteenth century, that one could uncover universal rules—the "deep structures"—that underlie the arts as forms of specialized knowledge.[123] Those rules could be taught, learned, and mastered, often through the very process of imitation itself. Artists were collectively defined by and through those rules, "fashioned" by them, to use a familiar term in the academy, as they exercised a profession rooted in an art. In this respect, these treatises were establishing a group identity defined by exemplary professional practice grounded in rational, determinate, rule-bound, communicable, and reliable knowledge. On the other hand, a number of the practitioners who turned to authorship in the Italian Renaissance were keenly aware that some people will be good at acquiring an art and some people will not, so that no matter how hard or diligently they work at it, an innate magical something, the mysterious raw talent of "ingenium," was ultimately required to allow a person to make that leap from being a dutiful learner to becoming a remarkable practitioner within a profession. This is not simply to say that a number of authors were articulating a notion of their art as stochastic, rather than exact, in nature, although that was indeed often the case. What it does mean is that some of the authors found themselves bumping up against the very limits of the educational process they putatively endorsed when they wrote their discourses, recognizing that one can communicate and teach but one cannot really adequately ensure success for anyone. Moreover, one finds expressed every now and then in these discourses a desire on the part of the writer practitioners to have someone stand out from that group of professionals fashioned within the discourse about an art and, at the same time, have that very same person—typically, but not necessarily, the author himself—emerge not only as a unique "individual" but also as someone who is truly inimitable. Try as you might (and indeed you are often invited or seduced by such author practitioners as Castiglione and Cellini into trying with all of your might), you simply cannot do what the brilliant individual practitioner author can do, or what someone else of spectacular talent identified in the discourse about the art can individually do, or, for that matter, what even a very small elite circle of individual experts can masterfully do.[124] Not for the life of you.

How is one expected to respond to these teasing assertions of inimitability ensconced within discourses that often inculcate the importance of imitation as a key process of indoctrination and edification? We are expected to respond, I take it, with "meraviglia,"[125] the all-important passion that fires the imagination and fuels the desire to imitate those masters (How marvelous if I can be just like those perfectly admirable persons!) but also calls attention to our inability to be just like those exemplary persons because they are so patently beyond our capabilities and ken, precisely because they come off as so eerily inimitable (How, we can only wonder with awe, do those astonishing people pull it off, even when all the information about their art is so openly disclosed to us in their discourses?). Hence we find ourselves repeatedly privileged to all those varied assertions of wonder. Fioravanti presents himself as a miracle worker even when he has divulged his key "secrets" of how to cure people of their often baffling illnesses. Cellini boasts about his accomplishments that inspire the act of marveling in the context of spilling all the beans about the art that makes up the profession of goldsmithing. Vasari characterizes Michelangelo as a figure of terrifying awe in a book that details at the outset how sculpting, architecture, and painting are in fact done by professionals thoroughly versed in the arts he discusses at such length. And Castiglione transforms the courtier into a person whose grace, however achieved (from Nature? from practice? from a gift bestowed from on high?), is so breathtakingly admirable that it elicits a sort of muted, decorous applause, a collective recognition of all its seemingly magical finesse, even as we are told from the very outset how to studiously acquire grace through sprezzatura. Professionally speaking, all that wonder and admiration and awe encoded into these discourses about arts highlight an individual *and* a group achievement, in which both the individual and the group are formed and transformed in relation to one another, the one dependent on the other. For it is only through the determinate, rational, rule-bound, and communicable knowledge of those arts practiced by a collectivity that certain individuals can position themselves in the first place as exemplary makers or doers capable of eliciting so much marveling through their socially prized achievements. And in turn it is through the achievements of such remarkable inimitable individuals worthy of wonder that the practitioners themselves turning to authorship can all the more firmly and persuasively establish the value of the arts generally—both the practical *and* the productive arts—as specialized forms of knowledge within the context of group professional life in Renaissance Italian culture.

Jacob Burckhardt, I would therefore like to argue in conclusion to this extended reflection, was once again both right and wrong. He was right in his foundational essay *The Civilization of the Renaissance in Italy* in seeing that the notion of "art"—or, more precisely, Kunst, in his terms—was central to the Italian Renaissance. In making this fundamental claim early on in his essay, in the very first chapter, "The State as a Work of Art [*Kunstwerk*]," Burckhardt did not frame the concept of Kunst in terms of the long historical tradition of the arts going all the way back to ancient Greece and its formative concept of techne.[126] Nevertheless, in his discussion about war itself as a work of "art," Burckhardt did recognize that "there existed a comprehensive science and art [*Wissenschaft und Kunst*] of military affairs," thus not only linking the concepts of Wissenschaft and Kunst through the ampersand but also effectively conflating them. In that case he certainly spoke, it would seem, about Kunst in a manner that would have resonated felicitously with what people, both practitioners and non-practitioners, in not only the Italian Renaissance but also the classical period and the Middle Ages, were thinking about when they wrote about the arts as forms of specialized knowledge, as some sort of "science," as—indeed—a kind of Wissenschaft.[127] However, when Burckhardt spoke of Kunstwerk he meant something quite different from what writers from classical antiquity to the Italian Renaissance were talking about when they discussed the arts. In framing much of the Italian Renaissance in the context of Kunstwerk, Burckhardt, as Lionel Gossman has observed, meant that such things as the state and military affairs, once secularized and emancipated from religion and tradition,[128] were deemed "not natural, but the products of artful calculation,"[129] although no one from antiquity to the Italian Renaissance, it bears mentioning in passing, would have spoken of an "art" (understood as techne, ars, or arte) as something absolutely distinct from the "natural."[130] Above all, in an effort to heighten the sense of newness of the period that he was most interested in and that he saw genealogically, as well as problematically and pessimistically, as the harbinger of his own, Burckhardt—after equating Kunst with Wissenschaft—asserted that "here, for the first time," in Renaissance Italy, "neutral joy is taken in the proper conduct of war as such [*hier zuerst begegnen wir einer neutralen Freude an der korrekten Kriegführung als solcher*]." Yet taking a sort of objective pleasure ("neutral joy") in an art as something self-defined, "as such" (als solcher), was not, it is essential to emphasize, a feature of ancient concepts of techne or ars. Similarly, taking a sort of objective pleasure ("neutral joy") in an art as something self-defined, "as such" (als solcher), was not a feature of Italian Renaissance concepts of ars or arte. Rather, in the Italian Renaissance the putative "joy" experienced on the part of the practitioner, as well as the potential "joy" experienced on the part of others bearing witness to the art of the practitioner (the "joy" of a patron, say, or like-minded practitioners, or virtually anyone else observing the masterful "artist" at labor), was by no means imagined as neutral or detached. Nor was that "joy" viewed as primarily aesthetic in nature, although there would always be an element of aesthetic appreciation involved in the realization of an art produced or practiced by someone with exceptional skill. Instead, the "joy" experienced on the part of the practitioner, as well as the "joy" experienced on the part of others bearing witness to the art of the practitioner, was above all the product of the recognition of a job well done in the service of an activity that had a social function as a form of recognized and valued work; that was conceived as possessing not only purposive social value but, it would seem in many cases, inherent personal value for practitioners by nurturing their sense of self-worth as they served others and benefited the community in various ways through their work; and that was deemed intensely partisan in nature within a competitive system of professions in a complex, hierarchical society.

Burckhardt never explicitly applied his appreciation of the centrality of Kunst in the Italian Renaissance to his notion of the new modern "individual" that emerged in the same period, with the individual presumably fashioned, like the state and military affairs, as a self-consciously crafted work of art—as an "artificial construct," to use Gossman's phrase[131]—that could elicit "neutral joy" and could be appreciated with some aesthetic pleasure in and of itself, "as such" (als solcher), as something conceptually bracketed and self-defined.[132] It was left to others to formulate the connections between Kunstwerk and the individual and, in time, debunk aspects of them. Those connections were perhaps most memorably drawn in our own time by Stephen Greenblatt, for whom the notion of the highly controlled and controlling "individual" with a "pure, unfettered subjectivity" could only be viewed as an enabling illusion perfectly suited for a nineteenth-century European bourgeoisie that had a deeply vested interest in imagining itself in bad faith as free and full of independent, autonomous selves.[133] In any event, a hallmark of Greenblatt's largely anthropological and Foucauldian approach is to envision the "individual" as being shaped by his or her culture in a process wherein the self is viewed as the product of an art. In this way, in viewing the individual as a "cultural artifact," as someone who is powerfully and thoroughly constructed, Greenblatt appropriates the Burckhardtian notion of the centrality of Kunst but radically alters it, transforming the Renaissance individual as the "first-born among the sons of modern Europe," who possesses complete self-control and has an identity firmly grounded in self-determination,[134] into effectively the firstborn among the sons (and daughters) of the postmodern era, who possesses only the illusion of self-control and at any given moment performs an identity that occupies a subject position within an overarching, determining structure and has no essential, personal core to it. In appropriating and adapting Burckhardt, Greenblatt does not evoke the long tradition of the arts in his discussion of cultural self-fashioning, although the art of rhetoric underpins much of what he has to say. But he could have done so. And arguably, in light of his take on Burckhardt, he should have done so.

"Despite its age and its well-documented limitations," Greenblatt writes in
his chapter on Edmund Spenser, in which he synthetically captures Burckhardt's notion of Kunst and applies it to the process of identity formation of
the "individual,"

> one of the best introductions to Renaissance self-fashioning remains
> Burckhardt's *Civilization of the Renaissance in Italy*. Burckhardt's crucial
> perception was that the political upheavals in Italy in the later Middle
> Ages, the transition from feudalism to despotism, fostered a radical
> change in consciousness: the princes and *condottieri*, and their secretar-
> ies, ministers, poets, and followers, were cut off from established forms
> of identity and forced by their relation to power to fashion a new sense
> of themselves and their world: the self and the state as works of art. But
> his related assertion that, in the process, these men emerged at last as
> free individuals must be sharply qualified. While not only in Italy, but in
> France and England as well, the old feudal models gradually crumbled
> and fell into ruins, men created new models, precisely as a way of con-
> taining and channeling the energies which had been released.[135]

Rhetoric, Greenblatt then directly goes on to say, was "the chief intellectual and
linguistic tool in this creation" of new models of selfhood. But this vision of the
role and value of rhetoric in the period, which is a fairly characteristic vision
endorsed in a variety of scholarly readings of the Italian Renaissance, is only
partly true.[136] For it was "art" itself—art understood in its broadest sense, as a
specialized form of knowledge that *included* rhetoric (one of the great, para-
digmatic technai in antiquity)—that helped usher in many of the "new models"
of selfhood Greenblatt eloquently speaks about, with practitioners increasingly
turning to authorship in the Italian Renaissance so that they could advocate
forcefully for the value of the specialized knowledge underpinning a profession
and, at the same time, advocate for an individual's exceptionality and inimitability within the very same profession by virtue of his extraordinary ability to
adhere to *and* transcend the rules themselves associated with the art. The Italian
Renaissance exploration of what the Greeks once called techne by practitioners
engaged in the practical and productive arts, with their notable and unprecedented expansion of what constituted a profession grounded in an art, thus
disclosed to men an array of possibilities for conceiving of themselves as being
part of a new sort of group bound by new sets of strategies for professional
success *and* as individuals seeking to liberate themselves from the very constraints of collective professional self-definition that they helped give shape to

in concrete terms through their discourses about arts. And in this way practitioners in Renaissance Italy writing discourses about arts—from Castiglione and Cellini to Biringuccio, Fioravanti, and Vasari—offered a variety of individual men embedded in and constrained by communities an additional, and extremely powerful, "way of containing and channeling the energies which had been released" from the sorts of sociopolitical shifts that had taken place in the peninsula.

In a number of ways, then, our extended reflection on the historical reach of techne has brought us in the end to view techne itself, as the concept gradually evolved over time into ars and arte, as a feature essential to a fuller appreciation of the Italian Renaissance sense of male identities. Indeed, Italian men during the period were obsessed with the arts in a variety of ways. They identified themselves with an art and in the process worked hard to define the nature of that art as essential to a profession. They explored how to achieve success within a specific profession thanks to their command of the art. They searched for a language, and sometimes invented a language, to describe how to achieve success through an art in a specific profession. They labored to enhance socially a profession by insisting that it indeed had an art. They characterized a particular profession as new and demanded a new form of specialized knowledge to achieve success in it and stand out from the crowd, sometimes conspicuously, sometimes not. They orchestrated whole ceremonies dedicated to the proposition that a long-lost profession, along with the art underpinning it, had been revived from antiquity after a long, sad, dismal period of cultural amnesia.[137] They articulated appropriate habits of conduct and codified personal attributes either required or desired to be more winning within a profession defined by an art. They transgressed the rules codified within discourses about an art as a form of specialized knowledge. They fashioned tastes related to the art and crafted historical narratives about the development of the art as a form of specialized knowledge. They explored an art as a matter of philosophical concern, as a cognitive act. They made a case for the significance of the place of an art in a (new) profession. They embedded arts in institutional practices and co-opted notions about various arts from the past. They broadened the purview of what constituted a profession with its own legitimate art underpinning it. They framed the work done as something of inherent personal value thanks to one's mastery in a specific art. They transformed practitioners into authors writing about the value of their art within the context of professional life and experience. And they adopted a language of marveling associated with specific practitioners whose achievements in a determined profession grounded in an art rendered them not only exemplary but also inimitable. Or, rather, they adopted a language that made one remarkable practitioner after another appear to be a "great mystery," to use one of Greenblatt's more quizzical phrases when he writes about "how Shakespeare became Shakespeare" and still cannot in the end fully demystify Shakespeare's exceptionality—or what was traditionally dubbed his "natural genius"—even after Greenblatt has so very rationally (and imaginatively) embedded Shakespeare within the discursive, economic, gendered, sexual, ritual, penal, pedagogical, religious, political, institutional, linguistic, and, yes, distinctly techne-defined "professional" and "artisan" practices of the culture that ostensibly produced him.[138]

The Italian Renaissance, in a phrase, was thus from beginning to end all about "art." But it was not about art in the sense that one might associate with Burckhardt's notion of Kunst, in which something arouses a detached emotional response of "neutral joy" and is appreciated in and of itself, "as such" (als solcher), as something conceptually bracketed, contained, and self-defined—as a complete "artificial construction." Nor, for that matter, was it about art in the sense that one might associate with Greenblatt's notion of self-fashioning, in which identities are embedded in the cultures that always necessarily bracket, contain, and define them—as a complete "cultural artifact." The Italian Renaissance was instead, on its own terms, all about "art" as a determinate, rational, rule-bound, communicable, and reliable form of knowledge that was shaped principally by men and that profoundly shaped their lives; that offered men both in groups and as individuals the possibility of controlling, or hedging their bets against, chance in a world of immense flux—a world that left men feeling so painfully vulnerable in the face of shifts of fortune in a constantly changing political and social landscape; and that allowed men the opportunity to find immense personal satisfaction in the value of their work done as expert practitioners. Above all, thanks to their command over their art as a highly specialized form of knowledge, a variety of men, as we have seen in this chapter, identified profoundly with the products of their labor; fantasized about social mobility; attained through their efforts some status, prosperity, happiness, and fame; and, last but not least, explored who they and others were within the very limits of the constraints of the professions they helped give shape to, while recognizing at the same time that a certain mystery—an ineffable, eerie quality that makes up a certain *nescio quid*—often enough lay at the heart of what made for extraordinary individual success.

CHAPTER 2

ဢ

Reflections on Professions and Humanism
in Renaissance Italy and the Humanities Today

HUMANISM, I MAINTAINED IN THE PREVIOUS CHAPTER, WAS A LANGUAGE-based educational and cultural program in Renaissance Italy that did not, in point of fact, have a particular professional bent to it. Yet humanists in Renaissance Italy, the vast majority of them of course being men, did have professional identities, even if humanism itself was "*not*," as Lisa Jardine emphatically observes, "job-specific."[1] Humanists typically worked as secretaries, notaries, chancellors, ambassadors, courtiers, editors, and schoolteachers in private, civic, courtly, business, and ecclesiastical settings. They thus tended to occupy, as Paul Oskar Kristeller observed long ago, certain professions throughout the Italian Renaissance, and many pursued careers in the legal, medical, and religious fields.[2] There is also strong evidence that humanism in Italy emerged out of the notarial profession, although "the beginning humanists," Ronald G. Witt has shown, "did not intend to displace medieval Latin with classicizing Latin" all at once but first experimented with their new style in poetry and "other genres of private rhetoric." Only later, according to Witt, did humanists in Italy extend their influence to other more public forms of rhetoric as humanism achieved widespread appeal and humanists could express themselves in different, more culturally entrenched genres with greater freedom, given the "institutional constraints" within which they operated.[3] Italian humanists at the origins, then, had professional identities as they put into practice their arts as forms of determinate, rational, rule-bound, communicable, and reliable knowledge. And while there may not have been much give-and-take between humanism and professions at the outset, there was eventually a fruitful exchange between the two in the mid-fourteenth, fifteenth, and sixteenth centuries, from roughly the time that Petrarca shaped humanism as an innovative program outside the academy, particularly with his highly choreographed coronation oration trumpeting the profession of the poet, to the time that humanism had become so thoroughly disseminated and institutionalized as an educational program that it was virtually required of all men to participate in it in some form or manner before they could eventually take up their roles as dutiful functionaries or, in some instances, ideally enlightened leaders. Even so, humanists did not receive—nor did they impart as educators—disciplined training for any specific professions, it bears repeating. Humanism, as Donald R. Kelley has succinctly argued, concentrated on the *trivium*, principally the two arts (technai) of grammar and rhetoric as forms of specialized knowledge. It therefore focused on, and consequently sought to elevate in status and appeal, arts related to traditionally trivial things—trivial but by no means unimportant for humanists, for those trivial things prepared people for a virtuous, good, and active life in the community, even if they did not prepare men for any one profession in particular.[4]

Nevertheless, Italian humanists contributed significantly to the formation of professional identity in the Italian Renaissance as they exercised or wrote about professions and the specialized forms of knowledge underpinning them. This contribution took place at a time when there was, more generally, an increased concern for, and arguably more developed and variegated discourse about, professional choice and experience in high and low culture. As George McClure has argued, from the mid-fifteenth to the end of the sixteenth century, Italy experienced a profound shift in a "rhetoric of profession," with rhetoric here understood not just as the formal art of persuasion (although McClure does consistently focus throughout his excellent study on an epideictic rhetoric of praise and rebuke) but as a discourse that is bounded with traceable *topoi* (commonplaces) and that is historically and culturally determined. This shift in a rhetoric of professions involved, among other things: a marked attention to professional self-definition; a truly broad-based cultural exploration, leveling, and secularization of professions; an increased attention to the value of vocational choice and work as a source of happiness and self-worth; a popularizing of these issues through the commercial press and in the vulgar tongue; an astonishing proliferation of the topic of professions in a variety of less learned cultural forms, from encyclopedic compendia to chronicles, to jokes, to civic rituals, to carnival songs, to parlor games; and an extraordinary increase in—as well as cultural acceptance of and resistance toward—different professions as indeed professions. The contribution of humanists was one among many, all of which culminated in Garzoni's cornucopian *La piazza universale di tutte le professioni del mondo* and included poems and descriptions of virtually every profession under the sun, including, as we shall see in the final chapter of this book, even discussions and observations about the mundane work of barbers, who were trained, among other things, to clean and trim beards.[5]

The humanist contribution to this broad-based discourse of professionalism in the Italian Renaissance is particularly interesting for a number of reasons, even if it is typically a bit highbrow (they did not, say, focus on the work of barbers) and even if it was directed primarily at and for men. There were, to be sure, female humanists who adapted and revised humanism to suit their needs and circumstances, but secular professionalism was not a key interest of theirs, nor were they advised to think in those terms by male humanists as women gradually retreated, or were forced to retreat, into "book-lined cells" in the fifteenth and sixteenth centuries and find their voices in the traditional sphere of the household.[6] To begin with, the humanist investment in professionalism retains certain familiar dimensions over roughly two and a half centuries. Italian Renaissance humanists wrote about professions in often strikingly similar ways. Hence as Italian humanists assisted in constructing professional identities and the specialized knowledge of the arts underpinning them, professional identity did not fundamentally alter, although it did have an impact on, the way in which these men wrote or viewed the world as humanists. Second, Italian humanists not only had a systemic understanding of professions as they marked out distinctions between professions and entered into new and traditional rivalries, but they also felt comfortable bridging divisions, moving fluidly between professions, even if they were not always comfortable with the professions they occupied. Having one profession did not at all exclude having another, and in many respects having multiple professions was a necessity and something of a norm. Humanist writings therefore sometimes contain within themselves traces of the presence of multiple professions at work at the same time, just as they sometimes contain within themselves traces of the overriding expectation that the individual humanist would in time take up his role within the dominant power structure and social order and fulfill the cultural expectations made of him.[7] This is not just to say that humanist writings are simply dialogic, in the sense that multiple discourses are always bound up in any words we use. Rather, it means that the discourses of professions specifically permeate humanist writings all at once. We can schematically separate those discourses of professions out as a heuristic device, but we can also detect them woven together into the fabric of particular texts. Third, there is at times a distinctly antiprofessional strain to the humanist rhetoric of professionalism, much as there is at times an antihumanist strain within humanism itself. The humanist rhetoric of professions can often enough be at odds with itself, something that in Stanley Fish's deconstructionist terms only means that the humanist rhetoric of professions is all the more intensely invested in professional identity exactly when, and precisely because, it expresses from time to time antiprofessionalism, as, for instance, Petrarca's and Castiglione's calculated rhetoric about professions occasionally seems to do.[8]

There are additional ways of reflecting on the interaction of humanism and professions in the Italian Renaissance, and I would like to explore one of them now as the centerpiece to this chapter, using the term "humanist," however, with some latitude to include Niccolò Machiavelli. Although arguably not a humanist in the manner of Ermolao Barbaro, Torquato Tasso, or Baldassare Castiglione (three other male Italian Renaissance authors briefly examined here), Machiavelli—even as he applied pressure on humanism and radically challenged some of its underlying strategies and presuppositions—had significant training in the studia humanitatis, repeatedly engaged the discourse of humanism in his writings, circulated his ideas among humanists, and was profoundly indebted to humanism as a cultural program that shaped the way he viewed and wrote about the world.[9] In particular, we shall see, Machiavelli shared with Barbaro, Tasso, and Castiglione a tendency to mystify professional activity in the very moment that he demystified it. Finally, after discussing at length issues related to work, professionalism, and discretion in Francesco Guicciardini's *Ricordi* in light of Walter Benjamin's notion of the collector, I will address some of the salient concerns raised by Anthony Grafton and Lisa Jardine almost three decades ago when they rapidly traced connections between the humanism of the Renaissance and the humanities of the present, between the studia humanitatis as a pedagogical and cultural program that privileged men, on the one hand, and, on the other hand, the sort of stuff that goes on in the humanities in colleges and universities across North America and Europe and that involves, and hopefully speaks to, both men and women in equal measure. In any event, how we reflect on humanism and professionalism in the Renaissance, I will argue at the end of this chapter, both matters a great deal and does not matter at all as we reflect on professionalism in the humanities today.

When I first began to examine the interaction of humanism and professions in Renaissance Italy almost twenty years ago, I did not expect to find that the humanist treatment of professions would be so rich, dense, and, at times, at odds with itself. Instead, I had in mind a rather grim notion of the relationship between humanism and professions that is perhaps familiar to some today and that in my most lugubrious fantasy made me think of the sorts of hideous transformations that take place in the 1978 sci-fi horror film *Invasion of the Body Snatchers*. My nightmarish vision ran something like this. A perfectly intelligent, well-spoken individual with a humanistic education (which is to say, someone trained in late twentieth-century or early twenty-first-century humanities rather than the studia humanitatis of poetry, rhetoric, grammar, moral philosophy, and history) eventually learns to speak a nearly unintelligible, specialized, overly technical, jargon-infected, and at times bureaucratized language after occupying (or being occupied by, as if being overtaken by some creepy, alien pod) a profession for an extended span of time. When I turned to the Italian Renaissance, however, and thus to the period when humanism originated and in which some in the academy today locate the roots of the humanities as both an educational and cultural program, I discovered that many humanist men valued their professions; that they were enriched by their professional experiences and their reflections on professional life; that humanism (at least judging from the cases I have studied closely) benefited from its interaction with professionalism; and that, in fact, a number of influential, valued works composed by Italian Renaissance humanist men had their roots in, and conceptually owed a great deal to, professional experience, including, say, such celebrated writings as Castiglione's *Il cortegiano*. This gave me some cause for cheer. Moreover, humanism, I discovered, was an extremely resilient educational and cultural program that not only helped define professionalism in the Renaissance but also allowed people from different areas and walks of life to communicate and understand one another thorough a shared mode of thought and language. Humanism, in this regard, provided extraordinary unity to a potentially disorienting array of work experiences in an increasingly complex and changing world. Humanism, moreover, seems to have provided a variety of people (overwhelmingly men, of course) with a flexible way of cohesively shaping professional experience in discursive form and of offering it to others as one way of thinking about and valuing professional experience.

There are, however, positive and negative ways of viewing this particular take on the humanist interaction with professions and the arts undergirding them. On the one hand, that we can identify common recurrent features to the humanist rhetoric of professions suggests that it is all, well, just rhetoric, or rhetoric in the worse sense of the term, as a matter of manipulated, codified style and nothing more, as vapid but elegant, stylized, and sometimes beguiling talk. That Tasso, for example, could write about the secretarial profession with such authority and aplomb without ever having practiced it, by only imaginatively occupying, that is to say, the role of the sort of practitioner-cum-author we examined in the previous chapter, certainly suggests that: (1) Tasso, whose job was to write poetry for his patron and not formal letters in the d'Este chancery of late Renaissance Ferrara, hasn't the faintest idea what he is really talking about; (2) Tasso has absolutely nothing concrete to offer those wishing to be secretaries, as one experienced secretary in fact asserted, since Tasso lacks the specialized knowledge to be one;[10] and (3) Tasso could just as easily have written about any other profession in its place, depending on who was making the request and what advantages Tasso, so well trained in the art of rhetoric, saw in responding to it: grab Cicero, say, adapt it, and you're off and running.[11] All this gives the humanist treatment of professions potentially a bit of a bad reputation. In rhetorical terms, Tasso here arguably lacks ethos, unlike the practitioner authors examined in the previous chapter. On the other hand, that there are indeed common features to the humanist rhetoric of professions does not necessarily mean that all their talk (and there was a fair amount of talk) was purely self-aggrandizing, meaningless, and derivative, a rote mindless exercise in, among other things, adapting, imitating, and emulating the classics whenever the occasion arose for any particular humanist to do so because he felt, for whatever particular reason, the impulse, duty, or need to do so. First of all, the humanist rhetoric of professions did attempt to expand the reach of selfhood within humanism to include professional experience, whether or not the humanist had any real familiarity with that experience as a practitioner. Second, by embracing professional experience, humanists made the studia humanitatis, for all that it was grounded in the trivium and thus concerned with apparently "trivial" things, appear more useful, more directly related to the praxis of work in life for men. It thus gave added professional value to an educational and cultural program that had no particular professional bent to it and no concrete job skills to offer. Third, in their talk about professions, humanists substantially complicated our understanding of what it means to occupy a profession and thus authoritatively apply an art as a form of specialized knowledge.

In his *Il secretario* (1587), for instance, Tasso may not have anything practical to say about being a secretary, in the sense that he does not really know or tell us anything about the nuts and bolts of secretarial work, which, by contrast, a number of more practical-minded writers do indeed attend to from the mid-sixteenth century through the seventeenth century in Italy in their treatises. But Tasso, who was intimately knowledgeable about court culture, does convey a keen understanding of the problems of the position of the secretary in relation to the current political and social order and how downright risky it is to occupy that position. He does convey a sense of the value of the profession and the usefulness of the studia humanitatis, as well as the tacit expectation that a secretary will have a thorough grounding in a humanist education, thus connecting the ideology of humanism with the practices to which it could strategically be put to use. Most important of all, Tasso does powerfully convey an understanding that even if you know all the ins and outs of secretarial work, even if you can read and beautifully imitate all the letter-writing strategies of the ancients and the moderns, even if you know how to address a letter properly with the right sort of handwriting, even if you know all the rules that can ever be known and have ever been set down in writing so that one might meticulously define the determinate, communicable, and reliable knowledge underpinning "secretaryship" as a profession, you may not, in the end, be a good, effective secretary, much less a perfect one, which is the kind of secretary that Tasso sought to fashion as he Platonizes the topic in a fairly typical Italian Renaissance manner. To become that sort of exemplary secretary, you need something else.

What that "something else" is is difficult to say. Tasso, true to form as a defiantly oblique and opaque writer, refuses to say what it is. And it goes by different names for different humanists when they talk about different professional activities in the world. For the distinguished Venetian humanist Ermolao Barbaro, writing his *De officio legati* (*On the Duty of the Ambassador*) at the end of the fifteenth century, either while he was in diplomatic service or directly after returning home (there is some question about the precise timing here), the something else you need in order to be a good ambassador is prudence. But Barbaro never concretely tells us how to acquire prudence, and he refuses to pin down what it is. "Although the precepts of this office can be set down," he writes at the outset, as he refuses to set them down, "nevertheless a certain I don't know what [*nescio quid*] depends more on the prudence of man than what can ever be committed to this treatise."[12] Barbaro's strategy is somewhat predictable within the overall humanist treatment of professions but also a bit frustrating. At the very beginning of his treatise we are not taught the precepts that Barbaro could transmit to us. That task is roundly dismissed, perhaps because the task of compiling those precepts would be long, dull, and tedious, even though Barbaro does give us some precepts, or just enough to construct a self-congratulatory narrative of himself and his father as Venetian ambassadors hard at work, expertly versed as polished practitioners in the specialized and reliable knowledge underpinning the art of being a seasoned diplomat. At the same time, we are not taught the prudence that is deemed absolutely essential to the ambassador. That discussion is swiftly swept under the rug, probably because covering that particular topic means pinning down something as elusive as an "I don't know what" (*nescio quid*). As such, Barbaro does not give us what we need and what, of course, Barbaro could presumably give us as a humanist who has evidently thought a lot about a particular profession as an accomplished practitioner of it. Instead what we do get, as Italians colloquially like to say today, is "a fistful of flies" (*un pugno di mosche*): the insistence that we need prudence; a handful of precepts; and half a dozen examples of Barbaro and his father in action, with the underlying—and typically humanist—assumption that the examples provided here (exclusively of father and son in action) will adequately instruct us on how to conduct ourselves as good, dissimulating, prudent ambassadors. Last but not least, we get the evasive will-o'-the-wisp expression "I don't know what" (*nescio quid*) as a way of explaining away, with the sleight of hand that humanists so deftly employ, what the slim

treatise refuses to cover and perhaps cannot cover but is deemed absolutely necessary to possess in order to know how to succeed as an ambassador.

Much of the same can be said about Castiglione's *Il cortegiano*. There is, to
be sure, a lot of talk in *Il cortegiano*, and perhaps even more in contemporary
critical prose on *Il cortegiano*, about all the dedicated work that is involved in
being a courtier and, at the same time, how one needs to adroitly hide all
that work. Being a good, effective courtier, we learn, requires immense skill at
manipulating self-representations, masking, deceiving, dissimulating, simulat-
ing, posing self-consciously as one pretends not to pose, translating poetic practice into shrewd interpersonal relations, artfully hiding one's own artfulness,
coping with all manner of surveillance, and making—more broadly—rhetoric
work as politics. But if doing all these things (and more) requires an incredible
amount of work, I am still not sure what that work really is and, just as important, how you go about systematically training for it by way of preparation to
become a courtier. In practical terms, do you stand alone, behind closed doors,
in front of a mirror practicing? Do you try out your best jokes on friends in
private and then hope for the best when you work them into conversation in
public? Beyond that, we are told, of course, that we need "grazia" and "sprezzatura" to be a good courtier. And it is clear you need to work hard—very, very
hard—to acquire "grazia" and "sprezzatura." But in the end, as I argued at
length in the previous chapter, it is not at all clear how you systematically train
to get "grazia" and "sprezzatura" if you do not already mysteriously possess
them. Indeed, Castiglione never gives us concrete steps to take to acquire
"grazia" and "sprezzatura" the way, say, a ballet teacher might instruct one on
how to take the steps—one step after another before a horizontal, full-length
mirror—to learn how to dance. Worse, Castiglione does not make being a
courtier look easy as a profession by the time we have finished his book. It is
not at all like riding a bike, which anyone can do after some training and a
rudimentary process of imitation, but it is also not at all like leaping across the
stage as a truly accomplished ballet dancer, which hardly anyone can do even
after years and years of rigorous training and studied attempts at laborious
imitation. Rather, the entire *Cortegiano* provides us with colorful examples of
courtiers acting and interacting (again, as for Barbaro, with the underlying
humanist assumption that these examples presented are both edifying and helpful). But the overall composite picture offered by Castiglione in his arresting
group portrait is of courtiers having a difficult go of it in this "new profession,"
struggling, laughing as much at each other as they are with each other, jockeying
for status and distinction, concerned not only about their place within the court
amid the other courtiers but also in relation to a powerful autocratic prince

(who is strategically absent during the discussions) and potentially other would-be courtiers (who may come one day to compete with these privileged courtiers and thereby displace them out of the closed circle of the cultural elite that, at least for the duration of the evening games, turns its back on the world in a harmonizing gesture of ideal intimacy and solidarity). For all their apparent and fashionable "coolness," there is a lot of sweating going on beneath the surface, and the perspiration sometimes, inadvertently, shows. The examples occasionally offer a rare glimpse into the strain, the struggle, the tension, and the pervasive anxiety amid all the suaveness, nonchalance, laughter, poise, and appealing nostalgia.

Similar issues are at stake in Machiavelli's *Il principe*. For Machiavelli, if you want to be a prince, you need *virtù*, but there is no more ambivalent term than "virtù" in *Il principe*, and it is not at all clear how you go about learning virtù in a way that makes it useful, much less reliable. Arguably, as both Wayne A. Rebhorn and Victoria Kahn have demonstrated in different ways, Machiavelli teaches us virtù by problematizing its meaning rhetorically in *Il principe*, by constantly shifting the meaning of virtù according to a variety of often contradictory contexts in which the term is strategically deployed.[13] Thus as the word "virtù" acquires a density and complexity as we move from one passage to the next in *Il principe*, we are always, according to this reading, forced to keep a watchful eye, implicitly taught to stay on our toes, even to the point where we learn that we can never grasp the real, full meaning of the term "virtù" because it is so overdetermined, so destabilized and conditioned by the contingent and the reading process. But even if this is the case, how, we may ask, do you get from the text to reality, from print to professional practice, from the page to the polished, successful performance of an art as a form of determinate, rule-bound, reliable, and communicable knowledge? How do you get from the recognition of the ambivalence of the term "virtù" at any given moment in *Il principe* to the ambivalence of what to do when you have to act with virtù as a prince, vigorously grasping the elusive, bald Fortuna by the forelock and wrestling her in a manly manner to the ground? Is the practice of reading and the edifying process of exemplarity really adequate preparation for the practice of ruling? If Machiavellian virtù is in large measure about risk, knowing and evaluating risk, taking risk, minimizing risk, as well as the recognition of the exorbitant price one has to pay for taking or not taking a risk at any given moment, in practical terms what exactly is the risk of misinterpreting the word "virtù" in *Il principe*? If you make a mistake, what will happen? Chances are you won't end up losing a princedom or your head. So you make a mistake, you go back, you read again.

All things considered, reading *Il principe* is not all that risky. Misreading the reality of any situation as a prince is, however, incredibly risky. In real life, as a new prince facing the loss of a hard-won princedom, you cannot afford not to act. In real life, as a new prince reading Machiavelli's *Il principe*, you can always afford not to read. Moreover, even if we maintain the fiction that *Il principe* is disclosing secret information that the prince desperately needs to know but somehow does not know (and this is indeed a fiction since princes had been busy doing for a long time what Machiavelli describes the prince should be doing with such prowess and guile, so the information is hardly arcane),[14] and even if we take seriously the implicit warning that the new prince better read this treatise and absorb the specialized knowledge it contains about the art of ruling or else the vulnerable prince, untutored in the ways of Machiavellian scheming, may wind up losing his princedom—even, as I say, if we take all these important issues into account, as indeed we should, we still need to square them with the fact that virtually all the examples in *Il principe* are of rulers who eventually lose power and mess up for one reason or another. Worse, Machiavelli himself announces toward the end of *Il principe* what we have all along no doubt gleaned from a careful reading of his duplicitous book: at any given moment there is a roughly fifty-fifty chance of success for the new prince as he faces one tough decision after another and, come what may, has to decide on what course of action to take, precisely because he cannot afford not to act. The secret information about the art of ruling a new principality so openly delivered in Machiavelli's innovative treatise in the spirit of full disclosure thus does not exactly inspire faith that it is information worth following. What sort of information is this? How helpful is it? We need virtù, we are told, but the examples of new princes exercising their virtù lead them sooner or later to ruin, of not being able to maintain their new princedom as they come up against tough choices or, as Fortuna would have it, tough luck.

Machiavellian virtù, then, is hardly something we need to develop in order to master an "exact" art, since Machiavelli cannot justifiably claim that exercising this virtù will absolutely ensure a practitioner will attain the desired outcome all the time as we assess and then act on risk in the art of ruling as new princes. And, all things considered, Machiavellian virtù doesn't even appear to be something we need to develop in order to master a "stochastic" art as new princes: after all, the results ultimately produced by exercising this sort of Machiavellian virtù are, in the end, so very aleatory that it is really not worth taking seriously into account the art of ruling explored in *Il principe* in order to preserve a body politic. Nor, just as important, can the term "virtù" itself be neatly defined, so slippery and overdetermined is the meaning of it. As such, Machiavellian virtù cannot be pinned down; it cannot guarantee success; it is hardly dependable "for the most part," judging from the repeated examples of failure that we are given, so there is every reason to doubt that the body of knowledge associated with it is something we need in order to practice a conjectural art;[15] and it cannot be readily translated, in the literal sense of "carried across," from the page to the polished performance. But, of course, we are told that we desperately need Machiavellian virtù, whatever it happens to be, if we are going to be successful as a new prince ruling a new princedom with any "art" whatsoever.

The "something else" you need to succeed in life in different sorts of activities, then, goes by different names for very different sorts of Italian humanists, for those who are self-evidently full-fledged humanists (Barbaro, Castiglione, and Tasso) and for those who are perhaps, for some, not-so-evidently humanists but were still trained in the studia humanitatis and certainly worked within, and often vigorously challenged, the strategies and presuppositions of humanism in their writings (Machiavelli). Depending on the humanist in question, that "something else" needed in order to succeed in life in different sorts of arts and activities can go by the name of "prudence," "grazia," "sprezzatura," or "virtù." Occasionally that "something else" cannot be concretely named at all (it is an "I don't know what," a *nescio quid*), or it can be named only by cleverly inventing a new term ("sprezzatura"), or it can be named only by radically complicating a well-established term in such a way that it becomes decidedly ambiguous in meaning ("virtù"). All this may seem as if humanists—as remarkably diverse as the men treated in this chapter—are just fudging. Yet, arguably, that is precisely the point. What makes one person truly successful at what he or she does (both now and in the past, I would argue) requires some mental fudging. It's not simple. It is complicated. It is indeed mysterious why some individuals are good at applying an art as a form of specialized knowledge and some are not, no matter how hard they work at it.[16] And this, I believe, is what Barbaro, Castiglione, Machiavelli, and Tasso—along with so many others in the Italian Renaissance who sought to expand the reach of humanism to include reflections on professional identity—are telling us when they play a language game and fudge, when they provide us with terms that seem to explain what we need to succeed in life but never adequately define the terms or account for how we can practically acquire those abilities through systematic training.

In this light, if these humanists are at all composing "how-to" books articulating an art as determinate, rule-bound, reliable, and communicable knowledge, they are composing "how-to" books that tell us how very difficult it is to actually do the things they describe.[17] They make it clear that doing these things constitutes work, but something still escapes the purview of the art that they seek to define for like-minded men who are engaged in, or wish to engage in, the art they discuss. The work described can be demystified insofar as we can say

it is work—that it requires dedicated practice and training of some sort—but it
is not at all clear what exactly makes up that practice and training and, more
important, why some men succeed at it and some do not. Personal "style,"
some sort of innate aptitude, the successful quality of an "individual" performer
with a particular mode of addressing the world: all these things cannot be easily
or systematically taught or learned when it comes to the sorts of language-based
and performance-oriented activities that these humanists privilege in their own
historically determined time, culture, and place. Using the words "prudentia,"
"virtù," "sprezzatura," "grazia," and "nescio quid" may certainly make some
people feel better about learning how to masterfully do certain things because
someone has concretely named what we need to succeed, but it only obscures
and mystifies the process further. Recognizing this is in itself a process of understanding. Recognizing that we try to name what we cannot systematically teach
or fully define or know frustrates our very desire to reduce human achievement
to some demystified "thing," rather than accept the fact that "something else"
accounts for true success—a "something else" that ultimately eludes our conceptual grasp and remains mysterious as a *nescio quid*.

Now Guicciardini's *Ricordi*, which is not a "how-to" book but is certainly a
book that discusses time and again how men need to get on in life and do
different sorts of things, addresses many of these problems in an extremely
complicated way. It does so in part because Guicciardini does not focus on any
one activity but discusses a multitude of them as they are bundled together in
the same maxim and laced throughout his text, in part because Guicciardini
challenges humanism so completely from within humanism, especially by questioning, as no one had fully ventured to do so before in such a far-reaching
manner in his time, the humanist faith in exemplarity and the assumed value
of the lessons of classical culture as trustworthy guides for action in the present.[18] Some of the professions Guicciardini reflects on—and I restrict my selection here to the "final" C version of the *Ricordi*—have to do with the work of
princes, kings, tyrants, popes, ministers (those working for popes, princes, and
tyrants generally in matters of affairs of state), ambassadors, astrologers, doctors, businessmen, courtiers, lawyers, historians, and military leaders (including
captains and the like). There are many roles for men to play in life, many
professions out there and many arts to learn that underpin them as specialized
forms of knowledge, Guicciardini lets us know. And what matters, as he puts it
tersely in one maxim (C 216), is not the actual role one plays but only how well
or poorly one plays the role, the "quality of the performance" ("ma solamente
si attende chi la porta meglio"). But what makes someone good at what he
does? How does one acquire quality? How do you learn to perform well?

"Believe me," Guicciardini insists, "in all matters, public or private, success depends on the right approach [*sapere pigliare el verso*]. Whether you succeed or fail in an enterprise depends on whether you handle it one way or another [*e però in una medesima cosa el maneggiarla in uno modo a maneggiarla in uno altro importa el conducerla a non la conducere*]."[19]

To help us find the "right approach," Guicciardini has all kinds of sage advice. Some of his advice, intended presumably for the male members of his family and perhaps even posterity, is fairly straightforward. Often it comes in the form of a personal maxim presented with the universalizing authority of a well-established, communally accepted proverb. Some advice, even when initially couched in proverbial form, is tortuously complicated. In a characteristically devious and Machiavellian fashion, Guicciardini makes a statement, qualifies it, qualifies the qualification, and continues to mull it over until it is nearly impossible to know how you are supposed to think much less act, although you know you must indeed think and act. Advice, which in Guicciardini's world is never in short supply, is good, although the wisdom underpinning good advice is painfully difficult to acquire, Guicciardini gives us to understand with elegiac force in a number of maxims (C 189, among others). And advice is very, very difficult to put to use: "Read these *Ricordi* often, and ponder them well. For it is easier to know and understand them than to put them into practice. But this too becomes easier if you grow so accustomed to them that they are always fresh in your memory" (C 9). Experience is also good: "Let no one trust so much in native prudence [*prudenzia naturale*] that he believes it to be sufficient without the help of experience. No matter how extremely prudent, any man who has been in a position of responsibility will admit that experience attains many things which natural gifts alone could never attain [*alle quali è impossibile che el naturale solo possa aggiugnere*]" (C 10). Experience refines our abilities; it is a great teacher. So it was for a host of humanists thinking about professions in Renaissance Italy, from Barbaro to Machiavelli to Castiglione to Tasso.

But to act successfully in a world in which "you cannot always abide by an absolute and fixed rule of conduct [*non si può in effetto procedere sempre con una regola indistinta e ferma*]" (C 186) and "in which success depends on the right approach" (C 198), you need discretion, that sharp and discerning eye that allows us to understand "the character of the person, of the case, and of the occasion [*la qualità delle persone, de' casi e de' tempi*]"—"for that," Guicciardini asserts, "discretion is necessary [*è necessaria la discrezione*]" (C 186). And if it is discretion that I most need, then it is discretion that I most want to learn in order to choose the "right approach" (C 198). For I need discretion not only to get by in life and perform well but also to realize that examples themselves are unreliable, that, as Michel de Montaigne would have it, they limp. I need discretion, it would seem, to undermine the humanist faith in exemplarity: "To judge by example is very misleading. Unless they are similar in every respect, examples are useless, since very tiny differences in the case may be a cause of great variations in the effects. And to discern these tiny differences takes a good and perspicacious eye [*buono e perspicace occhio*]" (C 117). Along with this, I need discretion—that good, keen, perspicacious, discerning eye (C 76, C 117)—to chart a path through some of the more dense, sinuous maxims. And I need discretion to make meaning of the maxims themselves as they unfold in this untidy collection. I need discretion, in short, to read the *Ricordi*. "'Little and good,' says the proverb. It is impossible for someone who says or writes many things not to put in a good deal of nonsense; whereas, few things can be well digested and concise. And so it may have been better to select [*scerre*] the best of these *ricordi* than to have accumulated so much material [*che accumulare tanta materia*]" (C 210). That process of selection, that ongoing process of sorting out and finding patterns of meaning, is not just the author's but the reader's work as he or she uses discretion, that sharp and discerning eye, to distinguish, sift through differences, and make sense of it all.

In this regard the *Ricordi*, which was composed in stages and has no real formal shape to it, is an extremely complicated text with no stable field of reference. It is a text composed in large measure of disconnected fragments, or, to invoke Benjaminian terms, it is a constellatory text as the work of a consummate collector. For in Walter Benjamin's scheme of things, true collectors care little about an overall ordered frame of reference in a collection, any more than they care if they have obtained all the works of specific authors or concentrated their holdings in a certain area. What matters most is that the collector creates a "constellation" of objects whose seemingly random arrangement sparks dialectical inquiry. And with every addition to, subtraction from, or rearrangement of the collection, one changes the dialectic of such a constellation, not completely but subtly, therefore sparking yet more inquiry and fresh patterns of meaning. As Susan Buck-Morss writes in a cogent description of the Benjaminian concept of constellation: "The role of the subject, to draw connections between the phenomenal elements, was not unlike that of the astrologer, who perceived figures in the heavens: 'Ideas are related to the phenomena as constellations to the stars.'"[20] At the same time, as the literary theorist and critic Terry Eagleton reminds us, the Benjaminian constellation radically upsets conventional aesthetics and desires for completeness, totality, wholeness. "The concept of constellation," Eagleton writes of Benjamin, is perhaps the most strikingly original attempt in the modern period to break with traditional versions of totality. . . . By revolutionizing the relations between part and whole, the constellation strikes at the very heart of the traditional aesthetic paradigm, in which the specificity of the detail is allowed no genuine resistance to the organizing power of the totality. . . . The constellation safeguards particularity but fissures identity, exploding the object into an array of conflictive elements and so unleashing its materiality at the cost of its self-sameness.[21]

In his *Ricordi*, Guicciardini gathers his thoughts and memories over time, and like Benjamin's collector, for whom there is continually a "dialectical tension between the poles of disorder and order" and whose "passion borders on the chaos of memories,"[22] Guicciardini reconfigures those isolated thoughts and memories—some of which are self-contained fragments, the by-products of other writings—into a constellation that defies totality and reconfirms instead the inherent unpredictability of all things in a world of flux. In this respect, Guicciardinian "discretion," as part of a Benjaminian epistemology, not only indicates how we should go about singling out everything from examples to "the character of the person, of the case, and of the occasion." It also indicates how one must go about reading his collected thoughts as one composes and recomposes patterns of ideas that "are related to the phenomena as constellations to the stars." One must therefore read with discretion a text that privileges discretion. For this reason, not even the early Q² version of the *Ricordi*, which scholars take to be the full germ of the later texts, displays order. And that, to be sure, constitutes the value and novelty of the *Ricordi* as an untidy, open-ended collection. For unlike Petrarca's *Rerum vulgarium fragmenta* (*Fragments Composed in the Vernacular*), the model Italian Renaissance collection of fragments in literary form, order is not formally or aesthetically imposed on the *Ricordi*. However scattered Petrarca's rhymes are, the number of them already imposes a coherent, unifying master narrative onto the collection: it matters if there is one more or one less. The number of poems (*rime*) marks a calendar year, at least once we exclude the opening sonnet as an obvious proemium to the whole collection. It is thus extremely calculated, just right. The fixed number emphasizes and reaffirms that Petrarca's collection is closed, an aesthetic whole, a corpus as beautiful and formally complete as Laura's body, which is reconfigured by him as a totality as he re-members her in his collection of "scattered rhymes" (*rime sparse*) and re-masters her absence and highly gendered feminine power as a stable, less threatening presence.[23] By contrast, Guicciardini openly admits that he really does not know if he has too many or too few maxims. The number of maxims he includes recalls no master narrative, imposes no obvious structure on the collection, and elicits no sensation of aesthetic completeness or wholeness from its author as a closed collection. Quite the contrary: the size and potential expansiveness of the *Ricordi* make him unmistakably uneasy.[24]

The *Ricordi* therefore requires no explanation for its dimension other than to acknowledge that *that* is how Guicciardini saw fit at a particular moment in time to put together this collection. Do with it what you will, as best you can. And since the *Ricordi* has no formal closed order to it and no unifying story to tell, order can only emerge from the text dialectically, as the product of a readerly process. It derives from discretionary work. But therein lies the problem. We desperately need discretion, but if discretion is "not given by nature," Guicciardini insists, it "can rarely be learned adequately from experience" and "can never be learned from books [*co' libri non mai*]" (C 186). "It is a great error," Guicciardini writes in another context,

> to speak of the things of this world absolutely and indiscriminately and to deal with them, as it were, by rule [*per regola*]. In nearly all things one must make distinctions and exceptions because of differences in their circumstances. These circumstances are not covered by one and the same manner of calculation [*non si possono fermare con una medesima misura*]. Nor can these distinctions and exceptions be found written in books. They must be taught by discretion [*e queste distinzione e eccezione non si truovano scritte in su' libri, ma bisogna le insegni la discrezione*]. (C 6)

Discretion thus teaches us how to act, but we cannot be taught discretion. Not even the *Ricordi*, nor any other book, can teach us discretion. Indeed, to the extent that Guicciardini conceptualizes discretion as a book, it is a book that is already in your mind, within your individual, particular nature, tucked away and thus invisible to your own good, keen, perspicacious eye. And in no way is it at all like the book we read: "These *ricordi* are rules that can be written in books. But particular cases have different circumstances and must be treated differently. Such cases can hardly be written anywhere but in the book of discretion [*si possono male scrivere altrove che nel libro della discrezione*]" (B 35). Discretion is therefore necessary in all things: in selecting maxims, in discerning, in judging, in making (or rather, in *not* making) use of exemplarity, in sorting out, in taking the right approach, in performing well, in doing well, in recording internally all the exceptional cases that are out there in the world to consider. Yet you either have discretion or you don't. It is not an acquired skill. It is an innate ability—something more like a "gift" or mysterious "talent," although the word "ability" captures the Guicciardinian concept better as an underlying force that is at once dynamic and enabling and generative. Discretion is capable of being, and in fact must be, refined and strengthened through experience—as well through the reading process. But it is not an ability that can be inculcated through a techne, a specialized form of knowledge. And yet at bottom discretion is, and always will be for Guicciardini, the underlying ability required for success in *whatever* we aim to do in life, much as "prudentia," "sprezzatura," "virtù," and "nescio quid" were for Barbaro, Machiavelli, Castiglione, and Tasso. In this respect, we all seem to desperately need that mysterious "something else" to succeed—that "something elusive," as Stephen Greenblatt somewhat surprisingly puts it when talking about one of Shakespeare's greatest comic theatrical creations, "that remains to be accounted for" but still, for all our best efforts to pluck out the mystery, nonetheless escapes our ken, "as if" Falstaff, he writes, like so many people in real life who seem to succeed with remarkable individual style, "had the power in himself to resist all efforts to explain or contain him."[25]

What, then, do these reflections potentially tell us about our *own* relationship to humanism and professionalism in the humanities today? Together the intellectual and cultural historians Grafton and Jardine raised a similar sort of question roughly three decades ago in their jointly authored *From Humanism to the Humanities*, and their response was decidedly negative and polemical. The calculated strategy of "mystification" that Renaissance humanism willfully engaged in, for Grafton and Jardine, can be laid bare by examining evidence. And if you look at the real, hard-core material evidence, at the class notes taken at the famous humanist school of Guarino da Verona, for instance, the entire male-directed and male-dominated humanist pedagogical program seems so transparently and relentlessly boring to them, so inept at inculcating how to move from the specific to the general, so incapable of teaching anyone (man *or* woman) how to grasp the forest for the trees, so mindlessly focused on trivial philological details rather than larger moral philosophical matters. Where is the concrete evidence here or anywhere else in the Italian Renaissance, Grafton and Jardine challenge, that the studia humanitatis delivered on its promise of enlightening people, liberating and enlarging their minds, training particular men to become leaders? Instead, they argue, humanism seems to instill docility, an obsequious acceptance of authority, confusion, a love for trifles, a passion for banalities. Surely Scholasticism, they insist, was better suited than humanism to prepare people for life in general and, more specifically, men for constructive work in professions grounded in specialized forms of knowledge. Moreover, if humanists did succeed in life, if they are at all innovative, there is no definitive proof, they tacitly assume, that the studia humanitatis had anything to do with it. And if we acknowledge for the sake of argument that a number of individual humanists were remarkable and innovative and that the studia humanitatis had everything to do with making them so, where does that leave everyone else, all the other everyday, hardworking, run-of-the-mill humanists who are collectively and individually incapable of making that "mysterious transition" from "routine competence" to "creative achievement"? Where indeed, they ask, is the end-product value of humanism, much less the "marketable end-product" value of the humanities?[26]

By way of response, it is worth noting from the outset that Grafton and Jardine are somewhat engaged in their own deft process of mystification, first when they claim that there has been a "long history of evasiveness" regarding the practical value of humanism and the humanities, for they do not then write that full-length history, understandably enough since it would perhaps be an onerous if not tedious undertaking.[27] Second, and more significant, they somewhat mystify matters when they seem too comfortable in moving so quickly, effortlessly, and seamlessly from Renaissance humanism (as Kristeller magisterially defined it well over half a century ago) to contemporary Western-styled humanities (as no one seems truly confident in defining it these days).[28] Renaissance humanism isn't at all the same as modern-day humanities: the two are far more different, I submit, than they are alike, not the least given the fact that the latter, judging by current university and college enrollments, is now dominated by women. But it is indeed significant that Grafton and Jardine do make the connection between Renaissance humanism and modern-day humanities and that they feel free to do so. There are doubtless a number of reasons why they feel free to do so. But one reason, I suspect, has to do with the fact that we have grown a bit too accustomed to a certain sort of narrative (in Hayden White's terms a certain kind of story with its own characteristic forms of emplotment) that helps us, or in generic terms conditions us, to understand our relationship to the past in a particular way.[29]

If I understand it correctly, the broad contours of the historical narrative at play here have the early modern period (formerly known as the Renaissance) and the postmodern period (for some still the modern period) as beginning and end points.[30] And the rest of the narrative runs something like this. Protocapitalism in the early modern period, which began to have a global reach and impact with the colonizing of the "New World" and far-flung trading companies, finds itself now undone by postcapitalism, which is exhausting itself in the postcolonial period and spinning out of control in a last-gasp state of global, multinational, multicorporate crisis. The emergence of the self and the "individual" in the early modern period finds itself now undone by the recognition that we only occupy subject positions, that we are ontologically split by conscious and unconscious drives, that half of what we say has already been said before, and that we are fashioned by structures and forces outside our control or ken (self-fashioning in this respect is pretty much an enabling illusion that nevertheless continues to sustain us, both men and women, in bad faith even as we endlessly deconstruct it in all our blindness and insight). The birth of a rigorous historicism, which recognizes differences and seeks a stable perspective through which we can place ourselves and measure our relationship to the past (much as one finds oneself placed in Renaissance one-point perspective as a fixed viewer in a relation to the objects in space forever pinpointed within the picture plane), is undone by the deeply ingrained postmodern habit of making a pastiche of styles in a manner that is heedless of historicity, of flattening out spatial relations and conflating the inside and outside in a manner that is at once disorienting and fragmenting, of valuing every perspective as equal to the point where pluralism becomes destabilizing relativism, and of undermining the very ground from which one can even begin to claim to hold a stable perspective. The birth of a sophisticated philology, which demanded understanding how a word was embedded and used in a specific cultural and historical context, is now undone by the postmodern habit of undermining our capacity to think historically, of substituting the copy for the original to the point where the referent has withered away, of relishing the endless deferral of meaning and the sometimes vertiginous play and clutter of signs, and of simply not giving a damn about reading texts in the original language because the principal concern is not with experiencing the meaning embedded in the form but in extracting the ideological code underlying a now just-as-well-translated text—or, for that matter, a text that can just as easily be fed into a computer and swiftly read by it in light of thousands and thousands of other digitally encoded texts. The story goes on and on.

Gazing at the early modern period, then, means gazing back at one's own origins according to this narrative, and it allows one to witness the birth of both what is coming apart and what we are actively dismantling in discourse and in the world in an act of creative destruction as we saw off the branch on which we stand within the humanities. It stands to reason, then, that humanism is meeting the same fate, following the same narrative structure within the historical paradigm limned above. If everything else is coming apart, undoing itself through the very process that once made it possible (whatever was once constructed can now be retroactively, and indeed endlessly, deconstructed), surely the antihumanist trend in the humanities finds its origins in the moment when humanism is thought to have begun. The mystification of humanism is now therefore being undone by the demystification of both humanism and the humanities by extraordinary, erudite scholars at such high-powered institutions as Cambridge and Princeton—not, incidentally, from the margins but from the dead center, from two of the most elite institutions in Europe and North America. And the charge these scholars have leveled against humanism and the humanities has been issued from one of the most prestigious publishing houses in the world, Harvard University Press. Now, not Eugenio Garin's and Hans Baron's enlightened Renaissance humanists are the heroes breathtakingly liberating minds and busting open the literary canon by hunting down books and reading the treasured insights contained within them in often startling new ways but, instead, our colleagues at universities as they justifiably battle pedagogical dogma and fight the tyranny of educational hype in Renaissance humanism and the humanities today. And as they set the record straight, we can all sit back and feel not the uplifting swoosh of the owl of Minerva taking off at dusk but the thrill (or, in some instances, dreadful panic) of finding that someone has at long last pulled the plug on the boat that keeps everyone in the already not-so-well-endowed humanities afloat, precisely—and probably not accidentally—in the very moment that professional schools increasingly dominate university and college campuses nationwide and absorb so many available institutional resources (and, more recently, in a period when major journalists and well-meaning academicians are increasingly registering alarm at the dramatically dwindling numbers of students majoring in the humanities at not only institutions of higher learning generally but elite ones as well).[31]

In seeking to demystify humanism and reveal the gap between ideals and practices in the humanities today, Grafton and Jardine have as their principal target of attack Garin and his cheerful assertion that humanism was truly liberating in so many of its forms—an assumption that of course needs to be, and has been very effectively, challenged seriously over the years. Historically speaking, there is much to say for debunking wholesale myths of presumed, but not adequately measured, success. However, it is also important to point out that when Grafton and Jardine examine student notebooks, they cannot in the end tell us what students learned. They can only tell us what they chose to record, and what students record is not always a fair indication, I'd wager, of what they have absorbed in class. In addition, many students obviously enjoyed the humanist education, even if it was perhaps not always as innovative, revolutionary, or mind opening as modern scholars have sometimes made it out to be. There is also reason to believe, moreover, that humanism did help some people think differently. The assumption, for instance, that we shape institutions as they shape us, that there is a constant, free-flowing give-and-take between the subject in the world and the world that constructs and gives meaning and shape to the subject, is perhaps already partly embedded in the structure of the Ciceronian periodic prose that the humanists so persistently and patiently imitated. There is some reason to believe, that is, that humanism was not only pleasurable[32]—a point that is worth stressing and often gets lost in the translation of academic studies—but that it also helped reconfigure the way people thought as dedicated humanists over time achieved real competence in imitating Cicero and thus began to experience in a new way their relationship to the world through his complex, layered style, a style that often confuses subjects and objects and places all sorts of structures between the agent and the object or person acted upon.[33] Some scholars, including those with a distinctly more theoretical and philosophical bent to them, have been maintaining for some time now that humanism reshaped thought and perception, especially as they focus on rhetoric and emphasize that particular art's contribution to, among other things, skepticism, visual insight, reading practices, the new science, pragmatism, and language theory.[34]

Along these lines, the humanist interaction with professions, I have here argued, had a cognitive edge to it as well. Humanist reflections on professional activities, I maintain, teach us over and over again to value complexity. We are given to understand that the codes within texts are extremely complicated and contradictory; that the codes in life, in actual work experience, are equally, if not more, complicated and contradictory; and that there is no reliable way of getting from the complexity of codes in texts to the complexity of codes in life. That path, from text to life, is itself complicated, fraught with pitfalls. For this reason we must accept epistemological uncertainty in whatever we do and profess we can do, dutifully armed as we may be with the foreknowledge that we will ultimately never know how best to act even though we know we must act. At the same time, we must accept that what makes some individuals successful and others unsuccessful as they are compelled to act as ambassadors or princes or secretaries or courtiers is, alas, a bit mysterious. Needless to say, Grafton and Jardine would like a bit more evidence, something objective and tangible to grasp, something that reveals a "regular and causal link between routine competence and creative achievement, let alone civic qualities of leadership and integrity."[35] Yet there is no such cut-and-dried link (I doubt one can find such a link in any educational and cultural program, no matter how much we increasingly attend in our schools, colleges, and universities to inputs, outputs, outcomes, and now something absurdly called "throughputs" in the spirit of performance-based measurement and evaluation). And humanists, I believe, are purposely showing us this time and time again, at least when these sorts of pedagogical issues are framed within the context of professionalism and the arts. How you acquire those creative qualities and remarkable abilities is, and always will remain, a mystery, just as it is a mystery for Barbaro, Castiglione, Machiavelli, and Tasso how you have or get "grazia," "sprezzatura," "prudentia," "virtù," or, to be sure, the ever-so-elusive "nescio quid." Thus Barbaro, Castiglione, Machiavelli, and Tasso can certainly name what you need to succeed, and by doing so they can make you feel, as you read their various writings, that you actually have an understanding of what you need to succeed. But they cannot in fact systematically teach you or give you what you need to ensure that your "performance" in whatever you happen to do in life will be—as Guicciardini puts it in another context (C 216)—of real social value in terms of quality (perhaps not necessarily marketable end-product value but value nonetheless). And there is, I frankly think, some value in knowing this, as scholars today occasionally seek to demystify the mystifying practices of humanists in Renaissance Italy and in the process mystify the institutional and historical connections between the humanities today and the studia humanitatis of the past.

PART II

✇

MAVERICKS

CHAPTER 3

ཅ

Constructing a Maverick Physician
in Print: Reflections on the Peculiar Case
of Leonardo Fioravanti's Writings

THE VARIOUS WRITINGS OF LEONARDO FIORAVANTI (FIG. 18), VIRTUALLY ALL
of which are dedicated to popular medicine, and certainly all of which stand at
the antipodes of the sorts of highbrow humanist writings we looked at in the
previous chapter, furnish an understanding of Renaissance culture in literary and
rhetorical terms in ways that have not always been adequately explored by scholars
attending to his life and work as a surgeon/physician. The historian William
Eamon, for example, brilliantly disclosed how Fioravanti, as a radical empiric
invested in discovering the "secrets of nature," contributed in a significant way to
the development of modern scientific inquiry, while the social and cultural historian David Gentilcore has solidly placed Fioravanti within currents of medical
charlatanism of his time. But Fioravanti was more than just an innovative empiric
working in the healing arts and more than just a model figure for a number of
charlatans throughout Europe, both during and after his lifetime. Moreover, he
was more than just an interesting, albeit minor, character within the grand sweep
of the history of medicine and natural philosophy, whose biography has been
elegantly written by both Eamon and Piero Camporesi and makes for fascinating
reading. Fioravanti was also a great medical communicator, and this mattered
then and should matter to us now as we seek to understand how he could have
possibly been so successful or have ever attracted such a following.

Fioravanti was in great measure successful and influential because he knew,
as Galileo Galilei did within the far different social setting of court culture, how
to play the game professionally. In late Renaissance and early modern Italy, as
challenging as it was to have interesting ideas, one had to know, Mario Biagioli
has perhaps best demonstrated in his studies of Galileo,[1] how to channel those
ideas in a persuasive manner through culturally normed vehicles for communication in order to have any impact at all. And this is what Fioravanti knew how

FIGURE 18. *Portrait of Leonardo Fioravanti.* From *Il tesoro della vita humana* (Venice: Appresso gli Heredi di Melchior Sessa, 1582), c8v. Reproduced by permission of the Harry Ransom Center, The University of Texas at Austin.

to do—or at least aggressively sought to do—professionally through the highly instrumentalized medium of print while he worked in the ambit of a group of men living as best they could off of the print industry centered in mid-sixteenth-century Venice, the so-called polygraphs (poligrafi). In the process Fioravanti, like the polygraphs, drew on not only his own vast body of personal experiences but also a communal storehouse of literary and cultural models. Like the polygraphs, he could also write in an entertaining manner and engage his readers in his stories, both about others and himself. And he could wage fierce battles with great stylistic verve and encode himself into his writings in subtle ways as he identified and warred with others and what they did. He could be at turn witty and aggressive, ordinary and extraordinary, "sincere" and duplicitous, supportive and subversive. Hence my broader aim in this reflection is to restore Fioravanti as not just a precursor to modern natural science, an important figure of medical charlatanism, or an interesting, colorful character in his own right but, as we shall see by looking closely at some curious practices and longstanding grudges in his life, a gifted narrator with a compelling and highly individualized voice. A maverick within his chosen profession, and admittedly not a household name to many today, he emerges through his writings as one of the most engaging figures of late Renaissance medicine, natural philosophy, and literary self-fashioning. In this way, as in so many others, the highly verbal, recalcitrant, restless, and endlessly self-promoting, marvel-making Fioravanti figures into the complex "story" of early modern science in an interesting manner for not only cultural but also literary historians—a story that involves, as Pamela H. Smith has most recently elucidated, in no small measure the "intersection of vernacular and scholarly culture, which brought about a new union of hand and mind, at the same time that a stark distinction came to be drawn between what counted as scientific knowledge and what was relegated to the category of old wives' tales."[2]

Unlike the real charlatans of his time, whose activities began to be regulated systematically by the authorities in early modern Italy, Fioravanti never mounted a makeshift platform to sell his medical products or himself, which is what charlatans—understood as expert "chatterers" (ciarlatori)—professionally did for a living as "mountebanks" (literally a person who "gets up on a bench," "monta in banco").[3] From what we know, Fioravanti never sang songs, put on theatrical masks, danced about, or acted out scripted or improvised roles in the public square, as if he were part of the burgeoning theatrical art form of the popular commedia dell'arte, which is again what many charlatans did for a living in order to captivate an audience and sell their newfangled products.[4] Rather, Fioravanti's gifted ability to fashion himself theatrically was realized within circumscribed domains (a patient's house, his own studio, a hospital),[5] not in wide-open public spaces, such as the piazza of San Marco in Venice where so many charlatans sought to sell their wares (fig. 19) or the town square of Palermo where carnival was taking place when Fioravanti first arrived in Sicily toward the beginning of his extensive travels and was auspiciously taken for a physician long before he officially became one.[6] Fioravanti's theatrical knack for putting on a good show found expression in singular performances that took place, presumably, with only a few spellbound onlookers present at his medical spectacles. On one occasion he ostensibly reaped the reward of astonishing some by appearing to bring back to life a patient, and he allegedly performed this feat in Venice, the one city he stayed in for the longest period of his life after 1548, when he cured the poet Dionigi Atanagi da Cagli with "miraculous success" after the unfortunate man was inadvertently shot in the head.[7] But Fioravanti did not make a point of appearing to bring people back to life (or feign to perform this sort of miracle) over and over again just to please an audience, as charlatans might well have done with their highly staged public performances.[8]

Moreover, and more important, Fioravanti's ability to put on a good show manifested itself above all within the minds of his readers, which is to say, privately and repeatedly in their *imagination* as they consumed the popular books he published in Venice, the city he effectively called his home during a most formative period of his adult professional life, beginning with his *De' capricci medicinali* (*Concerning Medical Whims*, Avanzo, 1561) and extending on to his *Secreti medicinali* (*Medical Secrets*, Avanzo, 1561), *Del compendio dei secreti rationali* (*Concerning a Compendium of Rational Secrets*, Valgrisi, 1564), *Dello specchio di scientia universale* (*Concerning a Mirror of Universal Knowledge*, Valgrisi, 1564), *Del reggimento della peste* (*Concerning a Regimen for the Plague*, Ravenoldo, 1565), *La cirugia* (*Surgery*, Sessa, 1570), *Il tesoro della vita humana* (Sessa, 1570), and *Della fisica* (*Of Physic*, Sessa, 1582).[9] In virtually all of these books, several of which went into multiple printings during and after his lifetime (a few were also translated into German, French, and English), Fioravanti at some point or other interrupts his discourse on the topic at hand to place vividly before our eyes his own spectacular role as an energetic miracle worker. In this respect, Fioravanti's role as a "charlatan" manifested itself within the wide public arena *exclusively* in the medium of print.[10] Here is where he "chattered" away and rendered himself so visible as a radical empiric who had traveled about the world. Here is where he gathered a following and became one of the privileged models for so many charlatans who came after him. Here is where

Intartenimento che dano ogni giorno li Ciarlatani in Piazza di S. Marco al Populo.
d'ogni natione che mattina e sera ordinariamente, ui concore
Giacomo Franco Forma con Priuilegio

FIGURE 19. *Intartenimento che demo ogni giorno li Ciarlatani.* From Giacomo Franco, *Habiti d'huomeni et donne venetiane: Con la processione della ser.ma signoria et altri particolari cioè. Trionfi feste et cerimonie publiche della nobilissima città di Venetia* (Venice: G. Franco, 1610). The Metropolitan Museum of Art, NY. Image copyright © The Metropolitan Museum of Art. Image source reproduced by permission of Art Resource, NY. Mountebanks in Piazza San Marco, Venice, with two charlatans standing on a platform, one holding a snake, selling their concoctions to the right of a lutist, with a *Pantalone* (a principal stock character of the commedia dell'arte) performing in profile on the other side.

he also emerged as one of the great medical communicators of his age, sought out clients through clever strategies of self-advertisement,[11] and displayed to the broadest group possible his obvious charisma.

Fioravanti loved print. That love finds expression in the many books that he wrote while working in the circle of the polygraphs, the loquacious, professional adventurers of the pen of late Renaissance Venice.[12] Fioravanti's love for print also found concrete expression in some of the statements he made about the democratizing power of print within those very books that appealed to such a vast potential audience, both in Italy and abroad.[13] Print conferred fame, he also reminds us, as he participates in a widespread discussion of the period about the value of print publication.[14] But Fioravanti, it is important to stress, did not exactly love a good deal of bookish culture, at least as he tells the story of his development as a surgeon (whose job it was to treat external ailments) and then, once he acquired a degree in 1568, as a physician (whose job it was to treat an individual patient's diet and thus the internal workings of the body).[15] Fioravanti's career, which benefited from print culture generally and his familiarity with the strategies of the Venetian polygraphs specifically, emerged largely out of a battle with books and the bookish, elite, Latin-based medical culture he disdained. As he tells the story in the second part of his *Tesoro*, a treatise written in part to celebrate his new role in life as a credentialed "physician," Fioravanti left Bologna in 1548 when he was about thirty years old (not, that is, when he was a young man) in order to acquire knowledge about the art of healing directly from experience in the world, rather than indirectly from books. To be sure, Fioravanti's ongoing quarrel with university-taught medicine had different dimensions to it, and it may have partly stemmed from an unhappy experience he had as a student if he ever attended the great school of medicine in Bologna (if he did matriculate, he certainly never graduated). Perhaps Fioravanti's vehement attacks against university-taught medicine also grew out of a career-path decision he may have made early on in his life regarding whether he would become either a healing surgeon or an anatomist-style surgeon who routinely disclosed the insides of a dead body.[16]

Either way, at the center of Fioravanti's complaint against physicians, as he tells it in a number of places in his writings, lay a profound disgust for the familiar medical practice of disputation. That learned practice, he insisted, was born from, dependent upon, and nurtured by the very books physicians assiduously studied and whose content so many physicians felt compelled to reproduce in a self-serving manner. They did so to secure their position within the medical hierarchy and sustain the public's belief in the value of their profession as one with, in Fioravanti's mind, its own narrowly construed and impoverished art. Hence when physicians talked, it was as if the patient disappeared in their presence. Their bookish nonsense took over and they competed, with all their vainglorious desire to outdo one another, in spouting yet one more useless piece of advice.[17] Much of what theory-based physicians did, he avowed, derived from their narcissistic desire to hold sway over others through a false rhetoric that obscured the truth.[18] When Fioravanti left Bologna in 1548, then, he was consciously turning his back on the bookish world of medicine in all its institutionalized forms, with its specialized vocabulary, elitist discursive practices, and concern for "theory" (*theorica*) at the expense of "practice" (*pratica*) and "experience" (*esperienza*).[19] "So," he observed at the end of his *Specchio*,

> I went seeking truth in many parts of the world, and I learned this truth from different sorts of people and from the animals and the plants of the earth; and this [process of acquiring knowledge through traveling] has had no other purpose than to aid the world and allow me to practice the truth, so as not to walk blindly as many do for not having walked about the world and witnessed the great diversity of things of nature, as I have seen in the great amount of time that I went traveling about the earth, sailing through the sea, and experiencing maritime and land wars, as well as having lived through floods, winds, earthquakes, tempests, fires, beneath the ground, in baths and caverns, amid thunder and lightning, all in the process of seeing things that would bring terror to even those in hell [*cose da mettere terrore nell'inferno*]—things, however, that are still necessary in order to practice our medicine. (308v)[20]

Fioravanti's epic- and romance-style travels, which would evidently "bring terror to even those in hell," took him on a fabulous quest for truth through "various and different regions of the world," not only in provinces in Italy but also North Africa, Spain, the western coast of current Croatia, and, he boasts, parts of Asia, although there is no reason to believe that he actually made it that far in his restless wanderings.[21] The overall significance of Fioravanti's movement in his medical odyssey is largely twofold for the purposes of this chapter. First, Fioravanti's movement, as Eamon has demonstrated, constitutes a journey into acquiring firsthand knowledge of medical secrets. Those secrets, which Fioravanti then exploits and often divulges in his writings in a spirit of full disclosure, can only be acquired directly from people and not indirectly from books. As healers, we need to be there, on the scene, listening, observing, and actually putting that knowledge into practice, in experiments, to see if it works.[22] This is how healers can acquire the real specialized knowledge underpinning their profession. To this end, doctors must immerse themselves in different cultures and be willing to talk to all sorts of people, from illiterate old men with a developed trick of the trade to a little old lady with a hand-me-down remedy.[23] Popular culture all over the world had simply amassed an enormous quantity of helpful information that could assist the practical-minded doctor who aimed to heal rather than just converse. Physicians invested in academic institutions of medical learning woefully neglected that culture, precisely because for Fioravanti they aimed to secure their position within the medical hierarchy by distancing themselves as much as possible from the unlettered and uninitiated. Physicians did not seek to learn from peasants, shepherds, soldiers, the religious, old and vulgar women, and every other sort of common folk,[24] yet, according to Fioravanti, they should do so, just as they should be willing to learn from members of society who hold culturally elevated positions in it yet do not possess recognizable credentials in the form of a degree.[25] What is more, they should present the information gleaned from their work openly,[26] unveiling the secrets of the art they put into practice in the spirit of full disclosure, rather than cloaking that hard-won knowledge in a fanciful technical language, as institutionally trained physicians often did, according to Fioravanti, in order to bolster their own sense of exclusivity within a profession.

Second, Fioravanti's movement in his travels as a radical empiric constitutes a journey, as edifying odysseys often do, from the margins back to the center, from the "primitivism" of the south, as Eamon cogently puts it, where "natural methods still survived among the common people as unwritten 'rules of life,'"[27] back to the north, where medicine had its firmly ingrained institutionalized practices and highly choreographed procedures for professional advancement.[28] In this context Fioravanti's journey also constitutes a movement from the foreign back to the familiar and thus, in the long run, from professional anonymity (Fioravanti is unmistakably a nobody "surgeon" when he first sets out from Bologna on his journeys) to fame (he is a recognized master "physician" with a following and the title of "knight" at the end of his life).[29] Having set out to "walk about the world,"[30] Fioravanti, thanks to that instructive journey, becomes the distinguished man who writes the books we read. And we, the indoctrinated readers, occasionally have the pleasure of tracing his development, much as if we were examining a sort of formative precursor to the bildungsroman. The second part of Fioravanti's autobiographically inspired *Tesoro*, for instance, unfolds as a story of self-growth full of adventures, gaffes, misfortunes, villains, conflicts, and stupendous successes. Furthermore, in literary terms, Fioravanti's movement in his travels from the margins back to the center constitutes a journey from oral to print culture, from the illiterate surgeons, shepherds, hags, and dispossessed peasants of popular culture in Sicily to the highly literate polygraphs, physicians, and merchants of vibrant, commercial, republican Venice. In this respect, having once immersed himself in different cultures whose information was transmitted to him orally, Fioravanti becomes not just a repository of all that information. He also becomes, as he puts that information into print, a translator and organizer of it for a broad literate audience, as well as a keen interpreter of it.[31] Fioravanti, we soon come to realize in reading his writings, is the person who can tell us what people think works, and since he has tried different ways of practicing and perfecting the art of medicine through studied experimentation, he can also tell us reliably what does and does not work as he seeks to present himself as a one-of-a-kind, superlative master in his chosen medical profession. Such, for instance, is the case when he tells the fascinating story about how he learned to distinguish the odors of urine, meticulously experimenting in the strangest of ways with all sorts of specimens, as well as when he tells the equally engaging story about how he ingeniously put into practice on the spur of the moment the long-lost art of rhinoplasty. These two stories, which will take center stage in the following section, exemplify some of the more eccentric aspects of this man as he presents himself in print in the role of a maverick physician. In the final section of this chapter I turn to examine Fioravanti's entrenched battle with anatomists, whom he casts as his demonic doubles and envisions as the true villains operating at the heart of the medical profession.

ॐ   ॐ   ॐ

In his medical treatise *De urinis* (*Concerning Urines*), contained within his *De excrementis* (*On Excretions*), the learned physician Giovanni Battista da Monte (1498–1551), perhaps best known for integrating clinical practice into his teaching, insisted that urine needed to be analyzed in terms of not only color and consistency but also odor.[32] He devoted an entire chapter, titled "De odore" (Concerning Odor), to the crucial topic of the role of smells and smelling in diagnostic practice, and he offered in this medical book, printed posthumously in 1554, the following straightforward information: "Therefore, either urine will be odorous or deprived of odor," meaning it could smell either "good" (it has no real odor) or "bad" (it has a putrescent odor, which is to say, prosaically, it stinks).[33] Da Monte made similar claims regarding the analysis of excrement, which we should understand to denote not only feces and urine but also anything excreted from the body, including tears. It was deemed necessary to detect, among other symptoms, the odor of "certain redundant matter in the body."[34] But da Monte's rhetorically unembellished observations, which rehearse the position of the great classical medical man Galen, raise a troubling question. What doctors in their right minds would ever want to stick their noses in the putrid places of a patient or the potentially putrid excretions of a patient? The Paduan physician Gabriele Zerbi (1445–1505) seems to have had this nagging question in mind when he refused to smell the breath of a patient: "that he admitted as much in a book on the physician and his conduct, published in 1495," the medical historian Richard Palmer observes, "suggests that Zerbi did not expect reproach."[35] In theory, a physician was supposed to diagnose the cause of a disease through smell, which in all likelihood meant that he had to get his trained nose fairly close to the "redundant matter in the body," but perhaps in practice this was not always a desirable thing to do. Two centuries before da Monte wrote about excrement, the laureate poet Francesco Petrarca, who often warred with the medical profession in his humanist diatribes and letters, took great pleasure in ridiculing what he perceived to be the inherently filthy habits of physicians. They turned pale, as he cruelly put it in his *Invective contra medicum* (*Invective Against a Physician*, 1355), from inhaling so much excremental odor of feces and urine.[36] According to Petrarca, physicians not only exercised a profession unworthy of being considered so elevated by the cultural elite but also engaged in activities that were done in decidedly bad taste.

At least one man of medicine—a near contemporary of da Monte—avidly analyzed every aspect of urine so as to become exceedingly knowledgeable about it, or at least he confessed to having done so with bold, self-aggrandizing pride. That man was, of course, the unconventional and iconoclastic Fioravanti, who informs us in his *De' capricci medicinali*, a medical compendium published seven years after da Monte's *De urinis*, how he was tricked in his professional development as a doctor because he was handed some "Trebbiano wine" instead of urine to analyze.[37] Because of its yellowish color ("zalletto"), the Bolognese Fioravanti takes the "urine," which he examines on the basis of its color alone, to signify that the ailing person suffers from excess "choleric humor" (46r). Because of his professional mistake, which is narrated in the form of a cautionary tale, Fioravanti urges doctors who actually practice medicine, rather than those who just theorize about it and are full of useless book knowledge, to learn how to distinguish real urine from other substances that might be fobbed off as a ruse on an unsuspecting doctor. Fioravanti himself, as he tells his exemplary story about his medical blunder, explains how he went about systematically acquiring that knowledge. He engaged members of his own household to provide him with samples of their urine to analyze "every day," as well as the urine of different animals, from dogs and donkeys to horses and mules, for purposes of careful studied comparison. In this way Fioravanti could presumably conduct his experiments in a methodical and empirical manner with a variety, as well as readily available supply, of urine to compare, both human and nonhuman.[38] Evidently his unorthodox plan seemed to have worked, for in the end Fioravanti does become, he proudly asserts, a true expert in urine, thanks to his dogged dedication to a rather peculiar form of controlled, firsthand observation and experimentation:

> I had all the experiences that were possible to do, so that I would not be tricked another time by urine; and in this I made a most great study. . . . and many times I have found myself in some city where there have been bizarre folks who wanted to check me out, put me to the test, by showing me the urine of horses, lye, wine, and vinegar, and similar stuff. But it was to no effect, because I had become an expert in that profession, [so that] all the times that they'd wanted to trick me, they instead remained tricked [*tutte le volte, che altri hanno voluto burlarmi, sono restati loro i burlati*]. (46v)

In one remarkable instance, suspecting that he has been handed vinegar to examine by some pranksters, he sticks his finger into the suspicious fluid and actually tastes it.[39] It was, he mercifully assures us, "most perfectly vinegar [*aceto perfettissimo*]" (47r).

Given Fioravanti's tendency to vaunt his unusual methods in self-celebratory autobiographical vignettes placed within his popular and edifying discourses on medicine, we may be inclined to think that doctors in general did not taste urine or, for that matter, stick their noses near or deeply into the "orinale" (an alembic-shaped urine flask, fig. 20) in order to analyze carefully a patient's health, however much they were advised to perform the latter in the Italian Renaissance medical community. That Fioravanti is first tricked because he merely looks at the color of the urine handed to him and makes a diagnosis of the humoral imbalance on the basis of the color alone suggests that it was a far more common practice to distinguish primarily by color, perhaps because European languages possess a limited vocabulary for talking about odors generally.[40] Smelling urine may therefore have been advised in theory, as Palmer observes, but it was perhaps less done in practice than Petrarca implies in his highly colorful and rhetorical attack against physicians—a distinctly humanist diatribe partly inspired by a reading of Pliny the Elder's *Naturalis historia* (*Natural History*) and aimed at mocking, among other things, his detractor's smugness, ignorance, and false sense of distinction. In any event, it is evident that the empiric Fioravanti wishes us to believe in his *De' capricci medicinali* that he went one step further than most doctors of the time, in particular the academic doctors he deplored, and used almost all his senses, from sight to taste to smell to touch, when it came to analyzing specimens of "nature" isolated for investigation—in this case the varied specimens of urine collected for experiments, as

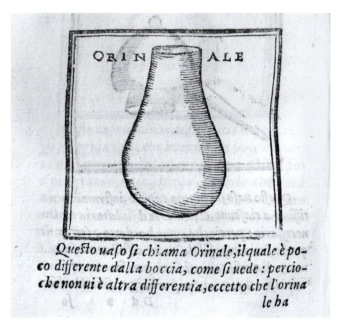

ORIN   ALE

Questo uaſo ſi chiama Orinale, ilquale è po-
co differente dalla boccia, come ſi uede : percio-
che non ui è altra differentia, eccetto che l'orina
le ha

FIGURE 20. Leonardo Fioravanti, *De' capricci medicinali* (Appresso Lodovico Avanzo, 1573), 202v. 1.Mx.107.no.2. Reproduced by permission of Countway Library of Medicine, Harvard Library. Image of an "orinale."

well as the specimens handed to him for examination by clients.[41] "I took the 'orinale' [from them]," he maintains, "and I went into my study and I smelled that urine [*annasai quell'orina*]" (47r). Rhetorically, Fioravanti's assertion here is vigorous. Far from appearing as a bland precept or observation delivered in a medical treatise on urine in order to tell other doctors what they should or should not do in general, Fioravanti's description here appears as an exemplary model of lived, rather than theorized, practice. And it takes place within a narrative that is concrete, dramatic, autobiographical in nature, and full of local color and detail. It also serves to render Fioravanti all the more unique within the context of the curious empirical practices he occasionally engaged in as a man so deeply invested in the profession of medicine and in search of a specialized knowledge underpinning it through his allegedly new way of healing.

The maverick Fioravanti was a doctor at once typical and atypical of his times, as Eamon and Camporesi have best demonstrated. He was entrenched in the medical community, familiar with its practices and many of its canonical texts, and proud of being acknowledged a credentialed physician later in life.[42] Becoming a physician meant that Fioravanti could prescribe cures "by mouth" and therefore devote himself to the inner workings and diet of the individual patient. Being a physician also elevated Fioravanti generally within the hierarchy of Renaissance medicine, although Fioravanti, it should be said, had effectively occupied the de facto position of a physician while working as an officially licensed surgeon, whose job it was, technically speaking, to perform only operations on the body and treat just the patient's external ailments.[43] But Fioravanti was also something of an institutional gadfly, a scourge of doctors, much as Pietro Aretino was an intractable scourge of princes.[44] He loved to critique his profession from within, and many, it would seem, loved to critique him. Men have plotted against him, he complains in his *De' capricci medicinali*, much as he did in his autobiographical *Tesoro*, where he laments about having been persecuted.[45] Indeed, Fioravanti was often taken to task by physicians and attacked by them and the governmental agencies that regulated their work, he asserts. In Rome, where he lived for three years, from 1555 to 1558, he fell into disfavor with some influential members of the profession. In Venice, where he worked for roughly fifteen years, from 1558 to 1573, and where he seems to have made a home for himself for a long period, he was influenced by the polygraphs and took on the role of a practitioner author, incurring the wrath of the medical establishment from time to time. In Milan, he was briefly thrown into prison in 1573 for allegedly killing patients with his unorthodox cures. And in Madrid, some time between 1576 and 1577, he was put on trial for, among other things, medicating without a license.[46]

Fioravanti's emphasis on his own experience and professional commitment in his analysis of urine is typical of this maverick surgeon who both did and did not fit into the medical community, and it demonstrates his willingness to go to extremes in order to achieve recognition and acquire practical expertise as a unique radical empiric. Consider, for instance, yet another moment when Fioravanti reveals himself to be worthy of note as he constructs his professional persona as a maverick physician in print. This moment occurs precisely when the nose, the organ implicitly evoked when Fioravanti systematically studies the various smells of urine, comes prominently into play in his *Tesoro*, his book of medical secrets full of colorful information about his own life.[47] On one occasion in it, he tells how in 1549 he traveled to Calabria to observe the famed Vianeo brothers perform the art of rhinoplasty, a form of specialized knowledge that had been long lost until its revival in southern Italy in the mid-fourteenth century. Given his vehement anti-academic bias, there are obvious reasons why Fioravanti would have traveled to a remote fishing village perched above the northern coast of Calabria in order to witness the somewhat novel art of rhinoplasty. As he tells it in his *Tesoro*, after making a name for himself in Sicily and getting a propitious start there in the medical profession, he gradually moved north, curing people of various ailments as he traveled about. All the while, he aroused wonder as he accomplished these feats and furthered his career through all kinds of seemingly miraculous means. Learning how to fashion the nose on the face of a patient lacking one would have therefore represented just one more of the many wondrous "secrets" that Fioravanti would have wanted to have learned directly, rather than bookishly and indirectly, during his life and extensive travels. Additionally, learning how to fashion the nose on the face of a patient lacking one would have represented yet another significant way in which Fioravanti sought to undermine institutionalized medicine since he, and not the university-trained physicians he constantly challenged for their slavish attachment to books, could now vaunt a cure that had escaped their ken, thanks to his willingness to travel the world and acquire through direct experience a valuable form of determinate, rational, rule-bound, communicable, and reliable knowledge—in essence an "art" understood in the classical sense of the term as a techne.

Moreover, as he tells the story of how he came to acquire this particular surgical knowledge, it becomes clear that what is being fashioned in Fioravanti's *Tesoro* is not just the nose of a patient in the Vianeos' operating room but also Fioravanti's own spectacular life as a resourceful and somewhat peculiar, iconoclastic doctor. The complex nature of Fioravanti's gaze as he furtively studies the novel surgical procedure is indeed particularly telling in this regard. To begin with, at the most basic level, Fioravanti's gaze is highly technical in nature. He looks carefully at the surgical procedure, studying it closely in order to gather requisite information, which he relates in some detail. On the basis of that information, we can ascertain with some reliability that Fioravanti was present at the operation, that he actually saw what he maintained he witnessed firsthand, and that he did indeed learn the complicated surgical procedure of rhinoplasty. At the same time, Fioravanti's gaze is an appreciative one as he describes this dramatically staged event and operation as a "great experience [*grande esperienza*]" (47v). He bears witness to a job being well done, and he comments on this fact as he records with delight how the nose gets tweaked and set with consummate care, as well as how the practitioners of this particular art used a variety of specialized surgical tools to bring the operation to completion (figs. 21 and 22). His gaze, to be sure, is also a sneaky one. Masquerading as someone else, Fioravanti cunningly pretends not to watch the operation so that he can in fact observe with pleasure what he would have otherwise been forbidden to see:

> Finding myself then easily by horse in Turpia and with a servant, I went to the house of these two doctors [*medici*], telling them that I was a Bolognese gentleman and that I had come there to talk to them, because I had a relative who, fighting his enemies, had lost his nose in the battle of Saravalle in Lombardy, and he wanted to know if he should or should

Icon Prima.

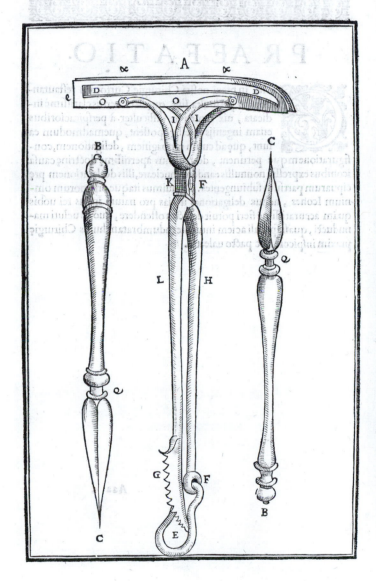

FIGURE 21. Gaspare Tagliacozzi (1545–1599), *De curtorum chirurgia* (Venice: Apud G. Bindonum iuniorem, 1597). fTyp 525 97.820. Reproduced by permission of Houghton Library, Harvard Library. Tools for performing the procedure of rhinoplasty.

FIGURE 22. Gaspare Tagliacozzi (1545–1599), *De curtorum chirurgia* (Venice: Apud G. Bindonum iuniorem, 1597). fTyp 525 97.820. Reproduced by permission of Houghton Library, Harvard Library. Example of the surgical procedure of rhinoplasty.

not come. . . . And every day I would go to their house, those [doctors] who had five noses to fix, and when they wanted to do those operations, they called me to see them, and pretending not to see such a thing, I turned my face aside, but the eyes saw it perfectly [*io fingendo di non poter veder tal cosa, mi voltava con la faccia a dietro, ma gli occhi vedean benissimo*]. And so I saw the entire secret, from top to bottom [*E così viddi tutto il secreto, da capo a piedi*].[48]

Furthermore, there is something of a receptive artist's gaze at work here in Fioravanti's story. Getting a nose job done in Fioravanti's time was not, to be sure, a matter of aesthetic concern: if people did not happen to like their noses in sixteenth-century Italy, they still had to live with them, so there were, to be glib about it, obvious limitations to "Renaissance self-fashioning" when it came strictly to how one could artistically shape one's own body in a manner that we simply do not have to contend with today, thanks to advanced forms of plastic surgery. But performing the art of rhinoplasty could nevertheless become a matter of some aesthetic appreciation for a man like Fioravanti, whose admiration as a surgeon lay not only in the result achieved but also in the elegance of the method involved—a method that is here found to be, in a word, "bellissima" (most beautiful, 47v).

Finally, writing about the nose job also has aesthetic interest for the reader of the *Tesoro* as Fioravanti transforms this particular part of his autobiographical medical treatise into a sort of colorful extended novella that defines him as such an innovative and unconventional physician. Fioravanti, who tellingly began his renewed medical career in the *Tesoro* by being mistaken for a physician during carnival, presents himself here as a sort of astute medical sleuth and sly master of disguise—a veritable trickster making up fantastic stories to advance his career and espy new secrets. And we are meant to applaud Fioravanti's performance as an impostor as he simulates and dissimulates in order to gather the coveted information that the Vianeo brothers have for so long successfully kept hidden from others. If Fioravanti deftly disguises himself among the Vianeo brothers, who perform the operation, and thus seeks to be, in a sense, invisible to them as a fellow practitioner seeking to abscond with their art as a valuable form of specialized knowledge, he stands out for us all the more as a clever, resourceful doctor within his narrative. And Fioravanti's cleverness and resourcefulness are then rendered even more evident later in the *Tesoro* when he tells us how, not long after watching the brothers perform the operation, he had the opportunity in 1550 to put into practice some crucial aspects of the novel art of rhinoplasty when he was working as a surgeon in North Africa for the Spanish navy. In that instance Fioravanti adds a particular, and indeed peculiar, medical touch all his own as he describes how he came to the aid of a wounded officer who had lost his nose in a swordfight. While holding in his hand a lopped-off nose encrusted with sand, Fioravanti, thanks to his own quick-wittedness, expediently and spontaneously sanitizes it by using his own naturally cleansing, ammonia-based urine:

> During this time I was in Africa a very great event occurred, one fine to tell. It was this, that is, a Spanish gentleman named Messer Andrés Gutiero, twenty-nine years of age, was strolling through the camp one day and had words with a soldier. They drew weapons and with a back-hand stroke the soldier cut off Messer Andrés's nose, which fell in the sand, and I saw it because we were together. The quarrel ended and the poor gentleman remained without a nose. And I, who had it in my hand full of sand, urinated on it, and having washed it with urine, I attached it to him and sewed it on very well, and I medicated it with balsam and bandaged it. And I had him remain thus for eight days, believing it would have gone to rot. However, when I untied it, I found it was well attached once again, and I returned to medicate it only once more, and he was healthy and free, and all Naples marveled at it [*che tutto Napoli ne restò maravigliato*]. And this was indeed the truth and Messer Andrés can tell of it because he is still alive and healthy. (64r)[49]

In telling this extraordinary tale, Fioravanti not only describes how he reconstructed a nose on a wounded man's face as he plots out the narrative of his life and professional development and seeks to render himself so unique. He also reaffirms our impression of him as a medical marvel, someone who is at once inimitable and exemplary. Once more Fioravanti is the great practical, charismatic fixer of things, using this time not only his ingenuity as a radical empiric but also his warm bodily fluids to cure a man who has lost that most virile member on the face: the nose. For cutting off the nose—the object that sticks out so conspicuously on the face and that disappears so readily, to be sure, on ancient statues—was viewed in Fioravanti's time as a particularly shameful punishment in acts of vengeance.[50] Cutting off a man's nose in sixteenth-century Italy symbolically amounted, we might say prosaically, to cutting off a penis—a penis that was in effect rendered visible to the world by virtue of the conspicuous presence of the nose, which according to some, such as the Neapolitan magus Giovan Battista della Porta, in its turn let everyone know how large or small that penis *really* was in material form.[51] Conversely, putting a nose back on a face was no small achievement in Renaissance Italy. It amounted to reconstituting a virility (as well as potentially a positive character trait, ranging from innate wit to sagacity to political prowess)[52] that had been conspicuously marred.

For Fioravanti, then, putting a nose back on a face meant that this wonder of all wonders, this bizarre, iconoclastic, adventurous medical man, could stick something back on a man's face that was essential to his identity, much as the penis was putatively essential to it. At the same time, in performing this operation well before anyone else in northern Italy had mastered it, Fioravanti could foreground himself in his colorful narrative as an outstanding physician who could judiciously and uniquely heal a severely wounded man—heal him, that is, thanks to a needle and thread, a healthy balm, and, last but not least, his own warm purifying urine. In this way, as in so many others, Fioravanti presented himself as a maverick to the medical community and to the reading public at large. Not only would this unusual medical man go to extraordinary lengths to train his nose to allow him to become an expert in distinguishing odors when analyzing the contents of an "orinale," as he insists in his *De' capricci medicinali*. He could also, as he demonstrates in his autobiographical *Tesoro*, expediently and ingeniously reattach a nose, even under the most pressing circumstances, on a patient's conspicuously dismembered face.

I turn now to a very different sort of Fioravanti represented in print, one whose voice is not that of a sly, charismatic trickster or a romance hero fueled by wanderlust setting out on a peripatetic, questing adventure to grasp the secrets of the world. Instead, it is that of a professional who has a deep, abiding grudge. And the grudge Fioravanti bore, which was buried inside him like a profound itch that he repeatedly felt the need to scratch, was against anatomists in particular. To see how this is so, the remainder of this chapter focuses almost exclusively on Fioravanti's *Specchio*, a popular and influential book that continued to be published into the late seventeenth century and was translated into French during his lifetime.[53] The *Specchio*, which Garzoni pillaged and used as a model in the writing of his monumental *Piazza universale di tutte le professioni del mondo*, and thus served as a seminal thesaurus for matters of professional self-definition, is unusual in Fioravanti's oeuvre. It is unusual because, unlike Fioravanti's other books, the *Specchio* is more openly encyclopedic in nature and, at least on the surface, does not purport to focus explicitly on the arts of healing. Like Garzoni's *Piazza universale*, Fioravanti's *Specchio*—which reads in many instances as an encomium to Fioravanti's then adopted home city of Venice[54]— surveys a broad array of professions in what can be best described as a rhetoric of praise and blame, with some professions occupying positions of superiority over others. Nevertheless, Fioravanti's primary concern in his *Specchio* is with one form of specialized knowledge above all others: the art of healing and its deep, abiding investment in the body. More specifically, in his *Specchio* Fioravanti not only participates in the ongoing rivalry of professions of the period in deploying a rhetoric of praise and blame, particularly with regard to the traditional, competing, communicative professions of law and preaching (the one grounded in the well-established rhetorical *ars arengandi*, the other in the *ars praedicandi*).[55] Fioravanti also stages in his *Specchio* a rivalry for jurisdictional claims over techne-oriented *competence* within the profession of medicine itself. For traditionally in the hierarchical medical culture of which Fioravanti was so vitally a part, it was assumed that physicians occupied the highest position of authority. The *Specchio*, written a few years before Fioravanti officially acquired his degree, attacks this assumption radically. With his *Specchio*, Fioravanti reverses longstanding expectations by privileging the mechanical arts over the intellectual ones as the basis for accounting for the origins and accumulation of professional know-how. Interestingly enough, because surgeons use their hands and are, in a very literal way for Fioravanti, close to nature (they are, in fact, for Fioravanti very much like farmers and thus, by association, are indirectly engaged in the classically valued techne of husbandry on the part of diligent landowners), surgeons—and not the institutionally trained physicians—turn out to possess the greatest understanding of how to treat the ailing human body.[56]

Paradoxically, then, surgeons, the professionals within the art of healing whose focus was supposed to be on the surface ailments of a patient, possess a deep "inside" understanding of disease and cures. Conversely, physicians, the very professionals within the art of healing whose privileged position allowed them to concentrate on and treat the inner workings of the patient, are condemned to having only a superficial knowledge of medicine because their understanding of the human body is ultimately grounded not in experience but books, not in tactile encounters but civil conversations, not in nature but, for Fioravanti, something more akin to literary fantasy.[57] More to the point, we are led to believe through a reading of his *Specchio* that it is above all Fioravanti who can properly anatomize culture because he has traveled far and wide and directly experienced the world. Indeed, because he has built his specialized knowledge on a solid, broad-based, empirical foundation, Fioravanti as a surgeon can uniquely provide us with a full, deep, and unifying understanding of how we all fit into an intricately connected world. Where all these issues best get played out in the *Specchio*, we shall see, is, first, in Fioravanti's vigorous debunking of anatomy in the medical culture of his time and, second, his rhetorical desire to convince his readers that they should trust him—and him alone—when it comes to offering sound advice on how they should perceive the nature of the medical profession; the breadth and limits of human knowledge within that profession; and, finally, what it is that men in the healing arts are really doing when they do the different things that occupy them professionally in their daily working lives.

Although Fioravanti has witnessed many anatomies, including those performed in such major cities as Rome, he has never learned anything from them, he insists, and not because he lacks intelligence, he rather immodestly assures us.[58] One cannot acquire reliable knowledge through anatomies, according to Fioravanti in his *Specchio*, because the individual organs isolated for inspection within a dead body during a dissection no longer function the way in which they did when the body was alive. Those organs are in essence inert. Consequently, studying dead organs for Fioravanti is, as it was for the classical empiricists centuries long before him, like looking at a flute that no longer has sound because it is not animated by living breath.[59] It therefore puzzles Fioravanti, as he casts a critical glance about the medical community of his age, that "among all of us doctors we don't argue over anything except those things which the human mind cannot grasp, which is to say those infirmities within, about which we want to know precisely what makes the patient suffer more inside" (13v–14r). However, for Fioravanti, if you want to know what is going on inside the ailing body, and if you want to cure it, the last thing you should do is anatomize a cadaver and, by doing so, end up desecrating the human body, a body for him crafted in the image and likeness of God yet here mangled in the most outrageous of ways: "we suffer," he observes in his *Specchio*, "in performing such cruelty on the bodies of our own kind" (51v).[60] Rather, if you want to know what is going on inside a patient suffering from an ailment, simply make the person cough up what bothers them inside, force them to "empty the body through vomit" (14v).[61] For this reason Fioravanti concentrates intensely on the stomach and the uses of such fanciful homemade medicines as his "elettuario angelico" (angelic elixir), which effect the "purgation of the body" (14v). With these handy, all-purpose medications, Fioravanti renders the inside apparent. And in the process he expediently brings to light not inert body parts that make up the "fabbrica dell'huomo" (the human frame), as anatomists do to no positive curative effect, he maintains, but astonishing things—some of them quite alive, massive in shape, and wondrous[62]—that must be emitted in a blast of cathartic vomit so that the internal workings of the patient can find their way back to natural harmony again.[63] "Let physicians go ahead and still do what they do," he admonishes, "because in knowing the interior anatomy of human bodies they will know nothing, since when one is sick, it is necessary to know how to purge the body of the illness from the stomach, extracting what indisposes the patient" (51r). To bring an ailing body back into its "pristine state": *that*, in the end, encapsulates the entire project of the doctor, as Fioravanti observes over and over again in his *Specchio*.[64]

What is more, we can open up a body and display every single part of it, Fioravanti avers, but in the end we cannot use what we have disclosed in an anatomy lesson to substantiate any of the claims that physicians have put forward and rely on when they talk about things that are invisible to the eye, such as choleric humor or vital spirits, much less the nature of the rational "soul," which anatomists actively sought to locate in their dissections as natural philosophers.[65] Opening up and dissecting a body only reveals that it contains, to put it colloquially, stuff. Examining that stuff can perhaps even serve to show us how the body is composed of multiple interconnected parts and thereby fashioned integrally as a "machina."[66] As a result, we can put individual parts of the body in their proper place thanks to anatomy, although perhaps our knowledge of what part goes where may be slightly distorted, Fioravanti argues, because the organs that actually function in living, breathing bodies differ in shape and substance from those that lie inert in corpses.[67] But nothing disclosed in a dissection can ever be reasonably used to support accepted medical knowledge taught in universities and circulated as accepted truth. Quite the contrary, what is disclosed in an anatomy lesson, Fioravanti insists in his subsequent *Cirugia*, "is only a manifest sign that they"—namely, the anatomists presiding over the dissection with their books—"have written about what is not there," and they have done this because "they want to medicate something that one cannot find" (51v).[68]

Consequently, the further you go inside the body in an anatomy lesson the further you distance yourself from the truth and enter the realm of pure supposition, if not downright fantasy. "When I saw an anatomy done, I have never seen that they have shown me phlegm, nor choler, nor melancholy," Fioravanti contends in his *Cirugia*, "but they have shown me very well the tongue, lungs, heart, liver, spleen, ventricle, diaphragm, bowels, kidneys, bladder, vesicular fat, nerves, veins, tendons, flesh, skin and bones, but certainly never any of the abovementioned things" (51r).[69] "How, then," Fioravanti asks, mindful that in performing dissections anatomists aimed to disclose the "secrets" of the body,[70] "can we believe in those things that are so hidden that they cannot even be found?" ("Come adunque potiamo noi prestar fede a quelle cose che sono così occulte che non si possono trovare?" 51r). Accordingly, as Fioravanti asserts in the section dedicated to the art of dissection in his *Specchio*, everything taught in connection with the anatomy lesson should be taken as make-believe. To be sure, all that fantasy finds expression in books. And all those books, which are born out of fancy, become the foundational texts for demonstration and explication in a circular logic that only reinforces the status quo by reaffirming the educational value of dissecting the human body in the first place: "they continually dispute and read these fabulous things [*materie favolose*], and none of them has ever been sufficient to let anyone know how a specific part of the interior works with all its particularity, but only by groping about [*ma solamente alla ventura*], and with their imagination and chimeras [*e per imaginationi, e chimere loro*] they go about imagining these things in their minds" (50v).[71]

Rhetorically, one of Fioravanti's underlying purposes in attacking the art of anatomy is to police his own profession and the various arts underpinning it, which can be construed as medicine generally and, at the time of the composition of the *Specchio*, surgery specifically. During the period in which he was writing, anatomical dissection was something of a rage. It had acquired status as an essential part of medical knowledge, with anatomists emerging as notable authorities among physicians, thanks to their distinctive art. The knowledge of the human body on the part of anatomists, Andrea Carlino observes, functioned as "a mark of cultural, and thus also of social and professional, distinction that set those physicians endowed with university educations apart from that mass of healers—from surgeons to charlatans—who operated in the therapeutic marketplace of the ancien régime and were therefore products of an intellectually and epistemologically lower sphere."[72] The medical historian Katharine Park concurs, making substantially the same argument. By the mid-sixteenth century, she writes, "anatomical knowledge based on human dissection was generally accepted as one of the foundations of learned medicine and natural philosophy."[73] To be sure, the story of the rise of anatomical dissections during the sixteenth century in Italy has been told a number of times, especially in the context of Renaissance and Reformation Europe, and it need not be rehearsed here. Nevertheless, four aspects of the development of anatomy in the period are important to review briefly for our present purposes.

First, according to the Hellenist physician Alessandro Benedetti (ca. 1450–1512), writing at the end of the fifteenth century, the anatomy lesson purported to unveil "the inner secrets of nature," with the anatomist in charge presenting himself as the person who harbored the secrets of the microcosm and harnessed an intellectual form of knowledge, not a mechanical one, much less a strictly therapeutic one.[74] Second, the public anatomy lesson took place often during carnival and thereby participated in various aspects of that ritualized period of cultural inversions as a throng of pullulating onlookers jostled for position in a crowded setting to witness the winter spectacle of an opened, rather than classically "closed," body on display.[75] Third, the anatomy lesson provided spectators with engrossing carnal theater, and it brought different cultures together within a setting that was consciously fashioned as a theater, replete with a stage, hierarchically arranged seating arrangements, and an usher or two at the door.[76] Fourth, the entire anatomical procedure took its legitimacy from the canonical text read by the *lector* (lecturer), with the dissected cadaver occupying the status of an illustration. In what has been referred to in modern scholarly medical literature as the "quodlibetum" or "quodlibetarian" model of public anatomical dissection, the surgeon as the designated *sector* (cutter) functioned as an agile, and often illiterate, "mechanical" worker. His specific job was to bring to light in material form the idea embedded in the text and then physically located, item by item, by the attending *ostensor* (demonstrator). The ostensor's task within the quodlibetarian model of dissection entailed identifying the parts singled out for public view, commenting occasionally upon those isolated parts, and translating sometimes from Latin into Italian the material read out loud by the lector so that the sector, an "idiota" often in his inability to understand Latin, would know where to make the proper cuts (fig. 23).[77]

Andreas Vesalius, as numerous medical historians have observed, made a point of dramatically altering this accepted anatomical procedure by performing the dissection himself. He thereby combined at once theory and practice in the same medical figure: the inquisitive anatomist physician whose distinctive use of his own hand became a hallmark of Vesalius's novel method of actively participating in the dissection himself (fig. 24).[78] If prior to Vesalius, as Carlino points out, "in the anatomy lesson conducted according to the quodlibetarian model it is the text that produces the dissection" (with the lector often on a raised platform reading *ex cathedra*, the sector cutting by the cadaver, and the ostensor identifying the individual parts exposed to view), "here it is the dissection that produces the text."[79] Indeed, Vesalius often talks about the body as a material text. And as the Vesalian anatomist became an attentive reader scrutinizing the body perceived as a book of nature, surgeons and barbers suddenly found themselves, at least in theory, marginalized from the anatomy lesson. In Vesalius's scheme of things it would not be too far-fetched to propose that surgeons and barbers—who once played at least an active, although still somewhat ancillary, role in the dissection procedure—were banished from participating in the anatomy theater in any meaningful way. Barber-surgeons therefore appear in the famous woodcut forming the frontispiece to Vesalius's *De humani corporis fabrica* (*On the Fabric of the Human Body*, 1543) crouching by the dissection table, "now polemically relegated to a secondary unimportant role: that of

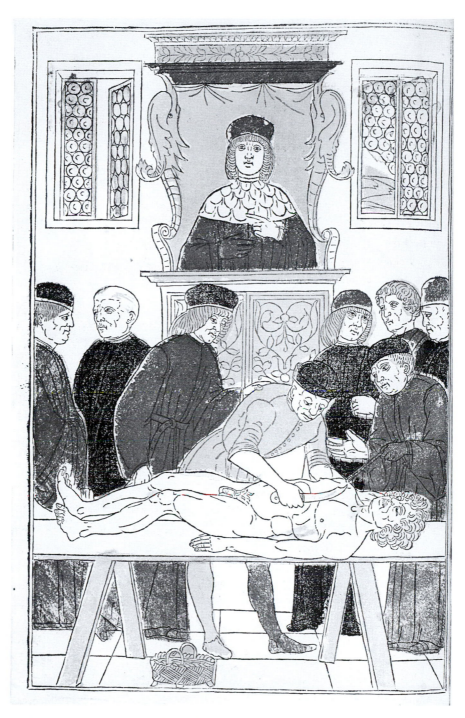

FIGURE 23. Johannes de Ketham (fl. fifteenth century), *Fasciculus medicinae* (Venice: Gregorio de Gregoriis, 1493). Oxford Science Archive, Oxford, Great Britain. Reproduced by permission of HIP/Art Resource, NY. Image of the quodlibetarian model of the anatomical procedure, with the lector, ostensor, and sector.

FIGURE 24. Andreas Vesalius (1514–1564), *De humani corporis fabrica* (Basel: Ex officina Joannis Oporini, 1543). Reproduced by permission of Snark/Art Resource, NY.

sharpening the blades used by the anatomist in his dissection." Perhaps, as
Carlino further suggests, Vesalius's barber-surgeons are even squabbling among
themselves as to who merely earns the pathetic privilege of performing the
menial, routine task of sharpening the anatomist's tools (fig. 25).[80] To be sure,
the established quodlibetarian model for enacting public dissections in anatomy

FIGURE 25. Andreas Vesalius (1514–1564), *De humani corporis fabrica* (Basel: Ex officina Joannis Oporini, 1543). Bibliothèque Nationale de France, Paris. Reproduced by permission of Snark/Art Resource, NY. Frontispiece.

lessons persisted in the period and was never entirely replaced by the one pro-posed by Vesalius.[81] But some physicians clearly desired to make the attending anatomist the sole reigning authority. And those desires had already been voiced at the end of the fifteenth and beginning of the sixteenth centuries in the writ-ings of Benedetti and Jacopo Berengario da Carpi (1460–1530).[82]

With this in mind, it is not difficult to imagine that Fioravanti's hostility toward anatomy arose directly out of competition over medical showmanship. Fioravanti as an inveterate chatterer in print was not a charlatan in the precise sense of the term, as we have seen, but he does make it abundantly clear in all his writings how he adored being the center of attention and how theatrical he could be in his medical performances. Anatomists, to be sure, could draw a large crowd when they conducted public dissections, which is what Fioravanti ostensibly aimed to do through his activities in one form or another. People came to Fioravanti's house in droves, rich and poor, educated and illiterate, we are led to believe from his writings.[83] And every time they came, they remained spellbound by his feats as a unique doctor, so much so that Garzoni would later dub him "that man famous/glorious from strange miracles [*quel glorioso uomo dai miracoli nuovi*]."[84] Fioravanti clearly reveled in the attention and cherished being viewed as a theatrical miracle worker, a sort of celebrity figure whose art as a specialized form of determinate, rational, rule-bound, communicable, and reliable knowledge rendered him one of a kind, inimitable. Hence, much as physicians occasionally resented Fioravanti for his ability to appear as a marvel performing unheard-of cures, so Fioravanti no doubt at times resented those in the medical profession, such as anatomists, who could attract so much attention and held such broad public appeal. Anatomists and Fioravanti were, in a real sense, rivals for early modern forms of spectatorship within the medical community.

Finally, in the terms advanced by the sociologist Andrew Abbott, we are dealing here with a medical practitioner competing for a "jurisdictional claim" within a highly stratified, hierarchical profession.[85] For during this period, the traditional role of a surgeon, as the deft yet mute carver at the anatomy lesson, experienced a direct challenge from the physician in charge. In theory, Vesalius and his close followers had usurped one of the essential, albeit specifically mechanical, roles of the surgeon. Professionally speaking, it is only natural that Fioravanti might have been offended by the dramatic change of function allot-ted the surgeon within the anatomy lesson as it was pictured and imagined by Vesalius and his followers, especially since experience—the kind of firsthand, trustworthy experience the anatomist now claimed for himself by performing the dissection by hand—played such an essential role in Fioravanti's way of thinking about his own particular method for acquiring medical knowledge and his own specific reserve of talents as a radical empiric surgeon traveling about the world.[86] Needless to say, it could have only made matters worse that one of Fioravanti's greatest enemies in Rome, Realdo Colombo (ca. 1516–1559), was both a prized follower of Vesalius and an influential anatomist who had himself pictured on the cover of his anatomical treatise not only performing the dissection by hand but also, perhaps, correcting (rather than slavishly relying on) the canonical, anatomical text held up for him to view (fig. 26).[87] For Fioravanti, anatomists like Colombo, whom he disparagingly referred to as "Dogfish" (Palombo), claimed an authority within the medical profession that did not rightly belong to them.[88] An anatomist like Colombo may appear knowledgeable and occupy one of the more important and prestigious positions in the medical community of Rome as a teacher at the Sapienza enjoying papal privilege, but in truth he produced nothing more than empty, useless spectacle as he engaged in an overall medical art that was, as Fioravanti contemptuously phrased it in his *Specchio*, both "impious and cruel [*empia e crudele*]" (51v).

If in Fioravanti's time, then, anatomy had conventionally come to represent the one prestigious medical art that was undeniably about penetrating the surface of the body to reveal the deep hidden secrets of the human organism, and if through that process of dissection anatomists had gradually acquired distinction in late Renaissance Italy as elevated and privileged authorities within the medical profession itself,[89] for Fioravanti anatomy was instead ultimately about doctors putting on a spectacle for gross, unenlightening entertainment; it was about doctors advancing their own crass professional interests; and it was about doctors impiously transforming a once living human being made in the image of God into an unreliable source for medical knowledge.[90] In effect anatomy substituted the real body of knowledge—the live human patient who can at times isolate his or her own ailments and communicate them to the attending doctor[91]—for a body of textual evidence that in no way conformed to the truth.[92] Worse, in the case of surgeons, performing anatomies transformed these medical practitioners into heartless, bloodthirsty, Sweeny Todd–like men who became all too eager to cut up even patients who were alive. Surgeons who had practiced anatomy became savage as they fiendishly applied their specialized skills in the field. "There are then the surgeons," Fioravanti warns,

> who want to maintain that they were the inventors of anatomy, insisting that in the public forums they continuously cut up dead humans, performing anatomies on them, in order to teach students the composition of human bodies, so that they know how to medicate properly when they practice surgery. . . . [And these surgeons maintain] that whoever as a surgeon is not a good anatomist, that person will not be a good

FIGURE 26. Realdo Colombo (ca. 1516–1559), *De re anatomica* (Venice: Ex typographia N. Beuilacquae, 1559), QM25.C7. Reproduced by permission of Countway Library of Medicine, Harvard Library. Frontispiece.

doctor. But in my opinion I have always seen that surgeons who are good anatomists, when they treat wounds, always want to perform anatomies [on their patients] with their tools, cutting up the poor human flesh, as if it were a pork chop [*co i loro ferri tagliando le povere carni humane, come se fossero brasuole di porco*]. (49v–50r)

Anatomies, it would seem, bring out the worst instincts in people. They transform highly trained surgeons into villainous butchers, whose art, Fioravanti claims, is more like the anatomist's than any other "since both do the same thing, namely skinning, dismembering, cutting up, and taking apart a body into so many pieces [*scorticare, smembrare, tagliare, e disfare un corpo in molti pezzi*]" (52v).[93] To the butcher's advantage, at least his art does not harm others: "In this way, then, we can call the art of the butcher a second anatomy, but one cannot too much liken the butcher to the anatomist, since there is a great difference between the two, in that the butcher never errs in such a way that he harms others. . . . But if because of anatomy some surgeon should make a mistake, it would not harm him but only the person who had him as a doctor, and, of course, all his household, such as his wife, children, brothers, and all his other relatives" (52v–53r). So much for the anatomist. From occupying a position of privileged authority within the highly stratified medical profession of sixteenth-century Italy, he has been demoted by Fioravanti—precisely in a manner that effectively reverses the judgment of barber-surgeons advanced by Vesalius[94]—to being a mere mechanical carver of flesh, a depraved butcher of men and women irreverently cutting up a slab of human meat for all to see.

At what point, we might therefore ask, should someone in the medical community pierce the skin and open up the body? After all, wasn't that in some measure the presumed job of the surgeon: to cut into the body when necessary and disclose some of its parts, all that was discreetly tucked away within the human frame, thereby disclosing its vital secrets? And wasn't that why the surgeon was typically chosen to be the sector at the anatomy lesson, along with the barber-surgeon who was trained in bloodletting? Fioravanti, of course, is keenly aware of the surgeon's role as a doctor trained to cut flesh. However, he has grave misgivings about that particular role conventionally assigned to the surgeon, and not just with respect to the surgeon's function as potentially the attending mute worker at the anatomy lesson who slices open the cadaver. Penetrating the surface of the live, ailing human body raises a number of concerns for Fioravanti. One concern is ethical and thus, by extension, professional in nature. In particular Fioravanti is concerned with the unjustifiable habit among some members of the medical profession of using their patients as guinea pigs so that they can both perfect their craft and try out new operations on unsuspecting, vulnerable patients, as if they were engaged in deplorable acts of vivisection.[95] Hence he warns in the chapter dedicated to their profession in the *Specchio* that surgeons must above all "not innovate in any manner by performing cuts with tools, as most happen to do, for which reason the sick patient often dies from pain; and watch out about wanting to learn this art at the expense of someone else, because more often than not it would be better for one not to be medicated than to let someone [treat you] who wants to gain experience [by cutting a patient open]" (19r).

By the same token, he asserts, "the surgeon must not therefore be cruel in medicating with his cuts and inflict gashes [*squarci*] on the members of the wounded" (19r). It was bad enough, we might surmise, that there are wars, which traditionally provided many surgeons with the occasion and opportunity, he points out early on in his *Specchio*, to learn how to heal wounds and thus acquire through immediate tactile experience a basic knowledge about their art within the profession of medicine. This, to be sure, was standard operating procedure, with a long and venerable history to it as a form of hands-on instructional practice. But a surgeon should never press the matter by additionally wounding people, cutting them open, not only when people are dead, as cadavers stretched out on the slab of the anatomy table, but also, just as important, when they are alive. Hence the fundamental role of the surgeon is *not* to cut, we learn, but, as Fioravanti never wearies of repeating, to help nature.[96] The surgeon, he observes over and over again, "is nothing other than a helper of nature [*adiutorio di natura*]" (18r). This does not mean that the surgeon never has to cut.[97] What it does mean, however, is that the fundamental, guiding model for Fioravanti is a *natural* one when it comes to understanding how we must go about figuring out what is going on inside the infirm body and how we must attend to curing the suffering patients of any particular ailment afflicting them: "I would advise surgeons," he warns, "that they try to be imitators of nature in medicating the wounded and scarred and not become masters in dismembering them living and dead [*e non maestri per ismembrarli vivi, e morti*]" (52r).

It is for this reason that surgery for Fioravanti is best envisioned as a "farming of men [*un'agricoltura d'huomini*]" (18v) and thus finds itself indirectly associated with the highly valued techne of husbandry among virtuous landowners in classical antiquity. Much as a farmer will bandage a plant to allow it to heal itself, so too a surgeon, who likewise exercises a manual trade and is close to nature, should allow the human body to discover its own instinctive, natural path back to health.[98] More broadly, the ecologically minded Fioravanti asserts that this is what doctors should always do. To this effect, doctors should generally look closely at nature. More specifically, they should look attentively at the habits of animals. By doing so doctors will acquire a greater understanding of what it is they are supposed to do and why they should do it. "The first inventors of [medicine]," he asserts, "were the irrational animals, which possessed a knowledge of medicine through the grace of God and as a gift of nature, as we can see well from experience that all animals know how to cure themselves of their illnesses, and not with any other science [meaning a form of knowledge] than their own natural instinct" (12v).[99] Fioravanti's habit of looking closely at nature and deriving principles of medical practice from it is part and parcel of what Eamon has cogently dubbed Fioravanti's "medical primitivism."[100] Not surprisingly, Fioravanti's love for nature as the guiding model for the medical arts also accounts for why he places surgery—a quintessential manual art—above all the other arts underpinning the profession of medicine, including those more typically envisioned as "intellectual" and traditionally placed in a more elevated position: "And so I say that surgery is nothing other than an aid to nature, through which the wounds and the wounded are returned to their pristine state by means of that [art], and it is the most necessary art that exists among all the other medicinal arts [*e è un'arte la più necessaria, che sia intra tutte l'altre arti medicatorie*]" (18v).

For this same reason the art of anatomy should yet again be viewed as an offense, although this time anatomy is not an offense to the profession of the healing arts but to "nature" itself. As Fioravanti points out,

> We see dogs that never bother at all the bodies of dead dogs, and so too wolves, foxes, cats, and all sorts of birds that are in the world, and this is because nature doesn't permit it [*la natura nol comporta*], and we all plead the excuse of learning in order to perform such cruelty, for which we are well punished and castigated [*siamo ben puniti, e castigati*], such that the majority of those that perform this so-called anatomy, die a violent death and almost in despair, as we continually see [*si muoiono di morte violenta e quasi disperati, come ben continuamente si vede*]; and so I would advise everyone not to meddle in this matter of anatomy in order to not take apart human bodies, which God our lord made, because in doing so one sins against the law of nature and offends one's own kind [*i quali ha fatto Iddio nostro Signore, perché si pecca in legge di natura, e si offende il prossimo suo*]. (51v–52r)[101]

Once more Fioravanti has come to set the record straight in his encyclopedic *Specchio*. And in doing so he polices his profession so that it conforms not to misguided social hierarchies, the very hierarchies he aims to subvert, correct, and reconstruct throughout much of the *Specchio*,[102] but to the "natural" order of things that ultimately connects us all in a divinely ordained world.

What are we to make of Fioravanti's process of self-fashioning in light of some of his writings that we have sampled in this chapter? What, in sum, is the nature of this peculiarly enlightened and adventurous man, and how can we characterize his manner of addressing the world? An encyclopedist; a trickster; a romance hero driven by wanderlust setting out on one peripatetic, questing adventure after another; a subversive rogue; a medical sleuth spying on others to garner and then expose professional secrets; a bizarre, iconoclastic figure of curious (and perhaps somewhat questionable) experimental practices; a resourceful surgeon ingeniously applying his craft and employing his urine on the spur of the moment to heal a victim of an ignominious wound; a rebellious challenger of established authorities; an unorthodox upstart and aggressive social climber eager to acquire status and honor; a magician-like physician captivating an audience with his wonder-eliciting cures; a moralizing, bellicose professional with a deep grudge against rivals applying their art within an increasingly important sector of his profession; a popularizing performer competing for spectatorship within the medical marketplace; a lover of nature swept away by the green world of the soft pastoral where the animal kingdom benignly teaches humans how to cure themselves: Fioravanti emerges from his colorful writings as a masterful impresario who can deftly pick his way through a storehouse of cultural and literary strategies, both high *and* low in nature, and readily deploy them when he wishes and how he wishes. He thus emerges above all as a man profoundly in control of what he does and how he would like us to perceive him and the trajectory of his career through his writings. For if we say that established roles radically constrained him, hemming him into a sort of predetermined mode of behavior, as if he were over and over again ineluctably forced to adhere to a cultural script like a character caught within the irresistible tug of a powerful totalizing genre and an all-embracing social structure, then we also have to acknowledge at the same time that Fioravanti deliberately chose those scripts, freely manipulated those genres in all his agency, lucidly adopted those manifold roles, both those that captured him in the elevated position of a credentialed physician robed in scarlet and those that displayed him potentially sipping urine to make sure pranksters would never get the better of him. And he played those various roles willingly and joyously to the hilt, according to his needs and, one suspects, his changing, eclectic moods. Moreover, he did so with remarkable acumen and, it would seem, often enough with apparent dazzling success as he tried to make himself appear one of a kind, a master second to none within his profession, and a man who cannot easily be pinned down.

Venice, the great center of the printing industry in Renaissance Europe, was no doubt the perfect place for Fioravanti as a practitioner versed in the art of medicine and a professional surgeon/physician to take on the role of authorship, which would also turn out to be the one role that ensured that his name would endure in time, although he never acquired the lasting fame that he probably thought he deserved and yearned to obtain. Venice, after all, was the city where Aretino (yet another remarkable iconoclast) had earlier settled down and where the polygraphs, who followed in Aretino's trailblazing path, had sought to eke out a living through the print industry, cobbling together earnings as editors, hack writers, copyeditors, proofreaders, translators, and plagiarizers. But in one important way Fioravanti, in a manner that renders him all the more outstanding, was very different from the polygraphs with whom he otherwise shared so many affinities, in terms of his bold, aggressive comportment and his freewheeling, garrulous, digressive, and unpolished narrative style. Fioravanti, like the polygraphs, could be endlessly gassy, yammering away in the vernacular as a disembodied presence in print as he seems to have dashed off his writings with lightning speed. But unlike the polygraphs, Fioravanti was not, nor did he ever claim to want to be, a professional writer, a journalistic-like master of the pen. Quite the contrary, Fioravanti was a professional surgeon/physician, he makes plain over and over again, who made his living from curing people of all sorts of strange ailments and who, in the process, fashioned himself as an inimitable yet still exemplary healer who enjoyed upsetting established hierarchies, institutions, and conventions. Hence his writings, for all that they allow Fioravanti the iconoclast to take on the role of the author, never for a moment present him abandoning his identity as Fioravanti the stalwart, dedicated, pugnacious medical practitioner bent on teaching everyone concerned the one true way to heal people of their sometimes dire and baffling ills as he urges them to walk along "the straight path" (*la retta strada*), guiding them to leave behind the "darkness" (*tenebre*) for the "light" (*luce*).[103] To be sure, Fioravanti's writings, even his encyclopedic *Specchio*, which seeks to cover every topic under the sun and even presents him coming up with all sorts of cockamamy inventions such as a ship that will never sink (313v–315v), all the more reinforce our impression of him as a man bound to the profession of medicine that defined him and, at the same time, allowed him to stand out and assert himself for the public at large as a maverick with a distinctly individual, personalized voice.

∾

Visualizing Cleanliness, Visualizing Washerwomen in Venice and Renaissance Italy: Reflections on the Peculiar Case of Jacopo Tintoretto's *Jews in the Desert*

"The history of cleanliness," the historian Peter Burke observed in an article devoted to the topic of cultural history as polyphonic history, constitutes "a meeting-point between studies of the body as a physical object and studies of the wider culture, between purity in the literal and in the metaphorical senses."[1] Anyone who has thought seriously about the history of cleanliness can certainly attest to the polyphonic nature of it. Historiographically, the history of cleanliness yields no linear master narrative, although some have tried to fashion one.[2] More to the point, the history of cleanliness must engage multiple sources, from low to high culture, from verbal to visual material. And it requires drawing on a host of fields, from religion to architecture, anthropology to economics, medicine to urban planning, environmentalism to natural philosophy, literary studies to visual studies. Put differently, the pleasure of thinking about the history of cleanliness—not to sound too coy about it—is that it makes for such a delightfully "messy" subject of study. It is conceptually so much about purity yet methodologically so impure. It forces scholars to weave back and forth between, say, abstract symbolic structures (see, for instance, Mary Douglas's classic *Purity and Danger*) and gritty material culture (see, for instance, Bas van Bavel and Oscar Gelderblom's splendid essay "The Economic Origins of Cleanliness in the Dutch Golden Age," which grounds the obsession with cleanliness in seventeenth-century Holland in, of all places, the quotidian material practice of making first-rate, marketable butter).[3] It is hardly accidental, then, that Burke, a scholar so invested in thinking about where various disciplines intersect, identified the history of cleanliness as a privileged "meeting-point" in current academic studies to exemplify how cultural history can indeed become polyphonic history.

This chapter reflects on one aspect of that polyphonic history described by
Burke in light of the topic of cleanliness and the overriding concerns of this
book, in particular the value of thinking about the individual in the period
within, to be sure, broader cultural, artistic, and intellectual contexts. It does so
by looking closely at Venice, the great commercial maritime city that we examined briefly at the end of the previous chapter and that curiously found itself
presented as particularly clean in the long sixteenth century. At the same time,
this chapter investigates at length a stunningly complex, large religious canvas
with two washerwomen conspicuously centered in it by an unconventional
painter, Jacopo Tintoretto (fig. 27), a man who barely budged from Venice
throughout his entire life, who is so often associated with the artisan culture of
the city, and who, like Fioravanti, is affiliated with the polygraphs and their
somewhat maverick habits of appearing and appealing to the world through
their bold, aggressive, and energetic styles of expression.[4] In the context of
thinking about individuals and identities in Renaissance Italy, one of my specific
aims in focusing on Venice and Tintoretto is to address a matter that has not
been adequately explored by scholars who have thought seriously over the past
few decades about the history of cleanliness. Simply put, the matter is this: How
has cleanliness been visualized in the past and how has it been gendered visually? Or to frame the question in Burke's terms, in which "cultural history"
dovetails with "polyphonic history," how does the visualizing of cleanliness
in the past become a "meeting-point" for a host of different competing and
complementary interests?

These sorts of questions are important. For scholars who have focused on
the history of cleanliness, at least with regard to Europe and America, have
tended to use images as transparent documents, *not* as complex works of art
with their own historically determined formal and aesthetic concerns.[5] We see
a picture of bathers, for instance, and we instinctively assume that that is, well,
how people bathed, and then we blithely leave it at that, as if there were somehow a neat, one-to-one correspondence between the image as putative
"evidence" and a presumed "event." Yet as Burke has made clear in his
Eyewitnessing: The Uses of Images as Historical Evidence,[6] and as art historians
have for so long advocated and cautioned, we must be careful in deploying
images within cultural history, in simply relegating images to the status of illus-
trations that serve to support texts and textual readings—in treating images
monolithically as evidence in an arsenal of facts rather than as carefully con-
trived objects of invention that offer up a multiplicity of voices in an overall
complex, polyphonic history. To this end, we must be aware of the local cultures
and communities that gave rise to those images, the sophisticated visual vocabu-
laries in play, the compositional and formal choices available, the modes of

FIGURE 27. Tintoretto (Jacopo Robusti, 1518–1594), *Self-Portrait*, 1588. Louvre, Paris. Reproduced by permission of Erich Lessing/Art Resource, NY.

artistic production at hand, the rivalries among artists that fed so much of the competitive spirit within the visual arts over time, the artistic traditions in which those images were embedded and the actual places within which they were ensconced, and, yes, the uniquely "individual" personalities of the artists in question who created those images. So it is with regard to the way the topic of cleanliness was deployed by visual artists within the local culture of Renaissance Venice, beginning, as we shall see, with the independent-minded Tintoretto and his unique mode of painting and rendering the world. Indeed, as I aim to underscore in this chapter through a reading of Tintoretto's *Jews in the Desert*, it

FIGURE 28. Tintoretto (Jacopo Robusti, 1518–1594), *Communion of the Apostles*, 1591–1592. San Giorgio Maggiore, Venice. Reproduced by permission of Cameraphoto Arte, Venice/Art Resource, NY.

is entirely apt that the art historian Tom Nichols labeled Tintoretto a "maverick individualist"—a label, it is important to mention from the outset, that would not in any way, shape, or form be viewed in positive terms by the cultural elite privileging selfless conformity in Renaissance Venice.[7] Nor, for that matter, would that particular label be viewed positively in the context of the unifying myth of Venice—a myth that served to explain the long-lasting harmony of the "most serene" (*serenissima*) republic by praising the complete absorption of male individuals within the idealized fabric of the larger social collectivity: within, that is to say, Venice's famed and cohesive sense of unanimity (*unanimitas*).

∾ ∾ ∾

Tintoretto's *Jews in the Desert* (1591–1592) hangs where it was originally installed on the northwest wall of the chancel, facing the *Communion of the Apostles*, in the Benedictine church of San Giorgio Maggiore in Venice (figs. 28, 29, and 30). Like the *Communion of the Apostles*, the *Jews in the Desert* is a late work, certainly one of Tintoretto's last large paintings. For this reason alone it should hold interest for scholars, along with the *Communion of the Apostles*, as marking the end to an important artist's career. The painting, completed in Tintoretto's

FIGURE 29. Tintoretto (Jacopo Robusti, 1518–1594), *Jews in the Desert*, 1591–1592. San Giorgio Maggiore, Venice. Reproduced by permission of Cameraphoto Arte, Venice/ Art Resource, NY.

early seventies, bears witness to his dramatic and expressive use of light, color, and shadow.[8] It also bears witness to his strikingly innovative handling of paint, as well as his ability to create the appearance of representing *prestezza* (speed) with his vigorous, overlapping brushstrokes. Finally, the *Jews in the Desert* bears witness to Tintoretto's characteristic interest in featuring common laborers, *popolani*, often to express the virtue of poverty but also to emphasize the value of hard work. Tintoretto adopted this strategy from time to time in such iconoclastic paintings as the *Last Supper* of San Trovaso, in which the astonished disciples hurl themselves around the canvas like drunk Venetian dock workers hanging out at a boisterous tavern, with one man even raucously reaching back for a large brown jug of wine (fig. 31). At the same time, the hard work exemplified in the labors of the popolani in the *Jews in the Desert* can only remind us of the concentrated hard work that Tintoretto valued in his own professional life and ultimately allowed him, an indefatigable artist who executed so many of his canvases rapidly, to succeed over time as a highly competitive painter engaged, somewhat like those very workers depicted in his canvases, in technically a "mechanical art."[9] However, Tintoretto, it should be stressed, at the same time strove throughout his career to present himself as a man of ideas who exercised an elite "intellectual art," much like his principal Venetian rivals Titian and Veronese, two men whose

Figure 30. Andrea Palladio (1508–1580), San Giorgio Maggiore, Venice. Reproduced by permission of Cameraphoto Arte, Venice/Art Resource, NY. Interior seen from the entrance.

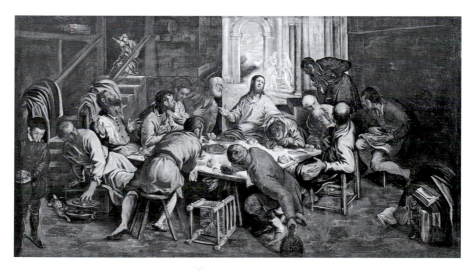

Figure 31. Tintoretto (Jacopo Robusti, 1518–1594), *Last Supper*, 1592–1594. San Trovaso, Venice. Reproduced by permission of Cameraphoto Arte, Venice/Art Resource, NY.

works instead typically eschew representations of and identifications with the base. In this way, like Fioravanti working in Venice in roughly the same period, Tintoretto was something of a cultural mediator who sought to bridge the high and low, connecting the realm of complex ideas with the realm of concentrated physical labor, the elite with the popolani, the sublime with, at times, the ridiculous.

As an idea, however, the *Jews in the Desert* appears to be somewhat confusing at first glance. When compared to the facing *Communion of the Apostles*, it seems all the more confusing. The *Communion of the Apostles* contains for the most part a clear narrative structure and remains centered on the apostles, servants, Christ, Judas, and angels arranged about a brightly lit table that recedes obliquely into a dark, claustrophobic indoor space. Moreover, in the *Communion of the Apostles*, Tintoretto rigorously controls our eye through a unifying yet tricky perspective governed by orthogonals that are accentuated in the coffered ceiling and angled floor pattern and that lead to a well-defined vanishing point.[10] By contrast, the *Jews in the Desert* posits no simple, readily readable core narrative. For a long time, in fact, the painting was erroneously thought to depict "The Miraculous Fall of the Manna" but is now understood to allude, rather vaguely and unsystematically, to a number of possible stories from the Old Testament without regard to unity of time, place, and action. Furthermore, in the *Jews in the Desert* Tintoretto encourages our eye to wander across the surface of a multitiered, variegated space that offers different visual foci, with individuals and groupings dispersed in a somewhat perplexing and disorienting format. One female figure in the foreground, for instance, seems to serve a purely allegorical function (fig. 29). Larger in size than any other figure in the painting, with the exception of Moses and Aaron, and more dramatically lit, she is set off spatially from the others by an incongruously draped bench upon which she decorously sits, and she bears attributes, two similar yet distinctly different leafy branches,[11] but her identity or purpose has never been adequately explained.[12] Likewise, it is not at all clear why the two half-naked men behind her are plucking or clutching branches, in both instances precisely the same type of branch on which the enigmatic allegorical figure rests her left hand as she leans back languorously into the action depicted within the canvas. Nor is it clear why the core of the painting focuses on women or what some of the people are even doing. Is the woman toward the center foreground braiding a companion's hair, delousing her, or waking her up to the presence of the manna on the ground? Is the man toward the right just leading the donkey, or is he a peddler?[13] Since the man poking his face and armored torso into the far right margin of the canvas is not the donor, as one might expect him to be,[14] who—we can only wonder—is he? Why is he there? What does he symbolize?

Although the *Jews in the Desert* is a somewhat confusing painting, and may forever remain confusing in parts, aspects of it can be clarified by examining it in relation to the *Communion of the Apostles*, which faces it directly across the chancel. Certainly the two paintings can be connected to the common theme of the Eucharist. The presence of the manna in the Old Testament scene—a puzzling presence since hardly anyone is gathering or noticing it—prefigures the presence of the bread in the New. Moreover, the two paintings may be connected in that they tell stories about biblical events staged *sub lege* (under the law) and *sub gratia* (under grace) with Moses and Christ figured in their respective canvases as lawgivers, a fairly familiar correspondence in the Italian Renaissance that finds its most famous articulation in the series of frescoed panels along the walls of the Sistine Chapel. On the left side facing the altar, in the *Jews in the Desert*, Moses as a *typus Christi* (type of Christ) rests his left arm on the tablet of the Ten Commandments and presides authoritatively with his cupped right hand over a respectful, harmonious, chosen community in the desert. Typically that community had *not* been obedient but now seems to be receiving Moses' benediction and shows itself to be dutifully absorbed amid its wandering in suitable life-enhancing tasks or activities: making or fixing shoes, working as ironsmiths, catching ducks in the stream, cooking, sewing, spinning wool, attending to a baby's needs, washing, reading, sleeping, and resting. On the right side facing the altar, in the *Communion of the Apostles*, Jesus, wearing the same-colored clothes as Moses and bearing almost identical physical features,[15] stands among his apostles, a few of whom are dutifully imitating his actions as he proffers the bread and lays down the rules of the new dispensation of communion in a full-fledged representation of the "Institution of the Eucharist." Jesus performs this act so that His apostles—with the notable exception of Judas at the far end of the table to the right—can be fully indoctrinated into the priesthood and, of course, continue to be with Him corporeally and thus saved through Him spiritually after His death as members of a respectful, harmonious, chosen community.

We can therefore offer various ways of relating these two paintings that were commissioned by the same patron, the prior of San Giorgio Maggiore, Michele Alabardi.[16] And we can certainly imagine how the members of the Benedictine monastic community, which was part of the reformist Cassinese congregation, would have been sensitive in the Counter-Reformation to the topics of law, obedience, hard work, and the Eucharist staged in them, particularly the implied emphasis on the *real* presence of the body of Christ at the moment in which the sacrament of communion is enacted and the underlying stress is placed on the importance of the priesthood in administering the host. In this regard, it is perhaps not insignificant that the two paintings offer us very different visual and interpretive experiences as they appear on either side of the main altar, precisely where the host itself would have been housed and then held aloft and celebrated during holy mass before a congregation that would have formed, ideally, a respectful, harmonious, chosen, and hardworking community. If formally and conceptually both our eyes and minds are rigorously controlled in the *Communion of the Apostles* and encouraged to wander in the *Jews in the Desert*, it may be because Tintoretto wished to place his viewers in analogous positions to the male and female figures depicted within the respective canvases as he tells stories about, on the one hand, an event experienced during a period *sub gratia*, when the Truth was finally revealed, ethereal light—here intensely pouring out of a lamp—proved so victorious over the dark, and everyone was allowed to see matters clearly, and, on the other hand, an event experienced during a period *sub lege*, when the Truth was glimpsed dimly and everyone (here ironically bathed in a sharp, angular, late-afternoon sunlight) was forced to see matters through a glass darkly.

In Pauline terms, then, it is fitting that the *Jews in the Desert* presents itself to the viewer as an object of intense contemplation with many enigmas incorporated into it. Like the Israelites, we are perhaps collectively and individually meant to err, in this case as we struggle to make full sense of the mysterious painting as a whole and in parts. Or like the enigmatic female figure in the foreground, we are expected to look directly across the chancel toward the *Communion of the Apostles* for clarification, so that we may see the Truth, as she does, face-to-face. Surely the fact that she is well lit with an otherworldly radiance to her; that she crosses her torso in a familiar gesture of piety; that she covers her naked breast almost visible beneath a transparent blouse in the manner of the classical Venus pudica; that her hair is let down like a young Venetian woman about to be wed, thus alluding once more to her purity;[17] and that she looks across the chancel with a heavy-lidded, rapturous gaze toward Christ, as if half dazed she had just witnessed something sublime and was responding theatrically to it: all these factors would seem to suggest that she functions within the overall canvas as a figure of innocence, redemption, or purification of some sort, even if we cannot assign a secure allegorical meaning to her iconographically by virtue of the attributes of leafy branches that she bears. Within the Eucharistic space of the sanctuary, then, which was "experienced by the monks as actors in the liturgical rituals" and constructed according to post-Tridentine design to maximize the visibility of the elevated host, Tintoretto's two large canvases on facing walls—"the right, evangelary side associated with the Old Testament, and the left, epistolary side with the New Testament"—hold a dynamic function for the viewers.[18] How we read the paintings and, more important, how we are *invited* to read them, along with how we bodily move within that sacred space, matter spiritually. Tintoretto in fact makes the dynamic function of the paintings all the more evident by having the dramatically foregrounded table in the *Communion of the Apostles* visibly appear to shift position before the viewer depending on how we physically approach the canvas and interact with it. This is indeed a curious optical trick that was lauded by the earliest chronicler of the church, Fortunato Olmo, as a "marvelous" invention. And it only serves to remind us how Tintoretto rigorously controlled our gaze in this particular canvas through a clever compositional use of perspective but conversely encouraged it to wander in the *Jews in the Desert*.[19]

Apart from being a complex work of art in Tintoretto's oeuvre for a host of reasons, some of which have been outlined already, the *Jews in the Desert* also holds interest, more specifically, for anyone curious about the history of the representation of cleanliness in the period. All things considered, it is one of a handful of paintings in Renaissance Italy that addresses so very prominently the topic of cleanliness. Arguably it is the only major painting by a major artist of the period that treats the topic of cleanliness in such an up-front, bold, and unprecedented way. Tintoretto in fact represents two washerwomen, truly unusual subjects of focus in the art of the period, at the precise center of the canvas (fig. 29).[20] This is not to say that the *Jews in the Desert* simply documents habits of cleanliness of the time, as if it were nothing more than a straightforward illustration of contemporary patterns of behavior in the Benedictine monastic community of San Giorgio Maggiore (unlikely, since the monastery was an all-male community), Venice (unlikely, because there were no such rocky, woodland streams in the city), or the Venetian mainland territories, its so-called *terrafirma* (perhaps, but still a stretch). Rather, it is to say that with this painting Tintoretto engaged the topic of cleanliness—with the word "topic" here understood to mean a rhetorical topos—in a period when material *and* spiritual cleanliness had become a matter of widespread cultural concern, and when artists and writers from time to time incorporated the topic into their visual and verbal works of art, although never so conspicuously or uniquely as Tintoretto did in this instance.[21]

To get a better grasp of how this is so and to appreciate the full significance of how Tintoretto uniquely engaged the topic of cleanliness within the local culture of Venice of which he was a part, we first need to examine earlier representations of cleanliness in the verbal and visual tradition of Venetian Renaissance culture. By doing so, we will be in a better position to see how Tintoretto took a topos that helped define the myth of Venice both materially and spiritually and transformed it into a way of subtly defining himself as an individual within his art. More precisely, the maverick Tintoretto, I will argue in the central portion of this chapter, used the occasion of including washerwomen in his

Jews in the Desert to situate himself within the Venetian culture to which he felt so bound; to highlight the subject matter of religious purity as part of the appropriate ritual context that bound a spiritual community together; and to set himself apart as an individual artist—to stand out and make a case for his own uniqueness with his distinctive, signature style. In closing, we shall examine briefly in an epilogue yet another rare instance in the Italian Renaissance when a washerwoman appears so distinctly and prominently in religious art: the *Mourning of the Dead Christ* (ca. 1521), produced roughly seventy years before Tintoretto's *Jews in the Desert* by the Ferrarese artist Giovanni Battista Benvenuti, otherwise known as Ortolano (fl. ca. 1500–after 1527).[22] A comparison between the two painters and their treatments of both washerwomen and the topos of cleanliness is admittedly not entirely fair since the two address different subject matters and emerge out of distinctly different traditions and styles of making visual art in the Italian Renaissance. But the comparison, despite these caveats, is still an instructive one. In the end it will allow us to better gauge Tintoretto's remarkable painterly innovations within the context of the representation of cleanliness in not just Venice but also, more broadly, Renaissance Italy.

In his novel panegyric on the city of Florence, *Laudatio florentinae urbis* (*Encomium of the City of Florence*, ca. 1403–1404), the young Leonardo Bruni showcased his talents as an accomplished orator by waxing eloquent on the topic of cleanliness. He did so at excessive length, in a pristine humanist Latin, in a well-crafted Ciceronian prose, and with a great deal of self-aggrandizing fanfare, cognizant that much of what he said was pure exaggeration: "history is one thing," he aptly observed in an epistle, "panegyric another."[23] Bruni even introduced the topic of cleanliness at the very beginning of his *Laudatio*, just to be sure he caught his readers' or listeners' attention, so that everyone could admire his rhetorical mettle and novel power of *inventio* (invention) right from the start. Florence, he astonishingly claimed at the outset, was not just the cleanest city in the world but also, of all things, the cleanest that had ever existed, including ancient Athens or Rome.[24] And yet, despite Bruni's rhetorical exuberance, it was Venice that was more consistently presented in the visual and verbal arts as the cleanest of all possible cities in the Italian Renaissance. Perhaps, as Robert C. Davis and Garry R. Marvin have maintained in their often witty and ingenious *Venice, the Tourist Maze: A Cultural Critique of the World's Most Touristed City*, Venetians also had good reason for thinking so. All things considered,

Venice was probably, if not "objectively," as Davis and Marvin contend, "one of Europe's cleanest cities" during the Italian Renaissance,[25] even as it was one of its more populous, reaching roughly 106,000 inhabitants (well over the size of Bruni's Florence) at the beginning of the sixteenth century. Keeping a city of that size clean without modern hygienic technology was, to be prosaic about it, not exactly the Herculean feat of ridding the Augean stables of filth in a single day, but it was certainly far more easily said than done. As is so often the case in talking about Renaissance Venice, what was myth and what was actual historical fact are never easy to tell. In the end the two, as numerous historians have demonstrated, are interconnected, if not at times virtually indistinguishable.[26]

Consider, for instance, the Venetian patrician Giovanni Maria Memmo's *Dialogo, nel quale dopo alcune filosofiche dispute, si forma un perfetto Prencipe, e una perfetta Republica, e parimente un Senatore, un Cittadino, un Soldato, e un Mercatante* (*Dialogue in Which After Some Philosophical Disputes, a Perfect Prince, a Perfect Republic, and in the Same Way a Senator, Citizen, Soldier, and Merchant Are Formed*, 1563). In this late Renaissance treatise, which stages a refined dialogue at a Venetian ambassador's palace in Rome, Memmo praises through one of the interlocutors the "*rii* and canals" of Venice because they make for magnificent waterways and protective boundaries but also, he claims through the same interlocutor, because "they purge the city of all its garbage."[27] In making this claim, Memmo repeats something of a commonplace about the city, which had been articulated in various ways by Venice's visitors, long-term residents, and citizens. The Castilian pilgrim Pero Tafur, for instance, arriving in Venice for the first time in 1438, briefly noticed that it stood out as a remarkably clean city: "the sea rises and falls there," he recorded enthusiastically, "and cleans out the filth from the secret places."[28] The patrician poet, humanist, and historian Andrea Navagero reminisced, in a somewhat homesick mood, about Venice along much the same lines while laboring in the early sixteenth century as the resident ambassador to Spain.[29] Surely this was a unique urban feature to a unique city. Venice's large-scale urban sewage system, unlike any other in Italy, was a strikingly "natural" one, having been built directly into the structure of the city from its inception. And that intricate sewage system was always necessarily incorporated into the city's physical makeup as Venetians engaged in a long-term ecological relationship with the marshland and the sea that they claimed as their home. As long as there was water, as long as there were inflowing and outflowing tides, as long as there were "rii and canals," Venice would forever be clean, even as it evolved and carved out more and more territory for itself out of the meandering, silt-rich, and brackish lagoon.

At the same time, Venice, with its labyrinthine purging rii and canals, always needed to work hard to have clean, fresh, potable water, despite the fact that

Venice rested, writer after writer observed as they took note of the city's many paradoxes, in the midst of water, so much so that it seemed to float magically upon it. "In recognizing truly the goodness of water," Memmo observes, echoing Petrarca's *Canzoniere* at one point,

> that water must be of good taste, which is to say it should not taste of anything, and so too it must be of good color in that it should lack altogether color. But let it be limpid, clear, and of little density, so that when spread upon a most clean piece [*una pezza nettissima*] it doesn't mar it [*non la macchi*], and when kept for a while in some vase, it doesn't leave any dregs. . . . And let it happen that beyond this that, above all, the palace should be full of sweet, clear, and fresh water [*dolci, chiare, e fresche acque*].[30]

Venetians consequently dedicated much time and effort to building quality wells, much as they exercised great ingenuity in constructing impressive aboveground and underground systems to gather and purify the runoff water. Those wells contained the precious drinking water used, among other things, to clean the laundry. In a wealthy patrician or citizen household, those wells—some of which featured elegant carvings—would have been located in the courtyard, while the laundries would have been located on the first floor, close to the kitchen where water could be easily heated. The servants, probably no more than one or two in the average wealthy patrician or citizen household, would have lugged the rinsed, damp laundry up to the top floor where it would be aired out to dry in the sun.[31] What was true for a wealthy patrician and citizen household, moreover, was ideally true for all households: "Every house," the polygraph Francesco Sansovino remarked in his *Venetia città singolare e nobilissima* (*Venice a Unique and Most Noble City*, 1581), "has a terrace on the roof made of brick or wood: these are called *altane* and are used for hanging out wash in the sun."[32] Venice, a city with a flourishing soap industry,[33] was purportedly proud to display *all* its linen in public. According to Sansovino it was also a city where the wealthy made sure that the multicolored stone floors in their houses, theoretically equipped with effective plumbing for sanitation and proper hygiene, were vigorously polished until they positively gleamed:

> They maintain [the floors in their houses] by rubbing them often either with a soft rag or sponge. And whoever desires that they remain shiny for a long time should drape them with coverings so that they do not get dirtied by people walking on them, in such a way that upon entering one of the rooms taken care of in this manner, you would say that you were

entering into a well-managed and clean/polished church of nuns [*ben culta & pulita Chiesa di suore*].[34]

Now, the quotidian act of witnessing women washing and hanging laundry out to dry; of seeing private and communal wells mounted in various paved and unpaved campi and courtyards; of recognizing that those handsomely decorated wells were constructed according to well-designed plans for purifying water; of visiting households where multicolored pavements gleamed like a nunnery thanks to the special waxes applied to them; in reading in architectural treatises about how those distinctly Venetian houses should be appropriately fitted with bathrooms;[35] and of knowing (or, better yet, *believing*) that urban refuse was expediently cleansed from the city through its maze-like network of interlocking rii and canals: all these aspects of Venice contributed to what it meant to be Venetian for those who lived there or visited the city. In this respect, the Venetian attention to cleanliness directly fed the Venetian sense of its own special "politia," a period term, the art historian Patricia Fortini Brown has shown, that signified "both refinement (as in aesthetic excellence) and civility (as in politic behavior)."[36] More broadly, the Venetian attention to cleanliness helped construct and affirm once more a specific, collective, civic identity within the all-embracing "myth of Venice." It helped Venetians and visitors to the city define who they were as a collectivity in relation to the city itself, each other, and outsiders. Moreover, if Venetians did not dwell on the topic of cleanliness with the outlandish effusiveness of Bruni, although they did sometimes deal with it at length in their writings, perhaps that was because they did not wish to exploit too egregiously a rhetorical topos in a manner that would undermine the sense of both the quotidian and the real that they aimed to convey in their accounts of the city, many of which could describe urban features in fine detail. It consequently went without being said that Venice was a city with a uniquely clean urban environment. Or, rather, it needed to be said only with appropriate decorum, in keeping with the longstanding Venetian adherence to the rhetorical, and by extension ethical, value of *mediocritas* (moderation). This, at least in part, constituted ideologically what it meant to be Venetian: you could claim with some authority, *pace* the classicizing Bruni, that you lived together, as a bounded and integrated community, in the cleanest city in the world, and you had the visible evidence to prove it: canals, wells, purifying aboveground and underground channels for runoff water, washerwomen, laundry, and polished, waxed floors that shimmered in the sun. Here, as Marc'Antonio Sabellico put it in his *Del sito di Venezia città* (*On the Site of the City of Venice*, 1502), even the common people ("volgo") dedicated to sailing ("navigare") maintain a lifestyle that is "rather clean/neat than sumptuous [*piuttosto è netto che sontuoso*]."[37]

FIGURE 32. Gentile Bellini (1429–1507), *Procession on the Piazza San Marco*, 1496. Accademia, Venice. Reproduced by permission of Erich Lessing/Art Resource, NY.

Much as writers of various stripes engaged the topic of cleanliness in Renaissance Venice and made it a matter of interest to a reading public, so too did visual artists for their viewing public. Most notably, some of the visual artists belonging to what Fortini Brown has identified as the "eyewitness school" of Venetian Renaissance art—Gentile Bellini, Giovanni Mansueti, and Vittore Carpaccio in particular—introduced in subtle, almost hidden ways the topos of cleanliness into the elaborate copia of their busy, documentary-style canvases and drawings.[38] In those canvases and drawings, for instance, we see such seemingly insignificant details as empty laundry poles leaning against the edges of buildings or over railings—poles that inevitably hint at the fact that laundry could be hung on them, thereby defining a presence through absence (figs. 32 and 33), as in Bellini's *Procession on the Piazza San Marco* (1496). We also see washerwomen working, as Sansovino said they did (or should), on or toward the top of houses (figs. 34 and 35), as in Mansueti's sketch for the *Miracle of the Relic of the Holy Cross in Campo San Lio* (ca. 1494) and Carpaccio's *Miracle of the Relic of the Cross* (1494). And we see laundry hanging from altane or dangling over ledges, busy canals, and dry, windswept campi. That laundry is often positioned in the distance, but it sometimes appears in plain view (figs. 32 and 34).[39] By discreetly including laundry poles, washerwomen, and laundry into their "eyewitness" paintings and drawings, Bellini, Mansueti, and Carpaccio, perhaps drawing inspiration from Mantegna's nearby *Martyrdom of St. Christopher* and the laundry curiously depicted in it (fig. 36),[40] no doubt reminded their viewers generally of an essential aspect of *venezianità*: its deep abiding concern for cleanliness within their unique urban setting—a concern that, like the limpidness of cleanliness

FIGURE 33. Gentile Bellini (1429–1507), *Procession on the Piazza San Marco,* 1496. Accademia, Venice. Reproduced by permission of Erich Lessing/Art Resource, NY. Detail of laundry poles on the rooftops, with a shirt hanging to dry over the ledge of an altana and, just to the right, a pole with laundry hanging from it.

itself, transparently bound a community together in its unanimitas. At the same time, these artists arguably reminded the *confratelli* (lay brothers) in particular who had commissioned the large canvases for their *scuole* (brotherhoods) that cleanliness was not only a Venetian virtue generally but a virtue of the confratelli specifically—a virtue that the confratelli themselves as a tightly bound group ideally put into practice through their charitable activities in the city. Venice, a city of pageantry like perhaps no other of the period, had—I think it is safe to assume—lots of laundry to clean. And the confratelli who commissioned those magnificent paintings could ideally see versions of themselves parading as an organized group ritually through the city with their crisp, gleaming garments— garments that had been cleaned by the very likes of the washerwomen pictured in those canvases and in the manner in which those garments were hung out to dry. In this way, the topos of cleanliness incorporated into some of these canvases called attention not just to a distinctly Venetian secular civic virtue of politia but also to a shared spiritual one of collective confraternal piety and purity.

FIGURE 34. Giovanni Mansueti (ca. 1465–1527, previously attributed to Gentile Bellini), sketch for the *Miracle of the Relic of the Holy Cross in Campo San Lio*, ca. 1494. Gabinetto Disegni e Stampe, Uffizi Gallery, Florence. By concession of the Ministero per i Beni e delle Attività Culturali e del Turismo. We can see on the altane three women, ostensibly the household *fantesche* (female servants) functioning as washerwomen, as they hang up laundered clothes to dry.

Needless to say, the artists of the eyewitness school introduced the topos of cleanliness into their canvases in a subtle, offhand manner. It surfaces in the guise of one item buried amid so many others, much the way the topic was introduced rhetorically in vernacular writings of the period, not ostentatiously but in passing, even if it could be addressed occasionally at some length. By contrast, Tintoretto introduced the topic of cleanliness into a visual format in a far bolder and determined manner and thus in a way, I will argue, that marked his individuality within the context of the collectivity of Venetian culture and its pervasive, sustaining myths. In the *Jews in the Desert* Tintoretto pictures two washerwomen engaged in virtually the same task of vigorously scrubbing soiled clothing (fig. 37). They work intently, thoroughly absorbed in their labor, with their heads turned down and their hair gathered up, one with it pinned into a tight bun, the other's loosely bound by a band. Between them, on the well-delineated steps leading down to the creek of cleansing water, lies a shared bundle of laundry in a wicker basket and a copper-colored pail that presumably contains the lye.[41] The washerwoman positioned to the left of the viewer leans

FIGURE 35. Vittore Carpaccio (ca. 1465–1525/1526), *Miracle of the Relic of the Cross*, 1494. Accademia, Venice. Reproduced by permission of Scala/Art Resource, NY. Detail of laundry hanging from poles over the Grand Canal, with in the distance some *fantesche*—one dusting—on an *altana*.

on a log while she works with a scrubbing board, which is in truth a makeshift wooden bench. Her face, completely averted, appears in partial shadow, with only the highlight of the curved upper lip of one ear clearly articulated. She applies her broad, bare, and fully illuminated shoulders to her task so forcefully that her white blouse seems to slip down, while the swooping, electrifying, and jagged folds of her pink dress convey a feverish energy to her work, particularly as they are drawn by Tintoretto in a painterly manner with his uniquely quick, loose, dry brush. The other washerwoman to the right, dressed in blue, also wears a white blouse. Kneeling down but more completely illuminated, she makes use of a nearby rock for cleaning. She has a gleaming forehead visible to

FIGURE 36. Andrea Mantegna (1431–1506), *Martyrdom of Saint Christopher*, 1448.
Chiesa degli Eremitani, Padua. Reproduced by permission of Scala/Art Resource, NY.
Detail of ancient column with laundry visible above it.

view, and she is stretched out as she devotes herself to her task, one bare foot
tucked behind her.

What is so striking about Tintoretto's washerwomen within the composition
of the *Jews in the Desert*, apart from the fact that they make a rare appearance
in a religious artwork of the period and appear nowhere else in Tintoretto's
extant oeuvre, is that they occupy such a visually prominent position in the
canvas. This is especially the case when we compare them to the minuscule
washerwomen who appear so remotely, for instance, in Mansueti's busy sketch,
the *Miracle of the Relic of the Holy Cross in Campo San Lio* (fig. 34). Draw two
diagonals from the four corners of Tintoretto's canvas: the intersecting lines
converge precisely on the basket of white gleaming laundry, which structurally
separates *and* formally unites the two washerwomen at the exact center. What

FIGURE 37. Tintoretto (Jacopo Robusti, 1518–1594), *Jews in the Desert*, 1592–1594. San Giorgio Maggiore, Venice. Reproduced by permission of Cameraphoto Arte, Venice/ Art Resource, NY. Detail of the two washerwomen.

is more, Moses' gently turned head with horns of light beaming out of it, along with the abruptly turned body of the man twisting about to Moses' right in a staged mannerist figura serpentinata pose, visually articulates for the viewer a diagonal movement extending upward from the bottom right corner of the canvas. That same dynamic diagonal, as it conditions our gaze and nudges it toward the center full of light, cuts directly through Aaron's right arm, which echoes the gesture of his arched left arm and carries forward the movement, spiritual energy, and authority of Moses' uplifted hand. In this way, as Aaron gestures to his right in response to the illuminated Moses, perhaps in an effort to call attention to the obedient community behind him and to demonstrate his own obedience himself, Aaron not only points in a vague sort of way toward the various activities taking place in the brightest portion of the canvas, activities that may have served to remind members of the Benedictine community themselves of some of the practical-minded or pleasurable activities that must have absorbed some of their time, from washing to reading. More specifically, as Aaron gestures backward at the beckoning of Moses, he points to, and indeed visually pinpoints with his extended index finger, a highly gendered female space with the two washerwomen and their shared basket of laundry at the exact structural center of the canvas (fig. 29). Surely one can find no more impressive, or for that matter unique, visual statement about the importance of washerwomen, and thus by extension the cultural centrality of the virtue of cleanliness, in the Venetian pictorial tradition of the Renaissance. If these wash-erwomen do not constitute the overriding visual key to this painting, they cer-tainly hold a key position in it.

But what, then, are these washerwomen exactly symbols of? At one level they are figures of energy, concentrated effort, and muscular force, while at another they are figures of purity in a painting that alludes through its calculated juxtapo-sition with the *Communion of the Apostles*, as well as in its privileged placement in the chancel, to the implied presence of the Eucharist and thus, by extension, to the purifying body of Christ. As the washerwomen in all their humility lower themselves to the ground as virtuous popolane to cleanse the clothes of quotidian impurities during a period when God tested his chosen people and forced them to act with all due deference toward Moses, so Christ, humbling Himself by sacri-ficing Himself for our sins, washes away the sin of Adam in his obedient flock through His real bodily presence in the raised and celebrated host and through His purifying, descending grace at the very moment in which the sacrament of communion takes place—a moment that indeed had to be prepared for liturgi-cally with the utmost purity.[42] The visual power and energy of these washerwomen at the precise structural center of the canvas thus symbolize renewal, the sort of uplifting, spiritual renewal that is not at all dependent upon the good deeds of hard work, as Protestants might have claimed, yet is certainly revealed through that work in a manner consistent with Counter-Reformation doctrine. However, at another level, as Tintoretto places these washerwomen in the center of the canvas, and as he thus strategically places himself as a man in the center of a typically Venetian tradition of representing cleanliness in visual and verbal form through the figure of laboring women, he also hints at his own special creativity as a unique Venetian painter who acquired recognition in part for working with such energy and speed; who so often represented common laborers to express through them the value of simple, hard work in a manner that from time to time egregiously defied conventions of decorum; and who aspired to be viewed as an intellectual artist of great inventiveness and originality even as he took obvious pride in designating himself as someone who came from humble origins and, by extension, identified indirectly with the common male and female laborers he so often depicted in his canvases.

Strikingly, the independent-minded painter whose nickname derived from his father being a dyer of cloth—"Tintore"/Tintoretto derives from the verb *tingere*—here represents and tinges cloth itself in the one art form, painting, that Leonardo da Vinci had famously defined in a paragone as particularly "clean" precisely because it should be deemed an intellectual art.[43] And as Tin-toretto does so, the highly individualized, muscular, and energetic women who would clean the fabric of the "colors" of undesirable filth in the very moment that they exercise a messy mechanical art are inversely colored themselves, visibly marked by Tintoretto's highly individualized, muscular, and energetic brush. In this way, these washerwomen within the *Jews in the Desert* can be viewed as not just the product of the local visual culture of which Tintoretto was always a part, a visual culture with a longstanding civic commitment to material *and* spiritual politia, but also the product of a highly distinctive visual style (*maniera*) and unique creative vision. What was marginal in earlier documentary-styled paintings of the "eyewitness school" thus becomes structurally and symbolically central in Tintoretto's late and highly self-reflexive religious painting as a way of allowing him to obliquely sign, as it were, his art. He appears once more through these washerwomen as a "clean," elite, intellectual, individualized male painter grounded all along in the very messy matter of the sort of mechanical labor he here depicts with thick, vigorous strokes of paint.[44] It is not, then, just Venice that is unique for being so clean as a community. It is also the maverick, individual Tintoretto who is here so unique for incorporating these unusual figures of washerwomen and the topos of cleanliness they inevitably represent into the exact structural center of his art in such a conspicuous, spiritually fitting, and artistically self-reflexive manner.

I close with a painting that Tintoretto would certainly not have known, and that is the only other one I can find from the Italian Renaissance that places washerwomen smack at the center of a visual experience: Ortolano's *Mourning of the Dead Christ* (fig. 38), now housed in the Capodimonte museum in Naples but originally and fittingly commissioned for the church of San Cristoforo alla Certosa in Ferrara—"fittingly," I say, because the painting conspicuously contains the image of St. Christopher within it in light of the fact that he is indeed the church's titular saint.[45] To be sure, pressing a formal comparison with Tintoretto's *Jews of the Desert* would only serve to highlight a number of all too obvious differences, the sorts of differences that one would naturally expect to find in placing side by side two works by such distinctly different exponents of painterly traditions of the Italian Renaissance: the one at the end of the sixteenth century in Venice with his loose, expressive brushwork, blurred outlines, dark, prepared backgrounds, and sensuous, chromatic coloring on a roughly textured canvas; the other toward the beginning of the sixteenth century in Ferrara with his crisp contours, meticulous, transparent finish, and vibrant coloring on a smooth, prepared surface. Nevertheless, Ortolano's treatment of washerwomen and the topos of cleanliness that they inevitably represent, while by no means as self-reflexive or highly individualized

FIGURE 38. Ortolano L' (G. B. Benvenuti, 1485–1527), *Mourning of the Dead Christ*, ca. 1521. Museo Nazionale di Capodimonte, Naples. Reproduced by courtesy of the Ministero Beni e Attività Culturali/Scala/Art Resource, NY.

as Tintoretto's, is still a compelling one. It is therefore worthy of consideration at the end of a reflection devoted to the problem of visualizing cleanliness and washerwomen in the broader context of thinking about the importance of the individual amid collectivities in Renaissance Italy.

In his *Mourning of the Dead Christ*, Ortolano positions a washerwoman standing in the well-defined, clear blue, windswept stream with chevrons of diminutive waves flowing down it. Unlike Tintoretto's washerwomen, Ortolano's washerwoman appears more relaxed and certainly better dressed as she performs the grunt work of plunging what appears to be linen into the water, scrubbing it over a perfectly flat surface and then gathering it neatly into a basket by her side. Unlike Tintoretto's washerwomen, Ortolano's washerwoman is also not singled out. Nicodemus, the blue-robed, standing figure in the foreground with the nails in his hand, looks back toward the washerwoman, thus guiding us into the general background area, but no one points directly at her. In fact, the other standing figure in the foreground, Joseph of Arimathea, who is holding the hammer and is robed in brown, looks at the implied beholder(s) of Ortolano's painting and, at the same time, points toward Golgotha, the crucial spot where we are no doubt supposed to dedicate some of our attention. There the crucifixion recently took place and the two dead or dying thieves hang upon their crosses, one cleansed of his sins through Christ, the other forever condemned to hell. That is the choice that we must all make, we are reminded, as our gaze is directed up to the lonely hill. There on the desolate and barren hilltop, at the edge of the cliff, is staged the fundamental, lasting choice between grace and sin, salvation and damnation, depending on whether we accept or reject Christ in our lives as our personal savior and act accordingly, cognizant of how high the stakes really are in *this* vulnerable, sublunary world.

Furthermore, unlike Tintoretto's washerwomen, Ortolano's washerwoman is decidedly small in proportion to the other major figures, although clearly larger than those in the background. And this is significant in helping us understand the washerwoman's symbolic function as a liminal figure placed so centrally in the middle of the composition and, to be sure, in the middle ground. For as she cleans linen, Ortolano's washerwoman belongs to the background world of the painting with all its tiny figures engaged in what appear to be fashionable, courtly activities: some are jousting, some are standing about conversing on a manicured lawn, some are walking about a partly crenellated castle with long, thin banners dangling from a balcony. In this respect, Ortolano's washerwoman is a figure of worldly politia, the sort of elegant refinement we might readily associate with what it meant to be, in Castiglione's terms, courteous ("cortese"). And Ortolano's washerwoman

FIGURE 39. Ortolano L' (G. B. Benvenuti, 1485–1527), *Mourning of the Dead Christ*, ca. 1521. Museo Nazionale di Capodimonte, Naples. Reproduced by courtesy of the Ministero Beni e Attività Culturali/Scala/Art Resource, NY. Detail of washerwoman.

appears to be, albeit a servant and a mechanical worker, suitably dressed for the part with her gleaming white dress and turban-style hat, as well as with her neatly creased and fluffy outer garment (fig. 39). Unlike Tintoretto's popolane washerwomen, Ortolano's is a person of some good manners ("bon costume"). However, as she cleanses, Ortolano's washerwoman also symbolically participates in the foreground world of the painting with all its prominent figures engaged in pious activities as they gesture in profound lament and mourn the death of Christ.[46] She is certainly positioned in an appropriate manner for the occasion, bent over in a posture of humility as she dutifully cleans. Indeed, she is positioned in a way that may well serve to evoke the spiritually cleansing rite of baptism. And, like the figure of Christ, she in essence purifies. In this regard it is not accidental that the lily, a familiar devotional sign of purity and piety often associated with the annunciation, rises up out of the foreground behind the head of the Virgin Mary and points, thanks to a strategically placed division in the petals of the flower, toward the washerwoman *and* the basket of laundry by her side.

Ortolano's washerwoman, framed so centrally between the arc of one arm and the outstretched hand of another holding a nail, is thus a key transitional figure in the painting. She serves to carry the viewer visually and conceptually across the stream as we are invited to move back and forth, between the foreground and the background and, consequently, between the secular and the religious, the material and the spiritual, the physically "clean" and the theologically "pure." What separates that background from the foreground is of course just the simple, purging, windswept, and white-capped stream within which the washerwoman cleanses her linen and across which St. Christopher confidently strides. That crystalline stream, which almost seems more refreshing than it does cleansing, appears to be narrow in width and easily traversed. But for an attentive beholder who has grasped the allegory of St. Christopher's presence as he dutifully shoulders the burden of the unbearably heavy Christ, that stream is in reality conceptually immense and extremely difficult to traverse. To cross it one needs to be, as St. Christopher proved to be in legend, pure in spirit and pure in heart, *not* fashionably and materially clean, as laudable as that communal civic virtue of cleanliness may appear to be in the courtly environment depicted within the background of the imaginary world of the painting. It is, after all, toward that refined courtly world—Castiglione's world of collective elegant comportment— that the figure to the side of the washerwoman bears her bundle of cleaned laundry. So the stream within which the washerwoman stands and cleanses her lily-white linen ultimately measures the theologically immense distance that separates the world of refined Castiglione-like grazia embodied in the graceful and presumably clean figures in the background and the world of rejuvenating transcendent grace embodied in the mourned and crucified Christ—a Christ who has just been, or is about to be, washed, we can tell from the presence of the holy Grail at the bottom of the canvas, [47] in preparation for being placed in the tomb.

In looking closely at the washerwomen in Ortolano's painting, then, and attending to the way those women are framed both visually and conceptually in light of significant formal and religious concerns, we are forced to choose between one distinct community and another, between a community concerned with worldly pleasures and quotidian refinement and a community concerned with divine suffering and ultimate salvation through death and resurrection. At the same time, as we are forced to choose between one distinct community and another, we are compelled to do so without any particular concern for the sort of artistry that we found so brilliantly and subtly explored in Tintoretto's visualizing of cleanliness in the *Jews of the Desert*. In that case, in Tintoretto's exceptionally complex and enigmatic painting, we witnessed an artistry that was grounded not only in a local community's binding concern for conformity through its collective process of mythmaking and practices of religious devotion but also, at the same time, in a maverick painter's signature assertion of himself as an individual within the cultural constraints that defined him and allowed him to operate and prosper so successfully well into old age.

Facing the Day: Reflections on a Sudden Change in Fashion and the Magisterial Beard

Look at any portrait of elite men in Renaissance Italy before 1500. Take, for instance, a sophisticated humanist: Angelo Poliziano, Pomponio Leto, Ermolao Barbaro, Leon Battista Alberti, Jacopo Sanazzaro, Lorenzo Valla, Bartolomeo Platina, or Giovanni Pontano, for whom wearing a beard, as it turns out, could at times constitute a hideous sight.[1] Or take a ruling-class Florentine patrician, such as Cosimo de' Medici, Lorenzo de' Medici, Piero de' Medici, or any other elite Florentine of the period, much less any other Italian man belonging to the cultural elite before 1500, such as those depicted with sometimes unflattering realism in Andrea Mantegna's *The Family and Court of Ludovico III Gonzaga* in Mantua (fig. 15) or those skillfully designed in Donatello's and Verrocchio's equestrian bronze statues of the celebrated condottieri Colleoni and Gattamelata in Venice and Padua (figs. 1 and 5). Go ahead. Try it. Select, if you want, individual portraits, group portraits, portraits that idealize male sitters, portraits that show every grubby little feature, such as the often anthologized one by Domenico Ghirlandaio, which reveals the unsightly protuberances—the putative cause of the malady of rhinophyma—on an elderly man's oversized, bulbous nose as he gazes fondly at his adoring grandson (fig. 40).

Then look at any portrait of elite men in Renaissance Italy shortly after 1500. Pick one. Any one. What do you invariably begin to see increasingly as time passes? Beards. Beards. And more beards. Beards, to be sure, are suddenly all over the place in Renaissance Italy after the first few decades of 1500. They are simply, unforgettably, enchantingly there. Sometimes they appear in low relief, as the mere shadow of the suggestion of a growth crawling around chins and jowls as marauding, darkened peach fuzz. Sometimes, at the other end of the extreme, they appear with such effusiveness and a bold elaborate shape to them that they seem to become, in the case of Parmigianino's marvelous rendition of the condottiere Gian Galeazzo Sanvitale, almost comically over the top, to the

FIGURE 40. Domenico Ghirlandaio (1448–1494), *Portrait of an Old Man and a Young Boy*, 1488. Louvre, Paris. Reproduced by permission of © RMN-Grand Palais/Art Resource, NY.

point where they could be twisted and twirled into a sort of extravagant mannerist, figura serpentinata–inspired, corkscrew and pinwheel design (fig. 41).[2]

Why? Why shortly after 1500 did men in Italy start wearing beards and, what is more, why did they eventually choose to address and impress the world with such a dazzlingly wide variety of them? This chapter attempts to provide an answer to that question by reflecting on it in light of a variety of issues related to collective and individual self-fashioning by using principally portraits and prose writings to try to pin down something so protean as a shift in fashion. The following chapter, which turns to primarily a work of imaginative literature, then examines how the topic of the beard becomes a unique matter of

FIGURE 41. Parmigianino (Francesco Mazzola, 1503–1540), *Portrait of Gian Galeazzo Sanvitale*, 1524. Museo Nazionale di Capodimonte, Naples. Reproduced by permission of Scala/Ministero per i Beni e le Attività Culturali/Art Resource, NY. Detail of face.

intense cultural concern in a late sixteenth-century comic play—a play that was never performed in the author's own lifetime but, as we shall see, is all about the performance of the beard in the everyday life of late Renaissance Italy.

∾ ∾ ∾

In a fascinating essay titled "The New World and the Changing Face of Europe," the Jewish studies scholar Elliott Horowitz advances an interesting and plausible explanation for the appearance of beards on the faces of Europeans generally in the sixteenth century.[3] Prior to the discovery of the New World, Horowitz argues, beards had been customarily associated with the Jew and Turk.[4] As a consequence, beards signaled the otherness of a foreign culture over and against

which Europeans as Christians collectively fashioned themselves. If the Jew and
the Turk routinely went bearded, and the beard became associated with them
as the quintessential Other, then Europeans collectively shaped their identity
negatively, as non-Jews, non-Turks, and thus as nonbearded people. However,
with the discovery of the New World, the "radical otherhood" traditionally
associated with the Jew and Turk shifted—according to Horowitz—to the indigenous people of the New World.[5] And one of the defining features of those
indigenous people was the absence of any facial hair, a fact made apparent not
only to the Europeans who were struck by the smooth-skinned faces of the
novel people they encountered but also to the indigenous people themselves
who were struck by the abundant growth of hair on the faces of the Europeans
(facial hair that the sailors had no doubt grown during the long voyage overseas). The otherness of the indigenous people of the New World created a peculiar problem, then, that the absence or presence of the facial hair resolved. For
the indigenous people were, like Europeans, deemed white in complexion, yet
unlike the Europeans, they lacked facial hair. To mark themselves off even more
from the indigenous people of the New World, to collectively differentiate their
true, authentic whiteness from the false whiteness of these "other" people of
the New World, Europeans according to Horowitz consequently grew beards
and cultivated them and their appearance. Additionally, this cultural displace-
ment of otherness focused on the signaling device of the beard could take place
in that precise period because by the end of the fifteenth century the Jew and
the Turk no longer represented the same economic, social, and political threat
that they had before.

Although Horowitz marshals considerable evidence to argue his point, it is
nevertheless difficult to imagine that the Jew and the Turk would have so
quickly disappeared as figures of "radical otherhood" in the European Renaissance in the sixteenth century. The natives of the New World may have begun
to occupy the status of "others," but one only need read Tasso's *Gerusalemme
liberata* (*Jerusalem Delivered*, 1581) to gauge the still vibrant perception of the
Turk and Jew as Other in the cultural imagination of sixteenth-century Italy.
Moreover, otherness is not a binary opposition in the Renaissance but a fluid
and dynamic concept: there was no more a single, stable category of "radical
otherhood" in the Renaissance than there was a single, stable currency. The
otherness of the indigenous people of the New World may have been on the
minds of the Spanish and Portuguese toward the beginning of the sixteenth
century, and that may account for their habit of adopting the fashion of wearing
beards to mark themselves off from the people they had conquered. Indeed,
Spain and Portugal were two countries that had a large-scale financial and cultural reason to shift their attention from the Far East to now the Far West, from

FIGURE 42. (left) Raphael (Raffaello Sanzio, 1483–1520), *Pope Julius II Rovere*, 1511. Uffizi, Florence. Reproduced by permission of Erich Lessing/Art Resource, NY. Detail of face.

FIGURE 43. (right) Agnolo Bronzino (1503–1572), *Portrait of Pope Clement VII (Medici)*, 1564–1570. Uffizi, Florence. Reproduced by permission of Scala/Art Resource, NY.

the old Indies to the new Indies. But Italy, we need to bear in mind, did not. Although Italians evinced a keen interest in the New World as soon as the discoveries overseas were made, they did not share the same large-scale involvement in it. As a result, the Other for Italians in the Renaissance in the sixteenth century remained, more appropriately, the Protestant, along with the Turk and Jew. Tasso, to be sure, collapses these categories and superimposes the religious erring of the Protestants and their fragmenting of Christendom onto the religious errancy of Islam, which the crusaders combat in his epic both by freeing Jerusalem and, in good post-Tridentine fashion, by unifying themselves into a single body with a single leader and a single goal. Lastly, the most noticeable and publicly recognized case of an "Italian" wearing a beard in the Renaissance had absolutely nothing to do with either the Jews and Turks or the indigenous people of the New World. It had to do with Julius II (Giuliano della Rovere) suddenly, and quite unexpectedly, growing a beard while ill and stalled in an entrenched war to regain the Papal States (fig. 42). Not until all the Papal States had been liberated would Julius II shave again. So, too, Clement VII (Giulio di Giuliano de' Medici) began wearing a beard after the sack of Rome.[6] For Julius II, as for Clement VII (fig. 43), growing a beard thus physically displayed mourning, a deep despondency, a sorrowful reclusion into hibernation. It registered at once Julius II's manliness (he would doggedly fight to the end) and amplified his pain (he let his beard grow untrimmed, like a "hermit," as he was described, dwelling in the wild).[7] The Italian custom of wearing a beard, as it was embodied in the figure of the pope based in Rome, was therefore born out of shame and sorrow, not a virile conquering of others. And it had little to do with imperial conquest. Nor, for that matter, does the abject example of the old and weary Julius II strike me as the likely, determining stimulus for this dramatic shift in fashion and ensuing trend that captured the imagination of so many men in sixteenth-century Italy and led them to sport all sorts of beards, from scraggly to abundantly thick and elaborately coifed ones.

If stylish Italians of the cultural elite did not begin to wear beards to distinguish themselves directly and agonistically from the indigenous people of the New World, and if they were not universally doing so—I think it is safe to assume—to express religious sorrow or penitential shame in the manner of a mourning warrior pope, why, then, did they do it? To answer, let us consider why they might have preferred not to wear beards before the sixteenth century, even though beards had long been associated with manliness, as we shall examine in even greater depth in the next chapter. One explanation for their desire to shave and go beardless might have to do with the process of urbanization that took hold firmly in Renaissance Italy during the fourteenth and fifteenth centuries. That spectacular process of rapid urbanization, which saw buildings and churches rise and tower magnificently over the city walls that were continually being enlarged, would have logically led Italians to prefer to go beardless. For the urban Italian, who collectively thought far more in local than regional terms, the aim was not so much to appear non-Turk as it was to not appear to have come from the nearby country. Everyone of means had financial investments in the country—it was part of the balanced economic portfolio of the wealthy to have farms—but the dominant investment, both intellectual and financial, was in the city, in such enterprises ideally as banking or large-scale trading. In Florence, for instance, the aim in many respects was to erase the original rustic tie with the country in order to present oneself as a well-ensconced urban dweller. Then, after having achieved a measure of financial success, the cultured urbanite built or bought a villa that architecturally transferred the image of the city to the *contado* (countryside), thus bringing the shape of urban experience to the outlying areas beyond the city walls.

Hence urban folk wanting to appear urbane went beardless because, quite simply, people from the country wore beards or were associated with wearing beards.[8] In Machiavelli's *Clizia* (1525), for instance, Eustachio, a family farmhand, is urged not just to fix himself up but also to clean himself up by Cleandro, a young man of some social standing in the urban community of Florence: "I'd like very much for you to fix yourself up a bit. You have this cloak that's falling off your back, this dusty cap, this shaggy beard [*barbaccia*]. Go to the barber, wash your face, dust off these clothes, so that Clizia won't reject you as a swine [*porco*]."[9] Structurally, given the established logical opposition in Renaissance Italy between the city and the country, it was only natural that a farmworker accustomed to handling and being around pigs would appear filthy—*porco* nicely rhymes with *sporco*[10]—within the walls of Florence (Bruni's ever-so-clean Florence, we may recall), even though pigs certainly roamed within them. Along with that, it was only natural that the farmhand should appear so vilely bearded and unkempt. To be bearded, it would seem, was as good as being filthy. In Mary Douglas's classic terms, it was as good as being "matter out of place" within the community of Renaissance urban life. Consequently, the urban elite, in order to differentiate themselves all the more from such vile, rustic workers, aimed to go beardless.[11] Get rid of the "barbaccia," Machiavelli's Cleandro insists, if you want to stay in the city and be treated properly.

Why the shift to beards, then? Could it be, perhaps, that the process of urbanization had reached such a point in time that Italians now felt secure in wearing beards? Had Italians in their cities, in other words, now sufficiently marked their identity as urbanites within the local culture that they no longer needed to fear any lingering association with their origins in the contado as they wore beards? I doubt it. I doubt, that is, that the opposition between country and city fundamentally had anything to do in a significant manner with the large-scale shift from a nonbearded Italian Renaissance to a bearded one in the sixteenth century. Rather, what partly propelled the change in fashion from a nonbearded to a bearded Italian face in the Renaissance was *insecurity*, the feeling on the part of so many Italians belonging to the elite or aspiring to be part of it that, despite all the colossal capital and urban planning and civic pride that went into constructing these marvelous cities that still seem to enchant us today, Italy was as weak and vulnerable as ever. Indeed, it was more vulnerable than ever. To be sure, the traditional date marking that sense of vulnerability was the end of the fifteenth century, and it has remained that way in the historiography of Italy. As Francesco Guicciardini puts it in the very first sentence of his massive *Storia d'Italia* (*History of Italy*, ca. 1536–1540; printed posthumously 1561), a book that is unique in its sophisticated understanding of how Italy figured into European politics generally:

I have determined to write about those events which have occurred in Italy within our memory, ever since French troops, summoned by our

own princes, began to stir up very great dissensions here: a most memorable subject in view of its scope and variety, and full of the most terrible
happenings since for so many years Italy suffered all those calamities
[*calamità*] with which miserable mortals are usually afflicted, sometimes
because of the just anger of God, and sometimes because of the impiety
and wickedness of other men.[12]

The date the French troops invaded Italy and upset the perfect balance of political parts fostered by Lorenzo de' Medici in his golden age of peace and stability
was 1494. Thereafter, as Guicciardini puts it in the tragic mode that dominates
his history, the "calamities" began. And those calamities only continued to
mount, culminating with the sack of Rome in 1527.

Then, not long after the invasion of the French in 1494, beards began appearing on the faces of urbane Italians. The process was slow. Italians did not all
suddenly begin to grow beards overnight, but by the second decade of the sixteenth century it was undoubtedly so fashionable to wear a beard that it is
difficult to think of famous men of the cultural elite who did not wear one. It
was certainly enough of a fashion, for instance, that Baldassare Castiglione,
probably among the most fashion-conscious Italians of his age, is depicted bearing a thick, lush beard, ever-so-slightly and suavely parted at the bottom, in the
famous portrait of him by Raphael completed between 1514 and 1516 (fig. 14).
Moreover, many of the male members of the group gathered together in 1507 at
Urbino to talk about the perfect courtier wore stylish beards at some point in
the early sixteenth century. To be sure, the comic playwright and cardinal Bernardo Dovizi da Bibbiena did not wear a beard (the portrait of him housed in
Palazzo Pitti shows him well shaven), and the jester Bernardo Accolti (Unico
Aretino) did not go bearded either (at least as he is represented in Raphael's
Parnassus in the Vatican). But both Pietro Bembo (fig. 4) and Giuliano de'
Medici, two outspoken members of the group, most likely did grow beards very
early on in the sixteenth century, as is suggested by surviving portraits of them
produced by Titian and Raphael. And Ottaviano Fregoso, yet another talkative
courtier in *Il cortegiano*, wore an ample white beard in a portrait depicting him
as the doge of Genoa, an office he acquired in 1513, just a few years after the
discussions in Urbino ostensibly took place. Surely, then, if these fine arbiters
of fashion were wearing beards so early in the sixteenth century, it was a broadly
accepted thing to do. Castiglione, Bembo, Giuliano de' Medici, and Fregoso
represented the very best of fashion from various parts of Italy, coming as they
did from Mantua, Venice, Florence, and Genoa.

In this light, there are two significant sociopolitical factors that can perhaps help account for the large-scale shift in fashion from a nonbearded Renaissance Italy to a bearded one, although it is important to stress that a direct cause-and-effect historical explanation for the appearance (or, for that matter, disappearance) of a fashion is supremely difficult to validate, and so the suggestions here should be taken as tentative and speculative but still, I think, probabilistic. The first contributing factor is the invasion of Italy by the French, an event that shook the peninsula and reshaped the balance of power forever in the Italian Renaissance, as Guicciardini melancholically pointed out at the beginning of his massive history. The second, an indirect consequence of the invasion first by the French and then by the German and Spanish imperial forces in 1527, was the fact that Italy became a more pronouncedly courtly society, whose ideal character is so memorably described by Castiglione. In both these cases, men in Italy were made to feel subordinate, no longer masters of their own destinies. The subjection of male Italians in relation to the lord they served in the court, or to the country that now controlled the balance of power in the peninsula, particularly after the conquest of Spain, placed men like Castiglione in a conspicuously subordinate position.

Hence *Il cortegiano*, as a number of scholars have pointed out over the past few decades, and as we explored at various moments in Chapter 1, gives expression to underlying anxieties on the part of elite men about seeming to be too effeminate.[13] The beard, I submit, effectively masks those anxieties and perhaps even relieves some of them.[14] At one level, the beard asserts the undeniable maleness of these courtiers, whose profession once was that of arms but is now that of posturing, negotiation, calculated talk, and graceful advice giving. For in theory men, and only men, can grow beards. A beard may not make the man, but—as we shall see in greater depth in the following chapter—it is an unmistakable and evident sign of maleness.[15] Needless to say, at a time when Italians suffered from feelings of inferiority in military prowess and when Spanish habits of appearance and comportment came to dominate Italian culture,[16] wearing a beard hides a weakness inherent in the culture: these men cannot for the life of them defend themselves against the dominant powers of Europe. In this respect, a beard conspicuously exhibits manhood in the very moment that the manhood of Italy was being questioned through a series of devastating invasions and, to be sure, at the very moment, as Castiglione observes in *Il cortegiano*, when Italians were quick to abandon (with an alacrity that elicits plaintive astonishment) their longstanding habits of fashion in order to adopt those very habits belonging to the new alien powers—powers, Federico Fregoso laments, that have made Italy the prey of all:

Messer Federico said: "I do not really know how to give an exact rule about dress, except that a man ought to follow the custom of the majority; and since, just as you say, that the custom is so varied, and the Italians are so fond of dressing in the style of other peoples [*gli Italiani son vaghi d'abbigliarsi alle altrui fogge*], I think that everyone should be permitted to dress as he pleases. But I do not know by what fate it happens that Italy does not have, as she used to have, a manner of dress recognized to be Italian: for, although the introduction of these new fashions makes the former ones seem very crude, still the older were perhaps a sign of freedom, even as the new ones [*novi*] have proved to be an augury of servitude [*augurio di servitù*], which I think is now most evidently fulfilled [*il quale ormai parmi assai chiaramente adempiuto*]. . . . Just so our having changed our Italian dress for that of foreigners strikes me as meaning that all those for whose dress we have exchanged our own are going to conquer us: which has proved to be all too true, for by now there is no nation that has not made us its prey. So that little more is left to prey upon, and yet they do not leave off preying [*così l'aver noi mutato gli abiti italiani nei stranieri parmi che significasse, tutti quelli, negli abiti de' quali i nostri erano trasformati, deve venire a subiugarci; il che è stato troppo più che vero, ché ormai non resta nazione che di noi non abbia fatto preda, tanto che poco più resta che predar e pur ancor di predar non si resta*]." (2.26)

Moreover, at a time when the emphasis was increasingly being placed on affect control, and when one had to be careful not to make a slip and reveal a socially undesirable emotion through a facial expression, a beard could always serve as a handy disguise. Wearing a beard, in this context, must have had its distinct social advantages in the tense courtly world of sixteenth-century Italy. At once declarative (I am a man, the beard announces; I can grow facial hair) and protective (I can conceal my expressions and my inability—as well as perhaps unwillingness—to fight to defend my territory or the prince's territory), the beard both masks and identifies, selectively conceals and reveals.[17] Needless to say, these strategies, like those of simulation and dissimulation, were prized in sixteenth-century Italy, especially in the court.[18] Indeed, if there is one thing *Il cortegiano* teaches us, it is that it is always better to reveal less than more. And a beard naturally reveals less of a person's emotional state, albeit a lot more of his body—or at least what the adult male body can grow abundantly on the face. Consequently, if it is true, as Horowitz argues, that the bearded European signaled "the virile conquest and domination of the newly discovered world to the West," and if, as he also argues, the fashion of wearing a beard in Italy was largely introduced from beyond its borders, from such countries across the Alps as France and across the Tyrrhenian Sea as imperial Spain (where beards were in fact likewise conventionally being worn by the cultural elite), then the wearing of a beard in Italy signaled not independence, a staking out of difference over and against the Turk or the Jew or the native people of the New World.[19] Instead, as Castiglione would seem to indicate in the context of talking about the Italian habit of adhering to new fashions of dress from conquering nations, the wearing of a beard signaled conformity to the fashion of the dominant alien powers, the very powers—in the case of France and then later Spain—that had invaded Italy, bringing with them one calamity after another into the peninsula and reducing it to a vulnerable "prey." In this way, by wearing a beard, the Italian male elite discreetly aligned themselves with the customs of the new dominant powers in Italy, thereby attempting to secure a posture of authority through identification, but ironically their collective alignment through fashion only called attention to their role as dominated. Theirs was, to be sure, the manly beard of "majesty," to borrow the terms of the anatomist Alessandro Benedetti, but—as we shall see in the case of Cosimo I in the next section to this chapter—it can also be viewed as an elegant and stylized quotation of the imperial majesty that Italians managed to make in good Renaissance fashion their own.[20]

Collectively Castiglione's group of courtiers discusses proper self-presentation for four evenings in a row, and on the last occasion even through an entire sleepless night. They also show that they are extremely concerned with how the body appears and emphasize how one must gesture appropriately in order to remain decorous. But they do not address whether a courtier should or should not wear a beard. Nor do they discuss directly whether a beard is inherently manly or not. They only mention that would-be courtiers should not pay too much attention to their beards, the way women, we are given to understand, attend too vainly to their appearance, thus privileging applied cosmetics over inner character or, in the Platonic terms Castiglione often adopts, appearance over essence. "But to say what I think is important in the matter of dress," the (perhaps bearded) Federico Fregoso says early on in Book 1,

> I wish our Courtier to be neat and dainty in his attire, and observe a certain modest elegance, yet not in a feminine or vain fashion [*ma non però di maniera feminile o vana*]. Nor would I have him more careful of

one thing than of another, like many we see, who take such pains with their hair that they forget the rest; others attend to their teeth, others to their beard [*altri di barba*], others to their boots, others to their bonnets, others to their coifs; and thus it comes about that those slight touches of elegance seem borrowed by them, while all the rest, being entirely devoid of taste, is recognized as their very own. And such a manner I would advise our Courtier to avoid, and I would only add further that he ought to consider what appearance he wishes to have and what manner of man he wishes to be taken for, and dress accordingly; and see to it that his attire aid him to be so regarded even by those who do not hear him speak or see him do anything whatever. (2.27)

If a beard signaled manliness in the cultural imagination of Italians in the sixteenth century, too much attention to a beard, Castiglione avers, can still be viewed as a sign of foppishness. How, then, should one wear a beard? How much attention to its appearance meets the requirement of locating that ideal Aristotelian mean that underpins Castiglione's treatise? What amount of attention constitutes too little or too much? Too little attention, no doubt, would lead a man to let the beard grow wild and thus make him look like a peasant, a recluse, or a mourning, embittered, bearlike pope.[21] Conversely, too much attention to the beard would perhaps turn a man into an effeminate and affected fop lacking sprezzatura. Moreover, since Castiglione suggests that the physically smaller is generally preferred to the bigger when searching for the proper mean between extremes, as he does, for instance, when discussing the ideal size of the perfect courtier, perhaps a smaller beard is better than a bigger one if there is any doubt about how big or small the beard should be. Needless to say, Castiglione does not address any of these matters in any detail in his treatise, since to codify anything too minutely in *Il cortegiano* would only defeat the purpose of its rhetorical strategy. One of Castiglione's aims is not to prescribe rules of fashion but to show through the edifying practice of exemplarity and carefully crafted descriptions that fashion is culturally—indeed even locally—determined.

Nevertheless, wearing a beard was unmistakably a widespread fashion, and like most fashions in Renaissance Italy, it led to reflection in other conduct and etiquette manuals. In the *Galateo*, for instance, the treatise that most openly codified conduct and etiquette in the late Renaissance, the topic of beards comes up briefly in the context of Giovanni della Casa's insistence—an insistence repeated over and over again throughout his treatise—that we must do everything we can to adopt the accepted current fashion of the people where we happen to reside. We should do this, we are told, not just so that we will not stick out conspicuously in the crowd but also so that we will not disturb or offend others.[22] As is so often the case in the *Galateo*, the aim is to please so as to be pleased. Adopting this behavioral strategy is a virtue, just as it is virtuous in an Aristotelian sense in the *Nicomachean Ethics* not to overstep boundaries. We must all find the equilibrated place between extremes. Above all, within civil society it is virtuous, for della Casa, to think and care about others in order to allow everyone with whom one has contact to feel at home. And beards, wearing them or not wearing them, directly figure into this civilizing process. As della Casa warns in the context of talking about custom and fashion:

> Everyone must dress well according to his status and age, because if he does otherwise it seems that he disdains other people. For this reason the people of Padua used to take offence when a Venetian gentleman would go about their city in a plain overcoat as if he thought he was in the country. Not only should clothing be of fine material, but a man must also try to adapt himself as much as he can to the sartorial style of other citizens, and let custom guide him, even though it may seem to him to be less comfortable and attractive than previous fashions. If everyone in your town wears his hair short, you should not wear it long; and where other citizens wear a beard, you should not be clean shaven [*o, dove gli altri cittadini siano con la barba, tagliarlati tu*], for this is a way of contradicting others, and such contradictions, in your dealings with others, should be avoided unless they are necessary, as I will tell you later. This, more than any bad habit, renders us despicable to most other persons.[23]

Knowing both where and when one should wear a beard, and what kind of beard one should wear, indicates an absence of selfishness. At the same time, it reveals worldliness and understanding and appreciation of otherness. It signals that you are cognizant that you have entered a culturally different space and know, as well as respect, the collectively accepted social customs governing it.

But not all beards are the same, and this was certainly the case in sixteenth-century Italy. On the one hand, wearing a beard might show some general degree of conformity and could therefore be construed as a matter of selflessly deferring to the taste, judgment, habits, and general well-being and comfort of others, of a collectivity. On the other hand, wearing a certain *type* of beard also revealed, given the constraints within which one necessarily operated, something about the self, and it signaled a discriminating claim that one personally and conspicuously asserted with respect to one's own particular identity, one's own individuality within a collectivity. And della Casa is aware of this, too. We

must wear a beard where it is appropriate to wear one, he insists, but the particular type of beard worn also all depends on the place, time, and circumstances,
although it is difficult, as Castiglione and della Casa knew, to pin down precisely
why fashion comes and goes:[24]

> You should not, therefore, oppose common custom in these practices,
> nor be the only one in your neighborhood to wear a long gown down to
> your feet while everyone else wears a short one, just past the belt. It is
> like having a very pug face, that is to say, something against the general
> fashion of nature, so that everybody turns to look at it. So it is also with
> those who do not dress according to the prevailing style but according
> to their own taste, with beautiful long hair, or with a very short-cropped
> beard or a clean-shaven face [*o che la barba hanno raccorciata o rasa*], or
> who wear caps, or great big hats in the German fashion.[25]

Although both Castiglione and della Casa assure the reader that their treatises
should not be read as self-portraits, the first overtly in the introduction to his *Il
cortegiano* and the second by having an "idiota" (idiot) narrator voice the concepts of the *Galateo*, we can nevertheless rest assured that both Castiglione and
della Casa, so conscious as they were of how fashion affects others and passes
with time, knew how to wear a beard. They knew, that is, what length the beard
should be and when it should or should not be trimmed according to the place
and circumstance. Indeed, both men certainly wore beards, and neither of them,
as it so happens, wore the "short-cropped" one. Della Casa's beard, as a matter
of fact, was rather long, flowing, and *abbondante* (fig. 44).

For both Castiglione and della Casa, then, wearing the right sort of beard
signaled some degree of conformity. It demonstrated publicly an understanding
of what sorts of beards are worn in specific places under specific circumstances.
This is important, since Renaissance Italians, along with Europeans generally in
the sixteenth century, had styles for beards that became associated in a vague
sort of way with the habits and customs of a specific place at a particular time,
much as della Casa observes that one should not wear a "plain overcoat" in
Padua, where it was not the custom to do so. Benvenuto Cellini tells us in his
autobiography, for instance, that the elderly Bembo was wearing "his beard
short after the Venetian fashion [*egli portava la barba corta alla veneziana*]"
when Cellini visited the great humanist in Padua and set out to make a medal
of him in 1537.[26] As we pass from the fifteenth to the sixteenth century, then, it
is not just a matter of thinking about the differences between a beardless and
bearded Renaissance but between a beardless one and one that became obsessed
with beards styled in so many varied and conspicuous ways. We pass, that is,

FIGURE 44. Pontormo (Jacopo Carucci, 1494–1557), *Portrait of Giovanni della Casa*, 1541–1544. Samuel H. Kress Collection, National Gallery of Art, Washington, DC. Reproduced by permission of the National Gallery of Art. Detail of face.

from virtually no hair on the face in the fifteenth century to all types of hair sprouting on the faces of urban Italian men. Wearing a beard thus signaled conformity to a general fashion, but the type of beard you wore could spell out publicly, and indeed conspicuously, your own affiliation with a particular style and, at the same time, provide the opportunity to assert your unique style within that group context as a mode of performatively addressing the world through your face. One could choose, for instance, the thick broad-fanning beard (represented by Lorenzo Lotto in a portrait of a man [fig. 45]); the long, venerable beard (represented by Pontormo in his portrait of della Casa [fig. 44]); the larger, bushier version of the same in so many portraits of Pietro

FIGURE 45. (top left) Lorenzo Lotto (ca. 1480–ca. 1557), *Portrait of a Couple*, 1523–1524. Hermitage, St. Petersburg, Russia. Reproduced by permission of Erich Lessing/Art Resource, NY. Detail of face.

FIGURE 46. (bottom left) Titian (Tiziano Vecellio, ca. 1488–1576), *Portrait of Pietro Aretino*, ca. 1545. Galleria Palatina, Palazzo Pitti, Florence. Reproduced by permission of Erich Lessing/Art Resource, NY. Detail of face.

FIGURE 47. (top right) Titian (Tiziano Vecellio, ca. 1488–1576), *Portrait of Count Antonio Porcia*, ca. 1548. Pinacoteca di Brera, Milan. Reproduced by permission of Scala/Art Resource, NY. Detail of face.

Aretino (such as the one painted by Titian in ca. 1545 [fig. 46], although Aretino, it is worth pointing out, also changed the look of his beard over time, as can be seen in an earlier portrait of him by Titian); the rather conventional cheek-and-jowl beard (represented in Titian's portrait of Count Antonio Porcia [fig. 47], the anonymous portrait of Leonardo Fioravanti [fig. 18], and Francesco Ferrucci del Tadda's profile portrait of Cellini [fig. 16]) or one of similar style with less beard covering the cheek and a bit of the chin showing beneath the furry underlip (represented in Raphael's double portrait of himself with his fencing master [fig. 48]); the stiletto-styled beard (represented, for instance, in images of Michelangelo [fig. 49]); the "tile beard" (a bushy square one represented by Bronzino in his portrait of Stefano IV Colonna [fig. 50]); the rather wooly, thick, mustachioed beard (represented in Tintoretto's self-portrait [fig. 27]); the truly elaborate one worn by Gian Galeazzo Sanvitale (represented by Parmigianino [fig. 41]); or the long, pointed beard parted the whole length down, like two stilettos (represented by Bronzino, for instance, in his portrait of Bartolomeo Panciatichi [fig. 51]).

Clearly, then, men in Italy invested a great deal of time in taking care of their beards and in choosing the right one for their particular, individual face. Some, such as Panciatichi, perhaps introduced new tastes into the reigning fashions of the day. And yet because beards were fashionable and signaled not just manliness but "majesty," as Benedetti put it in his treatise on anatomy, a problem potentially arose if you couldn't grow a beard, and a bigger problem potentially arose if you were a princely leader of men and really couldn't grow a full one. An interesting case in this regard would be the gradual—indeed, it would seem very gradual—appearance of a full beard on the face of Cosimo I. For Cosimo I began to grow his beard sometime after 1537, when he was only seventeen or eighteen years old, which was at least five years after the habit of wearing a beard became truly fashionable in Florence, according to the diarist Luca Landucci, although clearly the fashion had, I think it is safe to say, taken hold long before then.[27] In the earliest portrait of Cosimo I painted by Bronzino, and perhaps commissioned as a marriage gift for Eleonora of Toledo (fig. 52), the Duke of Florence is figured at the age of roughly twenty with only a few wisps of hair creeping up both sides of his cheeks, a barely visible moustache that transparently reveals the skin underneath it, and hardly a tuft of hair on the underside of his chin. This "coolly erotic" representation of Cosimo I, as Robert Simon has described it, may make some sense in that Bronzino here figures Cosimo I as the youthful Orpheus, whose iconography was occasionally deployed by the Medici to signal their calculated use of eloquence over force in order to protect Florence and its domains and thus maintain peace and stability—the longed-for *quies*—in the region, although the calculated mythological allusion in this instance could have also served to indicate to Eleonora that Cosimo I, like Orpheus, would even descend into hell for his beloved new bride.[28] In any event, however we read the symbolic significance of Orpheus in this painting, be it as a public or private message, if one of the well-established ways to convey visually the passage from adolescence to full-blown manhood to old age was the way the beard appeared or did not appear on the male face (as is clear in Giorgione's *Three Ages of Man* [fig. 53], for instance), then it

FIGURE 48. (top) Raphael (Raffaello Sanzio, 1483–1520), *Raphael (Self-Portrait) and His Fencing Master*, 1518. Louvre, Paris. Reproduced by permission of Erich Lessing/Art Resource, NY. Detail of faces.

FIGURE 49. (bottom left) Jacopino del Conte (1510–1598), *Portrait of Michelangelo Buonarroti*, ca. 1535. Casa Buonarroti, Florence. Reproduced by permission of Scala/Art Resource, NY. Detail of face.

FIGURE 50. (bottom right) Agnolo Bronzino (1503–1572), *Portrait of Stefano Colonna*, 1546. Galleria Nazionale d'Arte Antica, Rome. Reproduced by permission of Nimatallah/Art Resource, NY. Detail of face.

FIGURE 51. Agnolo Bronzino (1503–1572), *Portrait of Bartolomeo Panciatichi*, ca. 1540.
Uffizi, Florence. Reproduced by permission of Scala/Art Resource, NY.

certainly made good sense to portray Cosimo I with only a hint of a "wispy
beard," as Janet Cox-Rearick nicely puts it, in the painting of him as Orpheus
taming Cerberus.[29] Like Orpheus, Cosimo I—a devoted lover and a tamer of
the wild through his voice—must be portrayed as a young man whose age,
judging by the beard, would place him somewhere between the adolescent in
Giorgione's painting and the adult who instructs. However, in Bronzino's later
portrait of Cosimo I (fig. 54), which sets him in martial armor with his hand

FIGURE 52. Agnolo Bronzino (1503–1572), *Portrait of Cosimo I de' Medici as Orpheus*, ca. 1538–1540. Philadelphia Museum of Art. Reproduced by permission of the Philadelphia Museum of Art/Art Resource, NY.

resting on his helmet, we once again witness the duke—now around twenty-four years old—adorned with a delicate, thin beard, yet again appearing at a developmental stage somewhere between a boy and a man. In this three-quarter profile, the duke's boyish, wispy beard would seem to belie the very threat that the martial armor, with its jutting, highlighted spikes in the breastplates—the so-called besagues—pose to the viewer as sharp, pointed menaces.[30]

FIGURE 53. Giorgione (da Castelfranco, ca. 1477–1510), *The Three Ages of Man*, ca. 1500. Galleria Palatina, Palazzo Pitti, Florence. Reproduced by permission of Scala/ Art Resource, NY.

The official, political iconography of Cosimo I certainly mattered to the duke and his court, and it was something that they consciously wished to control.[31] When, for example, the Medici agent in Milan, Francesco Vinta, was collaborating with the sculptor Leone Leoni (who was also then master of the Milanese mint) on a new medal for Cosimo I, Vinta observed in a letter sent in 1550 to Pier Francesco Riccio, the majordomo of the court in Florence, that he was not at all confident that the medal he had in hand (and that was probably only a year old) offered an accurate, up-to-date likeness of Cosimo I because "His Excellence," he assumes, "has grown more beard [*ha messo più barba*]."[32] It was evidently important for Vinta and those at court back in Florence that Cosimo I's beard be presented just right, with the correct amount of hair on his face. The medal clearly called for "more beard," and more beard is what Cosimo I was bound to receive if a new medal were ever to be made.[33] For the beard mattered in terms of the male elite's manner of individual self-presentation, and there is clear visual evidence that Cosimo I made a conscious decision to grow a full, manly beard and that it took some time for him to do so. The early

FIGURE 54. Agnolo Bronzino (1503–1572), *Portrait of Cosimo I in Armour*, ca. 1543. Uffizi, Florence. Reproduced by permission of Scala/Art Resource, NY.

portraits modeled on the "official" one by Bronzino, which depicts Cosimo I in about 1543 in martial armor, continue to present the young duke with only a slight, thin beard that cannot cover the chin and, consequently, boasts only a faint brownish smudge under the bottom lip.

Then, some time after Cosimo I received the Order of the Golden Fleece in 1545, when he was about twenty-five, he was portrayed with a somewhat thicker beard. Evidently the two or more intervening years seemed to have made a difference. And for the next ten years, during which time Bronzino's original three-quarter portrait of Cosimo I served as the "official portrait of the duke," the beard gradually continued to grow.[34] Indeed, the beard as it grew over the years represented one of the few elements in the paintings modeled on Bronzino's early portrait of about 1543 that actually measured the passage of time in the natural aging and maturing process that we all, alas, have to cope with, for, as Langedijk observes, "in the case of Cosimo's likeness in particular a high degree of fixity prevails, both in the painted portraits and the sculptures."[35] There was thus not much change in the formal structure of the portrait of the first type, which resulted in a sort of iterative series based on Bronzino's painting, but there was a good deal of change in the beard, which grew bit by bit, in fits and starts.[36] Then, by about 1560, the model of likeness changed for a new series of official portraits of the duke (fig. 55). At this point Cosimo I, now aged forty or so, with little fear that Florence faced danger from foes near or far away, has himself portrayed without armor on but conspicuously wearing a thick, wooly beard. Thereafter the beard retains a sizable dimension, although it never did quite fully cover his chin. At best Cosimo I had there what is commonly referred to in contemporary American culture as a "soul patch," a dense, furry, triangular growth beneath the lower lip.

At one level, what is so intriguing about these portraits is that Cosimo I persisted in his efforts to grow a beard despite the fact that he had a difficult time, at least early on, growing a full, mature one. Cosimo I's insistence on growing a beard at once calls attention to his desire to impress on people in these official portraits an image of his "majesty," his legitimate princely right to rule. More specifically, it reveals his desire to have the official image he consciously controlled and presented of himself to the world conform to the image of majesty offered up by Charles V, whose portrait by Titian served as a model for Bronzino's early portrait of Cosimo I, the very portrait that would function as the model for so many others of Cosimo I.[37] At another level, what is also so intriguing about all the beards adorning Cosimo I's face in these portraits, from the ones portrayed in his youth to the ones of old age, is that they stand out as distinctive, although they were perhaps distinctive by accident. Everyone, from artists to patrons, courtiers to diplomats, as we have seen, wanted to make sure they maintained a certain, discriminating look with their beards, and their understanding of the beards they could design on their faces allowed for a wide range of possibilities and creative, individualizing shapes and sizes.[38] Renaissance Italians of some standing in the sixteenth century clearly aimed to acquire some measure of distinction by wearing a fashionable beard. Panciatichi surely aimed to flaunt his distinction through his elaborate beard in a portrait by Bronzino (fig. 51).[39] So distinctive is Panciatichi's highly textured beard that it stands out in the upper center of the canvas. His beard is also formally echoed in the poised forearms placed as perfectly parallel lines at slightly different levels,

FIGURE 55. Agnolo Bronzino (1503–1572), *Portrait of Cosimo I*, ca. 1560. Galleria Sa-
bauda, Turin. Reproduced by permission of Alinari/Art Resource, NY.

the fingers of the right and left hands coupled in balanced pairs, and, perhaps
most conspicuously, the sets of elegant, snail-shaped, ornamental window
braces receding into the background just to the left of the centrally located
beard, each of which represent so many smaller, architectural mirror images of
the beard. The inverted twin peaks of the beard, so centrally located in the
canvas, thus provide the model for the reiterated visual motifs within the canvas
itself. By contrast, Cosimo I's beard—in all of the versions of his painted
portraits—is not distinctive in the same way within the picture plane. It is not

distinctive, that is, because it is visually stunning or fashionable. Cosimo I's beard is distinctive because, it would appear, he simply could not seem to grow one that completely covered his chin. In the end, the beard Cosimo I grew, and that he had begun growing in earnest in 1537, was about the best he could manage to grow.

The beard in sixteenth-century Italy thus appears to be something unique to a man as it grows on his individual face in a peculiar way and on that person's face alone. At the same time the beard in sixteenth-century Italy appears as a sort of mask that can be shaped in a unique way and that serves as an adornment, as if it were something "worn." It can therefore be spoken of, as Castiglione and della Casa do, in the context of clothing, much as if it were apparel consciously and selectively worn in light of a widespread fashion that universally seized the imagination of a large body of men belonging to the cultural elite or those aspiring to be part of it. Even the language used to describe beards both now and in the Renaissance links these two opposing, yet still interrelated, concepts of identity formation. For one can speak in Italian of "wearing a certain style of beard" ("portare un certo tipo di barba") just as one can of "growing a certain type of beard" ("far crescere un certo tipo di barba"). The first phrase implies something exterior to the face that is actively applied to it. Francesco Vinta, the Medici agent in Milan, even used the verb *mettere* ("to put") to refer to the growth of the beard on Cosimo I's face, as if the beard were a cosmetic, something added—as if it were conceived even as a sort of prosthetic device. Conversely, the second phrase suggests something instead that passively emerges from within, piercing the surface of the skin to disclose biologically an essential part of the person contained inside. Together these concepts, embedded in different linguistic utterances about beards, articulate completely different notions of masculine identity as rooted in the male body. In one instance identity is what you have as a certain type of man: it's a given, just as the beard is what you have. You can't do much about it if you can't grow a beard over your chin, any more than you can alter your chin and place a dimple in the center because you happen to want one there, whether to be uniquely yourself or, for that matter, appear just like everyone else. Tough luck. In the absence of advanced cosmetic surgery in Renaissance Italy, you were who you were, with all the physical limitations of your individual body, just as your beard was your beard, although arguably it seemed to matter less if you were, as Cosimo I was, a powerful duke.[40] In another sense identity is what you make of it: it is something you can fashion, just as the beard can be manipulated, altered, dyed, thickened in representations, rendered more manly and majestic to suit the official portrait on a medal. When it comes to the beard as a peculiar facial feature in sixteenth-century Italy, then, you have some measure of control over self-presentation, some room for manipulating your facial features in public, some measure for engaging a personal, individualized, tailored style within the context of a broader collective fashion that aligned you with various groups and cemented alliances and loyalties. You may not be able to grow a certain kind of beard, to be sure, but you can still publicly and conspicuously stage the beard. At the very least, you can always go to the barbershop and, as Leonardo Fioravanti and others remind us, have the beard not only thoroughly washed but also properly trimmed so that you can go out and face the day.

❧

Manly Matters: Reflections on Giordano Bruno's *Candelaio*, and the Theatrical and Social Function of Beards in Sixteenth-Century Italy

I END THIS SERIES OF REFLECTIONS WITH A WORK OF IMAGINATIVE LITERA-
ture, Giordano Bruno's comedy the *Candelaio*, a rather curious and cumber-
some play that has sometimes been read in light of his philosophical positions
advanced in his more famous writings, such as his *De umbris idearum* (*Concerning the Shadow of Ideas*, 1582), *Ars reminiscendi* (*The Art of Memory*, 1583), and
De gl' heroici furori (*Concerning Heroic Furors*, 1585). But the play, I think it is
fair to say, does not seem to be philosophically serious in nature, the way, say,
some of Jean-Paul Sartre's existentialist plays are, and a case for a close connection between Bruno's philosophy and his one major work of fiction has never,
to my mind, been convincingly made.[1] For Bruno's play is not about dramatizing a philosophical position, even if elements of his philosophy can be uncov-
ered in the *Candelaio* in retrospect. Instead, like much Italian Renaissance
comedy of the sixteenth century, Bruno's *Candelaio* is about the conspicuous
staging of the self through role-playing. More specifically, it is at least in part
about the conspicuous staging of a performative male self through the putting
on and taking off of a particular part of the male body: a beard. Indeed, in his
Candelaio, Bruno—who incidentally bucked the trend and appears clean-
shaven with only a moustache, itself then something of an anomaly in Italy (fig.
56)[2]—focused on the beard to an unprecedented degree in Renaissance Italy
and in a manner not explored by any writer before him, including the classical
authors Plautus and Terence, whose comedies so often served as models for
Italian playwrights of the sixteenth century. Beards, in fact, not only appear
often in the play. One beard in particular becomes the focus of much discussion
at the very climax of the play, in the fifth and final act. As a result, beards, both
real and fake, acquire a special status in the *Candelaio* as symbolically charged
objects that reveal not only much about the individual characters and their

FIGURE 56. *Engraved Portrait of Giordano Bruno*, sixteenth century. Bibliothèque Nationale de France, Paris. Reproduced by permission of Bridgeman-Giraudon/Art Resource, NY.

functions within the play but also much about social norms and collective expectations regarding the performance of male sociability in sixteenth-century Italy. To this end, understanding the social and cultural context within which Italian men grew and cared for their beards during the period will help explain the meaning of a unique feature of Bruno's play, while examining Bruno's play will in its turn help dramatize more concretely a number of pervasive social and cultural anxieties about individual and collective self-presentation on the part of a variety of men in Bruno's time.[3]

The *Candelaio* contains many characters, no fewer than seventeen, and all of them are crowded into three loosely interwoven plots. The central plot, in which beards abound and have a crucial function, centers on Bonifacio, the character from whom the title of the play takes its name since he is, or has been known as, a "candlebearer," which in colloquial terms means a sodomite. For our purposes, the three plots themselves do not merit much summary here, but the principal characters and their roles do. Briefly, they are as follows. Bonifacio, the "candelaio," is a wealthy gentleman married to the beautiful, twenty-five-year-old Carubina. But now, "too old [*troppo attempato*]" (5.24), when "the first gray hairs appear and when desire normally cools" or "starts to cease" (1.3), he finds himself in his mid-forties (1.10) unexpectedly experiencing a rein-vigorated appetite for women. So he lusts after Vittoria, an attractive, conniving courtesan. For her part, Vittoria is bent on fleecing Bonifacio out of his money with the assistance of Lucia, Bonifacio's servant, who aims to get back at her master and help Carubina in exacting revenge against her disloyal husband. Bartolomeo, a greedy fool, spends all his money on a con man's promise of providing Bonifacio with easy riches, while Cencio, a traveling con man, in his turn tricks Bartolomeo by pretending to be an alchemist. Manufrio, a pedant, is robbed of his money by some pleasure-seeking knaves. Finally, Gianbernardo, a clever and resourceful painter, yearns for Carubina and puts together a plan to woo her, thanks to a hoax directed against Bonifacio and organized by the charlatan Scaramuré, the consummate trickster Sanguino—along with his mis-chievous cohorts in tomfoolery, Barra, Marca, and Corcovizzo (3.9)—and, in particular, Lucia, Bonifacio's malicious maid.

The extremely long and complicated play, which was perhaps sketched out in Naples before 1576 and then completed in Paris just before 1582, never did get performed in Bruno's lifetime.[4] And it never did meet with theatrical success over the next centuries, despite the critical acclaim it has sometimes received from modern scholars, who are typically interested not in the theatrical viability of the play as a staged performance but in its ingenious and playful manipulation of the Italian language at a time when the vernacular, for all that it had been brilliantly and expressively employed by a number of Renaissance Italian authors before

Bruno, was still in a formative state.[5] Scholars to this day thus tend to be more interested in Bruno's play on the page than on the stage. In any event, to the modern sensibility one additional reason why it would have been so difficult to pull off the *Candelaio* successfully—beyond the fact that it is chock full of characters who are difficult to keep track of—would have been that so many beards are used in it as a means of theatrical disguise.[6] In Bruno's *Candelaio* we are in fact talking about a lot of fake beards, no fewer than five: far more than one finds in any of Shakespeare's plays, for instance. At a certain point it may test not only the modern audience's credulity but also arguably its patience to see so many false beards being deployed as a reiterated mechanism of facial disguise.

The first to don a beard in this manner is the dim-witted, aging lover, Bonifacio, who attaches to his face a "barba negra posticcia" (a false black beard, 4.6), which is exactly the same beard as the one worn by the painter and prankster Gianbernardo. Bonifacio has sound reasons for adopting this particular disguise, which he procures from the local haberdasher (4.6): Gianbernardo is often seen entering Vittoria's house and spending time in her company. Counterfeiting the painter's identity by wearing his beard therefore makes good practical sense to Bonifacio, who has been advised to do so by the scheming Lucia (4.6). Disguised as Gianbernardo, Bonifacio can discreetly slip into Vittoria's house without arousing undue suspicion and, at least in theory, be admitted undetected into her room—or so Lucia convinces her master as she deviously plots against him. The next to put on a false beard is the trickster Sanguino. Pretending to be the police chief, Sanguino wears a "barba lunga e bianca" (long, white beard, 4.14). Then, as if this were not enough, the beard put on by Bonifacio, which is identical to the beard of the painter Gianbernardo, becomes the subject of some discussion when Sanguino and his cohorts—all knaves pretending to be guardians of justice and all of them incidentally wearing, we later learn, false beards as disguises—write down evidence regarding Bonifacio's crime of counterfeiting the painter's identity. Carubina, as it turns out, initiates the discussion over Bonifacio's fake beard by, as it were, "debearding" him. Entering into a ruse of her own, she has strategically occupied Vittoria's room, thanks to the help of Lucia and Vittoria herself (4.2), so that she can pretend to be the courtesan and catch her husband in his anticipated act of betrayal. Then, after having presumably crushed his testicles in private as she had planned to do (4.12), she publicly humiliates him by disclosing Bonifacio to the false guardians of justice (whom she initially believes are the real guardians of justice) as her husband who has, in fact, all along been wearing a false beard:

Carubina: Captain Palma—truth must out—this person in disguise [*travestito*] is my husband, Master Bonifacio; this other one is Gianbernardo. This is the truth and it can't be hidden.

Gianbernardo: And as confirmation, see if that is his real beard [*E per confirmazione, vedete si quella barba è sua*].

Bonifacio: I confess that it's false [*Io confesso che è posticcia*], but I put it on for a certain reason that concerns only my wife and myself.

Corcovizzo: Here's this good man's beard in my hands [*Ecco la barba cqua di questo uomo da bene nelle mie mani*].

Sanguino: Tell me, good man, is this your beard [*Dimmi, uomo da bene, è la barba tua questa*]?

Barra: Yes, sir, it is; after all, he bought it. (5.10)

Finally, we learn that virtually everyone else in the elaborate deception orchestrated by Sanguino, Gianbernardo, Scaramuré, and Lucia wears a beard:

Gianbernardo: Ha ha ha, the pedant [Manufrio] and Bonifacio should recognize them well enough. Have the others [Barra, Marca, and Corcovizzo—namely, Sanguino's cohorts] also put on [as in "disguised themselves with"] beards [*sono mascherati da barba*]?

Scaramuré: Every one of them; so much so that this seems to me to be a real stage comedy. All the pedant needs is a beard [*Al pedante non manca altro che la barba*]; Master Bonifacio already has one, if he should want to attach it [*se la vuole attaccare*]. (5.22)

Surely the false magus Scaramuré voices here what the audience already knows: this is "una comedia vera" (a real stage comedy), ostensibly nothing more, nothing less.

The overuse of a convention to foreground literary artifice—in this case to make sure that the audience knows that Bruno's comedy is indeed a comedy with actors playing out stock roles on the stage—is a familiar strategy deployed by self-reflexive artists. In Bruno's *Candelaio*, however, the beard as an overused disguise in a comic play foregrounds issues that are connected not only with metatheatrical artifice but also with collective and individual male identities in Renaissance Europe generally and Renaissance Italy in particular. For example, in perhaps one of the most memorable instances in modern historical accounts of a trickster successfully disguising himself in Renaissance Europe, it is primarily the appearance of the beard worn by Arnaud du Tilh (alias Pansette) that initially confuses Martin Guerre's young and independent-minded wife, Bertrande de Rols, and raises doubt in her mind that she is confronting her long-lost husband. On seeing her putative husband return after ten years of absence, the bewildered Bertrande cannot, in fact, tell right away if it is really Martin Guerre whom she sees standing before her because the man she examines wears a beard. As Natalie Zemon Davis tells the story in her now classic *The Return of Martin Guerre*, when Bertrande first beheld du Tilh, "she recoiled in surprise. Not until he had spoken to her affectionately, reminding her of things they had done and talked about, specifically mentioning the white hosen in the trunk, did she fall upon his neck and kiss him; *it was his beard that had made him hard to recognize*."[7] Needless to say, absolutely no one, we can safely assume, would have been duped had du Tilh marched back into town a week after Martin Guerre's departure, beard or no beard. The passage of time undoubtedly mattered in dislocating Bertrande's memory, thus rendering Bertrande's and the entire town's collective recollection of Martin Guerre both foggy and impressionable. It also mattered that du Tilh was a master trickster, just as it mattered that, without modern techniques for checking a person's true identity (fingerprints, photographs, computer-generated facial recognitions, dental records, DNA), it was supremely difficult to confirm a person's singular identity without the slightest doubt in Renaissance Europe generally. But a beard, it stands to reason, does make a difference in potentially disguising someone. So it is understandable why Martin Guerre's abandoned wife would have been perplexed initially before she could commit fully to the truth of her long-lost husband's specific, individual identity. After all, a beard can cover an immense portion of the adult male face, more than half of it, from cheek to chin, base of the nose to the bottom of the neck. It only makes sense, then, that a beard might be used in Bruno's play as a form of disguise by so many different men. The playwrights of the jovial Sienese Intronati drove home this point about the way a beard masterfully serves to disguise identity in their comic *Gli ingannati* (*The Deceived*, 1531) with the following observation delivered by the pedant in the play to one of the other characters: "I'm sure he won't recognize you either, what with how much you've changed. Moreover, you have that beard now which you didn't have before [*avete questa barba, che prima non la portavate*]."[8] Consequently, with a beard on the face, it is ostensibly difficult to say who you are, if you are one person or another—the real Martin Guerre, for instance, or a fake. By the same token, we are led to believe in the context of Bruno's play that it would be substantially difficult to tell the difference between the clever painter Gianbernardo or the numbskull Bonifacio once they are wearing the precisely same beard, the one, of course, having attached a false beard to his face, the other having actually grown it:

> *Gianbernardo*: Hey there, Master Black-Beard [*Olà, Messer de la negra barba*], tell me, who of the two of us is me, you or me? You're not answering?
> *Bonifacio*: You're you and I'm me [*Voi siete voi, ed io sono io*].

Gianbernardo: What do you mean I'm me? Thief, haven't you robbed me of
my identity/person [*Non hai tu, ladro, rubata la mia persona*]? (5.9)

It is also important to realize, however, that beards could never have been
used as such an efficient or verisimilar form of disguise in an Italian play composed prior to the beginning of the sixteenth century. Before that time, and thus
long before Bruno composed his *Candelaio*, beards, as we saw in the previous
chapter, were uncommon features on male faces in urban settings in Italy during the Renaissance—a fact that may still strike some readers as a surprise but
was in fact the case.[9] This does not mean that beards were not present in the
cultural imagination before they began to be worn and sometimes elaborately
styled by the urbane elite toward the beginning of the sixteenth century in Italy.
Beards abounded in literature and the visual arts in Italy well before the sixteenth century and thus, to be sure, well before Bruno wrote his comic play.
And many beards were deployed with consummate *fantasia* to establish in the
visual arts a formal balance or furnish a dynamic movement on a two- or three-
dimensional surface, much as they were treated on occasion as the concentrated
area on a canvas where painters could display a swashbuckling mastery over
their medium by building up a thick, colorful impasto. But it is also clear that
beards, once they began to be worn and cared for in sixteenth-century Italy,
became for many a highly charged focal point for the designing and fashioning
of the individual masculine self. As the polygraph Anton Francesco Doni (1513–
1574) observes in his *I mondi* (*The Worlds*, 1552–1553), many men in Renaissance
Italy were apparently obsessed with their beards, and they took great pains to
craft them so as to have a carefully cultivated and highly individualized "look."
Consider, for instance, the conversation staged by Doni between a barber, the
spirit Anima, and his inquisitive interlocutor, the satirical Momo:

Momo: Well, what then do you think about the world, since you say you
know so many things [about different people]?

Anima: The first thing you should know about my art [*all'arte mia*] is that
they all seem to me a caged gaggle of crazy people who live on the
earth, because of the thousands that I have shaved, washed, combed,
and slapped together, I fixed up one just as I did the other. . . . Many
want the long beard, many the beard cut half way, some in two parts,
rounded, shorn, with the moustaches, without moustaches, one who
shaved below, one who did so on top, on the scruff of the neck, beneath
the throat, and other bizarre things [*altre bizzarie*]. Young people all
keen on having a beard shave themselves often. Old men have their
beards dyed to look and feel young.[10]

It would also seem that even some women of sixteenth-century Italy took at least a passing interest in beards, if not necessarily a developed interest in the calculated interplay between a highly crafted male identity and the conscious shaping of beards as described by Doni in *I mondi*. The Venetian courtesan Elisabetta Condulmer, for instance, possessed a wardrobe that contained "three masks with beards for cross-dressing [*voltij tre barbi da stravestir. No. tre*]."[11] The inventory of Condulmer's trio of hirsute masks, as recorded dutifully by a notary after her death, does not distinguish one beard from another, so it is impossible to tell from the terse description he delivers if one of Condulmer's masks sported a "swallowtail" beard, "tile beard," or a short beard cropped *alla veneziana*, among so many other available styles to choose from in the period—or perhaps even something truly "bizarre," as Doni would have it.[12] Yet given the manner in which courtesans cherished variety in self-presentation, it is certainly plausible that the masks discovered in Condulmer's possession could have boasted distinctly different types of beards. Be that as it may, one can only wonder why the courtesan Condulmer felt compelled to possess such bearded masks. Perhaps, as Patricia Fortini Brown has suggested, Condulmer did so for the increased titillation of her eager male clients who may have fancied a slightly different sort of intimate encounter in the sexually stimulating and liberating spaces of a courtesan's boudoir: "cross-dressing," as Fortini Brown has observed, "was one more weapon in the courtesan's arsenal of seduction," and bearded masks may have suited this very purpose by functioning as sort of erotic prosthetic devices.[13] Or perhaps, we might reasonably imagine, Condulmer used those bearded masks when she periodically appeared in public: Venetian courtesans sometimes adopted disguises on outdoor social occasions, although appearances of courtesans as bearded in Venice have, to my knowledge, so far gone undetected in the visual and verbal records.[14] In any event, whatever reasons Condulmer had for possessing three bearded masks for the purpose of cross-dressing, the fact remains that she did indeed own them, which only reinforces the underlying assumption that women were not expected to grow facial hair, unless, of course, they somehow succumbed to an aberration in their normal biological development.

In this light we might consider how physicians in the sixteenth century understood why hair grew on faces in the first place. Take, for instance, the argument presented by the eminent physician and anatomist Alessandro Benedetti, whose writings we briefly sampled in Chapter 3 and whose notion of the "magisterial beard" underpinned parts of the argument of the previous chapter. In his *Anatomice* (1502), composed about half a century before Andreas Vesalius's monumental studies on anatomy, Benedetti explains why hair grows on the body and thus, as a result, why beards grow generally on the faces of men. The process, it turns out, is fairly straightforward according to the medical notions of humoral balances and excretions, and Benedetti's explanation represents a standard way of looking at the matter of hair—and by extension the growth of beards—in Renaissance Italy. "The material of the hair," Benedetti asserts in his *Anatomice*, "is made from the excrementitious humor and smoky vapor carried from the entire body to the skin."[15] Hair, like thick smoke or soot floating up through a chimney, is largely made from excess heat. As a result, a lot of hairs naturally sprout in the head, where the heat would be more concentrated and excreted through the pores. "Everywhere in the head," he writes,

> the natural heat has pierced the skin and opened passages, whence the viscose humor drawn outward and extended little by little in length and rendered equal or even by these punctures has spread it out into the slenderness of the hair and the humor turned back under the skin has put forth roots. For these reasons therefore the hairs grow in the skin; on account of the coagulation due to cold they have become harder than the skin and denser in substance. (112)

Of course, some hairs have a different feel, color, and thickness to them. This has to do with the nature and "quality of the skin" (113). Lepers, with their peculiar diseased skin, therefore sprout hairs different from those of other people. Moreover, hair, we learn, grows in different stages with respect to different parts of the body. We are born, for instance, with hair on the head, and we all have eyebrows and eyelashes at birth. Afterward we grow pubic hair around the genitalia and hair in the armpits. Lastly, Benedetti points out, we grow beards. At that point, Benedetti interrupts his sober anatomical treatise, which is filled with all sorts of medical insights, with a humorous anecdote in order to explain why men *alone* grow beards, or at least why they in theory should alone grow beards. "There is a story," he says, about a Greek peasant:

> He suddenly and with laughter asked a certain philosopher why the beard existed. The astonished philosopher made no reply. But the peasant said, with a jeer, "I who abide in the country shall tell you readily and properly. Since it is contained in the testicles, so the chin is adorned with Greek majesty [*mentum graeca maiestate barba cohonestari*]." (113–14)[16]

Arguably the heat of the man, characterized by his heat-generating testicles, produces the excess hair on the face and thereby allows for the creation of a beard, which in its turn was traditionally linked, as William Fisher has observed, to

the power—a distinctly male power grounded in the distinctly male testicles—
to beget children. No facial hairs, as the familiar quip had it in English, then
no heirs.[17]

Benedetti thus answers his own implied question "Why do men have
beards?" with a joke. At first glance, this may seem to be a rather odd way of
explaining the presence of beards on men, especially in a serious anatomical
treatise. But the reported quip of the peasant mocking the nonplussed philosopher does have the virtue of going directly to the heart of the matter, as jokes
often do.[18] Beards, like testicles, signal manliness. Hence beards adorn men's
faces to differentiate them all the more from women and, by extension, not
only boys but also young men who are on the verge of becoming full-fledged
adults. Beards consequently highlight the "virtue" of adult men *as* men, with
the emphasis tacitly placed on the first syllable, *vir*.[19] The stages by which hairs
grow on the human form indeed conventionally marked a natural break
between adolescence and manhood, between the time when the boy has just
smooth peach fuzz barely blooming on his cheeks and chin and seems effeminate, and the time when the mature man can instead grow a robust, virile beard
and proudly beget children. As the peasant would have the philosopher know,
the Greeks surely knew this. A beard in ancient Greece, he points out, signaled
"majesty," the kind of majesty that makes men naturally rule over boys, girls,
and women. And a beard had an intellectual quality for the Greeks, something
the speechless and puzzled philosopher queried and mocked by the peasant
should no doubt have known. A beard, in short, signaled an aggressive, rigorous, virtuous, and thus adult manly mind. It is not accidental, for instance, that
Hadrian, the most Hellenized of all the Roman emperors, grew a beard. He did
so not only to hide the blemishes of his skin, which were evidently quite noticeable, but also "to establish," as scholars of Roman portraits generally maintain,
"an association with Greece, especially Greek intellectuals."[20] Hadrian, who had
extended the Roman Empire to its limits and was known for his intellectually
curious and capacious mind, made wearing a beard an accepted sign of imperial
majesty among Romans. Consequently, after Hadrian's rule it became custom-
ary for Roman emperors to wear beards. Perhaps the best-known example of
the period, and the one prominently displayed in Renaissance Rome, can be
seen on the equestrian bronze statue in the center of Michelangelo's Campidoglio, with Marcus Aurelius—once considered to have been the emperor Con-
stantine—sitting stolidly on a horse, staring off across the eternal city toward
the walled Vatican complex with a sturdy, bearded face (fig. 3).[21] Needless to
say, in the century when Bruno wrote his play, one could readily adduce count-
less examples of men of significant stature donning beards, from emperors such

as Charles V to dukes such as Cosimo I, in order to enhance and project manliness, their putative intellectual and martial "majesty."

How, then, did men care for their beards in sixteenth-century Italy as they routinely sported them in public? And where, for that matter, did men go to have them properly trimmed and styled, if not also, as Doni indicates, to have them tinted and dyed so as to appear younger? Typically they went to the barbershop, a space that was itself highly gendered in the period and became a privileged place for male sociability. "Without barbers many men would live in a dirty way," Fioravanti opines in his *Dello specchio di scientia universale*. Indeed, people "go to the barber," he observes admiringly in a section devoted to the habits and art of the barber, "and they wash their hair, their beard gets fixed up, their hair cut, and so they leave the barbers neat and clean."[22] Likewise, Tomaso Garzoni, a finicky man always quick to seize on the topic of the clean and the unclean, has much say about barbers in his encyclopedic *La piazza universale di tutte le professioni del mondo*, and much of the information that he imparts about their profession is drawn directly from Fioravanti's *Specchio*, although he adds touches and details that are all his own.[23] At the same time, the barbershop, we learn, is not only the place where the individual male self is crafted in bodily form. The barbershop is also the place where the identity of a man is potentially revealed in the very moment that a beard is stylishly refined. Men, we learn from Garzoni, occasionally disclosed secrets about themselves in the barbershop, some essential matter of intrinsic worth, in the moment that they were constructing an exterior image of themselves, a carefully confected, individual "look," no doubt with the express aim of appearing to the world with the requisite politia, a period term that signaled in the Italian Renaissance "both refinement (as in aesthetic excellence) and civility (as in politic behavior)."[24]

This sort of imprudent behavior on the part of Italian men in barbershops is rather odd. Italian men of some social standing in the Renaissance, it is safe to say, worked extraordinarily hard to build up an image of themselves and strike a good impression, but then, it seems, they potentially let down their guard at the barbershop as they had their beards fashionably styled. "Regarding the poor barbers," Garzoni warns when commenting on their profession and the art underpinning it, "one cannot say anything but that they chatter in flocks usually like gabbling magpies, because all the gossipy news, rather all the tall stories rush about in barbershops, and blessed be the person who says all those things most freely. . . . And one should add also this: that confiding a secret to a barber is like confiding it to a Levantine Jew, as the example of the barber of King Midas (who revealed how the king had the ears of an ass) completely manifests it."[25] The barbershop in Renaissance Italy, it would seem, was a place of free-flowing, circulating information and gossip—a point confirmed by the social and cultural historians Elizabeth A. Horodowich and Filippo de Vivo in their studies of Renaissance and early modern Venice.[26] A man went in to get his beard cleaned and trimmed and he left having perhaps involuntarily offered up too much information about his own personal, individual matters—his "particolare," the always cautious, discriminating, and secretive Guicciardini would have no doubt declared. To be forewarned is thus to be forearmed, Garzoni would have us understand. So, too, Pietro Aretino would have us understand in his *Il marescalco* (*The Stablemaster*, 1533), when he has one comic character, Jacopo, inform another, Ambrogio, that he has received his gossip straight from a "first-rate source" (3.9): namely, the barbershop, which is elsewhere described in the same play as the "shop of truth" (1.3). "Who is it that knows so much news? [*Chi è costui, che sa tante novelle?*]," Ambrogio asks in the *Il marescalco*, to which Jacopo tersely retorts: "My barber." "Certainly a place worthy of credit," Ambrogio then jovially responds, "the barbershop, where all the travelers of the whole world come bearing news" (3.9).[27] Likewise, Doni, Aretino's friend and later bête noire, makes much the same claim in his *I mondi*. As Doni's barber spirit informs his interlocutor Momo, "if anyone knows the facts of the world, our barbers are the repositories of stories, because every sort of person ends up there to get cleaned, from various areas, of diverse apparel, of strange languages, of hideous mugs, of ugly physiognomies, and of truth and falsehood anyone [who comes] brings a big/heavy load [*e di verità e di bugie ciascuno ne porta un carico*]." And then Doni's barber concludes: "I wanted to tell you about the state of other men, because, in the course of discoursing while washing the pate of many, each one told me his own life's story" (113–14). The process of having a beard trimmed, shaped, or dyed thus rendered a man socially vulnerable within the cultural imaginary of sixteenth-century Italy, for men hankering for scuttlebutt must have congregated in barbershops in late Renaissance Italy, much as they sometimes still seem to do now.

With this in mind, I would like to return to Bruno's *Candelaio*, the play with which we began, for we are now in a better position to understand more fully how Bruno dramatizes different issues about masculine identity rooted in the male body in his unusually elaborate and unique treatment of the staged beard in late sixteenth-century Italian theater. At the heart of the matter lies the disclosed identity of Bonifacio, the previous sodomite and now grossly duped lover, who is unmasked and thus "debearded." With his beard removed, Bonifacio is revealed as just a fool tricked by his own vanity, unable to realize how he has been acting out a role orchestrated by Lucia, Scaramuré, Sanguino, and Gianbernardo within the play. At the same time, Bonifacio is disclosed to the audience with this unmasking as yet another character acting out a highly conventional role in Italian comedy generally, grounded as it is in ancient Roman theater, particularly the comedies of Plautus and Terence. His beard is removed much the way an article of clothing would have been taken off a character in a conventional act of undressing and unveiling in a comedy of the period. Bonifacio's scripted character—that of the aging, undressed, unmasked, foolish husband lusting after another woman—is thus an old and familiar one. His identity is supremely constructed. It is shaped by theatrical models that exceed his ken, fashioned by controlling schemers like Lucia, Scaramuré, Sanguino, and Gianbernardo—and, of course, by artist-philosophers like Bruno. For Bonifacio unwittingly lives, we can reasonably say, within a set of carefully scripted constraints. His life is not just structured but generically and culturally prestructured.

But the debearding of Bonifacio also, at first glance, seems to mark a change in Bonifacio's individual character as it is actively fashioned in the play. So his debearding calls attention to an aspect of an identity *essential* to him as a man, his would-be virile "majesty," as Benedetti might have phrased it. Indeed, Bonifacio's debearding adds insult to injury by transforming the once bearded, cocky suitor into a whining subordinate pleading for his survival. No sooner has Bonifacio been caught in his ludicrous scheme and carried off by Sanguino and his cohorts than he is reduced to a humiliated prisoner, groveling at the mercy of the men who have tricked him and publicly unmasked him. As Sanguino, pretending to be the chief of police, informs Scaramuré, pretending to be helping Bonifacio:

> *Sanguino*: He has been put into my hands by Gianbernardo, the painter, whom he was impersonating [*contrafacea*] with a false beard [*barba posticia*]. . . . The beard is here [*la barba è cqua*], in the keeping of my men and if you want to see how well it looks on him, come tomorrow at nine o'clock to Vicaria and you will laugh when we match them up together with their beards [*quando le confrontarremo insieme, co le barbe*].
> *Bonifacio*: Oh poor me, oh, for the love of God, help me! (5.18)

Having his fake beard removed from his face is thus emasculating for Bonifacio, so much so that he has lost not only his prior social standing as a "gentleman" of putative honor in sixteenth-century Italy through public shaming and ridicule but also his sexual potency, since his prior ardor for Vittoria has now noticeably cooled as he whines and prays over his abject plight. His debearding thus partly functions within the comedy as a symbolic act of castration, depriving the degraded Bonifacio of his individual manhood, both sexually and socially, in the very moment that it infantilizes him. Conversely, the artist Gianbernardo, whose beard Bonifacio had earlier worn in order to counterfeit the younger man's identity, will then have Bonifacio's alluring and beautiful wife, Carubina, for as long as he wishes (5.11). In this respect, Bonifacio's debearding has left him even more vulnerable than the other duped men in the play, Bartolomeo and Manufrio, who have at worst lost sums of cash. The dishonored and humiliated Bonifacio, without foreseeable conjugal relations with his now openly estranged wife, will henceforth be rendered a cuckold over and over again thanks to Gianbernardo, who has fittingly won the affections of the beautiful Carubina. "I can see now that you are all too clever [*scaltrito*] and you have woven this whole web [*avete saputo tessere tutta questa tela*]," Carubina informs Gianbernardo, impressed by his winning scheme; then, after a lengthy exchange in which she succumbs to his wooing, she says, "By your grace, let's go somewhere more private and not discuss such things here" (5.11). As a result, Gianbernardo, with his *real* black beard on his face, has emerged all the more within the comedy as the play's embodiment of an independent-minded man of true virile "majesty," not just intellectually because he has been so "clever" in putting together this intricate "web" of seduction but also, just as important, sexually because he has successfully wooed the woman he adores and has then been invited to pass time with her in a private space. Having or not having a beard consequently signals, among other things in the context of Bruno's play, the presence or absence of not just manly intellectual vigor but also male sexual prowess. "Let's go my sweet," Gianbernardo says, beckoning Carubina away, "for there are people coming" (5.11). Surely he will do more than just talk privately with her offstage.

At the same time, it is important to note that Bonifacio as an aging, infatuated man, whose desire was supposed to be waning as gray hairs began to sprout on his face in his mid-forties, was vulnerable long before he was even debearded. This was true, for instance, in the very moment that he put *on* the false beard as a mask, in an episode that offers yet more clues into the essential aspect of Bonifacio's comic character, who is portrayed as something of a wimp even in his moment of exhilarated cockiness. Significantly, just before the planned meeting with the courtesan Vittoria is supposed to take place, Bonifacio—for the first time visibly wearing the false beard of Gianbernardo—can barely restrain himself emotionally, much less contain himself physically. At the threshold of the tryst, shaking with trepidation in anticipation of his pent-up desire being satisfied, the overexcited Bonifacio fears he will ejaculate before the act of consummation commences. This falsely bearded man, whose lost appetite for women is now whetted to the point of exasperation, cannot seem to hold his semen inside him, that precious bodily fluid that distinctly marked manhood generally, as Patricia Simons reminds us.[28] And if his semen does indeed spurt out and splatter on the ground, the lubricious Lucia jests with the sin of Onan on her mind, then he'll just have to wait, work it up, and try again:

> *Bonifacio*: Ho ho ho ho ho. Let's go quickly because I can't hold it in any longer [*mi scappa*], ha ha ha ha.
> *Lucia*: Don't spill it on the ground if you don't want to draw down the wrath of God upon your head, ha ha ha; you make me laugh. If you lose this lot by frigging/shaking [*scrollandovi*] you can make some more.
> *Bonifacio*: That's true; but, ha ha ha ha ha ha . . .
> *Lucia*: Away, then. (5.1)

In every way, then, Bonifacio lacks the strength to persevere. As he wears Gianbernardo's distinctly black beard on his face, and thus as he wears a far more youthful beard in appearance than he could ever possibly grow as a man with graying hair (unless, of course, he had had it dyed at the barbershop), Bonifacio cannot seem to perform with the tacit control of the man whose identity he has stolen and who has, it so happens, demonstrated nothing but masterful self-discipline and lover's resolve by patiently longing for Carubina and artfully working over time to achieve his goal. In this respect, beards in Bruno's play mark not only gender, intellectual vigor, and sexual prowess but also, in the case of Bonifacio, an age-appropriate male capacity to consummate sexually with apposite restraint. Put differently, if taking off the false beard has a castrating effect on Bonifacio by emasculating him and robbing him publicly of his social standing, putting on a distinctly youthful-looking black beard inversely has an overstimulating effect on him, as if the all-too-eager aging and graying Bonifacio had swallowed a fistful of Viagra and then comically lost control of part of his body—that part of his body, of course, that he had previously been using as a candlebearer for slightly different libidinous purposes. Long before Bonifacio was unmasked, then, we can say that he was always ineluctably wearing something of a conventional comic mask—the dramaturgical mask of the lewd, aging, graying man with waning control over his still excitable yet vulnerable male body. As Marta, Bartolomeo's wife, earlier puts it, in keeping with the tacit laws of decorum that govern the genre of comedy, "Little girls for little boys and young women for young men. Old men need to content themselves with more stale/musty women [*più stantive*]" (4.8). Each, as Gianbernardo also imploringly puts it to Carubina, to his or her own:

I'm the one who loves you, I'm the one who adores you, and if the heavens had blessed me with what they gave to this silly, unappreciative fool, there would never have been a spark of love in my heart, as there is not now, for anyone else but you. . . . Let it not be, I beg you, that such beauty has been conferred on you in vain by the heavens which, being generous and liberal towards you in grace and features, have yet been miserly in not uniting you to a man who can appreciate them. (5.11)

Finally, the debearding of Bonifacio raises issues about identity grounded in the male body that are peculiar to the sixteenth century in Italy, and these issues tell us much about the anxieties of men both individually and collectively in the late Renaissance. Social and cultural historians have taught us over the past few decades that intense daily interactions defined the life of Italian men in the Renaissance, precisely the kinds of daily interactions that had men chitchatting in the highly gendered, theatrical spaces of barbershops, where they found themselves potentially spilling the beans as they momentarily and incautiously let down their guard while they were getting fixed up professionally to face the day with the proper politia and a highly individualized, but still collectively accepted, look.[29] As such, if in America today it is possible to stay home, order in, furnish a household, and conduct financial and social transactions by Internet or phone, thus effectively making it possible to remain indoors all the time, the opposite was ostensibly the case for men in Renaissance Italy. Renaissance Italy was an agoraphobic's nightmare: a man constantly had to involve himself with people in open and closed public spaces. How he presented his individual face—as well as how his face was represented in art forms, with or without a beard—mattered immensely. In this regard, shaping the beard constituted one more way in which Italian men negotiated their status amid the theatricality and sociability of everyday Renaissance life, especially as men needed to guard against revealing some aspect of their personal lives in such free-flowing, easygoing, conversational places as the barbershop. In short, the beard, as in the case of the painter in Bruno's play, occasionally made the man.[30]

As a result, it becomes a matter of *honor* how a man individually held onto his identity through his beard, as Gianbernardo observes. Someone, he laments, has dared to abscond with *his* identity by wearing *his* particular, identifying beard, and perhaps that person has inadvertently ruined the painter's individual reputation in the process in a small, status-conscious Neapolitan community where everyone's business is to know someone else's business: "And what about *my* person [character/persona] and *my* beard and *my* cloak and perhaps *my* honor? [*E la* mia *persona e la* mia *barba e la* mia *biscappa e forse il* mio *onore*]"

(5.23). As he speaks these words, Gianbernardo self-consciously acts out a pre-defined role in a carefully orchestrated scheme that serves to befuddle only further the already confused and easily duped Bonifacio. So the painter's stated concern about his identity and honor is openly feigned for the enlightened and detached audience both within and outside the play. But Gianbernardo's lament nevertheless voices a real social and cultural concern about how a man individu-ally needed to care for his reputation in sixteenth-century Italy and make sure that it was not being bandied about town in the most conspicuous of ways (5.9). For the male members of the audience viewing this play (had it ever been put on the stage in Bruno's own time), a ruined reputation would have been no small joke, not just for extended family members at large but also for the indi-vidual male members in question themselves. Or rather, it was a joke that could have served well to release tensions within the play about matters that undoubt-edly would have concerned an audience observing the play, particularly, if not exclusively, the individual, sociable male members of that audience, whether or not they sported well-trimmed beards and stroked them self-consciously during the course of the performance to see if they were indeed still there and in their proper shape.

In this context, one reason it would be so difficult to pull off Bruno's *Cande-laio* successfully today and thereby enjoy the humor of this "comedia vera," as Scaramuré phrases it, is that we no longer collectively and individually share the social and cultural concerns that Bruno's drama exploits about a single, yet highly performative, part of the male body: the beard. To wear a beard today speaks little about virile majesty, imperial aims, the power to beget children, sexual, intellectual, testicular, and martial prowess, politia, complex dress codes, or, in Gianbernardo's terms, manly "honor," the ego capital that greased the wheels of social interactions and made life run, for better or for worse, in the exceedingly status-conscious courtly and urban environments of sixteenth-century Italy. And the theatricality of life foregrounded by Scaramuré in his observation about the beards as masks in the play—a theatricality rendered all the more evident with so many actors donning beards on the stage—is now lost on us today in twenty-first-century America and Europe as something that is meaningful, expressive, and tangible in precisely the same way. Today a beard undoubtedly marks men both collectively and individually. In the late 1960s and early 1970s (when I grew up in New York City), growing a beard was arguably seen as a transgressive gesture that fashionably aligned a person with the count-erculture, thereby cementing an intuited alliance with a generation bent on appearing "cool," or, at the very least, with a flower-happy, anticonformist, psychedelic, and hip generation that imagined it was getting "back to nature" by letting facial hair "all hang out," even ever-so-nakedly in a rock 'n' roll

musical on the popular Broadway stage. But today—with the Red Sox going completely hirsute in defiance of their rivals, the always clean-shaven
Yankees[31]—wearing a beard no longer stages the same anxieties that the Italian
elite had about the self-presentation of a sometimes highly vulnerable individual
and collective male identity in the close-knit social world of sixteenth-century
Italy, with all its pressing concerns for honor, secrecy, gossip, name recognition,
reputation, and competitive interpersonal relationships—in a world, to be sure,
where cross-dressing Venetian courtesans sometimes even appeared, either
seductively in their private quarters or furtively in open public squares, donning
disguises of bearded masks. Staging facial hair in Bruno's *Candelaio* thus means
dramatizing issues about manly matters, both literal and figural, that are virtually lost on us today as we concern ourselves with other sorts of anxieties culturally grounded in the theatrical and social function of the performative male
body.

~

Epilogue

"WHO'S THERE?" THE GUARD CRIES OUT AT THE BEGINNING OF *Hamlet*, unsure of what he is going to discover in the dark and the mist and the cold. And the answer that comes back if we ask that question of the Italian Renaissance—as if we were engaged in an elaborate academic "knock-knock" game—is that it all depends on how people, both men *and* women, are seen to have dealt with the multifarious constraints in which they were compelled to live their everyday lives. We can therefore talk, for instance, about how people in the Italian Renaissance felt collectively rooted to parishes, confraternities, charitable organizations, and local religious institutions. We can demonstrate how they negotiated extended family relationships and, as families, were both loosely and tightly connected to one another through the law, patriarchy, marriage, baptisms, dowries, funerals, honor, property, business ventures, and enduring bonds of lineage. We can reconstruct intricate patronage relationships, social networks, and neighborhood ties that bound people together. We can explore how people conveyed ambiguous messages in private and public settings to collectively preserve honor and save face among friends and neighbors, as well as how gossip served to forge communities and facilitate their smooth, everyday workings. We can think about how gender and habits of channeling sexual desires conditioned communal behavior in manifold ways. We can situate people in local cultures with their own binding mythologies. We can articulate how people experienced a group identity by belonging to guilds, workshops, academies, and specific professions. We can talk about how people configured through exemplarity a collectivity through their presumed identification or rivalry with others. We can identify how certain groups of people collectively, ceremoniously, "nationally," and sometimes playfully occupied certain civic spaces.[1] We can document how secular, religious, and "deviant" heretical rituals and belief systems bound people together and determined worldviews. We can explain how people were absorbed into and shaped by different economies of production and exchange, as well as how gift-giving practices and eating habits cemented loyalties, created obligations, and forged collective identities. We can examine class conflicts, accepted racial distinctions, and religious affiliations as shapers of group identities. We can think about local politics and the rise of court culture as cohesive forces shaping collectivities, along with, of course, the longstanding ideology of corporatism. We can track shifts in fashion that compelled people to conform to all manner of appearances and how propriety, etiquette, cleanliness, and politeness became increasingly codified and routinely conditioned communal behavior. We can speculate about how diseases, violence, warfare, soldiering, dueling, feuding, and famine bound people together through a shared experience and codes of behavior. We can embed people in broadly shared sensibilities, habits of fashioning and participating in collective memories, tastes, educational strategies, linguistic outlooks, intellectual communities, reading, viewing, and listening practices, letter-writing tactics, leisurely pastimes, and artistic traditions. And we can look at how people found themselves enacting a variety of somewhat ready-made cultural scripts and constraining roles, be it in the inquisitor's tribunal, the court, the home, the loggia, the church, the court, the chancery, the piazza, or, among so many other spaces, the anatomy theater and the barbershop.

There were, in sum, lots of ways in which people experienced the world as a collectivity and implicitly thought in the first person plural rather than the first person singular. But there still remains another important way of answering the question "Who's there?" as we turn to the Italian Renaissance. And the answer is that the multifarious constraints within which people operated within collectivities, both men and women, also enabled them to forge individual identities and address the world in a particular manner. Needless to say, not everyone possessed the means, ability, or opportunity to assert or perform his or her own individuality, stand out, make vigorous claims of inimitability, advocate strenuously for a unique signature verbal or visual style, behave as a scourge or maverick, or appear so worthy of rapt attention that he or she could be configured as a marvel. Nevertheless, as I have argued in this book, a number of men from a variety of walks of life with very different degrees of educational training and resources at their disposal did lay claim to the singularity of their own identity, as well as the identities of other men, whether it be a charlatan-like surgeon searching for secret medical knowledge as he traveled restlessly about the world or, somewhat at the other end of the social spectrum, an elite humanist describing how to exercise sprezzatura and gravitate elegantly toward centers of courtly power. And how they did so, and the very fact *that* they did so, is significant as we reflect on the Italian Renaissance. It certainly tells us from the vantage point of our own culture—a culture so thoroughly invested in the notion of the individual in both crass and life-enhancing ways—that we do not have to embrace wholeheartedly Burckhardt's assertion that "man became a spiritual individual [*geistiges Individuum*]" for the first time in Renaissance Italy (an assertion that strikes me as both misguided and untrue) to find some use value in the concept of the individual as we explore the nature of identities, not only of men but also, to be sure, of women in the remote and recent past.[2]

This book has accordingly been predicated on the idea that there is indeed substantial value in thinking about the individual in the Italian Renaissance. It has done so by looking at men from the period, particularly those of the sixteenth century, and by examining writings and visual works that in some significant measure dramatize or reflect upon how the individual and the collectivity are dialectically engaged as well as historically determined. In the process of attending to these and other issues (such as wonder, work, politia, self-fashioning, and masculinities) and in the process of using a variety of sources (from discourses about techne to works of imaginative literature, religious paintings, and popularizing books of secrets), this book has labored to come to terms with what made some men peculiarly and singularly "themselves." At the same time, by gradually narrowing down its focus from matters of broad to local concern (by moving, that is to say, from professionalism to mavericks to beards in its three separate parts) and by gradually shifting its attention from matters of primarily intellective to bodily and physical concern (by moving, that is to say, from issues about humanism and theories of specialized knowledge underpinning the arts to issues about smelling urine, constructing noses, anatomizing corpses, performing surgeries, cleaning clothes, having sex, and donning beards), this book has also sought to address from distinctly different vantage points the ways in which some men used the discursive and representational strategies available to them to articulate a notion of what constituted the individual in light of their identities as men within their culture or, to be sure, the identities of other men within that culture. It has studied neither the individual in order to examine exclusively large-scale cultural, intellectual, artistic, and social trends nor exclusively such trends to get at the individual. It has tried to do both, cognizant that this approach will not lend itself to a vast swath of Renaissance society, centered as this book has been, and I suspect other books of this nature would always be, on the writings and visual works of the elite and those aspiring to be part of it, primarily because those people have, for better or for worse, left behind the most extensive traces of themselves as part of the historical record.

But the value of the approach adopted in this book is that it ultimately brings us back from matters of broad, generalizing, and contextualizing concern to specific, concrete people within communities, to the things they made or did in the past, the ways they imaginatively represented themselves and others (both real *and* fictionalized "others," I should emphasize), and how they perceived, described, thought about, felt about, and fantasized about the world in which they lived and were constrained to operate. More to the point, adopting this approach allows us to try to better grasp what potentially made some people in Renaissance Italy indeed appear to be compelling "individuals," without simply resorting to envisioning them as the demystified, interpellated, artful products of their culture or as socially determined and structured constructs, much less as the forerunners to the supposedly free, untrammeled, self-governing individuals of modernity or, for that matter, the rampant nationalist individuals of the European nineteenth century whom Burckhardt in his historical pessimism seems to have loathed, as opposed to the dutiful, civic-minded, community-oriented, patrician Swiss burghers that he valued for entirely different, and indeed often personal, reasons.[3] For in the end, while writings or works of visual art—the sometimes remarkable "things" that make up material culture—have profoundly touched many people's lives both now and in the past, perhaps even transforming those lives in manifold ways, it is still primarily people, I'd wager, individual people embedded in and constrained by communities, who have touched specific people's lives the most, either by making those very things available in the first place or by directly or indirectly opening us up to them in their own peculiar way, thereby endowing them with meaning.[4] All of which is to say that a multifaceted, interdisciplinary, "polyphonic" history of the individual (as opposed to separate, isolated, biographic histories of specific individuals) has yet to be fully explored, and it deserves much more of our ongoing scholarly attention as a topic of lasting importance.

NOTES

∾

INTRODUCTION

1. Lodge 1984, 134.

2. Greenblatt 1980, 1986, 1988, 1990; Martin 1997, 2004. In all fairness, Martin's study, with which I feel a great affinity, is not at all the same as Greenblatt's. Martin is a religious, cultural, and social historian who draws on extensive archival research; Greenblatt is a literary and cultural scholar who draws on the work of historians but is ultimately a close reader of texts, informed as those eloquent readings are by a variety of critical theories. And Martin takes aim at Greenblatt throughout his book, calling Greenblatt's assumptions and historical methodology into question, while recognizing the importance of what Greenblatt has done and the value of his scholarship for historians generally. But, and this is the key issue for me, both Greenblatt and Martin, albeit in strikingly different ways, do away with the notion of the "individual" when talking about the period. Martin, who cogently prefers to talk about "selves" (porous selves, layered selves, a whole variety of selves), drives this point home quite personally at the very outset of his book when he writes about Veronese and his conflict with the Inquisition. At first glance, Martin observes, everything about Veronese's *Feast in the House of Levi* (originally designed as a "Last Supper") strikes him as the product of an individual, until he looks closely at the historical context and then—poof—the individual, designated as such, effectively disappears from consideration as the producer of his remarkable, alluring work, even as Martin investigates issues throughout related to the interior self. Or, as Martin puts it emphatically at one point as he turns away from the concept of the individual to talk instead about "selves," "identity was *not* about individuality but rather explicitly about *the problem of the relation of one's inner experience to one's experience in the world*" (2004, 15)—a point reiterated at the very end of the book: "notions of individuality and individualism were not . . . part of the basic vocabulary of the Renaissance" (131). By contrast, my aim is to restore that individual, designated as an "individual," back into our discussion, to keep the individual—Veronese, say—from disappearing from our purview as we become sensitized to all the contextualizing historical constraints within which a particular person—again Veronese, say—operated. Needless to say, Burckhardt's seminal, but much contested, discussion of "individualism"—or, more precisely, the "individual"—appears in the second chapter of his landmark *The Civilization of the Renaissance in Italy*.

3. I am thinking, for instance, of Weissman 1989 and Wojciehowski 2011. The number of studies that have embraced the notion that the self is a cultural construct in one form or another in the Italian Renaissance, and the European Renaissance generally, is by now legion. I find myself in much sympathy with Davis 1986 and Burke 1997.

4. On Burckhardt's profound pessimism and disenchantment with the notion of the "individual" in his own time, which he roots back in the Italian Renaissance (and to a degree even ancient Greece, for that matter), see Gossman 1994 and 2000, as well as Murray's

introduction to the English translation of Burckhardt 1998, xi–xliv and in the same volume Burckhardt's lectures. In his *Civilization of the Renaissance in Italy*, Burckhardt, Gossman has taught us, envisions the "individual" as something profoundly ironic, so that when he called the Renaissance Italian in his seminal essay the firstborn of modernity, he meant it as more of a gross insult—something that has often been lost on scholars when they invoke Burckhardt or even call themselves, or are called in a pejorative fashion, Burckhardtian.

5. Consider, for instance, Cox 2008, 2011; Rosenthal 1992; Robin 2007; Benson 1992; Shemek 1998, forthcoming; Ross 2009; and Weaver 2002. This is, to be sure, only a partial list of works dedicated to women in Renaissance Italy, a field that has perhaps seen the greatest expansion in the past few decades. For scholars interested in women writers in the field of literary studies primarily, one should consult in particular the Other Voices series, published first by the University of Chicago Press and now by the University of Toronto Press.

6. *Vocabolario degli Accademici della Crusca*, http://www.lessicografia.it/index.jsp. "INDIVIDUO. *Definiz:* sust. Termine dialettico, e val cosa particolare, compresa sotto la spezie, e lo dicono in Lat. *individuum. Esempio:* Com. Inf. *c. 24.* Aggiugnere più individui in uno individuo." Williams 1983, 162, but see more generally his synthetic discussion, pp. 161–65.

7. *Vocabolario degli Accademici della Crusca*, http://www.lessicografia.it/index.jsp. "INDIVIDUO. *Definiz:* Sust. Cosa particolare, compresa sotto la spezie. Lat. **individuum. Esempio:* Com. Inf. *24.* Aggiugnere più individui in uno individuo. Varch. Ercol. *36.* Tutto quello, che conviene per natura a uno individuo ec. non convien egli anche di necessità a tutti gli altri individui di quella medesima spezie? E Varch. Ercol. *307.* Gl'individui sono quei particolari, ne' quali si divide le spezie, come donna Berta, e ser Martino. Fir. Rag. *156.* Dubitando, che per qualche accidente e' non nascesse alcuna differenza tra questi due individui. Red. Ins. *70.* Non mi da fastidio, che il volgo creda, e molti autori lo abbiano scritto, che veruno animale mangia gl'individui della propria spezie, imperciocchè ec."

8. For a concise synthesis of the notion of "individualism" as it applies to the historiography of the Italian Renaissance, see Connell 2002, 1–12 and esp. Martin 2004, 1–20, as well as Caferro 2011, 31–60, while Thomas 2009, esp. 37–43 (his entire book is really germane here, particularly the introduction and entire first chapter), provides an excellent synthesis for early modern England, roughly 1600–1800. There is still much to glean from Wittkower 1961. For a broad view of "individualism," along with "selfhood," see Lukes 1977; Taylor 1989; Seigel 2005; Guerevitch 1995; Renaut 1997; and Coleman 1996; but see also Weintraub 1978. For the value of the concept of the individual prior to the Renaissance and questions related to it, see in particular Bynum 1980; Morris 1987; and Ullmann 1966. For the evolution of the term "individualism," as opposed to "individual" or "individuality," see Moulin 1955. See as well Williams 1983, 161–63. For thoughts on the term and concept of the "individual" in the English Renaissance and after, as well as an argument that the individual did not exist in any form or manner when it comes to thinking about Shakespeare, see Stallybrass 1992, which puts it succinctly at one point: "Let me put my argument as crudely and controversially as possible: in what we now call 'Shakespeare,' no individual author, no individual word, no individual, in the modern sense. Just the signifier, 'individuall,' at a particular moment where it looks so impossible to us that it has been consistently emended" (609). Stallybrass's position is by no means provocative anymore and has now instead become the accepted view. Again, for an understanding of how we have misunderstood Burckhardt's notion of the individual and invoke his name to describe a phenomenon that he himself would have not recognized, see Gossman's studies mentioned in note 4. For a radical questioning of all these

terms and concepts, along with those related to the "self" and "individual," as they apply to the premodern period, see Reiss 2003.

9. There are now numerous scholarly studies on masculinity. My thoughts for the Italian Renaissance are particularly indebted to Rocke 1996; Finucci 2003; Simons 1994, 1997, 2008, 2009, and especially 2011; Springer 2010; Quondam 2003; Milligan and Tylus, 2010; Ruggiero 2006, 2007; and Milligan 2006, 2007a, 2007b. There is much to glean on the topic from scholarship on dueling; for a broad view, see Hughes 2007, but more specifically for the Italian Renaissance, see Weinstein 2000, along with Erspamer 1982 and Angelozzi 1998. For England, see Low 2003. For the European Middle Ages broadly, see Karras 2003. For aspects of competitive male showmanship and communal gamesmanship in the context of a large, open, public arena, see, for instance, Davis 1994.

10. On Cortesi, see his *Renaissance Cardinal's Ideal Palace* (1980).

11. This is most clearly enunciated at the opening of chapter 14, dedicated to "Quod principem deceat circa militiam": "Debbe adunque uno principe non avere altro obietto né altro pensiero, né prendere cosa alcuna per sua arte, fuora della guerra e ordini e disciplina di essa; perché quella è sola arte che si espetta a chi comanda" (Machiavelli 1971, 278).

12. Greenblatt 1980, 256.

13. On this sculpture generally, see Butterfield 1997, 158–83, 232–36; for the rather exaggerated and reiterated motif of testicles and their significance, see Simons 2011, 107–11.

14. Portraiture in the Renaissance is an immense topic among art historians, beginning with the foundational study of Pope-Hennessy 1966. In thinking about these matters generally, I have benefited most from Burke 1987, 150–67; Burke 1995a; Jacobs 2005; Fortini Brown 2000; Campbell 1990; Cranston, 2000; Levy 2006; Simons 1995; and Woods-Marsden 1987, 1998.

15. The phrase is Leonardo's, of course, on which see Pope-Hennessy 1966, 101–54.

CHAPTER 1

1. What was associated with the terms "productive" and "practical" arts changed significantly over time. My definitions in my discussion are therefore not meant to fit uniformly every classification from antiquity to the Renaissance. They serve heuristically to give shape to and help us make some organizational sense of a large body of material in a manner that for the most part globally reflects categories of thought active in the periods in question.

2. There is an extensive bibliography on the Greek concept of techne (and by extension the Roman concept of ars, which is closely aligned with its Greek ancestor), much of it scattered in various accounts of other issues, such as in the history of work. I have benefited from Vernant 1983, 237–301; Cambiano 1991; Dunne 1993; Cuomo 2007, 7–40; Ferrari and Vegetti 1983; Parente 1966; Lloyd 1991; Marrou 1956, 1969; Löbl 1997; Parry 2008; Nussbaum 1986, 94–96; Roochnik 1994, 1996; Schadewaldt 1979; Pleket 1973; Allen 1994; Ierodiakonou 1995; Boudon-Millot 2005; Solmsen 1963; Traina 1994; Atwill 1998; Angier 2010; Von Staden 2007; Schiefsky 2007; Woodruff 1990; and Detienne and Vernant 1978. For the medieval period, see Weisheipl 1965; Sternagel 1966; Whitney 1990; Chenu 1968, 38–46; Alessio 1965; Van Den Hoven 1996; and Ovitt 1983, 1986a, 1986b, 1987. For excellent broad overviews that I am especially indebted to, and that carry the concept up through the Middle Ages and/or Renaissance while discussing notions of work, see Long 2001; Rossi 1970; Whitney 1990; and Van Den Hoven 1996. Lis and Soly (2012) place the concepts of techne and ars periodically within the context of the history of work. See also White 1969 and, of course, the classic Kristeller 1951 and 1952, reprinted in 1965, 163–227, which is focused, however, on tracing the emergence of the concept of the "fine arts." For an elaboration of Kristeller in the context of

cultural history, broadening the time span under consideration to embrace a contemporary understanding of the fine arts within an overall "system of art," see Shiner 2001.

3. House building was probably the original craft associated with techne, but the concept of techne quickly evolved well beyond the productive arts to the practical ones, expanding wildly. Plato's writings, as is well known, are riddled with references to technai as models, and not just with respect to philosophical knowledge. On Plato's use of technai in the context of statecraft, see, for instance, Bambrough 1956. Banausic crafts constitute a lower order of technai and were uniformly regarded as base, not just in Plato but also in Greek thought generally.

4. In referring to such activities as military strategy, navigation, or medicine, all of which do not produce anything material or durable but are activities of doing, not making, Dunne (1993, 254) significantly observes: "If these cases diverge significantly from the standard paradigm of fabrication, . . . this fact does not seem to have impressed Aristotle. We do not find in his writing any explicit differentiation of them from the technai such as building that are exercised in simple reification." See, for instance, the locus classicus, *NE* 6.4. See as well *Meta.* 2.1.

5. See Roochnik 1996, 19 on tracing the Indo-European root of techne from "tek," meaning to put together parts of a building and, more generally, on tracing how the term evolved in Greek thought, from Homer on.

6. Roochnik 1996, 52 nicely evokes Stanley Fish's scholarship in talking about "rules of thumb" in relation to ancient Greek notions of techne.

7. I adapt my phrase from Roochnik 1996, 26.

8. See Vegetti 2010 on medicine, for instance, in antiquity, with the contrast formulated by Crisciani (2010) for the Middle Ages. For more of a synthesis about guilds in antiquity, see Long 2001, 75–78. For *collegia* in ancient Rome as occupational associations that functioned as "status groups," see, in the context of the history of work, Lis and Soly 2012, 74–75 and passim. For a long view of how schools fit into the development of educational programs in antiquity, beginning with the sophists as the first professionals teaching a techne, and how they were not geared to prepare students for a techne, see the classic study Marrou 1956, esp. 262–66, 303–4, 306, and passim.

9. My reference to Prometheus is not arbitrary but refers to a famous passage in Aeschylus, *Prometheus Bound*, 463–522 (see, for instance, Aeschylus 1998, 173–74), in which Prometheus claims that humans received all their technai from him.

10. Cuomo 2007, 37, 39.

11. Lis and Soly (2012), for instance, draw on Cuomo's argument a number of times as they argue for the polyphonic nature of the value of work in the classical period.

12. Stewart 2008, 10–38, esp. 19–20; Burford 1972.

13. Xenophon 1965, *Oeconomicus* 4.2–3, 6.5–8. On Xenophon's changing attitude toward work, and in particular toward wholesalers and shipowners involved in large-scale commerce, see Lis and Soly 2012, 39–40, but especially Johnstone 1994, on how aristocratic "toil" (hunting, agriculture, and the like) borne out of leisure, in contrast to the laborer's "work" borne out of necessity, produced—in Xenophon's scheme of things—not a product per se (food, say) but the lifestyle of being an aristocrat: the distinction of a "naturalized" habit of being in the world that legitimated elite power, virtue, and rule in the face of democratic claims. See also the comments of Pomeroy in Xenophon 1994, 235–37.

14. Cicero 1938, 1.150–51.

15. Cicero 1960, 1.4 (as well as Valerius Maximus 2000, 9.14.6), contrasted with Pliny 1938–63, 36.7. Pliny becomes the source for Castiglione and others in the Italian Renaissance

who use Fabius as an example to talk about the honor associated with the art of painting in antiquity, on which see McHam 2013, 106, 264, 270, 288, 292, 302–3.

16. Cicero 1942, 1.22.102 and passim and Quintilian 1922, 2.17–21 discuss if "rhetoric is an art." Cicero does not in fact use the phrase "vir bonus dicendi peritus" (it appears instead in Quintilian), but the concept is fully consonant with Cicero's conception of the orator.

17. The "liberal arts" took some time to crystallize into the medieval quadrivium and trivium, but they did retain much of the same general form in the previous periods of early and late classical antiquity. See, for instance, Stahl and Johnson 1971, 90–98, along with Marrou 1938, 211–35; Marrou 1956, passim; and Marrou 1969.

18. Plutarch 1961, 5.

19. Lis and Soly 2012, 51, but passim: the entire book, from beginning to end, explores the multiple voices articulating the positive and negative valorizations of work, grounding those voices often enough in a social context; the key, the authors observe, is that there was no monovocal approach to the notion of work itself: it all depends on who is voicing the concern, when, and why. Farr (2000) makes much the same observation in the first chapter, "The Meaning of Work: Ideology and Organization" (10–44), most emphatically from the very opening sentence: "From the Middle Ages to the industrial age men (and it was exclusively educated men who wrote about this) have had an ambivalent, even sometimes paradoxical, attitude toward work" (10)—an ambivalence that finds expression well into the Enlightenment (19). See also the earlier study of Geoghegan (1945). D'Arms 1981, 1–47, 149–71 concentrates on conflicting attitudes about commerce on the part of the Roman elite.

20. For the calculated placement and function of Trajan's column within the urban space of Rome, see Davies 2000.

21. Van Den Hoven 1996, 242. See also Lis and Soly 2012 in the context of the history of work.

22. Pleket 1973, 304.

23. Petersen 2003 examines the tomb of Eurysaces, the wealthy baker, who may or may not have been freeborn or freed; how Eurysaces champions himself, his profession, and his work with great pride in his tomb; and how we need to be careful not to view his tomb negatively through the cognitive filter of elitist perceptions of such workers and freedmen (what Petersen refers to, in light of Petronius's *Satyricon*, as the distorting "Trimalchio vision"). Joshel 1992 is also germane here.

24. It is nevertheless clear that many craftsmen valued their own work in antiquity, boasted about their accomplishments, and took pride in them. For a number of the testimonies of craftsmen taking pride in their work, particularly on gravestones and in epigraphs, but also on the very objects they produced as artisans, see Burford 1972, 207–10; Lis and Soly 2012, 47–51, 69–71, 80–84, and passim; Pleket 1973, 305–6; Joshel 1992; MacCormack 2001, 222–23; De Robertis 1979, 26–28 and passim; Clarke 2003, 118–21; and Geoghegan 1945, 24–27, 51–58. On Pliny's esteem of certain artists, and his view that the Greeks valued painting in some instances as a liberal art, see the concise remarks in McHam 2013, 39–52 and passim.

25. Lis and Soly 2012, 16–18, 550–51, 555–56 and Van Den Hoven 1996, 28–38 and passim are good on this issue, with respect to "ponos."

26. Whitney 1990, 66.

27. Ibid., 8. Whitney finds felicitous resonance in studies by some of the historians of work, such as Lis and Soly (2012).

28. Van Den Hoven 1996.

29. Augustine 1950, 22.24, on which see Whitney 1990, 52–55. More generally, on Augustine and work, see MacCormick 2001 and Arbesmann 1973, as well as Augustine 1952.

30. See Hugh of St. Victor 1991.

31. Ranft (2006) is not concerned with exploring the classifications of the arts in the period, but her observations are still germane.

32. See the challenges to this argument in Ovitt 1986b, 1987. Van Den Hoven 1996 argues strenuously for the continuity of thought regarding the value of the arts from the classical to the medieval periods, while Whitney 1990 argues for significant change. Ovitt provides the most balanced treatment. For a synthetic overview of the issue in the context of the history of work, tracing rapidly the positions of Weber and Benz and White to Ovitt, Le Goff, and Van Den Hoven, see Ehmer and Lis 2009, 10–15.

33. Le Goff 1980, 58–70, 107–21.

34. Whitney 1990, 147.

35. I draw the phrase from Ranft (2006), who is not invested in exploring the hierarchies of the arts but has much to say about the changing views about work among the religious, particularly from the eleventh to the fourteenth century. See, more broadly, Lis and Soly 2012.

36. Ovitt (1983, 1986a, 1986b, 1987) cogently observes that the practice of mapping one hierarchy onto another did not take place because thinkers in the period were responding to particular social changes. Rather, it occurred because thinkers inescapably processed the arts through a "metaphysical" or "salvationary" approach to knowledge, which always privileged the spirit over the body. For the purposes of this chapter, however, the issue is not whether social structures or metaphysics determined the hierarchies of the arts within the various classifications of the sciences in the Middle Ages. The fundamental issue is that the long-standing hierarchies within the sciences did indeed map themselves onto established social hierarchies, even if the latter did not determine the former.

37. Lis and Soly 2012, 138–39, for instance.

38. On Vitruvius and Renaissance commentaries, see especially Long 2001, 222–34; Long 2011, 62–93; and Long 1985. Among other relevant commentaries, see Drake and Rose 1971 on the pseudo-Aristotelian *Questions of Mechanics*, which was primarily a matter of Renaissance concern. I have not yet had a chance to examine in any detail medieval and Renaissance commentaries on Aristotle's *Ethics*, an essential text about ethics in the university system (on which see Lines 2002) and a locus classicus historically, along with Aristotle's *Metaphysics*, for notions about "techne."

39. Ovitt (1987, 43), who is quick to argue for technological progress in the Middle Ages, acknowledges that when it comes to the productive arts, "few craftsmen wrote anything at all" and that "most craftsmen were silent in the Middle Ages." Theophilus is an exception to the rule, and a comparison between his text and Renaissance discourses by practitioners is revealing about the marked differences. See Theophilus 1961; his knowledge about actual practice from experience appears only in the third book. On Theophilus, see Dodwel's introduction to *De diversis artibus* and Van Engen 1980. See also *The Trotula* 2001 and *Mappae clavicula* 1974. As Long (1997, 1–2) observes in talking about manuscript production on the productive arts in the fifteenth century, although she is not talking only of author practitioners, "there is simply no precedent for the great number and variety of such codices that appeared from the early years of the fifteenth century until its end." For the importance still of theory in the practice of the arts in the Middle Ages, see Ackerman 1949. With regard to the visual arts in the classical period, only Vitruvius's influential treatise in the Renaissance survives. Pliny 1938–63, 34.55, 34.65, 35.79, 35.76, and 36.39 has Polyclitus, Lysippus, Apelles, Euphranor, and Pasiteles writing about their arts—writings that are lost not only now but also back in the Renaissance, as Alberti was all too aware in his *De pictura* (see Alberti 1972, 2.26), along with Ghiberti in his *Commentarii* (see Ghiberti 1998, 1.9.2, 1.2.9) and Cennini in his *Libro dell'arte*. See McHam 2013, 84, 102, 110, 113, 376nn141, 142, but especially 308, where

she summarily observes that the realization on the part of Italian practitioners of the visual arts that artists in antiquity, as described by Pliny, "wrote treatises about art" helped "spur the outbreak of theoretical writings by artist-theorists in the sixteenth century."

40. Long 2001.

41. Long (2001) limits her range to the productive arts, those that she terms discourses of techne as opposed those of praxis.

42. On Biringuccio, I am indebted to Long 2001, 177–81; Long 1991; and Bernardoni 2011. I cite from Biringuccio 1959 and have consulted the original in Biringuccio 1540. For his life, see Tucci 1968, 625–31.

43. Abbott 1988.

44. For an application of Abbott's theories to Renaissance culture and professional experience, see Biow 2002. On Fioravanti, see Chapter 3.

45. On the changing value of curiosity in the period, from being a vice to becoming a virtue, see Daston and Park 1998; Findlen 1994; and Pomian 1990, 45–64.

46. See Du Cange 1954, 5.424, defined in the first lemma as "Mestier, ars," and the *OED* (under the lemma "mystery") for definitions of *misterium*.

47. Eamon 1994 in its entirety is germane here.

48. I place "market" in quotes only to indicate with some caution that in some areas there were and were not markets, as we understand the concept today.

49. See Chapter 3, note 11.

50. Fundamental here is the seminal work of Goldthwaite (1993). See as well adaptations of his position in Jardine 1996; Findlen 1998; Fortini Brown 2004; Welch 2005; and Thornton 1997, along with the thoughts in Campbell 2004, 29–57 and, for a later period, Ago 2013. The seminal sociological study on "distinction" as it is here characterized is, of course, Bourdieu 1984.

51. See, for instance, Kemp 1981, 1989, and 2006 and, more generally, Kemp 1990, ch. 1 for the place of such writings in the context of "the science of art." For his writings in translation, see Leonardo da Vinci 1970; see also Kemp and Barone 2009. For an overview of the professionalization of the painter in the Renaissance and the role of the court, see Kempers 1987, 219–309. For thoughts on the novel investment in theory (in this case imitative theory) as it pertains to painting in Cennini's *Libro dell'arte*, see Bolland 1996, and for Pliny's role, see McHam 2013, 84–87. McHam also notes that Cennini was likely inspired by the model of Apelles, whom Pliny describes as not only the master artist but also an author of writings about his art: "In Cennini's day, no trace of Apelles' writings or paintings survived, so not only could Cennini and his advisors anticipate that his book would be the first treatise explaining the style and techniques of 'modern' painting that had emerged in Italy (his term), but he may have thought it would be the first extant artistic treatise in the West" (84).

52. Rossi 1970, 32–33, 22. These observations should be tempered somewhat by the insights in Ackerman 1949.

53. Ames-Lewis 2000, 17–60 characterizes that evolution.

54. Long 2001, 249.

55. Amelang 1998. Much has been written on ego documents and life writing in the Italian Renaissance (and the Renaissance generally). I have benefited from Mayer and Woolf 1995; Bedford, Davis, and Kelly 2006; Guglielminetti 1977; McLaughlin 2002; Burke 1998; and Frazier 2013.

56. On Castiglione, I have benefited from Rebhorn 1978; Berger 2000; Cartwright 1908; Cian 1951; Woodhouse 1978; Burke 1995b; especially Saccone 1978, 1983, 1987; Menut 1943; Patrizi 1984; Ryan 1972; Javitch 1978; Whigham 1984; Quondam 2000, 2007a; Lipking 1966; Hale 1983; Finucci 1992, 1997; and Guidi 1973. On Cellini, I have found most useful Gallucci

2001, 2003; Rossi 1994, 1998, 2004; Borsellino 1979; Gardner 1997; Bonino 1979; Cervigni 1979; Tylus 1993, 2004; Pope-Hennessy 1985; Lucas 1989; Galetta 1995; Cole 2002; Goldberg 1974; Zatti 2013; Coates 2000; and Guglielminetti 1977, 292–383. On polygraphs, the major studies are Aquilecchia 1980; Filippo Bareggi 1988; Bragantini 1996; and Grendler 1969. I have discussed both Cellini and the polygraphs in ways that relate to my thoughts in this chapter in Biow 2010, 133–56, and Castiglione in Biow 2010, 35–59 and Biow 2002, 6–12.

57. In the classical period some remarkable artists could be admired, as in Pliny the Elder's discussion of Zeuxis, but, it is important to stress, we do not have extensive writings by those practitioners that set themselves up as figures worthy of such admiration.

58. On Vasari, see in general Rubin 1995; I have also found of value Satkowski 1993; Pozzi and Mattioda 2006; Clifton 1996; Stack 2000; and Pilliod 1998 and 2001. I refer to the 1568 edition throughout, unless otherwise indicated, and cite from Vasari 1991 with translations, modified on occasion, drawn from Vasari 1996; cited by page numbers in the text.

59. Lis and Soly 2012, 51.

60. Consider, for instance, Augustine 1984, 19 and *Saint Benedict's Rule for Monasteries* 1948, 67–70.

61. I have benefited here from Mondolfo and Duncan 1954; Balme 1984; Joshel 1992; Petersen 2003; Van Den Hoven 1996; Geoghegan 1945; Burford 1972; Whitney 1990; Ovitt 1983, 1986a, 1986b, 1987; Le Goff 1980; White 1962, 1963, 1968, 1978; Holdsworth 1973; Ranft 2006; Farr 2000; Welles 1967; and Lis and Soly 2012. On sweat as a divine offering, see Newman 2012. For a broad overview, see Applebaum 1992 and, of course, Lis and Soly 2012.

62. Farr 2000, 11–12.

63. Ovitt 1986b, 14, which is, of course, not what either hermetic or cenobitic life called for, even as it promoted work. For changing attitudes toward work in early modern England, which bears some affinities with this discussion, in which work is seen in many instances no longer as a curse but as a source of fulfillment, see Thomas 2009, 78–109. For Luther, as for Calvin, however, as for men religious generally in the period, "work had no intrinsic value and consequently must never become an objective in its own right" (Lis and Soly 2012, 151).

64. The reference is to Lis and Soly 2012. For a concise synthesis of work in relation to guilds, corporatism, and the political and social order in medieval and early modern Europe, see Farr 2000, 10–44.

65. Lis and Soly 2012, 550.

66. On a somewhat related note, the humanist Giannozzo Manetti, although he is not a practitioner writing about his art, builds his treatise on human dignity (1452–1453) on the notion that understanding and contemplation are not enough: people have to do, make, create things. This was a fairly current notion in the Italian Renaissance that Cellini is appropriately engaging.

67. Cellini 1985, 2.92. On the calculated role of spectatorship with regard to the *Perseus*, which transforms into stone through its gorgonizing gaze (in the sense of paralyzed astonishment) the viewers and the surrounding sculptures with which it playfully vies, see Shearman 1992, 48–58. The best study on the *Perseus* remains Cole 2002.

68. This aspect of Fioravanti comes through even in the early *Compendio di tutta la cirugia*.

69. See Fioravanti 1573, 89r–v; Fioravanti 1582b, 2r; and Fioravanti 1582c, b3r, 137v.

70. I investigated a number of these issues in Biow 2010.

71. The classic study on these sorts of artists, adopting a long view, is Wittkower and Wittkower 1963. Another delightful example, far more famous than that of Piero di Cosimo, has to do with "Maso" (short for Tommaso). He was so sloppy that people started calling him Masaccio (bad/dirty Tom). See also what Antonio Manetti says of the young Brunelleschi

and Donatello working in Rome somewhat like two "Bohemians" in Baldassarri and Saiber 2000, 198.

72. I owe this insight to a review of *In Your Face* by Nussdorfer (2011, 677).

73. Long 2001, 15, 211, 234, 243, 246.

74. The notion of the "period eye" is borrowed, of course, from Baxandall 1972.

75. For a good overview of major distinctions in the visual arts during the period, see Summers 1981 and Roskill 1968. On "disegno" in light of Foucault's notion of discursive practices, with apt references to Aristotelian notions of "techne," see Barzman 2000, 143–80; for an understanding of disegno in light of concepts related to techne, see Williams 1997.

76. My thoughts about these two narrative structures explicated in the following few paragraphs on Vasari, as well my understanding of the dialectic at play in Vasari's *Le vite*, are very much indebted to the excellent study by Ruffini (2011), whose splendid argument I here largely rehearse. On Vasari in general, see note 58.

77. Much has been written on Michelangelo's terribilità, but see the synthetic observations of Summers (1981, 234–41).

78. On the relationship between the Accademia and state formation, see Barzman 2000.

79. We should bear in mind, of course, that the nature of authorship in *Le vite* is, some scholars have argued, problematic, even if the book bears Vasari's name. Ruffini 2011 examines what was and was not written by Vasari and how many academicians were involved in the production of *Le vite*. What emerges from Ruffini's analysis, which draws on the scholarship of Hope 2005, is effectively this: *Le vite* not only talks about but also *enacts*, in the way in which it was both conceived and written, the tension between an individualistic and corporate notion of artistic production. Strikingly, *Le vite* is a book that is and is not Vasari's. Put differently, it is a book that boldly claims Vasari as the author on the title page and seems to be imbued with his presence throughout, but in reality, Ruffini argues, it is very much the collaborative handiwork of a host of thinkers and writers and nitpicking editors with whom Vasari had close associations. In this way, the tensions Ruffini finds conceptually at the heart of "Vasari's" *Le vite* (between heroic individualism, say, and group identities fashioned in terms of professionalization through institutional formation) are formally developed within the book that "Vasari," as the putative sole author, writes. Some related issues are traced in Bolland 2006. For resistance to Hope's position, see, for instance, Scapecchi 2011.

80. First published in 1568, accessible in Cellini 1980, and with serviceable English translation, Cellini 1967, cited by page number in my text.

81. Alberti 1966, with the English translation in Alberti 1986; Filarete 1972, with the English translation in Filarete 1965; Martini 1967; and Palladio 1980, with the English translation in Palladio 1997.

82. Cockle 1957; D'Ayala 1854.

83. Cennini 1971, with the English translation in Cennini 1933; Lomazzo 1974. On Piero della Francesca's *De prospectiva pingendi* as plausibly an instructive manual for an apprentice, see Field 1993, 82–83, 93. Ghiberti 1998 (English version 1948–67) is important for articulating the status of the artist, but not how to be one.

84. See Fioravanti 1561, 1582c; Nati 1588; Capaccio 1599; Ingegneri 1594; Guarini 1594; Zucchi 1600; Costo 1602; and Marzari 1602. The list of secretarial treatises goes on to include later ones, such as Persico 1620; Gramigna 1620; and Nardi 1711. See as well, for the others listed, Barbaro 1969; Maggi 1566; and Messisbugo 1549, 1564.

85. Machiavelli, *L'arte della Guerra* (the only work of his printed in his lifetime, in 1521), which can be accessed in Machiavelli 1971 and has been translated as *Art of War* (2003); Alberti 1972, with the English translation as Alberti 2011; and Tasso 1587, which can be accessed in Tasso 1875, 2.255–77.

86. Sansovino 1564, which was the first version of this treatise and can be accessed in Sansovino 1942; Cortesi 1510, parts of which have been translated and can be accessed in Cortesi 1980.

87. Zinano 1625.

88. This is key to the seminal argument in Long 2001, which I seek to qualify somewhat in the following section by examining how some of these discourses about arts by practitioners purport to be open but in truth are deeply secretive, and teasingly so, about what it takes to be a true master in a certain, specified art.

89. Erasmus is here drawing on a commonplace of humanist literature, which can be found, say, in Manetti's and Pico's orations on human dignity, both of which maintain that it is not enough to be born human: one must strive throughout to really achieve human dignity in the fullest sense by begetting oneself through contemplation and action. Greene 1968 and Greenblatt 1980 offer strikingly differing takes on this notion, of course, but the seminal study in English on the humanist investment in the "dignity of man" remains Trinkaus 1970.

90. I have used throughout the edition of *Il cortegiano* edited by Cian (1929) and the Singleton translation, Castiglione 1959, cited by page number.

91. "Noi in questi libri non seguiremo un certo ordine o regula di precetti distinti, ché 'l più delle volte nell'insegnar qualsivoglia cosa si sòle" (1.1). In this context, he has in mind Cicero's *De oratore* 1.6.22–23. But, we need to emphasize, he does provide rules—"alcune regole universali" (2.7)—throughout, even if this is not a conventional manual. And he expects those rules to be practiced.

92. Monk 1944.

93. On the topic of the "open secret," see the cogent observations in Miller 1988, 205–7.

94. Castiglione 1769, 1:193. On this, see Saccone 1978, 5–7 and Biow 2002, 6–12. See also Woodhouse 1978, 70, 189 on the "new professionalism" of the *Cortegiano*.

95. Farr 2000, 20. That said, when it comes to the visual arts, I am not aware of any examples of the "masterpiece" system in use by Italian Renaissance guilds, or by any other kind of training function. When the Accademia del Disegno is founded we get systematic pedagogy, but it is not connected with the guilds. It is an outgrowth of the artists' confraternity of St. Luke. Still, guilds oversaw the production of goods, and they certainly had a protectionist function, along with a social, political, and cultural one. In sum, in the visual arts, one had to belong to the guild (pay dues) to have the right to run one's own workshop. And paying dues entitled one to the various protections and benefits afforded by the guild. So when an artist does not appear on the guild rolls, it suggests the likelihood that he did not have an independent workshop, which is where the training in an art really took place.

96. On workshops, with reference to painters as a case study, and the role of apprentices, see Thomas 1995, esp. ch. 1, and 2006.

97. The relevant passage at 1.26 reads as follows: "Chi adunque vorrà esser bon discipulo, oltre al far le cose bene, sempre ha da metter ogni diligenzia per assimigliarsi al maestro e, se possibil fosse, transformarsi in lui. E quando già si sente aver fatto profitto, giova molto veder diversi omini di tal professione e, governandosi con quel bon giudicio che sempre gli ha da esser guida, andar scegliendo or da un or da un altro varie cose. E come la pecchia ne' verdi prati sempre tra l'erbe va carpendo i fiori, cosí il nostro cortegiano averà da rubare questa grazia da que' che a lui parerà che la tenghino e da ciascun quella parte che piú sarà laudevole."

98. See, for instance, the chapters on Petrarca in the seminal study by Greene (1982).

99. Castiglione reminds us in a number of places (including implicitly in the dialogic structure of the book) that courtiers must be prepared to converse on a daily basis on an

"infinity of topics" at the drop of a hat. See, for instance, 2.7, when he speaks of "conversar cottidiano."

100. This is not to say, of course, that poets did not engage in such a shame culture or ridicule and discredit one another. It is only to say that the shaming did not take place in a public forum when the activity associated with the art actually took place. On gossip in the Italian Renaissance, see Horodowich 2005, 2008.

101. On the bee's work as a paradigm for imitative practices, see, for Petrarca, for instance, Bosco 1961 and more generally Greene 1982, as well as Pigman 1980.

102. Dugan 2005, 75; Dugan also refers to it as "transgressive" and "revolutionary" on pp. 75–171.

103. On the *Rhetorica ad Herennium* in Renaissance Italy, see Ward 1978, 31–41; and Ward 1983, 1995. For its application to a reading of Machiavelli, see Cox 1997. On the *Ad Herennium* in Renaissance education, see Grendler 1989, 115–16, 212–14. On its widespread diffusion, making it, along with *De inventione* with which it was often paired, one of the most available and printed classical treatises of rhetoric, compared with the *De oratore*, for instance, see Mack 2011, 13–32.

104. Even if Castiglione is interested in how certain abilities are fashioned through work, he is supremely conscious, as the ancients were, that people have what he would call a natural aptitude, as when he speaks of someone having a "natural disposizione" (1.25) to do something, or a particular "ingegno" (talent) or a "native judgment." And yet a comparison with Cicero's *De oratore* is once more revealing about respective strategies, for Cicero, it strikes me, is far more outspoken than Castiglione in his book about the need that someone possess a certain natural talent—ingenium—for that person to succeed in the art in question. Put differently, Cicero in large measure *openly* mystifies what it takes to succeed, and in the process he provides us with a plethora of elaborate and thoroughly examined rules, whereas Castiglione in the main *covertly* mystifies what it takes to succeed, and in the process he fails to provide us with a plethora of rules.

105. On how-to books generally, see Bell 1999.

106. On male sensibilities in *Il cortegiano*, see, for instance, Finucci 1997, and for a discussion of the role of arms versus letters, Najemy 2006.

107. For this reading of Cicero, I am indebted to Connolly 2009, 154, 160, 213; Dugan 2005, 80–81; and Narducci 1992, 114–23.

108. For a standard modern long view of the defense of rhetoric, see Vickers 1988. Needless to say, the number of defenses of rhetoric is too vast to even begin to list them.

109. This is not to say, to be sure, that Cicero was not redefining the nature of the orator at all. It is only to say that the nature of that redefinition was not so wholesale as Castiglione's redefinition of the courtier, who transforms the courtier from one so thoroughly versed in arms as his principal profession to one much more versed in giving advice and the like. On Cicero's redefinition of the orator and how it helped reshape Renaissance humanism by uniting "wisdom" and "eloquence," and thus philosophy and rhetoric, see the classic study of Seigel (1968).

110. On the rising function of the secretary, see Nigro 1983, 1984, 1987, 1991; Quondam 1981, 1983; Bolzoni 1981; Basso 1990; Iucci 1995; Bonora 1994; the excellent study by Fiorato (1989a); Biow 2002, chs. 5, 6; and Simonetta 2004.

111. This is not to say that consumers of the book after its publication did not receive it as a manual of instruction, or that it was packaged as such (Burke 1995b, 39–54, esp. 44), even if it was not, in truth, structured as a manual of instruction, as Burke (1995b, 32) succinctly observes: "The book professes to teach what cannot be learned, the art of behaving

in a naturally graceful manner. One is reminded of Socrates and his belief that virtue cannot be taught—at least, not directly."

112. The phrase derives from Shearman (1967), in his catchy encapsulation of "mannerism."

113. For a study of these treatises, see Rossi 2004.

114. Cennini 1933, 1; Cennini 1971, 3. Cennini emphasizes from the outset that he is writing "for the use and profit of anyone who wants to enter this art [arte]"—a point he reiterates throughout his treatise. For a synthetic overview of his life, see Bacci and Stoppelli 1979.

115. On the false modesty topos, see Curtius 1990, 83–85.

116. See Thomas 1995 on the legal age-appropriateness of entering workshops in Florence.

117. In this respect, Cellini's treatise is far different from Cennini's *Libro dell'arte*, which, for all that it highlights the theoretical underpinnings to the art of painting, rarely places the author center stage and is indeed far more openly structured as a manual of instruction, geared "to minister to all those who wish to enter the art" (Cennini 1933, 2), rather than to a connoisseur or collector.

118. See, for instance, Waldman 1999, 26 and Geronimus 2002.

119. Often enough in Vasari's narrative, those conversations are not about "arte," in point of fact, but about amusing things, so that the artist can display his Boccaccesque wit while he is working and thus come off all the more as an intellectual in the process of engaging in a productive art, as in the case of Giotto with the king of Naples (1.107). But Vasari does not, from what I can tell, explain to patrons—or to men of judgment interested in or capable of understanding—the finer points of the technical and mechanical aspects of an art. They may want to know about all of that, but they do not seem to understand it, as when Brunelleschi sends a detailed letter explaining how he will construct a freestanding cupola for the Duomo to men who nevertheless remain clueless about what Brunelleschi is saying (1.339).

120. On Vasari's mythmaking, see Barolsky 1990, 1991.

121. Rajna 1975. I hasten to say the obvious: Ariosto's poem is indeed extremely novel and "original" even if it draws, as much sophisticated Italian Renaissance writing does, on a host of literary models. On origins and originality in Renaissance literature generally, the key work remains Quint 1983, and on imitation and originality, Greene 1982.

122. Della Casa 1986. The Italian, when accessed in my text, is taken from della Casa 1960. On the topic of propriety in his writings, see Biow 2006, 17–24.

123. This is true not only with regard to the arts we have been examining but also the arts of poetry and rhetoric, for instance, on which see Weinberg 1963 and Rebhorn 2000.

124. This very same process goes to the heart of what Petrarca often enough enacts in his major letter collections and, in a different way, in his staging of his coronation, on which see Biow 2002, ch. 1, esp. 27–36.

125. On the marvelous in the literary, see Biow 1996 for Italian literature and Biester 1997 for literature in England. More generally, for Italian criticism of the sixteenth century, see Hathaway 1968. For the marvelous in Europe as a cultural phenomenon, see Daston and Park 1998 and Greenblatt 1991.

126. The quotes in the paragraph are from Burckhardt 1960, 63, modified for accuracy, with the German taken from Burckhardt 1989, 107. My thoughts on Burckhardt are indebted to Gossman 1994, 2000, and 2002. There is much to glean about Burckhardt's notion of the individual as well from Murray's excellent introduction to the English translation of Burckhardt 1998. See also Cohn 1995.

127. As Murray in Burckhardt 1998, xv synthetically observes: "the first part treats of politics and warfare under the provocative heading, 'the State as a Work of Art.' That is to say, political life was no longer determined by traditional forms of government or by underlying forces revealed by the modern historian, but by the conscious knowledge of protagonists that there existed a science or art of government, which could be discovered either by experiment or by reflection."

128. Gossman 1994, 420.

129. Gossman 2000, 533n126.

130. Close 1969, 1971; Schiefsky 2007; Schadewaldt 1979; Solmsen 1963; Newman 1997, 2004; and Long 2011, 30–61.

131. Gossman 2000, 283. It is important to stress, as Gossman has observed (1994, 2000), that Burckhardt had a much more pessimistic view of the "individual" in his own time and in the past, viewing the concept as very much a mixed blessing.

132. Burckhardt (1960) nevertheless does move distinctly in the direction of making that connection, as in such statements (p. 223): "The demeanor of individuals, and all the higher forms of social intercourse, became ends pursued with a deliberate and artistic purpose." Or (p. 228): "The higher forms of social intercourse, which here meet us as a work of art." Or (p. 232): "This society, at all events at the beginning of the sixteenth century, was a matter of art." But he never solidly makes the connection between Kunstwerk in relation to the individual, as he does when he clearly draws out the connections between Kunstwerk and military affairs and statecraft in the first chapter.

133. Greenblatt 1980, 256.

134. Burckhardt 1960, 81.

135. Greenblatt 1980, 161–62, and 162 as cited in the following paragraph.

136. For a good, concise, and clear introduction to the centrality of rhetoric in the Renaissance and some of its applications, see Rebhorn 1995, 2000; for a history of it, see Mack 2011.

137. My reference, here, of course, is to Petrarca, who sought in his *Coronation Oration* and *Privilegium* to define the "profession of the poet" as a sort of professionless profession and in the process announced how he was reviving a practice that had lamentably fallen into profound cultural forgetfulness until his arrival on the Capitoline on Easter Sunday, April 8, 1341. I discuss this in Biow 2002, 27–36.

138. Greenblatt 2004, 12. On the topic of genius generally in the Italian Renaissance, see Brann 2002.

CHAPTER 2

1. Jardine 1983, 243.

2. This, of course, is the classic formulation in Kristeller 1961, 10. I investigated a number of issues related to humanism and professional identity in Biow 2002, which this chapter builds on and extends in a new direction. On professional identity in the Renaissance, see as well Vasoli 1990; Fiorato 1989b; McClure 1998, 2004; Bec 1983; De Caprio 1983; Douglas 1969; Garin 1947; Gilmore 1979; Martines 1968; the entire section titled "Humanism and the Professions" in Rabil 1988, 3.310–79; Fragnito 1998; Doglio 2009; McClure 2004; Grafton 2011a, 2011b; Nussdorfer 2009; and various chapters in Ferrari and Mazzarello 2010 and Rota 2009. For thoughts tracing the notion of "professione," see Becchi and Ferrari 2009. For a general view of humanism, see, along with the books cited later in this chapter, the articles collected in Rabil 1988, above all those in vol. 1 dedicated to humanism in Italy; Kraye 1996; and Garin 1965. Hampton 2009 examines issues related to diplomacy as part of a comparatist project that owes much to New Historicism and touches on professional identity.

3. Witt 2000, 491.

4. Kelley 1991, 24–74.

5. McClure 2004.

6. See, for instance, Jardine 1983; Grafton and Jardine 1986, 29–57; and King 1980. Ross (2009, 16) has pointed out that "there is an apparent paradox at the heart" of the story of Renaissance feminism: "The new category 'woman as intellect' derived its legitimacy and popularity by association with women's traditional place, the household." The notable achievements of women in the Italian Renaissance, at least within the context of humanism, did not traditionally take place in the public sphere in the realm of professions. For the professional courtesan, who was not a humanist or trained as a humanist, see the seminal study of Rosenthal (1992). The first professionally minded woman writer, whose humanist credentials are weak but not absent, was perhaps Isabella Andreini, a professional actress, on whom see Ray 2009, 156–83.

7. Jardine 1983, 243–44 is germane here: "The educational programme of the humanist pedagogues is *not* job-specific. But the *value* attached to humanist studies does depend upon a particular ideology, and in this important sense it is firmly tied to its civic context. . . . What I am stressing is that the independence of liberal arts education from establishment values is an illusion. The individual humanist is defined in terms of his relation to the power structure, and he is praised or blamed, promoted or ignored, to just the extent that he fulfills or fails to fulfill those terms."

8. Fish 1989, 197–246.

9. For new work on Machiavelli's education and his connection to humanism, see Black 2011; Black 2012; and Black 2013, 14–23. Virtually all the studies cited in note 13 presume a serious engagement with humanism on Machiavelli's part.

10. See Bonifacio Vannozzi to Bartolomeo Sozzifanti, as transcribed in Solerti 1895, 2.426. Vannozzi also wrote about secretaries in Vannozzi 1613, 399–400.

11. On Tasso's *Il secretario*, and the role of the secretary in his *Gerusalemme liberata* and its rivalry with the role of the ambassador (one a rhetor versed in writing, the other in speech), see Biow 2002, 181–96. On the function of the ambassador in Tasso's epic, see both Biow 2002, 181–96 and Hampton 2009, passim. Tasso's life has been nicely summarized in Brand 1965, 3–37, but for an in-depth biography, see Solerti 1895.

12. Barbaro 1969, 159: "Huius officii praecepta quamquam tradi possunt, plus tamen nescio quid in hominis prudentia situm est, quam quod mandari scripto queat." On Barbaro, I have benefited from Mattingly 1988, 94–102; Bigi 1964; Branca 1973, 1981; King 1986, 197–205; King 1976; Doglio 1983; Paschini 1957; Ferriguto 1922; Figliuolo 1999; and Fubini 1996. I have examined more closely Barbaro's treatise in light of the profession of the ambassador in Biow 2002, 101–27. For how Barbaro fits into the long tradition of treatises on the ambassador, see Bazzoli 2005.

13. Rebhorn 1988; Kahn 1986. The bibliography on *Il principe* in particular and Machiavelli more generally is, of course, immense. I have benefited most from Ascoli and Kahn 1993; Bock, Skinner, and Viroli 1990; Chabod 1964; De Grazia 1989; Donaldson 1988; Gilbert 1938; Gilbert 1939, 1949, 1984; Godman 1998; Najemy 1993, 2010; Cox 1997; Pocock 1975; Ridolfi 1963; Rubenstein 1956; Skinner 1981; Struever 1992, 147–81; and Ruggiero 2007. For a thought-provoking, polemical, and somewhat iconoclastic reading of *Il principe*, which transforms Machiavelli's treatise from being a foundational work of rational modern political thought and science (in the vein of the writings of John G. A. Pocock and Quentin Skinner, say) to being a foundational work of trauma within the context of religious history, mourning practices of the period, and what we might best term the irrational (or at least the irrational

driven by passions), see Frazier 2007, which is now being developed into a book tentatively titled *The Death of Pietro Paolo Boscoli: Religion and Politics in Machiavelli's Florence.*

14. Biow 2002, 161–73; Donaldson 1988.

15. I borrow the term "for the most part" in defining a stochastic art as a conjectural art that aims to hit the target but cannot exactly do so from Allen 1994. For more on the stochastic, see Ierodiakonou 1995; Boudon-Millot 2005; and Roochnik 1994, 1996.

16. Menand (2004) brilliantly captures the "mystery" I'm trying to get at better than I could ever possibly phrase it in his withering attack of Truss's "how-to" book (or seeming how-to book), *Eats, Shoots & Leaves: The Zero Tolerance Approach to Punctuation*, when he reflects on the mystery of how someone *somehow* acquires a distinctive, alluring authorial voice: "One of the most mysterious of writing's immaterial properties is what people call 'voice.' . . . There are probably all kinds of literary sins that prevent a piece of writing from having a voice, but *there seems to be no guaranteed technique for creating one.* Grammatical correctness doesn't insure it. Calculated incorrectness doesn't, either. Ingenuity, wit, sarcasm, euphony, frequent outbreaks of the first-person singular—any of these can enliven prose without giving it a voice. You can set the stage as elaborately as you like, but either the phantom appears or it doesn't. . . . Writing that has a voice is writing that has something like a personality. But whose personality is it? *As with all art, there is no straight road from the product back to the producer.* . . . Some writers, when they begin a new piece, spend hours rereading their old stuff, trying to remember how they did it, what it's supposed to sound like. This rarely works; nothing works reliably. Sooner or later, usually later than everyone involved would have preferred, the voice shows up, takes a bite of the apple, and walks onstage" (emphasis mine).

17. On how-to books, see Bell 1999.

18. On Guicciardini, I am indebted to Ridolfi 1968; Gilbert 1984; Palumbo 1987, 1988; Sasso 1984; Markulin 1982; Asor Rosa 1993; Ramat 1953; Bondanella 1976; Holmes 1999; and Phillips 1984. On Guicciardini and exemplarity, see the brief remarks in Hampton 1990, 72–74 and Biow 2002, 128–52.

19. Guicciardini 1994; translations, slightly modified on occasion, come from Guicciardini 1965. The maxim here is C 198. The A, B, and C versions were composed respectively in or about 1525, 1528, and 1530. The designations Q^1, Q^2, A, B, and C, it is worth clarifying, refer to the five different versions of the *Ricordi* as they evolved in various stages, from the first notebook of collected fragments composed in 1512 to the final collection composed in 1530. See Fubini 1948; Scarano 1970; and Gagneux 1984.

20. Buck-Morss 1989, 92.

21. Eagleton 1990, 330, which should be read in light of Jay 1984 in thinking about various Marxist understandings of totality.

22. Benjamin 1969, 60.

23. Vickers 1982. For salient thoughts on fragments generally in Renaissance Italy, with a focus on the visual arts, see Barkan 1999.

24. For one such "readerly" effort at finding a pattern, see Holmes 1999.

25. Greenblatt 2004, 222. My point, yet again, is that Greenblatt's position about the nonexistence of the "individual" in the European Renaissance has *always*, curiously enough, been at odds with itself.

26. Grafton and Jardine 1986, xiv, 27–28.

27. Ibid. xiv.

28. A distinctly classicizing, "great books," and Eurocentric vision of the humanities, or where the humanities could and should be according to one pedagogical program, is articulated in Proctor 1998. For a concise statement about how little agreement there is regarding what the humanities are, see Atwill 1998, 11–14.

29. Hayden White's classic studies on this are in White 1978 and 1987.

30. The bibliography on postmodernism is vast. I have profited mostly from Jameson 1991 and Collins 1992. On the turn from Renaissance to early modern studies, see Marcus 1992, along with Starn 2002.

31. I am thinking, of course, of http://www.humanitiescommission.org/_pdf/HSS_Report.pdf, about which both David Brooks and Stanley Fish have voiced their concerns in *New York Times* op-ed comments. See, for instance, Brooks, "The Humanist Vocation," http://www.nytimes.com/2013/06/21/opinion/brooks-the-humanist-vocation.html?partner = rssnyt&emc = rss, and Fish, "A Case for the Humanities Not Made," http://opinionator .blogs.nytimes.com/2013/06/24/a-case-for-the-humanities-not-made/?_r = 0.

32. Grendler (1989) has most vociferously argued for the pleasure of the humanist educational program. On humanism and education, see also Black 2001.

33. See, for instance, Leeds 2004, now in Leeds 2010.

34. I am thinking, for instance, of not only the classic studies of Eugenio Garin, who argued (against Kristeller) that humanism was significantly philosophical in its orientation, but also such varied studies as Struever 1970, 1992; Celenza 2004; Gouwens 1998; Kahn 1985; Rebhorn 1995; Baxandall 1971; Findlen 1994; and, leaving aside the polemical *From Humanism to the Humanities*, Grafton 1996, 1997, 1999, 2000.

35. Grafton and Jardine 1986, 28.

CHAPTER 3

1. Biagioli 1993. For a recent treatment of how Galileo employed conventions of the "literary" to package his ideas, see Hall 2013.

2. Smith 2009, 375.

3. Gentilcore 2006. On Fioravanti generally, see Camporesi 1990, 1997 and Eamon 1993, 1994, 2005, and especially 2010, to which I am indebted, as well as Eamon's other fine studies, for an understanding of Fioravanti's presentation of himself in his writings as a novel surgeon and empiric physician.

4. Eamon 1994, 235–50.

5. Fairly typical is the fact that, as his reputation grew, people—he claims—came in droves to his house, as in Fioravanti 1582b, 20r, as he starts out his career in Palermo, but also 21v, where he is compelled to get an even bigger house to accommodate all who came for his cures.

6. Fioravanti 1582b, 18r. Eamon 2010, 65 discusses the significance of this formative moment, when Fioravanti is taken as a physician during precisely carnival.

7. As told in Fioravanti 1582b, 84v–85r; see also 1564, 54r–v. On Dionigi Atanagi, see the entry in Mutini 1962.

8. However, Fioravanti does make a point of talking about how he often seemed to bring people back to life (by no means with any religious association attributed to the act of doing so) at length in Fioravanti 1573, 89r–v. And he was surely theatrical in displaying his achievements, as in 1582b, 26v–27r.

9. Eamon 2010, 322–23 provides a complete catalogue of Fioravanti's books.

10. As Eamon (1994, 173–82; 2010, 179 and passim) observes, Fioravanti's models were those of the polygraphs and the charlatans (on which see more later in the chapter). But we should not discount the models available to him from within the tradition of the literature on surgery (Fioravanti's profession), for, as Siraisi (1990, 170–72) observes, surgeons told stories full of anecdotes that were often miraculous in nature.

11. See Eamon 1994, 173. His medicines, as he points out in his Fioravanti 1582c, 3v, can be acquired through the mail. See also Fioravanti 1573, 96r, 235r. In Fioravanti 1564, 119r, he

even provides detailed information for the address for pregnant women who would like to know whether they will be having a boy or a girl.

12. On the polygraphs, see Grendler 1969; Filippo Bareggi 1988; and Aquilecchia 1980. On Fioravanti amid the polygraphs, see Eamon 1994, the section "Fioravanti *Poligrafo*," 173–82, and Eamon 2010, 179 and passim.

13. In Fioravanti 1583, 41r–v, as well as 69v–70r and passim (cited hereafter by page number in my text), Fioravanti is particularly eloquent about the power of print to "democratize" learning in the medical community and thus to loosen the hold that bookish, academic medicine had over people. On Fioravanti's desire to be understood and the calculated accessibility of his writing, see Camporesi 1997, 152, 243 and Eamon 2010. The topic of the democratizing of print is part and parcel of the ongoing discussion about the social and cultural value of print, on which see Richardson 1998, 2004.

14. Fioravanti 1565, 70r: "Only those who are written up in books stay alive forever, and their names will never die [*solamente quelli che sono scritti ne i libri, restano vivi per sempre*]."

15. Siraisi (1990, ch. 6, "Surgeons and Surgery") points out that the distinctions between the work of the surgeon and that of the physician were operative legally but not in practice—there was a great deal of overlap; see also Park 1985, 19–20, 62–66, 167–70 and Park 1998. For more on surgery in pre-Renaissance Italy, see Siraisi 1994a. For premodern Europe generally, see McVaugh 2000; Pouchelle 1990; Zuccolin 2010; a number of the chapters in García-Ballester et al. 1994; and Gnudi and Webster 1950, for a case study of a particularly famous surgeon who lived and worked shortly after Fioravanti. Surgeons tended to learn their craft as it was passed on from father to son.

16. Eamon (2010, 39–40) hypothesizes that Fioravanti may have been a university dropout, which was indeed not an unfamiliar development among many medical practitioners in the period. In Fioravanti 1582c he talks at length about anatomy, casting his final negative judgment on it in 143r–v, but in the course of doing so, he also gives us to understand that he had a career path open to him as an anatomist but chose not to pursue it, preferring to heal people rather than cut up cadavers for, as he puts it, no apparent curative purpose. Eamon 2010, 48 has Fioravanti studying medicine at sixteen and practicing by the time he was twenty-two.

17. See, for instance, Fioravanti 1582a, 179–80.

18. See, for instance, 1573, 35v: "che l'arte del medicare i corpi humani ha havuto origine dalla esperienza, la quale è maestra di tutte le cose create, e non hebbe mai origine dalle parole, come vogliono costoro: percioche essa medicina fu gratia del sommo Monarca, e dono della natura. E in queste nostre età il mondo comporta, che quelli, che sanno la verità della medicina, e tanto s'affaticano nella esperienza stieno sottoposti a quelli, che non sanno se non ciancare cose oscure, e incerte, e che i pratici stieno alla censura de' theorici, che non possono sapere cosa certa, se non col mezzo della esperienza." Fioravanti 1582b, 3r and passim on the state of confusion of medicine, in part because it is written in Greek, Latin, and Arabic, whereas Fioravanti has come to set the record straight in clear, accessible, vernacular prose because, as he puts it (3v), "è molto differente il medicar con parole, dal medicare coi fatti. . . . Chi avertirà dunque a tutto quello che io ho scritto, tanto in questo libro, quanto ancor ne gli altri, e procederà in questo modo, venirà a conoscer la verità, e uscirà delle tenebre, e verrà alla luce e caminarà per la retta strada: nella quale mai si può perire."

19. "Esperienza" is what Fioravanti had chosen to delve into, he maintains in Fioravanti 1564, 35v, in the search for truth. This is standard repertoire for Fioravanti. In Fioravanti 1573, b2r–b3v, he maintains, as he always does, that "l'esperienza" is "la madre di tutte le cose" (b2r), as well as in Fioravanti 1573, 7v–8r.

20. This is part of Fioravanti's standard repertoire. See not only, for instance, Fioravanti 1582b, 1r–v and 17v but also Fioravanti 1582c, b2v, in his "Discorso dell'Autore," and Fioravanti 1573, 279r: "sarà necessario che andiate peregrinando per il mondo, vedendo diverse genti, per intender le lor nature, e complessioni, e per intendere il loro medicamenti: et così facendo, trovarete gran diversità nelle cose di natura, gran varietà di gente, e gran differentie nella medicina. . . . O quanta dolcezza sento io, quando mi raccordo haver visto tante parti del mondo, tante sorti di genti, tanti modi d'agricoltura, tante sorti di medicamenti, tanta quantità di simplici, e tanti modi di medicare."

21. Fioravanti, 1573, 44r. On Fioravanti's claim to having been in Asia, see Fioravanti 1583, 100v–101r.

22. My use of the term "experiments" does not refer to laboratory-based, exploratory, hypothesis-driven investigations of the modern era but the practice of the early modern period of testing recipes, trying out remedies, and the like. In the end, as he points out in Fioravanti 1573, as elsewhere, theory and books are one thing, but experience and practice are everything: "O ciechi, che noi siamo. Perchè non cerchiamo con tutto il nostro poter di saper la verissima scienza, la quale la troveremo per il mezzo della esperienza?" (153r).

23. Fioravanti 1573, 20r–v; Fioravanti 1582b, passim, but certainly 3r, for instance, on the state of confusion in medicine. In Fioravanti 1573, 238v, the bad doctor "si consuma in disputare, e molte volte si disputa di cose, che non fanno niente in proposito per lo infermo, nè manco sono per risolvere la infermità; ma ben consigliarei ciascun medico, che havesse sempre l'occhio alla verità, e non si mettesse a disputare di fascarie." On a "little old lady" (*vecchierella*) with knowledge, see Fioravanti 1582a, a8v: "poi verrà una vecchiarella prattica, la quale con la regola di vivere, e con un servitiale li farà cessar la febre. Con una untione li farà mancare il dolore, e con qualche fomentatione lo farà dormire. E in tal causa la vecchiarella saperà più del medico." See also 1582b, 28v and Camporesi 1997, 14, 22, 25, 41, 46.

24. Fioravanti 1582b, 17v–18r: "vilani, pastori, soldati, religiosi, donniciole, e d'ogni altra qualità." See also 1573, 23v, 34r–v ("una vil feminella con un suo secretuzzo gli ha sanati, che pur m'è forza di dirlo, essendo la verità. Ma so bene, che questa verità non piace così a tutti: perchè sempre si suol dire, quod veritas odium parit"), 37v, 118r.

25. This is not to say that Fioravanti believed that *only* popular culture possessed this sort of knowledge. His point is that such knowledge exists outside institutionalized medicine and can be found in all sorts of places, including popular culture. See, for instance, Fioravanti 1573, 23v: "io ho veduto assaissimi pastori, e agricoltori, artigiani, cittadini, gentilhuomini, e signori, che senza saper pure un minimo punto del metodo medicinale, hanno inteso tanti bei secreti, e esperientie di cose medicinali, e ancora in cirugia." Earlier in the Renaissance, Park 2006 observes, physician-anatomists resisted learning directly from those of a lower social order for gendered reasons: they did not want to acquire knowledge, say, from midwives. This sort of gendering of knowledge does not seem to concern Fioravanti, and it does not seem to concern some physicians invested in natural philosophy in the sixteenth century, such as Aldovrandi, who were willing to learn from everyone and anyone, including women, although it was understood that who could understand that knowledge properly were not only men but also men invested in the "conversable art" of civility. On this, see Findlen 1994. On "conversable art," see the series of essays by (Tribby 1991, 1992a, 1992b). On popular culture, the classic work is Burke 1978.

26. Consider how Fioravanti (1582c, 2v) makes claims about his own openness, in which he will not write with "inganno o simulazione," so much so that, as he insists, "scrivendo solamente le cose vere e non simulate o finte; e perche la verità occupa pochissimo luoco, mi sforzarò a dirla con tanta chiarrezza, che non si truovi nessuno che la possi occultare." This

is standard repertoire for Fioravanti, as in 1582b, 1v–2r. On openness in topics of "techne," see Long 2001.

27. Eamon 1994, 187.

28. The literature on Renaissance and early modern medicine is enormous. For an overview, see Park 1985 and Siraisi 1990.

29. On Fioravanti's fame, see Camporesi 1997, esp. 226–43. Fioravanti, however, does not seem to feel that fame and recognition can be won in one's own hometown, so his return journey to the north of Italy is not entirely a complete one as far as odysseys go: see, for instance, Fioravanti, 1573, 43v: "Perchè sempre gli huomini sono più stimati fuori della lor patria: e non senza gran cagione."

30. Fioravanti 1582b, 17v.

31. Camporesi 1997, 62–63.

32. On da Monte, see Muccillo 1986; Franceschetti, Zanchin, and Agazia 2005; Ongaro 1994; and Bylebyl 1993.

33. I have consulted da Monte 1555 (first printed in 1554), 119r, in the chapter "de odore," 118v–119v.

34. Da Monte 1555, 6r, 4r–5v.

35. Palmer 1993, 67 discusses briefly how vision was preferred in diagnosis over smell in analyzing urine. Bylebyl 1993, 46 examines how da Monte "deployed a rich descriptive vocabulary."

36. Petrarca 1978, 155 (II.741–49). It is certainly a commonplace against physicians in Italian Renaissance literature. On Petrarca's warring with physicians, see McClure 1991 and Biow 2002, 39–40, as well as the bibliographies in these two studies.

37. See Fioravanti 1573, 46r (first printed in 1561, while he was still a surgeon). On this episode, and on this prank as a typical one against doctors, see Camporesi 1997, 131–33.

38. This is an impressive, and perhaps to the modern eye somewhat comical, example of Fioravanti's commitment to empirical medicine, as narrated in Fioravanti 1573, 46v: "Ogni mattina facevo orinare tutti di casa, per veder le differentie, che erano tra orina, e orina. Dipoi feci raccoglier orine di cani, asini, cavalli, muli, e altri animali, che potevo havere, e ne faceva tutte le isperientie, che era possibil fare, per non esser un'altra volta gabbato nelle orine" (Every morning I made everyone of the house urinate to see the differences that existed between one urine and another. Then I gathered together as many urines as I could have of dogs, donkeys, horses, mules, and other animals, and I made every possible experience of them, so as not to be mocked with regard to urines another time).

39. Fioravanti 1573, 47r: "l'infusi dentro un dito, e lo misi alla lingua."

40. Consider, for instance, the reflections of McVaugh 2002; Palmer 1993, 61n1; and Siegel 1970, 156–57. For a philosophical classical source on the matter, see *Timaeus*, 66d–67a in Plato 1961. For a broad view about odors and the descriptive limits of talking about them, see Classen, Howes, and Synnott 1994. See as well Jenner 2011.

41. Findlen 1994, 205–6 discusses the increased emphasis on "sight" over "smell" among the natural philosophers of the late sixteenth century and baroque in Italy.

42. On Fioravanti's credentials, see Camporesi 1997, 90 and Eamon 2010.

43. For an overview of the medical community in Renaissance Italy that takes into consideration popular medicine, see Eamon 1994 and Gentilcore 1998, although Gentilcore's focus is primarily on post-1600. On charlatans and medicine, and Fioravanti's position among them as a model, see Gentilcore 2006.

44. For a good overview of Aretino in English, see Waddington 2004.

45. In Fioravanti 1573, 89v, he speaks of the "congiura." See also Fioravanti 1582b, 2r, where he speaks of being "persecuted," along with 78r and 1582c, 14r. The *Tesoro* was a

popular book that went through multiple editions, right on up to the mid-seventeenth century. On the harsh treatment that Fioravanti received from members of his profession, particularly early on in Rome, see Camporesi 1997, esp. 127, 130–31, 139–42, 213–14, and Eamon 2010, passim.

46. The case brought against Fioravanti is discussed in Eamon 2005 and Eamon 2010, 283–93.

47. The nose, I would submit, is evoked by Fioravanti when he discusses the act of smelling, as it is when da Monte talks about the odor of urine, but that does not mean that the nose was conceived either by Fioravanti or da Monte or others in the medical community as the organ that actually did the smelling. In fact, according to the medical tradition of the time, the nose distinguished itself from the eye and ear and tongue by being not so much an organ as a channel for smell. The nose guided odors, agreeable and disagreeable, up through the cavities to the brain, which smelled those odors through an olfactory bulb or porous plate—some imagined it riddled with miniscule nipples—housed in the front of the cranium. Galen maintained that this was the case, and his view survived through the Renaissance. By contrast, Aristotle argued in *De anima* (II.9 421a26–27) and *De sensu* (5 442b25) that the nose actively did the smelling, with the sense organ appearing to reside inside the nostrils. See Palmer 1993, 61–62 for a clear, concise discussion of the medical understanding of the function of the nose in classical thought and the Renaissance, as well as Kemp 1997 and McVaugh 2000. For an extended discussion of Aristotle on olfaction, see the chapter titled "Smell" in Johansen 1998.

48. Fioravanti 1582b, 47r, in the twenty-seventh chapter, dedicated to the topic "about the way that these two brothers had in making noses." In numerous other places Fioravanti demonstrates his art of dissimulation as he tries to pry information loose from someone. Consider, for instance, the case of Mattio Guaruccio, in Messina (Fioravanti 1582b, 46r–v). This act of near voyeurism on the part of Fioravanti is important for yet another reason: Fioravanti's description of rhinoplasty indeed represents the first time that anyone had recorded in print the novel surgical procedure, one that would later find extended treatment in Gaspare Tagliacozzi's landmark *De curtorum chirurgia* (1597), which appeared roughly three decades after the publication of the *Tesoro*. On Tagliacozzi, and on rhinoplasty before Tagliacozzi, see Gnudi and Webster 1950.

49. This was not, to be sure, the only time that Fioravanti used urine as a cleanser. See, for instance, Fioravanti 1582b, 69v. And, of course, urine had been a conventional laundry cleaner in antiquity, on which see, for instance, Clarke 2003.

50. See Groebner 1995, now in Groebner 2004, and Ruggiero 1985, 35, 122.

51. I have consulted the Italian version, della Porta 1652, 157–80. For some helpful thoughts on noses in Renaissance Italy, see Barolsky 1990 and Quondam 1991. Aristotle set the stage for thinking about different noses and characters in his *Physiognomics*, a text that interested such pseudo-Aristotelian natural philosophers in Renaissance Italy as della Porta. On della Porta's *Physiognomonia* and its precursors, both classical and modern, see MacDonald 2005.

52. The nose in Renaissance Italy could be invested with a great deal of importance as a topic of focused or passing interest. A nose could lend a person or take away from that person dignity, self-respect, acumen, and power. It could reveal character. It could signal through its presence or absence in literature a degree of decorum appropriate to a particular genre: no noses in lyric poetry, many in novellas, satires, jokes, and carnival poems. And the nose could potentially disclose to passive bystanders the size of a man's covered, if not entirely occluded, genitalia. For these matters, see Caro 1967; Sowell 1991; Quondam 1991; Hegener 1996; and Barolsky 1990.

53. Judging by printing numbers alone (see Eamon 2010, 322–23), it was not as popular a book as Fioravanti's *De' capricci medicinali* or *Compendio di secreti rationali*, but it was as popular as his *Tesoro* and slightly more popular than his *Reggimento*, *Della fisica*, and *La cirugia*.

54. As in Fioravanti 1583, 81v–84v, where he discusses the "art" of fishing.

55. McClure 2004, 73–74 places the *Specchio* in the context of professional rivalries of the time. On the art of preaching, for instance, see the classic study of Murphy (1974).

56. See also Fioravanti 1582c, 8v–9r.

57. So, for instance, in Fioravanti 1573, 238v, 249r, 254r.

58. On Fioravanti and anatomy, see Camporesi 1997, 41–43, 47, 60, 236–38. In Fioravanti 1582c, 126v–127r, Fioravanti speaks of having witnessed various anatomies (along with, it seems, vivisections of some sort, insofar as deep cuts had to be made on the severely wounded in times of war): "ho fatto io notomia di huomini morti, e di vivi, quando mi sono trovato nelle imprese contra Mori infideli, quando ne sono stati alcuni feriti a morte. Ho ancor visto squartare homini vivi, e sani, per giustizia in Roma, dove sono stato presente, per poter a mio modo vedere tal caso, e ho visto far tante anotomie, che è cosa di stupore." He certainly makes it evident in ibid., 121r that he is aware of the nature of the public anatomy setting. Might he have witnessed anatomies in Bologna before leaving when he was thirty? He pretty much brushes anatomy aside in Fioravanti 1561, 131r, maintaining that knowledge of the "composition" of the body can be acquired without the study of it.

59. The option, of course, was vivisection, which became a topic of some interest in the Italian Renaissance with the printing of Celsus's *Medicina* in Florence in 1478. On vivisection, not of humans but animals, in the period, see some of the observations in French 1999; for a synthesis of the history of vivisection in the sciences, see Guerrini 2003 and Maehle and Tröhler 1987, 14–18.

60. At no point does Fioravanti object to anatomies—and he does ferociously object to them—because of some fear of contamination through impure contact with an opened body, which would seem to confirm the thesis of Park 1994. Fioravanti's position resembles that of the classic empiricists, who fiercely attacked the practice: see French 1999, 19–20 and Carlino 1999, 136–38, 157–60. Fioravanti's hostility toward anatomy does not, however, seem to be typical of surgeons, either in his own time or in the late Middle Ages and early Renaissance. Henry de Mondeville (d. 1325) and Guy de Chauliac (ca. 1300–1368), both famous and influential surgeons, argued that anatomy was essential for their practice. On surgery and anatomy in the Middle Ages, see Zuccolin 2010. By contrast, Fioravanti qua surgeon routinely expresses his hostility toward anatomy, which he sometimes still grudgingly accepts as important to the surgical practice at some level.

61. This is standard practice in Fioravanti's medical counsel. Eamon 1993 compellingly links this practice to a politics of purgation during the Counter-Reformation period. See also more generally Camporesi 1988 on the fascination with vomit and its potential connections with the catharsis of exorcism.

62. As in Fioravanti 1582b, 32v: "e trovai che ella havea vomitato gran quantità di materie cattive. E fra l'altre havea vomitato una mola grande, come una mano, e era viva. E io vedendo cosa che mai piu havea visto, restai stupefatto. La tolsi, e la feci portare alla speceria dell'eccellente medico Leonardo Testa, e la lasciai là, che tutta la città l'andò a vedere per miracolo." See also, for instance, Fioravanti 1582b, 49v–50r, 76r, and especially 81r, where what is vomited out is not only large but also, to the wonder of all, round, hairy, and alive.

63. On the importance of vomit in Fioravanti's thought in a broader context of purification, see Eamon 1993 and Eamon 1994, 183–93.

64. And, to be sure, his books in general.

65. On anatomy in the Renaissance as part of the classical philosophical project of locating the soul in the body, see Cunningham 1997.

66. Fioravanti 1583, 51r.

67. Fioravanti 1582c, 42r; see also Camporesi 1997, 238.

68. "Questo è pur segno manifesto, che scrissero quello che non è, poi che vogliono medicare una cosa, che non si truova."

69. "E quando ho visto fare la notomia, non ho mai visto, che habbino mostrato, flemma, nè colera, nè malenconia . . . si bene hanno mostrato la lingua, il canarozzo, il polmone, il cuore, il fegato, la milza, il ventriculo, la diafragma, le budella, i rognoni, la vesica, le songie, i nervi, le vene, i tendoni, la carne, la pelle, e l'ossa; ma non già mai quelle cose sopradette."

70. Fioravanti 1583, 52r.

71. Fioravanti 1582c, 129r: "scorrendo per i libri di notomia ho trovato tante fandonie che è cosa da stupire il mondo."

72. Carlino 1999, 227–28, although the anatomist, Carlino also observes, occupied by salary a position of somewhat lesser prestige within the medical academy (92).

73. Park 2006, 13. On anatomies during the period in Italy specifically and Europe generally, I am indebted to the above-mentioned studies by Park as well as Ferrari 1987; Carlino 1999; French 1999; Cunningham 1997; and Klestinec 2004, 2011. For a synthesis of anatomy before the sixteenth century, see Siraisi 1990, 78–97. Some important medieval and Renaissance texts on anatomy are available in English: Lind 1975 and Ketham 1925.

74. Lind 1975, 82; Ferrari 1987, 58. On Benedetti, see Ferrari 1996; French 1999, 74–78 and passim; Cunningham 1997, 66–73; and Klestinec 2011, 29–30. That anatomists were uncovering "secrets of nature," not just for the benefit of medicine but also philosophy, is a commonplace of Renaissance treatises on anatomy.

75. Ferrari 1987; Carlino 1999, 81; French 1999, 84. For a more literary, anthropological, and theoretical approach to the witnessing of the dead body taken apart, see Sawday 1995. See also Bohde 2003 and Jacobs 2005, 62–104. The atmosphere was much different in Padua in the public dissections performed by Fabricius, although private dissections seem to be highly interactive and potentially rowdy, on which see Klestinec 2004. See also on the civil atmosphere of Padua, Klestinec 2007, 2011, the latter of which calls attention to the decorum and control instead present in the public anatomies in Padua (see p. 76, for instance, with reference to the first permanent anatomical theater in Padua), although, as she observes, such public anatomies during the period always constituted a "spectacle," on which see pp. 16–54.

76. Ferrari 1987; French 1999, 78–82; Carlino 1999, 11; Cunningham 1997, 66–73; Klestinec 2004, 2011.

77. French 1999; Carlino 1999, 1–38, 85–86, and passim. Carlino discusses the professional hierarchy of the anatomy lesson as we move from the intellectual labor of the lector to the mechanical one of the barber or surgeon sector. For a modified view, see Bylebyl 1990. See now as well Klestinec 2011, 24–32.

78. On Vesalius, the standard monographic study is O'Malley 1964. See also Nutton 2007; French 1999, 144–50, 169–83, and passim; Cunningham 1997, 88–142; and Park 2006, ch. 5. On Vesalius's hand, see Cunningham 1997, 121–22; Park 2006, 252; and Siraisi 1994b. For a thoughtful essay on Renaissance hands and their function in Renaissance anatomies, see Rowe 1997.

79. Carlino 1999, 52.

80. Ibid., 48.

81. Ibid., 68, 86.

82. See, for instance, the synthetic discussion of Park 2006, 165–85. On Berengario, see Cunningham 1997, 73–79; French 1985, 1999; and Carlino 1999, 198–99.

83. As in, among so many instances, Fioravanti 1582b, 35r: "molti della città concorreano a me"; 52v, where he acquires rapid fame ("ne medicai infiniti"), along with 54r ("medicai un mar di gente inferma"), and again 55r and 83r.

84. Garzoni 1996, 752.

85. I refer to Abbott 1988; for an application of Abbott's theories to Renaissance culture and professional experience, see Biow 2002.

86. Fioravanti is keenly aware of the surgeon's work in anatomy and addresses it at length in much of the second part of his *Cirugia*, which was published after the *Specchio*.

87. Carlino 1999, 64; on Colombo, see Cunningham 1997, 143–66 and French 1999, 196–212.

88. Eamon 2010, 147–48, on Fioravanti and Colombo. Fioravanti 1582b, 73v–74r, where Fioravanti speaks of the "invidia" Colombo felt for him; see also Fioravanti 1573, 89r.

89. Carlino 1999, 226–30.

90. Fioravanti 1582c, 143r–v.

91. Consider, for instance, Fioravanti 1573, 37v.

92. See also Fioravanti 1582c, 132r, 133r.

93. See also ibid., 119v–120r. This is a standard attack against anatomists, rehearsed all the way back to antiquity as the position of the Empiricists was voiced against that of the Dogmatists (or Rationalists).

94. In Vesalius, *Fabrica*, the author attacks barber-surgeons, likening them to butchers; see Vesalius, *De humani corporis fabrica*, http://vesalius.northwestern.edu/flash.html, 2v–3r.

95. See also Fioravanti 1582c, 119r. On vivisection in the Renaissance, see notes 58 and 59.

96. So, too, in his later Fioravanti 1582c, 121v–122r. See also Fioravanti 1573, 257r, 269v.

97. To be sure, Fioravanti (1582b) provides us with concrete instances when he himself did have to pierce beneath the skin, open up the body, and remove offending parts to save a life.

98. Fioravanti 1583, 18v.

99. A point made as well, for instance, in Fioravanti 1573, 28v, 32v–33r, 233v and Fioravanti 1564, 4v.

100. Eamon 1993; Eamon 1994, 182–87.

101. See also Fioravanti 1582c, 118v–120r.

102. As in his Fioravanti 1582c, 126r, and passim, where he talks at length about anatomy.

103. See note 18.

CHAPTER 4

1. Burke 2010, 482, now incorporated into the second edition of Burke 2008.

2. The closest we have perhaps come in scholarship is the study by the medical historian Virginia Smith (2006). For a lively, popularizing attempt at constructing a history of cleanliness, see Wright 1960 and Ashenburg 2007, both primarily histories of bathing. For a full bibliography of the early modern period, see Biow 2006, to which one can now add some of the essays in Bradley and Stow 2012. There are important observations about barbers and professional habits of cleanliness in Cavallo 2007.

3. Douglas 1966; van Bavel and Gelderblom 2009. Van Bavel and Gelderblom are, of course, responding to Schama 1988, which attributes the Dutch passion for cleanliness not to material culture but instead, in a more top-down manner, to the ideas generated from Calvinism.

4. On *prestezza* as a shared value of polygraphs and visual artists in the sixteenth century, see D'Elia 2004; Nichols 1996; and Nichols 1999, 69–99. As D'Elia 2004 points out, speed was not necessarily associated only with the polygraphs. See, for instance, with regard to Michelangelo, Clements 1954, 301–10. On prestezza within the ambit of court culture, which could be construed as the virtuosity (*facilitas*) of putting things together rapidly on an impromptu basis, see Warnke 1993, 209–11.

5. This is true, say, beginning with the groundbreaking work of Vigarello; see Vigarello 1985, translated into English in 1988. Art historians have begun to show interest in the visualizing of cleanliness; see, for instance, Dickerson 2010.

6. Burke 2001.

7. Nichols 1999, 22.

8. There are, of course, many studies of Tintoretto, but I have benefited most from and am indebted to Nichols 1999, as well as the seminal study Rosand 1997. For careful, sensitive readings of the two paintings, see Cope 1979, 204–13 and Cooper 1990, 231–47. Of interest are also Bühler 1989, 77–85 for the paired San Giorgio paintings, although only 77 and 110n256 for the *Jews in the Desert*; Swoboda 1982; and Ilchman and Borean 2009.

9. Rosand 1997, 8.

10. Cope 1979, 132; see also, later in the chapter, the discussion of the dynamic aspect of Tintoretto's perspective.

11. Cope 1979, 207 identifies the branches as a familiar "symbol of Christ," but Tintoretto does make a point of representing two different types of branches (note the differences in leaves), neither of which has ever been identified or explained iconographically.

12. See Cooper 1990, 237–38 for an alternative reading.

13. Clearly, since hardly anyone is gathering the manna on the ground, the painting is *not* strictly about the gathering of the manna, which is what it was perceived to be about not long after Tintoretto painted the canvas. See, for instance, the observations of Tintoretto's first biographer, Ridolfi (Ridolfi 1984, 66). Cooper 1990, 236–37 persuasively refutes Ivanoff 1975.

14. Cooper 1990, 240 points out that "we tantalizingly lack the information to identify . . . the secular figure shown in armor gazing out of the painting." As Cope 1979, 208–9 observes, the figure looks out "toward the high altar where the Sacrament is kept in reserve," thus underscoring the important Eucharistic theme of the two canvases.

15. Emphasized in Cope 1979, 206.

16. For the price paid, which was higher than the canvases for the scuola of San Rocco, see Nichols 1999, 234.

17. Fortini Brown 2004, 142–43.

18. Cooper 1990, 231, 233.

19. Baldan 2011, 535: "Ed è maravigliosa arte nascosta in questa tavola, e forse ch'è stata da noi primi avvertita, che si rivoglie la mensa tutta in scorcio, come dicono, perché a quelli ch'entrati in Chiesa s'accostano all'altare, pare avere l'estremo della tavola, o mensa rivolta verso le stesse, e caminando poi più avanti fin dietro l'organo, si rivolge tutta al contrario, ed assai più lunga parendo viene ad aver rivolto il detto estremo nell'opposto di quello parera prima insieme con tutte le persone, che si veggono a tavola." Here is my rather "free" translation: "And there is a marvelous art/device hidden in this canvas, and perhaps it is being noticed the first time by us, that the entire table that is 'foregrounded,' as they say, seems to turn itself toward those who have entered the church and are nearing the altar, so that it seems that the far end of the canvas, or table, appears to be turned toward the viewers as they approach it, and then, as one walks farther down the church until one arrives behind the organ, the table turns completely around in the opposite direction; now appearing to be

much longer in dimension, the table has the same far end turned back, precisely in the opposite direction to the way it first seemed to be, and consequently all the people that one sees in this canvas seem to have changed position too."

20. On this see, generally, Biow 2006.

21. Biow 2006.

22. I take my dates from the entry "Ortolano," *Oxford Art Online*.

23. Bruni 1741, 2.112: "Aliud est enim historia, aliud laudatio. Historia quidem veritatem sequi debet, laudatio vero multa supra veritatem extollit."

24. Biow 2006, 39–40, 82–94. Bruni's panegyric can be consulted in Baron 1968, 217–63 and in the English translation in Kohl and Witt 1978, 135–75.

25. Davis and Marvin 2004, 183, but see the entire section on pp. 181–85.

26. For an overview of the myth of Venice and its complex treatment in Venetian historiography, see Grubb 1986 and Crouzet-Pavan 2002.

27. Memmo 1563, 65: "I quali rivi e canali purgano ancora tutte le immonditie della città. Per la quale, benché vi sieno tanti rivi, canali e acque, per tutta essa città, non di meno commodamente si può andare a piedi per tutta quella, per esser pianissma, e haver molti ponti commodi sopra."

28. Tafur 1926, 167, as cited in Davis and Marvin 2004, 183.

29. Navagero 1754, 334. There is a variation of this theme, for instance, in Sabellico 1985, 10: "La qual perpetua variazione del movimento del mare non consente, che in tanta copia di fango cosa alcuna nociva possa crescere."

30. Memmo 1563, 66, 80. The famous canzone 126, which begins as "Chiare, fresche et dolci acque," can be readily consulted in the bilingual edition Petrarca 1976.

31. See Fortini Brown 2004, 82 on laundry placement. On servants in Venice in the Renaissance, see Romano 1996.

32. Sansovino 1581, 140r: "Ogni casa ha la terrazza sopra il tetto, fatta o di muro o di legno: e si chiamano Altane, per uso di distendere i panni al Sole."

33. Lane 1973, 160–61; Lane 1966, 261.

34. Sansovino 1581, 141 r–v.

35. On bathrooms in architectural treatises that describe specifically Venetian palace structures, see Fortini Brown 2004, 67. She discusses Sebastiano Serlio but also notes that in reality "bathrooms . . . seem to have been unimportant" within the actual structure of those palaces (270n38).

36. Fortini Brown 2004, vii, 3–5.

37. Sabellico 1985, 33.

38. Fortini Brown 1988.

39. For additional instances of laundry in Renaissance Italian painting of the period, see Biow 2006, 105–40.

40. Where in fact these three painters located the visual precedent for drawing on the topos of cleanliness is not entirely clear. Perhaps they were just dutifully "recording," albeit with some *fantasia*, what they saw about them in Venice, which is no doubt what they would have us believe. And such an explanation constitutes an entirely plausible one as to why laundry appears in their artwork, just as it explains why writers incorporated the topic of cleanliness into their descriptions of Venice itself. But perhaps Bellini, Mansueti, or Carpaccio had noticed and been inspired by the anachronism of the laundry dangling inconspicuously in the Ovetari chapel in nearby Padua, in the *Martyrdom of St. Christopher* (ca. 1448) painted by Andrea Mantegna (1431–1506), Jacopo Bellini's son-in-law and Gentile Bellini's brother-in-law. Why Mantegna, one of the most rigorously classicizing painters of the Renaissance, included laundry dangling from a pole in his *Martyrdom of St. Christopher* is a bit puzzling,

since images of laundry aired out to dry had, to my knowledge, no classical precedent. Their inclusion thereby constitutes an obsequious intrusion of the present into an ostensibly third-century imperial past. Perhaps Mantegna purposely incorporated images of the present into a narrative that dealt with a saint who was acknowledged to be part of a fantastical legend, as opposed to a figure from "verifiable" history. In other words, Mantegna, who was always sensitive to the humanist concern for historical accuracy, could have felt free to conflate distinctly different temporal periods and introduce contemporary quotidian elements into a fresco that treated a core subject matter of acknowledged legend, as indeed he does throughout the *Martyrdom of St. Christopher*, whereas he did not feel he had the liberty to do so in other frescoes in the Ovetari chapel that treated core subject matters of acknowledged history, such as *St. James Led to His Execution* (ca. 1448). Hence the anachronism of the contemporary image of laundry dangling behind a perfectly reconstructed antique cornice. Then again, as Grafton 1999 reminds us in another context, even the most rigorous humanists freely conflated historical specificity with present-day concerns.

41. Cooper 1990, 239 instead treats the "gleaming metal vessel" as the "Golden Urn," the container used when "Moses commanded Aaron to keep some Manna for his descendants," as the narrative is told in Exodus 6:32–34.

42. See, for instance, Cope 1979, 138–40 on why the representation of the "Washing of the Feet" was an apposite topic paired with the Last Supper in chapels of the sacrament as a "type for the purification which should precede the taking of Communion."

43. Kemp 1989, 38–39.

44. On these two late paintings being particularly "self-reflexive," see Nichols 1999, 233.

45. Hence the figure of St. Christopher to the left, in the middle ground, who serves to remind us of the titular saint of the church. On the *Mourning of the Dead Christ*, see Paolucci et al. 1994.

46. I follow the identifications of Paolucci et al. 1994, 180–82: Mary Magdalene to the left, St. John and the Virgin Mary bearing Christ in the center, Martha of Bethany to the right, and the bearded St. Bernard of Clairvaux, Nicodemus, and Joseph of Arimathea behind.

47. Paolucci et al. 1994, 181: The "vaso a bocca larga" at the bottom center of the canvas "è probabilmente il Graal, il recipiente in cui, secondo le leggende medievali, Giuseppe d'Arimatea conservò l'acqua sporca di sangue con cui aveva lavato il corpo di Gesù prima di seppellirlo."

CHAPTER 5

1. Pontano, "On the Prince," in Kraye 1997, 83: "Is there anyone who does not shudder at the sight of a beard which flows down to a man's chest?"

2. I recognize that this is not a systematic form of data gathering or analysis, but it is, I think, somewhat revealing, at least anecdotally, that only four of all the men from the sixteenth century discussed at any length in this book—Biringuccio, Guicciardini, Bruno, and Machiavelli—went beardless in the period in question.

3. Horowitz 1997.

4. I would suspect that they were also associated with religious men of the Greek Orthodox Church, such as one depicted on Filarete's bronze doors to St. Peter's, but that is another matter.

5. Horowitz 1997, 1185.

6. Zucker 1977 provides an in-depth study of this. On the beard generally in history, see Reynolds 1950.

7. Zucker 1977, 526, quoting from the *Diario romano* of Sebastiano di Branca Tedallini (May–June 1511), in Muratori 1904, 321: "And the pope wore a beard like a hermit [*romito*], and no one can remember anything similar, that popes should wear a beard."

8. As Constable 1985, 92–93 summarily observes: "peasants were often shown with beards."

9. Machiavelli 1972, 1.3. There is nothing of this sort in Plautus's *Casina*, which is the classical model.

10. Isidore of Seville 1911, 12.1.25 draws the (false) etymological connection.

11. On the broader function of cleanliness in the period, see Biow 2006.

12. Guicciardini 1969, 1; Guicciardini 1988, 3.

13. Quint (2000) reviews the scholarship on the topic and adds his own observations about the way in which Castiglione's text is complicitous in this gender conflict. Of particular importance are Finucci 1992 and 1997. See as well a recent historical treatment of the topic in Horodowich 2008, 165–206.

14. I have addressed some of these matters in Chapter 6.

15. To be sure, this is not always or necessarily the case (as Karras 2003, 5 observes) in theory, but it was the case in Renaissance Italy.

16. On the influence of Spain in the fashion of male dress, see, for instance, Quondam 2007b.

17. Fisher 2001, 173 discusses this in the context of Renaissance England.

18. On simulation and dissimulation, see the synthesis in Snyder 2009.

19. Horowitz 1997, 1191.

20. See Chapter 6.

21. See Zucker 1977, 526 on Julius II characterized in 1511 as a bear.

22. For Renaissance strategies of being inconspicuously conspicuous, with a focus on Castiglione, see Biow 2010, ch. 1 and relevant bibliography.

23. Della Casa 1986, 12. The Italian is taken from Cellini 1960, 378.

24. Castiglione (1959, 1.1) on one occasion acknowledges that it is almost impossible to know why fashions change. On another occasion, however, he does note that the many invasions Italy suffered affected fashion: "By way of the wars and ruins of Italy, changes have come about in the language, in the buildings, dress, and customs" (Preface.2). In this last instance, Castiglione may have a historical *longue durée* in mind (the changes since the fall of the Roman Empire, say), but he surely has the ravages of recent invasions on his mind as well.

25. Della Casa 1986, 12. The Italian is taken from Cellini 1960, 378.

26. Bembo changed his facial features, going from being thickly bearded to mildly bearded to well shaven, or such is at least suggested by Cellini, who describes the matter in a letter about the making of the medal for Bembo. See Cellini 1968, 1000.

27. Landucci 1927, 294 (my emphasis): "In the year 1529 the custom of wearing hoods began to go out, and by 1532 not a single one was to be seen; caps or hats being worn instead. Also, at this time, men began to cut their hair short, everyone having formerly worn it long, on to their shoulders, without exception; *and they now began to wear a beard*."

28. Simon 1983, 527n2. See also Simon 1985 and Brock 2002, 172–74. For the painting in the context of homosociality, see Simons 1997, 31–32.

29. Cox-Rearick 1993, 377.

30. See Simon 1983 for a discussion and dating of the first portrait of Cosimo I in armor and the various versions, both by Bronzino and by his workshop.

31. See Foster 1971; Cox-Rearick 1984; and Langedijk 1981.

32. Edelstein 2000, 36, 42.

33. The medal was never actually made, but that does not detract from the point that the shape and size of the beard were important in the deliberations about the design.

34. Langedijk 1981, 82.

35. Ibid.

36. Brock 2002, 105.

37. Langedijk 1981, 86. On the three types of portraits that make up the official image of the duke presented to the world, see also pp. 79–120, 407–530.

38. The array available for design exceeded the limited number shown, for instance, in della Porta 1652, 237–38.

39. See Cropper 1985 on the *fiorentinità* of this and other portraits of the period.

40. See, for example, Gnudi and Webster 1950.

CHAPTER 6

1. On placing Bruno's *Candelaio* in his developing philosophy, see, for instance, Ciliberto 1990, 20–25; Lerro 2012; Saiber 2005, 71–87; and Moliterno's introduction to Bruno 2000, 9–49. Quotations from the *Candelaio* are from Bruno 2000, cited by act and scene numbers, modified at times for accuracy. Citations of the Italian text are from Bruno 1964.

2. Bruno's wearing of a moustache, if the portrait is accurate, seems to be fairly unique in the Italian Renaissance. In *I mondi* (1994) Doni talks about men wanting a beard with or without a moustache but not about men just wanting to sport a lone moustache. I have no idea why this is the case: why Italian men of the period did not wear just moustaches and, for that matter, why Bruno does wear one, at least in this image of him.

3. Although the play is full of devices that articulate a relationship with a public, Bruno himself in the prologue calls attention to the difficulties of the play being staged, a topic at times brought up in critical discussions, such as in Pesca-Cupolo 1999, among others.

4. Moliterno (introduction to Bruno 2000, 30–31) discusses the play's performance history, and as he points out, Bruno may well have never intended it to be performed, preferring it to have been staged, as it were, "*in* the mind, as a literary exercise to be read and played out on the stage of the imagination" (14). It is important to recognize, moreover, that plays were often meant to be read rather than performed in the Italian Renaissance. For the production history of comedies and performances, see Richard 1993.

5. Consider, for instance, the introduction by Squarotti to his edition of Bruno 1964, 5–15, as well as Squarotti 1958 and 1960. For additional readings of the play, all of which are concerned with it as a textual as opposed to staged performance, see Lerro 2012; Sottong 2011; Giannetti 2009, 188–90 in the context of the author's discussion of theatrics and sodomy, 153–92; Saiber 2005, 71–87; Hodgart 1997; Quarta 1985; and Barr 1971.

6. Although there are a lot of disguises in Roman comedy, there are no beards serving as disguises, to my knowledge. Only two men in Plautus and Terence are explicitly bearded, in *Menaechmi* and *Casina*. I have not located instances of other men in the *commedia erudita* of the Italian Renaissance disguising themselves with beards; typically they fake accents, alter their facial expressions, put on cloaks, and the like. Nor have I found examples of their use in theatrical productions in Italy, although Montaigne 1983, 139 does mention the need for a "false beard" being deployed by a friar, or a man dressed as a friar, in a public procession in Florence; Flaminio Scala, in his *Il teatro delle favole rappresentative* (1611), has at least one instance in which a fake beard is used as a prop in a commedia dell'arte (*The Dentist*): see McKee 1967, 88. Additionally, Martin 2004, 64 records from the archives that some journeymen employed a fake beard in their mock religious rituals. There is little doubt in my mind that beards were used in performances in Italy, much as they clearly were on the Elizabethan stage, on which see Fisher 2001 and Fisher 2006, 83–128. It is worth mentioning that in

Ariosto's *Orlando furioso* Melissa magically disguises herself with a beard (7.51); Ariosto 1982. The most famous examples of beards put on and taken off on the English stage occur, of course, in Shakespeare, such as in *Twelfth Night* and *Midsummer Night's Dream*. Beards have pride of place, from time to time, in classical literature, as in Martial 1993, 2.36, 4.36, 6.57, 8.47, 8.52, 9.47, 11.22, 11.39, 11.84. Perhaps the best-known example of a beard serving as a disguise in classical literature occurs in Homer's *Odyssey*, when Odysseus first appears, but does not yet fully reveal himself, to his son Telemachus. To complicate matters, we can readily imagine that the actor playing Gianbernardo may well have worn, of course, a fake beard.

7. Davis 1983, 42, my emphasis.

8. Bonino 1977; Giannetti and Ruggiero 2003, 263.

9. Horowitz 1997; Zucker 1977. On the beard generally in history, see Reynolds 1950.

10. Doni 1994, 113. For an overview of Doni in English, see Grendler 1969 and Biow 2010, 157–86.

11. Venice, Archivio di Stato, Cancelleria Inferiore, Miscellanea Notai Diversi B 37, n. 28, gr; cited in Fortini Brown 2004, 282n71.

12. See Chapter 5.

13. Fortini Brown 2004, 185. On women in general, and prostitutes in particular, dressing up their hair in a certain distinct manner of the period so that they appear coifed like men and, by so doing, excite men sexually (and thereby engage, according to law, in sodomy), see, for instance, Chambers and Pullan 1992, 123–24. For thoughts connecting beards to pros-thetics, in a wide-ranging study that draws on the work of Judith Butler, see Fisher 2006.

14. Fortini Brown 2004, 185–86.

15. Benedetti, *Anatomice*, in Lind 1975, 113, further cited in the text. On Benedetti's life and works, see Lind 1975, 69–80. The original, with Italian translation, is in Benedetti 1998, 240.

16. Neither Lind (1975, 114) nor Ferrari in Benedetti 1998, 241 can locate the source of the jocular anecdote, which Ferrari speculates may be Benedetti's invention.

17. As Fisher (2001, 174–75) points out, Shakespeare plays with the pun: "The link between facial hair and the production of semen is presented in a more socially accessible form in Shakespeare's plays through the common pun on 'hairs' and 'heirs.' In *Troilus and Cressida*, Pandarus describes how Helen had spied a white hair on Triolus' chin and said: 'Here's but two and fifty hairs on your chin—and one of them is white.' To which Troilus replies 'That white hair is my father, and all the rest are his sons' (1.2.146–51). He thus associates his own production of facial hairs with his procreative potential. As in the medical texts, Troilus creates a direct link between the growth of his facial hair and his virility." See also Simons 2011, 30 and Fisher 2006.

18. This point is emphasized in Darnton 1984, 5.

19. On this point, see Horowitz 1997; Reynolds 1950, 23–24; and Fisher 2001, 2006.

20. Puma 1988, 58. This is the standard interpretation, voiced, for instance, also in Kleiner 1992, 238. For a reassessment of how to read Hadrian's beard, see Vout 2006. The association between beards (and hairiness in general) and Greek intellectuals (philosophers in particular) is rendered comic in Martial 1993, 9.47.

21. Certainly this gendered concept having to do with facial hairs—a concept that associ-ates maleness with beards on men and femininity with smooth-skinned faces on women (who were not, of course, supposed to produce facial hair, any more than they were supposed to have testicles)—had a hold on authors of literature in the Italian Middle Ages and Renais-sance. Dante, for instance, voiced the concept in his *Convivio* when he observed, in the context of talking about goodness and quantity, that "every goodness proper to a thing is

deserving of love in that thing, as in masculinity to have a full beard [*sì com'è nella maschiezza essere ben barbuto*] and in femininity to have the entire face free of hair [*e nella femminezza essere ben pulita di barba in tutta la faccia*], just as in the foxhound to have a keen scent, and in the greyhound to have great speed" (I.12.8). I have adopted the translation from the *Princeton Dante Project*, http://etcweb.princeton.edu/dante/pdp/, which takes its text from Dante 1995. In the same way, the concept associating a full beard with male adulthood and the absence of one with youth—in particular the indeterminate stage called "adolescence"—had a hold on authors of literature in the Italian Middle Ages and Renaissance. For the most part, as Constable (1985, 60) argues in a study of beards in the early and late Middle Ages, "the capacity to grow a beard was regarded as essential for a man, and even in periods when beards were not commonly worn, there was a tendency to regard close shaving as effeminate and to seek some special justification for classes of men, like monks and clerics, who regularly shaved their beards." Bell 1999 discusses the difficulty in defining "adolescence."

22. Fioravanti 1583, 73v, my translation. On Fioravanti, see Chapter 3 and bibliography.

23. See Garzoni 1996, 1294, 1374–77. On Garzoni, see McClure 2004, 70–140 and Martin 1996. For Garzoni's fascination with cleanliness and dirt, see Biow 2006, 14–15, 47–48.

24. Fortini Brown 2004, vii, but see also 3–5: "The term *politia* had two distinct, if related, meanings in the sixteenth century. One usage derived from the Greek *politeia* and connoted good government, the political life, and civil comportment. Another came from the Latin *politus*, meaning refinement in fashion, politeness of behavior, or the display of luxury. The word is related, as well, to the Italian *pulita* or *polita*: a gleaming cleanliness and orderliness." For a broad treatment of the topic in the Italian Renaissance as it appeared in primarily verbal form, see Biow 2006.

25. Garzoni 1996, 1376–77, my translation. Barbers were not often discussed, from what I can tell, in classical literature, but see Martial 1993, 2.17, which mentions a "female barber," and 2.48, 3.74, 7.64, 7.83, 8.52.

26. The most famous instance of a barbershop becoming a place of social interaction is the one belonging to Il Burchiello, the Florentine barber poet, who engaged people in the space of his barbershop and whose poetry, which became popular in the sixteenth century among Anton Francesco Grazzini and others, reflects aspects of his profession, including the poem that compares the work of the barber to that of the poet: one polishes the face, the other the writing. Barbershops appear as locales for gossip in Venice; see Horodowich 2005, 35–36; Cowan 2008, 124–25; and especially Vivo 2007, 98–106, 142–56, in the sections appropriately titled "Before the Coffeehouse" and "Reason of State in the Barbershop." In the second treatise of his *Libraria*, Doni has Burchiello writing a book, probably an invention of Doni, titled *Nobiltà dell'arte del barbiere*, on which he provides an amusing commentary; see Doni 1972, 277. The notion of the barber as a font of gossip persists through the early modern period and beyond. For a Habermasian reading of the barber's role in the eighteenth and early nineteenth centuries in Europe (principally in England), tying the function of the barbershop to that of the coffeehouse as spaces for political discussion and dissent, see Herzog 1996, esp. 32–34. For a woman's manipulation of hair in the period as a mechanism for not only marking gender but configuring alliances and social position and cementing loyalties, see Welch 2008, 2009.

27. Aretino 1968. I cite, with only slight modifications, from the translation of Giannetti and Ruggiero (2003, 166–67).

28. This is the central argument of "semniotics" in Simons 2011.

29. Martines 2001; Weissman 1989; Martin 2004; Burke 1986; Cohen and Cohen 2001; Horodowich 2005, 2008.

30. See Fisher 2001 and 2006 for compelling reflections on how the beard "made the man" in English Renaissance drama.

31. See, on the Red Sox going bearded, http://www.bostonglobe.com/sports/2013/06/12/ hairy-situation-for-red-sox/VgRcFAFwFO2E2IdONWE2AM/story.htmllhttp://sports.yahoo .com/blogs/mlb-big-league-stew/red-sox-embracing-beards-scruffy-faces-giving-team-2327 38518—mlb.ht, along with Rushin 2013.

EPILOGUE

1. By "nationally" I am not referring to nationhood in the modern sense of the term but in the Renaissance sense that refers to a linguistically bound group, such as the various "nazioni" gathering together as collectivities at universities.

2. Burckhardt 1960, 81, with the German taken from Burckhardt 1989, 59.

3. See note 4 in this book's introduction. Gossman is essential for an understanding of Burckhardt's concept of the individual—a concept that we have attributed to him over time, for a variety of historical reasons, as a much more cheerful and positive one than how he ever intended it to be understood.

4. This is rather movingly brought home in the award-winning and popularizing Greenblatt 2011, which noticeably rehearses toward the beginning the by now accepted notion among many that there was in fact no such thing as the individual in the period when Greenblatt declares that "to prize a person for some ineffable individuality or for many-sidedness or for intense curiosity was virtually unheard of" (16). For, interestingly enough, in Greenblatt's narrative, Lucretius's highly idiosyncratic *De rerum natura* (*On the Nature of Things*) now all of a sudden has a powerful, heroic "many-sidedness" and "ineffable" quality to it that is capable of transforming sentiments and outlooks and the course of history, not the person who rediscovered the book in the first place and was willing, despite all obstacles, to travel far from home in his yearning to collect writings from antiquity and possess them in his hands—a longing doubled in Greenblatt's act of rummaging through used books in New Haven, whereupon, as a penny-pinching and curious graduate student at Yale, he unaccountably alighted upon Lucretius's didactic poem in a manner that would eventually haunt his life. Nor should we find Greenblatt's approach entirely surprising, I suppose. After all, it is Lucretius's book—a thing—that has touched Greenblatt's life, not Bracciolini—a rather curious, adventurous, and independent-minded person—who recovered it from oblivion, although, truth be told, the ghostly presence of Greenblatt's rather lugubrious mother—a person, to be sure—looms large in the background of Greenblatt's story from the outset and serves to explain why he was so intensely drawn to Lucretius's book in the first place and its calming Epicurean message of how to overcome a fear of death. For salient reservations about Greenblatt's book voiced by a Renaissance scholar steeped in Italian humanism, see Monfasani 2013, along with Greenblatt's fascinating response, in which he pleads "guilty to the Burckhardtianism of which John Monfasani accuses me."

BIBLIOGRAPHY

Abbott, Andrew. 1988. *The System of Professions: An Essay on the Division of Expert Labor.*
  Chicago: University of Chicago Press.
Ackerman, James S. 1949. "'Ars Sine Scientia Nihil Est': Gothic Theory of Architecture at the
  Cathedral of Milan." *Art Bulletin* 31: 84–111.
Aeschylus. 1998. *Prometheus Bound.* Trans. William Matthews. In *Aeschylus, 2,* ed. David R.
  Slavitt and Palmer Bovie, 151–96. Philadelphia: University of Pennsylvania Press.
Ago, Renata. 2013. *Gusto for Things: A History of Objects in Seventeenth-Century Rome.* Trans.
  Bradford Bouley and Corey Tazzara. Foreword by Paula Findlen. Chicago: University of
  Chicago Press.
Alberti, Leon Battista. 1966. *L'architettura (De re aedificatoria): Testo latino e traduzione.* Ed.
  Giovanni Orlandi. Introduction and notes by Paolo Portoghesi. Milan: Il Polifilo.
———. 1972. *"On Painting" and "On Sculpture": The Latin Texts of "De pictura" and "De
  statua."* Ed., trans., and intro. Cecil Grayson. London: Phaidon.
———. 1986. *The Ten Books of Architecture.* Trans. James Leoni. New York: Dover.
———. 2011. *On Painting: A New Translation and Critical Edition.* Ed. and trans. Rocco
  Sinisgalli. Cambridge: Cambridge University Press.
Alessio, Franco. 1965. "La filosofia e le 'artes mechanicae' nel secolo XII." *Studi medievali* 6:
  71–155.
Alighieri, Dante. *See* Dante Alighieri.
Allen, James. 1994. "Failure and Expertise in the Ancient Conception of an Art." In *Scientific
  Failure,* ed. A. I. Janis and T. Horowitz, 81–108. Lanham, MD: Rowman & Littlefield.
Amelang, James S. 1998. *The Flight of Icarus: Artisan Autobiography in Early Modern Europe.*
  Stanford, CA: Stanford University Press.
Ames-Lewis, Francis. 2000. *The Intellectual Life of the Early Renaissance Artist.* New Haven,
  CT: Yale University Press.
Angelozzi, Giancarlo. 1998. "Il duello nella trattatistica italiana della prima metà del XVI
  secolo." In *Modernità: Definizioni ed esercizi,* ed. Albano Biondi, 9–31. Bologna: CLUEB.
Angier, Tom. 2010. *Techne in Aristotle's "Ethics": Crafting the Moral Life.* London: Continuum
  International Publishing Group.
Applebaum, Herbert A. 1992. *The Concept of Work: Ancient, Medieval, and Modern.* Albany:
  State University of New York Press.
Aquilecchia, Giovanni. 1980. "Pietro Aretino e altri poligrafi a Venezia." In *Storia della cultura
  veneta,* vol. 3, pt. 2, 61–98. Vicenza: Neri Pozza.
Arbesmann, Rudolph. 1973. "The Attitude of Saint Augustine Toward Labor." In *The Heri-
  tage of the Early Church: Essays in Honor of G. V. Fiorovsky,* 247–59. Rome: Pontifical
  Institute Studiorum Orientalium.
Aretino, Pietro. 1968. *Tutte le commedie.* Ed. G. B. De Sanctis. Milan: Mursia.

Ariosto, Ludovico. 1982. *Orlando furioso*. Ed. Emilio Bigi. 2 vols. Milan: Rusconi.

Ascoli, Albert R., and Victoria Kahn, eds. 1993. *Machiavelli and the Discourse of Literature*. Ithaca, NY: Cornell University Press.

Ashenburg, Katherine. 2007. *The Dirt on Clean: An Unsanitized History*. New York: North Point Press.

Asor Rosa, Alberto. 1993. "*Ricordi* di Francesco Guicciardini." In *Letteratura italiana: Le opere*, vol. 2, ed. Alberto Asor Rosa, 3–94. Turin: Einaudi.

Atwill, Janet. 1998. *Rhetoric Reclaimed: Aristotle and the Liberal Arts Tradition*. Ithaca, NY: Cornell University Press.

Augustine, of Hippo. 1950. *The City of God*. Trans. Marcus Dods. New York: Modern Library.

———. 1952. *Work of Monks*. In *Saint Augustine Treatises on Various Subjects*, ed. Roy J. Deferraru, trans. Mary Sarah Muldowney, 321–94. New York: Fathers of the Church.

———. 1984. *The Rule of Saint Augustine: Masculine and Feminine Versions*. Trans. Raymond Canning. Introduction and commentary by Tarsicius J. Van Bavel. Kalamazoo, MI: Cistercian Publications.

Bacci, M., and P. Stoppelli. 1979. "Cennini, Cennino." In *Dizionario biografico degli italiani*. 23: 565–69. Rome: Istituto della Enciclopedia Italiana.

Baldan, Sergio, ed. 2011. "La storia del monastero di S. Giorgio Maggiore scritta dal Monaco Fortunato Olmo." *Studi veneziani* 63: 351–546.

Baldassarri, Stefano U., and Arielle Saber, eds. and trans. 2000. *Images of Quattrocento Florence: Selected Writings in Literature, History, and Art*. New Haven, CT: Yale University Press.

Balme, Maurice. 1984. "Attitudes to Work and Leisure in Ancient Greece." *Greece & Rome* 31: 140–52.

Bambrough, J. R. 1956. "Plato's Political Analogies." In *Philosophy, Politics and Society*, ed. Peter Laslett, 98–115. Oxford: Basil Blackwell.

Barbaro, Ermolao. 1969. *De coelibatu—De officio legati*. Ed. Vittore Branca. Florence: Olschki.

Barkan, Leonard. 1999. *Unearthing the Past: Archaeology and Aesthetics in the Making of Renaissance Culture*. New Haven, CT: Yale University Press.

Barolsky, Paul. 1990. *Michelangelo's Nose: A Myth and Its Mythmaker*. University Park: Penn State University Press.

———. 1991. *Why Mona Lisa Smiles and Other Tales by Vasari*. University Park: Penn State University Press.

Baron, Hans. 1968. *From Petrarch to Leonardo Bruni: Studies in Humanistic and Political Literature*. Chicago: University of Chicago Press.

Barr, Alan. 1971. "Passion, Extension, Excision: Imagistic and Structural Patterns in Giordano Bruno's *Il candelaio*." *Texas Studies in Literature and Language* 13: 351–63.

Barzman, Karen Edis. 2000. *The Florentine Academy and the Early Modern State: The Discipline of Disegno*. Cambridge: Cambridge University Press.

Basso, Jeannine. 1990. *Le genre épistolaire en langue italienne, 1538–1662: Répertoire chronologique et analytique*. Rome: Bulzoni.

Battaglia, Salvatore. 1961–. *Grande dizionario della lingua italiana*. Turin: Unione Tipografico-Editrice Torinese.

Baxandall, Michael. 1971. *Giotto and the Orators: Humanist Observers of Painting in Italy and the Discovery of Pictorial Composition, 1350–1450*. Oxford: Clarendon Press.

———. 1972. *Painting and Experience in Fifteenth-Century Italy: A Primer in the Social History of Pictorial Style*. Oxford: Oxford University Press.

Bazzoli, Maurizio. 2005. "Ragion di Stato e interesse degli stati: La trattatistica sull'ambasciatore dal XV al XVIII secolo." In *Stagioni e teorie della società internazionale*, ed. M. Bazzoli, 267–312. Milan: Edizioni Universitarie di Lettere Economia Diritto.

Bec, Christian. 1983. "Lo statuto socio-professionale degli scrittori (Trecento e Cinquecento)." In *Letteratura italiana: Produzione e consumo*, ed. Alberto Asor Rosa, vol. 2, 229–67. Turin: Einaudi.

Becchi, Egle, and Monica Ferrari. 2009. "Professioni, professionisti, professionalizzare: Storie di formazione." In *Formare alle professioni: Sacerdoti, principi, educatori*, ed. E. Becchi and M. Ferrari, 7–27. Milan: FrancoAngeli.

Bedford, Ronald, Lloyd Davis, and Philippa Kelly, eds. 2006. *Early Modern Autobiography: Theories, Genres, Practices*. Ann Arbor: University of Michigan Press.

Bell, Rudolph. 1999. *How to Do It: Guides to Good Living for Renaissance Italians*. Chicago: University of Chicago Press.

Benedetti, Alessandro. 1998. *Historia corporis humani, sive Anatomice*. Ed. Giovanna Ferrari. Florence: Giunti.

Benjamin, Walter. 1969. *Illuminations*. Trans. H. Zohn. New York: Schocken Books.

Benson, Pamela Joseph. 1992. *The Invention of the Renaissance Woman: The Challenge of Female Independence in the Literature and Thought of Italy and England*. University Park: Penn State University Press.

Berger, Harry, Jr. 2000. *The Absence of Grace: Sprezzatura and Suspicion in Two Renaissance Courtesy Books*. Stanford, CA: Stanford University Press.

Bernardoni, Andrea. 2011. *Conoscenza del fare: Ingegneria, arte, scienza nel "De la pirotechnia" di Vannoccio Biringuccio*. Rome: L'Erma di Bretschneider.

Biagioli, Mario. 1993. *Galileo, Courtier: The Practice of Science in the Age of Absolutism*. Chicago: University of Chicago Press.

Biester, James. 1997. *Lyric Wonder: Rhetoric and Wit in Renaissance English Poetry*. Ithaca, NY: Cornell University Press.

Bigi, E. 1964. "Barbaro, Ermolao." In *Dizionario biografico degli italiani*, 6: 96–99. Rome: Istituto della Enciclopedia Italiana.

Biow, Douglas. 1996. *Mirabile Dictu: Representations of the Marvelous in Medieval and Renaissance Epic*. Ann Arbor: University of Michigan Press.

———. 2002. *Doctors, Ambassadors, Secretaries: Humanism and Professions in Renaissance Italy*. Chicago: University of Chicago Press.

———. 2006. *The Culture of Cleanliness in Renaissance Italy*. Ithaca, NY: Cornell University Press.

———. 2010. *In Your Face: Professional Improprieties and the Art of Being Conspicuous in Sixteenth-Century Italy*. Stanford, CA: Stanford University Press.

Biringuccio, Vannoccio. 1540. *De la pirotechnia. Libri .x. dove ampiamente si tratta non solo di ogni sorte e diversita di miniere, ma anchora quanto si ricerca intorno a la prattica di quelle cose di quel che si appartiene a l'arte de la fusione over gitto de metalli come d'ogni altra cosa simile a questa*. Venice: Rossinello.

———. 1959. *The Pirotechnia*. Trans. Cyril Stanley Smith and Martha Teach Gnudi. New York: Basic Books.

Black, Robert. 1991. "Italian Renaissance Education: Changing Perspectives and Continuing Controversies." *Journal of the History of Ideas* 52: 315–34.

———. 2001. *Humanism and Education in Medieval and Renaissance Italy*. Cambridge: Cambridge University Press.

———. 2011. "New Light on Machiavelli's Education." In *Studies in Renaissance Humanism and Politics: Florence and Arezzo*, 391–98. Burlington, VT: Ashgate Varorium.

———. 2012. "A Pupil of Marcello Virgilio Adriani at the Florentine Studio." In *Umanesimo e università in Toscana (1300–1600): Atti del Convegno internazionale di studi (Fiesole-Firenze, 25–26 maggio 2011)*, ed. Stefano Ugo Baldassarri, Fabrizio Ricciardelli, and Enrico Spagnesi, 15–32. Florence: Le Lettere.

———. 2013. *Machiavelli*. London: Routledge, Taylor & Francis Group.

Bock, Gisela, Quentin Skinner, and Maurizio Viroli, eds. 1990. *Machiavelli and Republican-ism*. Cambridge: Cambridge University Press.

Bohde, Daniela. 2003. "Skin and the Search for the Interior: The Representation of Flaying in the Art and Anatomy of the Cinquecento." In *Bodily Extremities: Preoccupations with the Human Body in Early Modern European Culture*, ed. Florike Egmond and Robert Zwijnenberg, 10–47. Aldershot, UK: Ashgate.

Bolland, Andrea. 1996. "Art and Humanism in Early Renaissance Padua: Cennini, Vergerio and Petrarch on Imitation." *Renaissance Quarterly* 49: 469–87.

———. 2006. "From the Workshop to the Academy: The Emergence of the Artist in Renais-sance Florence." In *Renaissance Florence: A Social History*, ed. Roger J. Crum and John T. Paoletti, 454–78. Cambridge: Cambridge University Press.

Bolzoni, Lina. 1981. "Il segretario neoplatonico (F. Patrizi, A. Querenghi, V. Gramigna)." In *La Corte e il "Cortegiano,"* ed. Adriano Prosperi, vol. 2, 133–69. Rome: Bulzoni.

Bondanella, Peter E. 1976. *Francesco Guicciardini*. Boston: Twayne.

Bonino, Guido Davico, ed. 1977. *Il teatro italiano, II: La commedia del Cinquecento*. Vol. 2. Turin: Einaudi.

———. 1979. *Lo scrittore, il potere, la maschera: Tre studi sul Cinquecento*. Padua: Liviana.

Bonora, Elena. 1994. "Tra oratori, cortigiani e uomini di lettere: Il trattato sul segretario." In *Ricerche su Francesco Sansovino imprenditore librario e letterato*, 139–62. Venice: Istituto Veneto di Scienze, Lettere ed Arti.

Borsellino, Nino. 1979. "Cellini, Benvenuto." In *Dizionario biografico degli italiani*, 23: 440–51. Rome: Istituto della Enciclopedia Italiana.

Bosco, Umberto. 1961. *Francesco Petrarca*. Bari: Laterza.

Boudon-Millot, Véronique. 2005. "Art, Science and Conjecture, from Hippocrates to Plato and Aristotle." In *Hippocrates in Context: Papers Read at the XIth International Hippocra-tes Colloquium, University of Newcastle upon Tyne, 27–31 August 2002*, ed. Philip J. van der Eijk, 87–99. Leiden: Brill.

Bourdieu, Pierre. 1984. *Distinction: A Social Critique of the Judgment of Taste*. Trans. Richard Nice. Cambridge, MA: Harvard University Press.

Bradley, Mark, and Kenneth Stow, eds. 2012. *Rome, Pollution and Propriety: Dirt, Disease and Hygiene in the Eternal City from Antiquity to Modernity*. Cambridge: Cambridge Univer-sity Press.

Bragantini, Renzo. 1996. "Poligrafi e umanisti volgari." In *Storia della letteratura italiana*, ed. Enrico Malato, vol. 4, *Il primo Cinquecento*, 681–754. Rome: Salerno.

Branca, Vittore. 1973. "Ermolao Barbaro and Late Quattrocento Venetian Humanism." In *Renaissance Venice*, ed. John R. Hale, 218–43. London: Faber.

———. 1981. "L'umanesimo veneziano alla fine del Quattrocento: Ermolao Barbaro e il suo circolo." In *Storia della cultura veneta*, ed. G. Arnaldi and M. Pastore Stocchi, vol. 3/I, 123–75. Vicenza: Neri Pozza.

Brand, Charles P. 1965. *Torquato Tasso: A Study of the Poet and of His Contributions to English Literature*. Cambridge: Cambridge University Press.

Brann, Noel L. 2002. *The Debate over the Origin of Genius During the Italian Renaissance: The Theories of Supernatural Frenzy and Natural Melancholy in Accord and in Conflict on the Threshold of the Scientific*. Leiden: Brill.

Brock, Maurice. 2002. *Bronzino*. London: Thames & Hudson.

Brown, Katherine T. 2000. *The Painter's Reflection: Self-Portraiture in Renaissance Venice, 1458–1625*. Florence: Olschki.

Brown, Patricia Fortini. 1988. *Venetian Narrative Painting in the Age of Carpaccio*. New Haven, CT: Yale University Press.

———. 2004. *Private Lives in Renaissance Venice: Art, Architecture, and the Family*. New Haven, CT: Yale University Press.

Bruni, Leonardo. 1741. *Leonardi Bruni Arretini epistolarum libri VIII*. Ed. Lorenzo Mehus. 2 vols. Florence: Ex typographia B. Paperinii. Anastatic reprint with an introduction by James Hankins. Rome: Edizioni di Storia e Letteratura, 2007.

Bruno, Giordano. 1964. *Il candelaio*. Ed. Giorgio Bàrberi Squarotti. Turin: Einaudi.

———. 2000. *The Candlebearer*. Trans. Gino Moliterno. Ottawa: Dovehouse Editions.

Buck-Morss, Susan. 1989. *The Dialectics of Seeing: Walter Benjamin and the Arcades Project*. Cambridge, MA: MIT Press.

Bühler, Claudia. 1989. *Ikonographie und Entwicklung der Abendmahlsdarstellung im Oeuvre Tintorettos*. Köln: J Eul.

Burckhardt, Jacob. 1960. *The Civilization of the Renaissance in Italy*. Trans. S. G. C. Middlemore. London: Phaidon Press.

———. 1989. *Die Kultur der Renaissance in Italien*. Frankfurt am Main: Deutscher Klassiker Verlag.

Burford, Alison. 1972. *Craftsmen in Greek and Roman Society*. Ithaca, NY: Cornell University Press.

Burke, Peter. 1978. *Popular Culture in Early Modern Europe*. New York: Harper & Row.

———. 1986. *The Italian Renaissance: Culture and Society in Italy*. Rev. ed. Princeton, NJ: Princeton University Press.

———. 1987. *The Historical Anthropology of Early Modern Italy: Essays on Perception and Communication*. Cambridge: Cambridge University Press.

———. 1995a. "The Renaissance, Individualism and the Portrait." *History of European Ideas* 21: 393–400.

———. 1995b. *The Fortunes of the "Courtier": The European Reception of Castiglione's "Cortegiano."* Cambridge: Polity.

———. 1997. "Representations of the Self from Petrarch to Descartes." In *Rewriting the Self: Histories from the Renaissance to the Present*, ed. Roy Porter, 17–28. London: Routledge.

———. 1998. "Individuality and Biography in the Renaissance." In *Die Renaissance und die Entdeckung des Individuums in der Kunst*, vol. 2, *Die Renaissance als erste Aufklärung*, 65–78. Tübingen: Mohr Siebeck.

———. 2001. *Eyewitnessing: The Uses of Images as Historical Evidence*. Ithaca, NY: Cornell University Press.

———. 2008. *What Is Cultural History?* Cambridge, MA: Polity.

———. 2010. "Cultural History as Polyphonic History/Historia Cultural Como Historia Polifónica." *ARBOR Ciencia, Pensamiento y Cultura* 186: 479–86.

Butterfield, Andrew. 1997. *The Sculptures of Andrea del Verrocchio*. New Haven, CT: Yale University Press.

Bylebyl, Jerome J. 1990. "Interpreting the *Fasciculo* Anatomy Scene." *Journal of the History of Medicine and Allied Sciences* 45: 285–316.

———. 1993. "The Manifest and the Hidden in the Renaissance Clinic." In *Medicine and the Five Senses*, ed. W. F. Bynum and R. Porter, 40–60. Cambridge: Cambridge University Press.

Bynum, Caroline Walker. 1980. "Did the Twelfth Century Rediscover the Individual?" *Journal of Ecclesiastical History* 31: 1–17.

Caferro, William. 2011. *Contesting the Renaissance*. Malden, MA: Wiley-Blackwell.

Cambiano, Giuseppe. 1991. *Platone e le tecniche*. Bari: Laterza.

Campbell, Lorne. 1990. *Renaissance Portraits: European Portrait-Painting in the 14th, 15th, and 16th Centuries*. New Haven, CT: Yale University Press.

Campbell, Stephen J. 2004. *The Cabinet of Eros: Renaissance Mythological Painting and the "Studiolo" of Isabella d'Este*. New Haven, CT: Yale University Press.

Camporesi, Piero. 1988. *The Incorruptible Flesh: Bodily Mutation and Mortification in Religion and Folklore*. Trans. Tania Croft-Murray and Helen Elsom. Cambridge: Cambridge University Press.

———. 1990. *La miniera del mondo: Artieri, inventori, impostori*. Milan: Il Saggiatore.

———. 1997. *Camminare il mondo: Vita e avventure di Leonardo Fioravanti, medico del Cinquecento*. Milan: Garzanti.

Capaccio, Giulio Cesare. 1599. *Il secretario*. Venice: Vicenzo Somascho.

Carlino, Andrea. 1999. *Books of the Body: Anatomical Ritual and Renaissance Learning*. Trans. John Tedeschi and Anne C. Tedeschi. Chicago: University of Chicago Press.

Caro, Annibale. 1967. *Commento di ser Agresto da Ficaruolo sopra la prima ficata del Padre Siceo*. Bologna: Commissione per i Testi di Lingua.

Cartwright, Julia Mary. 1908. *Baldassare Castiglione: The Perfect Courtier, His Life and Letters, 1478–1529*. 2 vols. New York: E. P. Dutton and Company.

Castiglione, Baldassare. 1769. *Lettere del Conte Baldessar Castiglione, ora per la prima volta date in luce e con annotazioni storiche illustrate*. Ed. Pierantonio Serassi. Padua: Presso Giuseppe Comino.

———. 1929. *Il cortegiano*. Ed. Vittorio Cian. 3rd ed. Florence: Sansoni.

———. 1959. *The Book of the Courtier*. Trans. Charles S. Singleton. Garden City, NY: Doubleday.

Cavallo, Sandra. 2007. *Artisans of the Body: Identities, Bodies and Masculinities*. Manchester: Manchester University Press.

Celenza, Christopher. 2004. *The Lost Italian Renaissance: Humanists, Historians, and Latin's Legacy*. Baltimore: Johns Hopkins University Press.

Cellini, Benvenuto. 1960. *Opere di Baldassare Castiglione, Giovanni della Casa, Benvenuto Cellini*. Ed. Carlo Cordié. Milan: Ricciardi.

———. 1967. *The Treatises of Benvenuto Cellini on Goldsmithing and Sculpture*. Trans. C. R. Ashbee. New York: Dover.

———. 1968. *Opere: Vita, trattati, rime, lettere*. Ed. Bruno Maier. Milan: Rizzoli.

———. 1980. *Due trattati uno intorno alle otto principali arti dell'oreficeria. L'altro in materia dell'arte della scultura; dove si veggono infiniti segreti nel lavorar le figure di marmo, e nel gettarle di bronzo*. Florence: Per Valente Panizzij, & Marco Peri, 1568.

———. 1985. *Vita*. Ed. Ettore Camesasca. Milan: Biblioteca Universale Rizzoli.

Cennini., Cennino. 1933. *The Craftsman's Handbook: The Italian "Il libro dell'arte."* Trans. Daniel V. Thompson Jr. New York: Dover.

———. 1971. *Il libro dell'arte*. Ed. Franco Brunello. Intro. Licisco Magagnato. Vicenza: Neri Pozza.

Cervigni, Dino. 1979. *The "Vita" of Benvenuto Cellini: Literary Tradition and Genre*. Ravenna: Longo.

Chabod, Federico. 1964. *Scritti su Machiavelli*. Turin: Einaudi.

Chambers, David, and Brian Pullan, eds. 1992. *Venice: A Documentary History, 1450–1630*. Oxford: Blackwell.

Chenu, Marie-Dominique. 1968. *Nature, Man, and Society in the Twelfth Century: Essays on New Theological Perspectives in the Latin West*. Ed. and trans. Jerome Taylor and Lester K. Little. Chicago: University of Chicago Press.

Cian, Vittorio. 1951. *Un illustre nunzio pontificio del Rinascimento: Baldassar Castiglione*. Città del Vaticano: Biblioteca Apostolica Vaticana.

Cicero. 1938. *De officiis*. Trans. Walter Miller. Cambridge, MA: Harvard University Press.

———. 1942. *De oratore*. Trans. E.W. Sutton and H. Rackham. 2 vols. Cambridge, MA: Harvard University Press.

———. 1960. *Tusculanae disputationes*. Trans. J. E. King. Cambridge, MA: Harvard University Press.

Ciliberto, Michele. 1990. *Giordano Bruno*. Rome: Laterza.

Claeys, Gregory. 1986. "'Individualism,' 'Socialism,' and 'Social Sciences': Further Notes on a Process of Cultural Formation, 1800–1850." *Journal of the History of Ideas* 47: 81–93.

Clarke, John R. 2003. *Art in the Lives of Ordinary Romans: Visual Representation and Non-Elite Viewers in Italy, 100 B.C.–315 A.D.* Berkeley: University of California Press.

Classen, Constance, David Howes, and Anthony Synnott. 1994. *Aroma: The Cultural History of Smell*. London: Routledge.

Clements, Robert J. 1954. "Michelangelo on Effort and Rapidity in Art." *Journal of the Warburg and Courtauld Institutes* 17: 301–10.

Clifton, James. 1996. "Vasari on Competition." *Sixteenth Century Journal* 27: 23–41.

Close, Anthony J. 1969. "Commonplace Theories of Art and Nature in Classical Antiquity and in the Renaissance." *Journal of the History of Ideas* 30: 467–86.

———. 1971. "Philosophical Theories of Art and Nature in Classical Antiquity." *Journal of the History of Ideas* 32: 163–84.

Coates, Victoria C. Gardner. 2000. "'Ut vita scultura': Cellini's Perseus and the Self-Fashioning of Artistic Identity." In *Fashioning Identities in Renaissance Art*, ed. Mary Rogers, 149–62. Aldershot, UK: Ashgate.

Cockle, Charles J. D. 1957. *A Bibliography of Military Books up to 1642*. London: The Holland Press.

Cohen, Elizabeth S., and Thomas V. Cohen. 2001. *Daily Life in Renaissance Italy*. Westport, CT: Greenwood Press.

Cohn, Samuel. 1995. "Burckhardt Revisited from Social History." In *Languages and Images of Renaissance Italy*, ed. Alison Brown, 217–34. Oxford: Oxford University Press.

Cole, Michael Wayne. 2002. *Cellini and the Principles of Sculpture*. New York: Cambridge University Press.

Coleman, Janet, ed. 1996. *The Individual in Political Theory and Practice*. New York: Oxford University Press.

Collins, Jim. 1992. "Television and Postmodernism." In *Channels of Discourse, Reassembled: Television and Contemporary Criticism*, ed. Robert C. Allen, 2nd ed., 246–65. London: Routledge.

Connell, William J., ed. 2002. *Society and Individual in Renaissance Florence*. Berkeley: University of California Press.

Connolly, Joy. 2009. *The State of Speech: Rhetoric and Political Thought in Ancient Rome*. Princeton, NJ: Princeton University Press.

Constable, Giles. 1985. Introduction to *Apologiae duae: Gozechini epistola ad Walcherum; Burchardi, ut videtur, Abbatis Bellevallis Apologia de barbis*, ed. R. B. C. Huygens, 47–150. Turnholti: Brepols.

Cooper, Tracy Elizabeth. 1990. "The History and Decoration of the Church of San Giorgio Maggiore in Venice." Ph.D. diss., Princeton University.

Cope, Maurice E. 1979. *The Venetian Chapel of the Sacrament in the Sixteenth Century*. New York: Garland.

Cortesi, Paolo. 1510. *De cardinalatu*. San Gimignano: Symeon Nicolai Nardi.

———. 1980. *The Renaissance Cardinal's Ideal Palace: A Chapter from Cortesi's "De Cardina-latu."* Trans. Kathleen Weil-Garris Brandt. Rome: Edizioni dell'Elefante, American Academy.

Costo, Tomaso. 1602. *Discorso pratico fatto ad un suo nipote ad alcune qualità che debba haver un buon segretario.* Venice: Barezzo Barezzi.

Cowan, Alexander. 2008. "Gossip and Street Culture in Early Modern Venice." In *Cultural History of Early Modern Streets*, ed. Riitta Laitinen and Thomas V. Cohen, 119–39. Leiden: Brill.

Cox, Virginia. 1992. *The Renaissance Dialogue: Literary Dialogue in Its Social and Political Contexts, Castiglione to Galileo.* Cambridge: Cambridge University Press.

———. 1997. "Machiavelli and the *Rhetorica ad Herennium*: Deliberative Rhetoric in *The Prince.*" *Sixteenth Century Journal* 28: 1109–41.

———. 2008. *Women's Writing in Italy, 1400–1650.* Baltimore: Johns Hopkins University Press.

———. 2011. *The Prodigious Muse: Women's Writing in Counter-Reformation Italy.* Baltimore: Johns Hopkins University Press.

Cox-Rearick, Janet. 1984. *Dynasty and Destiny in Medici Art: Pontormo, Leo X, and the Two Cosimos.* Princeton, NJ: Princeton University Press.

———. 1993. *Bronzino's Chapel of Eleonora in the Palazzo Vecchio.* Berkeley: University of California Press.

Cranston, Jodi. 2000. *The Poetics of Portraiture in the Italian Renaissance.* Cambridge: Cambridge University Press.

Crisciani, Chiara. 2010. "La formazione del medico nel medioevo: Dottrina ed etica." In *Formare alle professioni: Figure di sanità*, ed. Monica Ferrari and Paolo Mazzarello, 36–57. Milan: FrancoAngeli.

Cropper, Elizabeth. 1985. "Prolegomena to a New Interpretation of Bronzino's Florentine Portraits." In *Renaissance Studies in Honor of Craig Hugh Smyth*, ed. Andrew Morrough et al., vol. 2, 149–60. Florence: Giunti Barbèri.

Crouzet-Pavan, Elisabeth. 2002. *Venice Triumphant: The Horizons of a Myth.* Baltimore: Johns Hopkins University Press.

Cunningham, Andrew. 1997. *The Anatomical Renaissance: The Resurrection of the Anatomical Projects of the Ancients.* Aldershot, UK: Scolar Press.

Cuomo, Serafina. 2007. *Technology and Culture in Greek and Roman Antiquity.* Cambridge: Cambridge University Press.

Curtius, Ernst Robert. 1990. *European Literature and the Latin Middle Ages.* Trans. Willard R. Trask. Princeton, NJ: Princeton University Press.

da Monte, Giovanni Battista. 1555. *De excrementis.* Paris: Apud Aegidium Gourbinum.

Dante Alighieri. 1995. *Convivio.* Ed. Franca Brambilla Ageno. Florence: Le Lettere.

D'Arms, John H. 1981. *Commerce and Social Standing in Ancient Rome.* Cambridge, MA: Harvard University Press.

Darnton, Robert. 1984. *The Great Cat Massacre and Other Episodes in French Cultural History.* New York: Basic Books.

Daston, Lorraine, and Katharine Park. 1998. *Wonders and the Order of Nature, 1150–1750.* New York: Zone Books.

Davies, Penelope. 2000. *Death and the Emperor: Roman Imperial Funerary Monuments, from Augustus to Marcus Aurelius.* Cambridge: Cambridge University Press.

Davis, Natalie Zemon. 1983. *The Return of Martin Guerre.* Cambridge, MA: Harvard University Press.

———. 1986. "Boundaries and the Sense of Self in Sixteenth-Century France." In *Reconstructing Individualism: Autonomy, Individuality and the Self in Western Thought*, ed. Thomas C. Heller, Morton Sosna, and David E. Wellbery, 53–63. Stanford, CA: Stanford University Press.

Davis, Robert C. 1994. *War of the Fists: Popular Culture and Public Violence in Late Renaissance Italy*. New York: Oxford University Press.

Davis, Robert C., and Garry R. Marvin. 2004. *Venice, the Tourist Maze: A Cultural Critique of the World's Most Touristed City*. Berkeley: University of California Press.

D'Ayala, Marian. 1854. *Bibliografia militare italiana, antica e moderna*. Turin: Dalla Stamperia Reale.

De Caprio, Vincenzo. 1983. "Aristocrazia e clero dalla crisi dell'Umanesimo alla Controriforma." In *Letteratura italiana: Produzione e consumo*, ed. Alberto Asor Rosa, vol. 2, 299–361. Turin: Einaudi.

De Grazia, Sebastian. 1989. *Machiavelli in Hell*. Princeton, NJ: Princeton University Press.

D'Elia, Una Roman. 2004. "Tintoretto, Aretino, and the Speed of Creation." *Word & Image* 20: 206–18.

della Casa, Giovanni. 1960. *Opere di Baldassare Castiglione, Giovanni della Casa, Benvenuto Cellini*. Ed. Carlo Cordié. Milan: Ricciardi.

———. 1986. *Galateo*. Trans. Konrad Eisenbichler and Kenneth R. Bartlett. Toronto: Centre for Reformation and Renaissance Studies.

della Porta, Giovanni Battista. 1652. *La fisonomia dell'huomo*. Venice: Presso Sebastian Combi.

De Robertis, Francesco M. 1979. *Lavoro e lavoratori nel mondo romano*. New York: Arno Press.

Detienne, Marcel, and Jean-Pierre Vernant. 1978. *Cunning Intelligence in Greek Culture and Society*. Trans. Janet Lloyd. Hassocks, Sussex: Harvester Press.

Dickerson, C. D., III. 2010. *Raw Painting:* The Butcher's Shop *by Annibale Carracci*. New Haven, CT: Yale University Press.

Doglio, Maria Luisa. 1983. "Ambasciatore e principe: L'*Institutio legati* di Ermolao Barbaro." In *Umanesimo e Rinascimento a Firenze e Venezia*, vol. 1, 297–310. Florence: Olschki.

———. 1993. *Il segretario e il principe: Studi sulla letteratura italiana del Rinascimento*. Alessandria: Edizioni dell'Orso.

———. 2009. "Politica, esperienza e *politesse*: La formazione dell'ambasciatore in età moderna." In *Formare alle professioni: Diplomatici e politici*, ed. Arianna Arisi Rota, 25–55. Milan: FrancoAngeli.

Donaldson, Peter S. 1988. *Machiavelli and Mystery of State*. New York: Cambridge University Press.

Doni, Anton Francesco. 1972. *La libraria*. Ed. Vanni Bramanti. Milan: Longanesi.

———. 1994. *I mondi e gli inferni*. Ed. Patrizia Pellizzari. Intro. Marziano Guglielminetti. Turin: Einaudi.

Douglas, Mary. 1966. *Purity and Danger: An Analysis of the Concept of Pollution and Taboo*. London: Routledge.

Douglas, Richard M. 1969. "Talent and Vocation in Humanist and Protestant Thought." In *Action and Conviction in Early Modern Europe: Essays in Memory of E. H. Harbison*, ed. T. K. Rabb and J. E. Seigel, 261–98. Princeton, NJ: Princeton University Press.

Drake, Stillman, and Paul Lawrence Rose. 1971. "The Pseudo-Aristotelian Questions of Mechanics in Renaissance Culture." *Studies in the Renaissance* 18: 65–104.

Dresbeck, Leroy. 1979. "*Techne, Labor et Natura*: Ideas and Active Life in the Medieval Winter." *Studies in Medieval and Renaissance History* 2: 83–119.

Du Cange, Charles Du Fresne. 1954. *Glossarium mediae et infimae Latinitatis*. Graz: Akademische Druck-U. Verlagsanstalt.

Dugan, John. 2005. *Making a New Man: Ciceronian Self-Fashioning in the Rhetorical Works*. New York: Oxford University Press.

Dunne, Joseph. 1993. *Back to the Rough Ground: "Phronesis" and "Techne" in Modern Philosophy and in Aristotle*. Notre Dame, IN: Notre Dame University Press.

Eagleton, Terry. 1990. *The Ideology of the Aesthetic*. Cambridge, MA: Blackwell.

Eamon, William. 1993. "'With the Rules of Life and an Enema': Leonardo Fioravanti's Medical Primitivism." In *Renaissance and Revolution: Humanists, Scholars, Craftsmen and Natural Philosophers in Early Modern Europe*, ed. J. V. Field and Frank A. J. L. James, 29–44. Cambridge: Cambridge University Press.

———. 1994. *Science and the Secrets of Nature: Books of Secrets in Medieval and Early Modern Culture*. Princeton, NJ: Princeton University Press.

———. 2005. "The Charlatan's Trial: An Italian Surgeon in the Court of King Philip II, 1576–1577." *Cronos* 8: 3–30.

———. 2010. *The Professor of Secrets: Mystery, Medicine, and Alchemy in Renaissance Italy*. Washington, DC: National Geographic.

Edelstein, Bruce. 2000. "Leone Leoni, Benvenuto Cellini and Francesco Vinta, a Medici Agent in Milan." *The Sculpture Journal* 4: 35–45.

Ehmer, Joseph, and Catharina Lis. 2009. "Introduction: Historical Studies in Perceptions of Work." In *The Idea of Work in Europe from Antiquity to Modern Times*, ed. Joseph Ehmer and Catharina Lis, 1–32. Burlington, VT: Ashgate.

Erspamer, Francesco. 1982. *La biblioteca di don Ferrante: Duello e onore nella cultura del Cinquecento*. Rome: Bulzoni.

Farr, James R. 2000. *Artisans in Europe, 1300–1914*. Cambridge: Cambridge University Press.

Ferrari, Gian Arturo, and Mario Vegetti. 1983. "Science, Technology and Medicine in the Classical Tradition." In *Information Sources in the History of Science and Medicine*, ed. Pietro Corsi and Paul Weindling, 197–220. London: Butterworth Scientific.

Ferrari, Giovanna. 1987. "Public Anatomy Lessons and the Carnival: The Anatomy Theatre of Bologna." *Past and Present* 117: 50–106.

———. 1996. *L'esperienza del passato: Alessandro Benedetti filologo e medico umanista*. Florence: Olschki.

Ferrari, Monica, and Paolo Mazzarello, eds. 2010. *Formare alle professioni: Figure di sanità*. Milan: FrancoAngeli.

Ferriguto, Arnaldo. 1922. *Almorò Barbaro, l'alta cultura nel settentrione d'Italia nel '400, i "sacri canones" di Roma e le "santissime leze" di Venezia*. Venice: A spese della R. Deputazione.

Field, J. V. 1993. "Mathematics and the Craft of Painting: Piero della Francesca and Perspective." In *Renaissance and Revolution: Humanists, Scholars, Craftsmen and Natural Philosophers in Early Modern Europe*, ed. J. V. Field and Frank A. J. L. James, 73–96. Cambridge: Cambridge University Press.

Figliuolo, Bruno. 1999. *Il diplomatico e il trattatista: Ermolao Barbaro ambasciatore della Serenissima e il "De officio legati."* Naples: Guida.

Filarete. 1965. *Treatise on Architecture; Being the Treatise by Antonio di Piero Averlino, Known as Filarete*. Translation, introduction, and notes by John R. Spencer. New Haven, CT: Yale University Press.

———. 1972. *Trattato di architettura*. Ed. Anna Maria Finoli and Liliana Grassi. Introduction and notes by Liliana Grassi. Milan: Il Polifilo.

Filippo Bareggi, Claudia di. 1988. *Il mestiere di scrivere: Lavoro intellettuale e mercato librario a Venezia nel Cinquecento*. Rome: Bulzoni.

Findlen, Paula. 1994. *Possessing Nature: Museums, Collecting and Scientific Culture in Early Modern Italy*. Berkeley: University of California Press.

———. 1998. "Possessing the Past: The Material World of the Italian Renaissance." *American Historical Review* 103: 83–114.

Finucci, Valeria. 1992. *The Lady Vanishes: Subjectivity and Representation in Castiglione and Ariosto*. Stanford, CA: Stanford University Press.

———. 1997. "In the Name of the Brother: Male Rivalry and Social Order in Baldassare Castiglione's *Il libro del cortegiano*." *Exemplaria* 9: 91–116.

———. 2003. *The Manly Masquerade: Masculinity, Paternity, and Castration in the Italian Renaissance*. Durham, NC: Duke University Press.

Fiorato, Adelin Charles. 1989a. "Grandeur et servitude du secrétaire: Du savoir rhétorique à la collaboration politique." In *Culture et professions en Italie (fin XVe–début XVIIe siècles)*, ed. A. C. Fiorato, 133–84. Paris: Publications de la Sorbonne.

———, ed. 1989b. *Culture et professions en Italie (fin XVe–début XVIIe siècles)*. Paris: Publications de la Sorbonne.

Fioravanti, Leonardo. 1561. *Compendio di tutta la cirugia*. Venice: Appresso Lodovico Avanzo.

———. 1564. *Del compendio dei secreti rationali*. Venice: Appresso Vincenzo Valgrisi.

———. 1571. *Reggimento della peste*. Venice: Appresso gli Heredi di Melchior Sessa.

———. 1573. *De' capricci medicinali*. Venice: Lodovico Avanzo.

———. 1582a. *Della fisica*. Venice: Per gli Heredi di Melchior Sessa.

———. 1582b. *Il tesoro della vita humana*. Venice: Appresso gli Heredi di Melchior Sessa.

———. 1582c. *La cirugia*. Venice: Appresso gli Heredi di Melchior Sessa.

———. 1583. *Dello specchio di scientia universale*. Venice: Heredi di Marchiò Sessa.

Fish, Stanley. 1989. *Doing What Comes Naturally: Change, Rhetoric, and the Practice of Theory in Literary and Legal Studies*. Durham, NC: Duke University Press.

Fisher, William G. 2001. "The Renaissance Beard: Masculinity in Early Modern England." *Renaissance Quarterly* 54: 155–87.

———. 2006. *Materializing Gender in Early Modern English Literature and Culture*. Cambridge: Cambridge University Press.

Fortini Brown, Patricia. *See* Brown, Patricia Fortini.

Foster, Kurt W. 1971. "Metaphors of Rule: Political Ideology and History in the Portraits of Cosimo I de' Medici." *Mitteilungen des Kunsthistorischen Institutes in Florenz* 15: 65–104.

Fragnito, Gigliola. 1998. "Buone maniere e professionalità nelle Corti Romane del Cinque e Seicento." In *Educare il corpo, educare la parola nella trattatisica del Rinascimento*, ed. Giorgio Patrizi and Amedeo Quondam, 77–109. Rome: Bulzoni.

Franceschetti, Diego, Giorgio Zanchin, and Bruno Agazia. 2005. "Giovanbattista da Monte (Montanus) padre della moderna clinica medica." *Medicina nei secoli, arte e scienza* 17: 151–59.

Frazier, Alison K. 2007. "Machiavelli, Trauma, and the Scandal of *The Prince*: An Essay in Speculative History." In *History in the Comic Mode: Medieval Communities and the Matter of Person*, ed. R. Fulton and B. Holsinger, 192–202. New York: Columbia University Press.

———. 2013. "Biography as a Genre of Moral Philosophy." In *Rethinking Virtue, Reforming Society: New Directions in Renaissance Ethics, c. 1350–1650*, ed. David A. Lines and Sabrina Ebbersmeyer, 215–40. Turnhout: Brepols.

———. Forthcoming. *The Death of Pietro Paolo Boscoli: Religion and Politics in Machiavelli's Florence*.

French, Roger. 1985. "Berengario da Carpi and the Use of Commentary in Anatomical Teaching." In *The Medical Renaissance of the Sixteenth Century*, ed. A. Wear, R. French, and I. M. Lonie, 42–74. Cambridge: Cambridge University Press.

———. 1999. *Dissection and Vivisection in the European Renaissance*. Aldershot, UK: Ashgate.

Fubini, Mario. 1948. "Le quattro redazioni dei *Ricordi* del Guicciardini." In *Studi sulla letteratura del Rinascimento*, 138–207. Florence: Sansoni.

Fubini, Riccardo. 1996. "L'ambasciatore nel XV secolo: Due trattati e una biografia (Bernard de Rosier, Ermolao Barbaro, Vespasiano da Bisticci)." *Mélanges de l'école française de Rome* 108: 645–65.

Gagneux, Marcel. 1984. "Reflets et jalons de la carrière d'un homme politique: Les trois rédactions des *Pensées* de François Guichardin." In *Réécritures II: Commentaires, parodies, variations dans la littérature italienne de la Renaissance*, 69–99. Paris: Université de la Sorbonne Nouvelle.

Galetta, Maria. 1995. "Tradizione ed innovazione nella *Vita* di Benvenuto Cellini." *Romance Review* 5: 65–72.

Gallucci, Margaret A. 2001. "Cellini's Trial for Sodomy: Power and Patronage at the Court of Cosimo I." In *The Cultural Politics of Duke Cosimo I de' Medici*, ed. Konrad Eisenbichler, 37–46. Aldershot, UK: Ashgate.

———. 2003. *Benvenuto Cellini: Sexuality, Masculinity, and Artistic Identity in Renaissance Italy*. New York: Palgrave Macmillan.

García-Ballester, Luis, Roger French, Jon Arrizabalaga, and Andrew Cunningham, eds. 1994. *Practical Medicine from Salerno to the Black Death*. Cambridge: Cambridge University Press.

Gardner, Victoria G. 1997. "*Homines non nascuntur, sed figuntur:* Benvenuto Cellini's *Vita* and Self-Presentation of the Renaissance Artist." *Sixteenth Century Journal* 28: 447–65.

Garin, Eugenio. 1947. Introduction to *La disputa delle arti nel Quattrocento*, xi–xxviii. Florence: Vallecchi Editore.

———. 1965. *Italian Humanism: Philosophy and Civic Life in the Renaissance*. Trans. Peter Munz. New York: Harper & Row.

Garzoni, Tomaso. 1996. *La piazza universale di tutte le professioni del mondo*. Ed. Paolo Cherchi and Beatrice Collina. 2 vols. Turin: Einaudi.

Gentilcore, David. 1998. *Healers and Healing in Early Modern Italy*. Manchester: Manchester University Press.

———. 2006. *Medical Charlatanism in Early Modern Italy*. Oxford: Oxford University Press.

Geoghegan, Arthur T. 1945. *The Attitude Towards Labor in Early Christianity and Ancient Culture*. Washington, DC: Catholic University of America Press.

Geronimus, Dennis V. 2002. "Arbitrating Artistry: The Case of Domenico di Michelino in 1483." *Burlington Magazine* 144: 691–94.

Ghiberti, Lorenzo. 1948–67. *The Commentaries of Lorenzo Ghiberti*. Trans. with notes by members of the staff of the Courtauld Institute of Art. London: Courtauld Institute of Art.

———. 1998. *I commentarii (Biblioteca Nazionale Centrale di Firenze, II, I, 333)*. Ed. and intro. Lorenzo Bartoli. Florence: Giunti.

Giannetti, Laura. 2009. *Lelia's Kiss: Imagining Gender, Sex, and Marriage in Italian Renaissance Comedy*. Toronto: University of Toronto Press.

Giannetti, Laura, and Guido Ruggiero, trans. 2003. *Five Comedies from the Italian Renaissance*. Baltimore: Johns Hopkins University Press.

Gilbert, Allan H. 1938. *Machiavelli's "Prince" and Its Forerunners: The "Prince" as a Typical Book de Regimine Principum*. Durham, NC: Duke University Press.

Gilbert, Felix. 1939. "The Humanist Conception of the Prince and the *Prince* of Machiavelli." *Journal of Modern History* 11: 449–83.

———. 1949. "Bernardo Rucellai and the Orti Oricellari: A Study on the Origin of Modern Political Thought." *Journal of the Warburg and Courtauld Institutes* 12: 101–31.

———. 1984. *Machiavelli and Guicciardini: Politics and History in Sixteenth-Century Florence.* Reprint. New York: Norton.

Gilmore, Myron P. 1963. *Humanists and Jurists: Six Studies in the Renaissance.* Cambridge, MA: Harvard University Press.

———. 1979. "*Studia Humanitatis* and the Professions in Fifteenth Century Florence." In *Florence and Venice: Comparisons and Relations*, ed. S. Bertelli, N. Rubinstein, and C. H. Smyth, vol. 1, 27–40. Florence: La Nuova Italia Editrice.

Gnudi, Martha Teach, and Jerome Pierce Webster. 1950. *The Life and Times of Gaspare Tagliacozzi, Surgeon of Bologna, 1545–1599.* New York: Herbert Reichner.

Godman, Peter. 1998. *From Poliziano to Machiavelli: Florentine Humanism in the High Renaissance.* Princeton, NJ: Princeton University Press.

Goldberg, Jonathan. 1974. "Cellini's *Vita* and the Conventions of Early Autobiography." *Modern Language Notes* 89: 71–83.

Goldthwaite, Richard A. 1993. *Wealth and the Demand for Art in Italy, 1300–1600.* Baltimore: Johns Hopkins University Press.

Gossman, Lionel. 1994. "Cultural History and Crisis: Burckhardt's *Civilization of the Renaissance in Italy*." In *Rediscovering History: Culture, Politics, and the Psyche*, ed. Michael S. Roth, 404–27. Stanford, CA: Stanford University Press.

———. 2000. *Basel in the Age of Burckhardt: A Study in Unseasonable Ideas.* Chicago: University of Chicago Press.

———. 2002. "Jacob Burckhardt: Cold War Liberal?" *Journal of Modern History* 74: 538–72.

Gouwens, Kenneth. 1998. "Perceiving the Past: Renaissance Humanism and the 'Cognitive Turn.'" *American Historical Review* 103: 55–82.

Grafton, Anthony. 1996. "The New Science and the Traditions of Humanism." In *The Cambridge Companion to Renaissance Humanism*, ed. Jill Kraye, 203–23. Cambridge: Cambridge University Press.

———. 1997. *Commerce with the Classics: Ancient Books and Renaissance Readers.* Ann Arbor: University of Michigan Press.

———. 1999. "The Humanist as Reader." In *A History of Reading in the West*, ed. Guglielmo Cavallo and Roger Chartier, trans. Lydia G. Cochrane, 179–212. Cambridge: Polity.

———. 2000. *Leon Battista Alberti: Master Builder of the Italian Renaissance.* New York: Hill and Wang.

———. 2011a. *The Culture of Correction in Renaissance Europe.* London: British Library.

———. 2011b. *Humanists with Inky Fingers: The Culture of Correction in Renaissance Europe.* Florence: Olsckhi.

Grafton, Anthony, and Lisa Jardine. 1986. *From Humanism to the Humanities: Education and the Liberal Arts in Fifteenth- and Sixteenth-Century Europe.* Cambridge: Cambridge University Press.

Gramigna, Vincenzo. 1620. *Il segretario dialogo.* Florence: Pietro Cecconcelli.

Greenblatt, Stephen. 1980. *Renaissance Self-Fashioning: From More to Shakespeare.* Chicago: University of Chicago Press.

———. 1986. "Psychoanalysis and Renaissance Culture." In *Literary Theory/Renaissance Texts*, ed. Patricia Parker and David Quint, 210–25. Baltimore: Johns Hopkins University Press.

———. 1988. *Shakespearean Negotiations: The Circulation of Social Energy in Renaissance England*. Berkeley: University of California Press.

———. 1990. *Learning to Curse: Essays in Early Modern Culture*. New York: Routledge.

———. 1991. *Marvelous Possessions: The Wonder of the New World*. Chicago: University of Chicago Press.

———. 2004. *Will in the World: How Shakespeare Became Shakespeare*. New York: Norton.

———. 2011. *The Swerve: How the World Became Modern*. New York: Norton.

Greene, Thomas. 1968. "The Flexibility of the Self in Renaissance Literature." In *The Disciplines of Criticism: Essays in Literary Theory, Interpretation, and History*, ed. Peter Demetz, Thomas Greene, and Lowry Nelson Jr., 241–64. New Haven, CT: Yale University Press.

———. 1982. *The Light in Troy: Imitation and Discovery in Renaissance Poetry*. New Haven, CT: Yale University Press.

Grendler, Paul F. 1969. *Critics of the Italian World, 1530–1560: Anton Francesco Doni, Nicolò Franco, and Ortensio Lando*. Madison: University of Wisconsin Press.

———. 1989. *Schooling in Renaissance Italy: Literacy and Learning, 1300–1600*. Baltimore: Johns Hopkins University Press.

Groebner, Valentin. 1995. "Losing Face, Saving Face: Noses and Honour in the Late Medieval Town." Trans. Pamela Selwyn. *History Workshop Journal* 40: 1–15.

———. 2004. *Defaced: The Visual Culture of Violence in the Late Middle Ages*. Trans. Pamela Selwyn. New York: Zone Books.

Grubb, James. 1986. "When Myths Lose Power: Four Decades of Venetian Historiography." *Journal of Modern History* 58: 43–94.

Guarini, Giambattista. 1594. *Il segretario, dialogo*. Venice: Megietti.

Guazzo, Stefano. 1993. *La civil conversazione*. Ed. Amedeo Quondam. 2 vols. Ferrara: Franco Cosimo Panini.

Guerevitch, Aron. 1995. *The Origins of European Individualism*. Trans. Katherine Judelson. Oxford: Blackwell.

Guerrini, Anita. 2003. *Experimenting with Humans and Animals: From Galen to Animal Rights*. Baltimore: Johns Hopkins University Press.

Guglielminetti, Marziano. 1977. *Memoria e scrittura: L'autobiografia da Dante a Cellini*. Turin: Einaudi.

Guicciardini, Francesco. 1965. *Maxims and Reflections of a Renaissance Statesman*. Trans. Mario Domandi. Intro. Nicolai Rubinstein. New York: Harper & Row.

———. 1969. *History of Italy*. Ed. and trans. Sidney Alexander. Princeton, NJ: Princeton University Press.

———. 1988. *Storia d'Italia*. Ed. Ettore Mazzali. Intro. Emilio Pasquini. 3 vols. Milan: Garzanti.

———. 1994. *Ricordi*. Ed. Giorgio Masi. Milan: Mursia.

Guidi, Josè. 1973. "Baldassar Castiglione et le pouvoir politique: Du gentilhomme de cour au nonce pontifical." In *Les écrivains et le pouvoir en Italie à l'époque de la Renaissance*, ed. André Rochon, vol. 2, 243–78. Paris: Université de la Sorbonne Nouvelle.

Hale, John R. 1983. "Castiglione's Military Career." In *Castiglione: The Ideal and the Real in Renaissance Culture*, ed. Robert W. Hanning and David Rosand, 143–64. New Haven, CT: Yale University Press.

Hall, Crystal. 2013. *Galileo's Reading*. Cambridge: Cambridge University Press.

Hampton, Timothy. 1990. *Writing from History: The Rhetoric of Exemplarity in Renaissance Literature*. Ithaca, NY: Cornell University Press.

———. 2009. *Fictions of Embassy: Literature and Diplomacy in Early Modern Europe*. Ithaca, NY: Cornell University Press.

Hathaway, Baxter. 1968. *Marvels and Commonplaces: Renaissance Literary Criticism*. New York: Random House.

Hegener, Nicole. 1996. "Angelus Politianus enormi fuit naso." In *Antiquarische Gelehrsamkeit und Bildende Kunst: Die Gegenwart der Antike in der Renaissance*, ed. Katharina Corsepius, Ulrich Rehm, Lothar Schmitt, and Gunter Schweikhart, 85–121. Köln: W. König.

Heller, Thomas C., and Christine Brooke-Rose, eds. 1986. *Reconstructing Individualism: Autonomy, Individuality, and the Self in Western Thought*. Stanford, CA: Stanford University Press.

Herzog, Don. 1996. "The Trouble with Hairdressers." *Representations* 53: 21–43.

Hodgart, Buono. 1997. *Giordano Bruno's "The Candle-Bearer": An Enigmatic Renaissance Play*. Lewiston, NY: E. Mellen Press.

Holdsworth, Christopher J. 1973. "The Blessings of Work: The Cistercian View." In *Sanctity and Secularity: The Church and the World*, ed. Derek Baker, 59–76. Oxford: Blackwell.

Holmes, Olivia. 1999. "Order in Discord: Guicciardini's *Ricordi*." *Italica* 76: 314–34.

Hope, Charles. 2005. "Le 'Vite' Vasariane: Un esempio di autore multiplo." In *L'autore multiplo*, ed. Anna Santoni, 59–74. Pisa: Scuola Normale Superiore.

Horodowich, Elizabeth A. 2005. "The Gossiping Tongue: Oral Networks, Public Life, and Political Culture in Early Modern Venice." *Renaissance Studies* 19: 22–45.

———. 2008. *Language and Statecraft in Early Modern Venice*. New York: Cambridge University Press.

Horowitz, Elliott. 1997. "The New World and the Changing Face of Europe." *Sixteenth Century Journal* 28: 1181–1201.

Hugh of St. Victor. 1991. *The Didascalicon of Hugh of St. Victor: A Medieval Guide to the Arts*. Ed., trans., and intro. Jerome Taylor. New York: Columbia University Press.

Hughes, Stephen C. 2007. *Politics of the Sword: Dueling, Honor, and Masculinity in Modern Italy*. Columbus: Ohio State University Press.

Ierodiakonou, K. 1995. "Alexander of Aphrodisias on Medicine as a Stochastic Art." In *Ancient Medicine in Its Socio-Cultural Context: Papers Read at the Congress Held at Leiden University, 13–15 April 1992*, ed. Ph. van der Eijk, H. F. J. Horstmanshoff, and P. H. Schrijvers, vol. 2, 473–85. Amsterdam: Rodopi.

Ilchman, Frederick, and Linda Borean. 2009. *Titian, Tintoretto, Veronese: Rivals in Renaissance Venice*. Boston: MFA Publications.

Ingegneri, Angelo. 1594. *Del buon segretario libri tre*. Rome: Presso a Guglielmo Faciotto.

Isidore of Seville. 1911. *Etymologiae*. New York: Oxford University Press.

Iucci, Stefano. 1995. "La trattatistica sul segretario tra la fine del Cinquecento e il primo ventennio del Seicento." *Roma moderna e contemporanea* 3: 81–96.

Ivanoff, Nicola. 1975. "Il ciclo eucaristico di S. Giorgio Maggiore a Venezia." *Notizie da Palazzo Albani* 4: 50–57.

Jacobs, Fredrika Herman. 2005. *The Living Image in Renaissance Art*. Cambridge: Cambridge University Press.

Jameson, Fredric. 1991. *Postmodernism, or, The Cultural Logic of Late Capitalism*. Durham, NC: Duke University Press.

Jardine, Lisa. 1983. "Isotta Nogarola: Women Humanists—Education for What?" *History of Education* 12: 231–44.

———. 1996. *Worldly Goods: A New History of the Renaissance*. New York: Nan A. Talese.

Javitch, Daniel. 1978. *Poetry and Courtliness in Renaissance England*. Princeton, NJ: Princeton University Press.

Jay, Martin. 1984. *Marxism and Totality: The Adventures of a Concept from Lukács to Habermas*. Berkeley: University of California Press.

Jenner, Mark S. R. 2011. "Follow Your Nose? Smell, Smelling, and Their Histories." *American Historical Review* 116: 335–51.

Johansen, T. K. 1998. *Aristotle on the Sense-Organs*. Cambridge: Cambridge University Press.

Johnstone, Steven. 1994. "Virtuous Toil, Vicious Work: Xenophon on Aristocratic Style." *Classical Philology* 89: 219–40.

Joshel, Sandra R. 1992. *Work, Identity, and Legal Status at Rome: A Study of the Occupational Inscriptions*. Norman: University of Oklahoma Press.

Kahn, Victoria. 1985. *Rhetoric, Prudence, and Skepticism in the Renaissance*. Ithaca, NY: Cornell University Press.

———. 1986. "Virtù and the Example of Agathocles in Machiavelli's *Prince*." *Representations* 13: 63–83.

Karras, Ruth Mazo. 2003. *From Boys to Men: Formations of Masculinity in Late Medieval Europe*. Philadelphia: University of Pennsylvania Press.

Kelley, Donald R. 1991. *Renaissance Humanism*. Boston: Twayne.

Kemp, Martin. 1981. *Leonardo da Vinci, the Marvelous Works of Nature and Man*. Cambridge, MA: Harvard University Press.

———, ed. 1989. *Leonardo on Painting: An Anthology of Writings by Leonardo da Vinci with a Selection of Documents Relating to His Career as an Artist*. Trans. Martin Kemp and Margaret Walker. New Haven, CT: Yale University Press.

———. 1990. *The Science of Art: Optical Themes in Western Art from Brunelleschi to Seurat*. New Haven, CT: Yale University Press.

———. 2006. *Leonardo da Vinci: Experience, Experiment and Design*. Princeton, NJ: Princeton University Press.

Kemp, Martin, and Juliana Barone. 2009. "What Might Leonardo's Own Trattato Have Looked Like? And What Did It Actually Look Like Up to the Time of the *Editio Princeps*?" In *Re-Reading Leonardo: The Treatise on Painting Across Europe, 1550–1900*, ed. Claire Farago, 39–60. Burlington, VT: Ashgate.

Kemp, Simon. 1997. "A Medieval Controversy About Odor." *Journal of the History of the Behavioral Sciences* 33: 211–19.

Kempers, Bram. 1987. *Painting, Power, and Patronage: The Rise of the Professional Artist in Renaissance Italy*. Trans. Beverley Jackson. London: Penguin.

Ketham, Johann de. 1925. *Fasciculo di Medicina, Venice 1493*. Ed. and trans. Charles Singer. 2 vols. Florence: Lier.

King, Margaret L. 1976. "Caldiera and the Barbaros on Marriage and the Family: Humanist Reflections of Venetian Realities." *Journal of Medieval and Renaissance Studies* 6: 19–50.

———. 1980. "Book-Lined Cells: Women and Humanism in the Early Italian Renaissance." In *Beyond Their Sex: Learned Women of the European Past*, ed. Patrizia H. Labalme, 66–90. New York: New York University Press.

———. 1986. *Venetian Humanism in an Age of Patrician Dominance*. Princeton, NJ: Princeton University Press.

Kleiner, Diana E. E. 1992. *Roman Sculpture*. New Haven, CT: Yale University Press.

Klestinec, Cynthia. 2004. "A History of Anatomy Theaters in Sixteenth-Century Padua." *Journal of the History of Medicine and Allied Sciences* 59: 375–412.

———. 2007. "Civility, Comportment, and the Anatomy Theater: Girolamo Fabrici and His Medical Students in Renaissance Padua." *Renaissance Quarterly* 60: 434–63.

———. 2011. *Theaters of Anatomy: Students, Teachers, and Traditions of Dissection in Renaissance Venice*. Baltimore: Johns Hopkins University Press.

Kohl, Benjamin G., and Ronald G. Witt. 1978. *The Earthly Republic: Italian Humanists on Government and Society*. Philadelphia: University of Pennsylvania Press.

Kraye, Jill, ed. 1996. *The Cambridge Companion to Renaissance Humanism*. Cambridge: Cambridge University Press.

———. 1997. *Cambridge Translations of Renaissance Philosophical Texts*. Vol. 2, *Political Philosophy*. Cambridge: Cambridge University Press.

Kristeller, Paul Oskar. 1951. "The Modern System of the Arts: A Study in the History of Aesthetics. Part I." *Journal of the History of Ideas* 12: 496–527.

———. 1952. "The Modern System of the Arts: A Study in the History of Aesthetics. Part II." *Journal of the History of Ideas* 13: 17–46.

———. 1961. *Renaissance Thought: The Classic, Scholastic, and Humanist Strains*. New York: Harper & Row.

———. 1965. *Renaissance Thought, II: Papers on Humanism and the Arts*. New York: Harper & Row.

Landucci, Luca. 1927. *A Florentine Diary from 1450–1516*. Trans. Alice de Rosen Jervis. London: Dent.

Lane, Frederic. 1966. *Venice and History: The Collected Papers of Frederic C. Lane*. Baltimore: Johns Hopkins University Press.

———. 1973. *Venice: A Maritime Republic*. Baltimore: Johns Hopkins University Press.

Langedijk, Karla. 1981. *The Portraits of the Medici*. Vol. 1. Florence: Studio per Edizioni Scelte.

Leeds, John C. 2004. "Against the Vernacular: Ciceronian Formalism and the Problem of the Individual." *Texas Studies in Language and Literature* 46: 107–48.

———. 2010. *Renaissance Syntax and Subjectivity: Ideological Contents of Latin and the Vernacular in Scottish Prose Chronicles*. Burlington, VT: Ashgate.

Le Goff, Jacques. 1980. *Time, Work, and Culture in the Middle Ages*. Trans. Arthur Goldhammer. Chicago: University of Chicago Press.

Leonardo da Vinci. 1970. *The Notebooks of Leonardo da Vinci: Compiled and Edited from the Original Manuscripts*. Ed. Jean Paul Richter. 3 vols. New York: Dover.

Lerro, Alessio. 2012. "Le anticamere della filosofia: Paratesto e componimenti proemiali ne 'Il candelaio' e 'De umbris idearum' di Giordano Bruno." *Critica letteraria* 155: 327–46.

Lind, L. R. 1975. *Studies in Pre-Vesalian Anatomy: Biography, Translations, Documents*. Philadelphia: American Philosophical Society.

Lines, David A. 2002. *Aristotle's "Ethics" in the Italian Renaissance (ca. 1300–1650): The Universities and the Problem of Moral Education*. Leiden: Brill.

Lipking, Lawrence. 1966. "The Dialectic of *Il cortegiano*." *Publications of the Modern Language Association* 81: 355–62.

Lis, Catharina, and Hugo Soly. 2012. *Worthy Efforts: Attitudes Toward Work and Workers in Pre-Industrial Europe*. Leiden: Brill.

Lloyd, Geoffrey E. R. 1991. "The Definition, Status, and Methods of the Medical τέχνη in the Fifth and Fourth Centuries." In *Science and Philosophy in Classical Greece*, ed. Alan C. Bowen, 249–60. New York: Garland.

Löbl, Rudolf. 1997. *Techne: Untersuchung zur Bedeutung dieses Wortes in der Zeit von Homer bis Aristoteles; Band I: von Homer biz zu den Sophisten*. Würzburg: Königshausen & Neumann.

Lodge, David. 1984. *Small World: An Academic Romance*. New York: Warner Books.

Lomazzo, Gian Paolo. 1974. *Trattato dell'arte della pittura, scoltura et architettura (Milan, 1584)*. In *Scritti sulle arti*, vol. 2, ed. Roberto Paolo Ciardi. Florence: Marchi & Bertolli.

Long, Pamela O. 1985. "The Contribution of Architectural Writers to a 'Scientific' Outlook in the Fifteenth and Sixteenth Centuries." *Journal of Medieval and Renaissance Studies* 15: 265–89.

———. 1991. "The Openness of Knowledge: An Ideal and Its Context in 16th-Century Writings on Mining and Metallurgy." *Technology and Culture* 32: 318–55.

———. 1997. "Power, Patronage, and the Authorship of Ars: From Mechanical Know-How to Mechanical Knowledge in the Last Scribal Age." *Isis* 88: 1–41.

———. 2001. *Openness, Secrecy, Authorship: Technical Arts and the Culture of Knowledge from Antiquity to the Renaissance.* Baltimore: Johns Hopkins University Press.

———. 2011. *Artisan/Practitioners and the Rise of the New Sciences, 1400–1600.* Corvallis: Oregon State University Press.

Low, Jennifer A. 2003. *Manhood and the Duel: Masculinity in Early Modern Drama and Culture.* New York: Palgrave Macmillan.

Lucas, Corinne. 1989. "L'artiste et l'écriture: *Il dire* et *il fare* dans les écrits de Cellini." In *Culture et professions en Italie (XVe–XVIIe siècles)*, ed. A. C. Fiorato, 67–97. Paris: Publications de la Sorbonne.

Lukes, Steven. 1971. "The Meanings of Individualism." *Journal of the History of Ideas* 32: 45–66.

———. 1977. *Individualism.* New York: Harper & Row.

MacCormack, Sabine. 2001. "The Virtue of Work: An Augustinian Transformation." *Antiquité Tardive* 9: 219–37.

MacDonald, Katherine. 2005. "Humanistic Self-Representation in Giovan Battista della Porta's *Della fisionomia dell'uomo*: Antecedents and Innovation." *Sixteenth Century Journal* 36: 397–414.

Machiavelli, Niccolò. 1971. *Tutte le opere.* Ed. Mario Martelli. Florence: Sansoni.

———. 2003. *Art of War.* Ed. and trans. Christopher Lynch. Chicago: University of Chicago Press.

Mack, Peter. 2011. *A History of Renaissance Rhetoric, 1380–1620.* Oxford: Oxford University Press.

Maehle, Andreas-Holger, and Ulrich Tröhler. 1987. "Animal Experimentation from Antiquity to the End of the Eighteenth Century: Attitudes and Arguments." In *Vivisection in Historical Perspective*, ed. Nicolaas A. Rupke, 14–47. London: Croom Helm.

Maggi, Ottaviano. 1566. *De legato libri duo.* Venice: Ruscellius.

Malatesta, Maria. 1995. "Introduction: The Italian Professions from a Comparative Perspective." In *Society and the Professions in Italy, 1860–1914*, ed. M. Malatesta, trans. Adrian Belton, 1–23. Cambridge: Cambridge University Press.

Mappae clavicula: A Little Key to the World of Medieval Techniques. 1974. Ed. and trans. Cyril Stanley Smith and John G. Hawthorne. Philadelphia: American Philosophical Society.

Marcus, Leah S. 1992. "Renaissance/Early Modern Studies." In *Redrawing the Boundaries: The Transformation of English and American Literary Studies*, ed. Stephen Greenblatt and Giles Gunn, 41–63. New York: Modern Language Association of America.

Markulin, Joseph. 1982. "Guicciardini's *Ricordi* and the Idea of a Book." *Italica* 59: 296–305.

Marrou, Henri-Irénée. 1938. *Saint Augustin et la fin de la culture antique.* Paris: E. de Boccard.

———. 1956. *A History of Education in Antiquity.* Trans. George Lamb. New York: New American Library.

———. 1969. "Les arts libéraux dans l'Antiquité classique." In *Arts libéraux et philosophie au Moyen Âge*, 6–27. Paris: Vrin/Montréal: Institut d'études médiévales.

Martial. 1993. *Epigrams.* Trans. D. R. Shackleton Bailey. 2 vols. Cambridge, MA: Harvard University Press.

Martin, John Jeffries. 1996. "The Imaginary Piazza: Tommaso Garzoni and the Late Italian Renaissance." In *Portraits of Medieval and Renaissance Living: Essays in Memory of David*

Herlihy, ed. Samuel K. Cohn Jr. and Stephen A. Epstein, 439–54. Ann Arbor: University of Michigan Press.

———. 1997. "Inventing Sincerity, Refashioning Prudence: The Discovery of the Individual in Renaissance Europe." *American Historical Review* 102: 1309–42.

———. 2004. *Myths of Renaissance Individualism*. New York: Palgrave Macmillan.

Martines, Lauro. 1968. *Lawyers and Statecraft in Renaissance Florence*. Princeton, NJ: Princeton University Press.

———. 2001. *Strong Words: Writing and Social Strain in the Italian Renaissance*. Baltimore: Johns Hopkins University Press.

Martini, Francesco di Giorgio. 1967. *Trattati di architettura ingegneria e arte militare*. Ed. Corrado Maltese. Transcription by Livia Maltese Degrassi. Milan: Il Polifilo.

Marzari, M. Giacomo. 1602. *La prattica e theorica del cancelliere*. Vicenza: Giorgio Greco.

Mattingly, Garrett. 1988. *Renaissance Diplomacy*. New York: Dover.

Mayer, Thomas, and D. R. Woolf, eds. 1995. *The Rhetorics of Life-Writing in Early Modern Europe: Forms of Biography from Cassandra Fedele to Louis XIV*. Ann Arbor: University of Michigan Press.

McClure, George. 1991. *Sorrow and Consolation in Italian Humanism*. Princeton, NJ: Princeton University Press.

———. 1998. "The *Artes* and the *Ars moriendi* in Late Renaissance Venice: The Professions in Fabio Glissenti's *Discorsi morali contra il dispiacer del morire, detto Athanatophilia* (1596)." *Renaissance Quarterly* 51: 92–127.

———. 2004. *The Culture of Profession in Late Renaissance Italy*. Toronto: University of Toronto Press.

McHam, Sarah Blake. 2013. *Pliny and the Artistic Culture of the Italian Renaissance: The Legacy of "The Natural History."* New Haven, CT: Yale University Press.

McKee, Kenneth, trans. 1967. *Scenarios of the "Commedia dell'Arte": Flaminio Scala's "Il teatro delle favole rappresentative."* New York: New York University Press.

McLaughlin, Martin. 2002. "Biography and Autobiography in the Italian Renaissance." In *Mapping Lives: The Uses of Biography*, ed. Peter France and William St. Clair, 37–65. London: Oxford University Press.

McVaugh, Michael R. 2000. "Surgical Education in the Middle Ages." *Dynamis* 20: 283–304.

———. 2002. "Smells and the Medieval Surgeon." *Micrologus* 10: 113–32.

Memmo, Giovanni Maria. 1563. *Dialogo, nel quale dopo alcune filosofiche dispute, si forma un perfetto Prencipe, e una perfetta Republica, e parimente un Senatore, un Cittadino, un Soldato, e un Mercatante*. Venice: Gabriel Giolito de' Ferrari.

Menand, Louis. 2004. "Bad Comma: Lynne Truss's Strange Grammar." *New Yorker*, June 28. http://www.newyorker.com/archive/2004/06/28/040628crbo_books1.

Menut, Alfred D. 1943. "Castiglione and the *Nicomachean Ethics*." *Publications of the Modern Language Association* 58: 309–21.

Messisbugo, Cristoforo. 1549. *Banchetti compositioni di vivande, et apparecchio generale*. Ferrara: Per Giovanni De Buglhat et Antonio Hucher Compagni.

———. 1564. *Libro novo nel qual s'insegna a far d'ogni sorte di vivanda secondo la diversità de i tempi, cosi di carne come di pesce. Et il modo d'ordinar banchetti, apparecchiar tavole, fornir palazzi, e ornar camere per ogni gran principe. Opera assai bella, e molto bisognevole a maestri di casa, a scalchi, a credencieri, e a cuochi: composta per m. Christofaro di Messisburgo, e hora di nuovo corretta, & ristampata. Aggiuntovi di nuovo, il modo di saper tagliare ogni sorte di carne, e uccellami. Con la sua tavola ordinata, ove agevolmente si troverà ogni cosa.* Venice: Appresso Francesco de Leno.

Miller, David A. 1988. *The Novel and the Police*. Berkeley: University of California Press.

Milligan, Gerry. 2006. "The Politics of Effeminacy in *Il cortegiano*." *Italica* 83: 345–66.

———. 2007a. "Behaving like a Man: Masculinity and Masquerade in *Gli ingannati*." *Forum Italicum* 41: 23–42.

———. 2007b. "Masculinity and Machiavelli: How to Avoid Effeminacy, Perform Manliness and Be Wary of the Author." In *Seeking Real Truths: Multidisciplinary Perspectives on Machiavelli*, ed. Patricia Vilches and Gerald E. Seaman, 149–72. Leiden: Brill.

Milligan, Gerry, and Jane Tylus. 2010. Introduction to *The Poetics of Masculinity in Early Modern Italy and Spain*, ed. Gerry Milligan and Jane Tylus, 13–40. Toronto: Center for Reformation and Renaissance Studies.

Mondolfo, Rodolfo, and D. S. Duncan. 1954. "The Greek Attitude to Manual Labor." *Past and Present* 6: 1–5.

Monfasani, John. 2013. Review of *The Swerve*: How the Renaissance Began (review no. 1283). http://www.history.ac.uk/reviews/review/1283.

Monk, Samuel Holt. 1944. "A Grace Beyond the Reach of Art." *Journal of the History of Ideas* 5: 131–50.

Montaigne, Michel de. 1983. *Montaigne's Travel Journey*. Trans. Donald M. Frame. San Francisco: North Point Press.

Morris, Colin. 1987. *The Discovery of the Individual, 1050–1200*. Toronto: University of Toronto Press in association with the Medieval Academy of America.

Moulin, Leo. 1955. "On the Evolution of the Meaning of the Word 'Individualism.'" *International Social Science Bulletin* 7: 181–85.

Muccillo, Maria. 1986. "Da Monte (De Monte, Del Monte) Giovanni Battista, detto Montano." In *Dizionario biografico degli italiani*, 32: 365–67. Rome: Istituto della Enciclopedia Italiana.

Muratori, Lodovico A., ed. 1904. *Rerum italicarum scriptores: Raccolta degli storici italiani*, vol. 23, pt. 3. Città di Castello: S. Lapi.

Murphy, James Jerome. 1974. *Rhetoric in the Middle Ages: A History of Rhetorical Theory from Saint Augustine to the Renaissance*. Berkeley: University of California Press.

Murray, Oswyn. 1998. Introduction to Jacob Burckhardt, *The Greeks and Greek Civilization*, xi–xliv. London: HarperCollins.

Mutini, Claudio. 1962. "Atanagi, Dionigi." In *Dizionario biografico degli italiani*, 4: 503–6. Rome: Istituto della Enciclopedia Italiana.

Najemy, John M. 1993. *Between Friends: Discourses of Power and Desire in the Machiavelli-Vettori Letters of 1513–1515*. Princeton, NJ: Princeton University Press.

———. 2006. "Arms and Letters: The Crisis of Courtly Culture in the Wars of Italy." In *Italy and the European Powers: The Impact of War, 1500–1530*, ed. Christine Shaw, 207–38. Leiden: Brill.

———, ed. 2010. *The Cambridge Companion to Machiavelli*. Cambridge: Cambridge University Press.

Nardi, Isidoro. 1711. *Il segretario principiante, ed istruito*. Bologna: Longhi.

Narducci, Emanuele. 1992. *Introduzione a Cicerone*. Rome: Laterza.

Nati, Andrea. 1588. *Trattato del segretario*. Florence: Giorgio Marescotti.

Navagero, Andrea. 1754. *Opera omnia*. Ed. J. A. Vulpius and C. Vulpius. Venice: Remondiniana.

Newman, Martha. 2012. "Labor: Insights from a Medieval Monastery." In *Why the Middle Ages Matter: Medieval Light on Modern Justice*, ed. Celia Chazelle, Simon Doubleday, Felice Lifshitz, and Amy G. Remensnyder, 106–20. London: Routledge.

Newman, William R. 1997. "Art, Nature and Experiment Among Some Aristotelian Alchemists." In *Texts and Contexts in Ancient and Medieval Science: Studies on the Occasion of*

John E. Murdoch's Seventieth Birthday, ed. Edith Dudley Sylla and M. R. McVaugh, 305–17. Leiden: Brill.

———. 2004. *Promethean Ambitions: Alchemy and the Quest to Perfect Nature*. Chicago: University of Chicago Press.

Nichols, Tom. 1996. "Tintoretto, *Prestezza* and the *Poligrafi*: A Study in the Literary and Visual Culture of Cinquecento Venice." *Renaissance Studies* 10: 72–100.

———. 1999. *Tintoretto: Tradition and Identity*. London: Reaktion.

Nigro, Salvatore. 1983. "*Scriptor necans*." Introduction to Torquato Accetto, *Della dissimulazione onesta*, ed. S. Nigro, 19–26. Genoa: Costa & Nolan.

———. 1984. "Le livre masqué d'un secrétaire du XVIIe siècle." *Le Temps de la réflexion* Fall: 183–211.

———. 1987. "Lezione sull'ombra." Introduction to Torquato Accetto, *Rime amorose*, v–xxi. Turin: Einaudi.

———. 1991. *Il segretario di lettere*. Palermo: Sellerio.

Nussbaum, Martha C. 1986. *The Fragility of Goodness: Luck and Ethics in Greek Tragedy and Philosophy*. Cambridge: Cambridge University Press.

Nussdorfer, Laurie. 2009. *Brokers of Public Trust: Notaries in Early Modern Rome*. Baltimore: Johns Hopkins University Press.

———. 2011. Review of Douglas Biow, *In Your Face*. *Journal of Modern History* 83: 677.

Nutton, Vivian. 2007. Introduction to *De humani corporis fabrica*, ed. Daniel H. Garrison and Malcolm Hast. http://vesalius.northwestern.edu/flash.html.

O'Malley, Charles D. 1964. *Andreas Vesalius of Brussels, 1514–1564*. Berkeley: University of California Press.

Ongaro, Giuseppe. 1994. "L'insegnamento clinico di Giovan Battista da Monte (1489–1551): Una revisione critica." *Physis* 31: 357–69.

Otetea, André. 1926. *François Guichardin: Sa vie publique et sa pensée politique*. Paris: Librairie Picart.

Ovitt, George, Jr. 1983. "The Status of the Mechanical Arts in Medieval Classifications of Learning." *Viator* 14: 89–105.

———. 1986a. "The Cultural Context of Western Technology: Early Christian Attitudes Toward Manual Labor." *Technology and Culture* 27: 477–500.

———. 1986b. "Manual Labor and Early Medieval Monasticism." *Viator* 17: 1–18.

———. 1987. *The Restoration of Perfection: Labor and Technology in Medieval Culture*. New Brunswick, NJ: Rutgers University Press.

Palladio, Andrea. 1980. *I quattro libri dell'architettura*. Ed. Licisco Magagnato and Paola Marini. Intro. Licisco Magagnato. Milan: Il Polifilo.

———. 1997. *The Four Books on Architecture*. Trans. Robert Tavernor and Richard Schofield. Cambridge, MA: MIT Press.

Palmer, Richard. 1993. "In Bad Odour: Smell and Its Significance in Medicine from Antiquity to the Seventeenth Century." In *Medicine and the Five Senses*, ed. W. F. Bynum and Roy Porter, 61–68. Cambridge: Cambridge University Press.

Palumbo, Matteo. 1987. "Guicciardini, Gramsci e la forma-ricordo." *Modern Language Notes* 102: 76–95.

———. 1988. *Francesco Guicciardini*. Naples: Liguori.

Paolucci, Antonio, et al. 1994. "'Compianto di Cristo morto': 'L'Ortolano,' datato 1521, Napoli, Pinacoteca del Museo Nazionale di Capodimonte." *Restauro: Rivista dell'Opificio delle Pietre Dure e Laboratori di Restauro di Firenze* 6: 180–87.

Parente, Margherita Isnardi. 1966. *Techne: Momenti del pensiero greco da Platone ad Epicuro*. Florence: La Nuova Italia Editrice.

Park, Katharine. 1985. *Doctors and Medicine in Early Renaissance Florence*. Princeton, NJ: Princeton University Press.

———. 1994. "The Criminal and the Saintly Body: Autopsy and Dissection in Renaissance Italy." *Renaissance Quarterly* 47: 1–33.

———. 1998. "Stones, Bones and Hernias: Surgical Specialists in Fourteenth- and Fifteenth-Century Italy." In *Medicine from the Black Death to the French Disease*, ed. Roger French, Jon Arrizabalaga, Andrew Cunningham, and Luis García-Ballester, 110–30. Aldershot, UK: Ashgate.

———. 2006. *Secrets of Women: Gender, Generation, and the Origins of Human Dissection*. New York: Zone Books.

Parry, Richard. 2008. "*Episteme* and *Techne*." In *The Stanford Encyclopedia of Philosophy*, ed. Edward N. Zalta. http://plato.stanford.edu/archives/fall2008/entries/episteme-techne/.

Paschini, Pio. 1957. *Tre illustri prelati del Rinascimento: Ermolao Barbaro, Adriano Castellesi, Giovanni Grimani*. Rome: Facultas Theologica Pontificii Athenaei Lateranensis.

Patrizi, Giorgio. 1984. "Il *Libro del Cortegiano* e la trattatistica del comportamento." In *Letteratura italiana*, ed. Alberto Asor Rosa, vol. 3, pt. 2, 855–90. Turin: Einaudi.

Persico, Panfilo. 1620. *Del segretario del Sig. Panfilo Persico*. Venice: Zenaro.

Pesca-Cupolo, Carmela. 1999. "Oltre la scena comica: La dimensione teatrale bruniana e l'ambientazione napoletana del *Candelaio*." *Italica* 71: 1–17.

Petersen, Lauren Hackworth. 2003. "The Baker, His Tomb, His Wife, and Her Breadbasket: The Monument of Eurysaces in Rome." *Art Bulletin* 85: 230–57.

Petrarca, Francesco. 1976. *Petrarch's Lyric Poems: The "Rime Sparse" and Other Lyrics*. Ed. and trans. Robert M. Durling. Cambridge, MA: Harvard University Press.

———. 1978. *Invective contra medicum: Testo latino e volgarizzamento di ser Domenico Silvestri*. Ed. Pier Giorgio Ricci. Rome: Edizione di Storia e Letteratura.

Phillips, Mark. 1984. "F. Guicciardini: The Historian as Aphorist." *Quaderni d'italianistica* 2: 110–22.

Pigman, G. W., III. 1980. "Versions of Imitation in the Renaissance." *Renaissance Quarterly* 33: 1–32.

Pilliod, Elizabeth. 1998. "Representation, Misrepresentation, and Non-Representation: Vasari and His Competitors." In *Vasari's Florence: Artists and Literati at the Medicean Court*, ed. Philip Jacks, 30–52. Cambridge: Cambridge University Press.

———. 2001. *Pontormo, Bronzino, Allori: A Genealogy of Florentine Art*. New Haven, CT: Yale University Press.

Plato. 1961. *The Collected Dialogues of Plato*. Ed. Edith Hamilton and Huntington Cairns. Princeton, NJ: Princeton University Press.

Pleket, Harry W. 1973. "Technology in the Greco-Roman World." In *Fourth International Conference of Economic History*, ed. Frederic C. Lane, 303–34. Paris: Mouton.

Pliny the Elder. 1938–63. *Natural History*. Trans. H. Rackham. 10 vols. Cambridge, MA: Harvard University Press.

Plutarch. 1961. *Plutarch's Lives*. Trans. Bernadotte Perrin. Vol. 3. Cambridge, MA: Harvard University Press.

Pocock, John G. A. 1975. *The Machiavellian Moment: Florentine Political Thought and the Atlantic Republican Tradition*. Princeton, NJ: Princeton University Press.

Pomian, Krzysztof. 1990. *Collectors and Curiosities: Paris and Venice, 1500–1800*. Trans. Elizabeth Wiles-Portier. Cambridge: Polity.

Pope-Hennessy, John Wyndham. 1966. *The Portrait in the Renaissance*. New York: Bollingen Foundation.

———. 1985. *Cellini*. New York: Abbeville Press.

Porter, Roy, ed. 1997. *Rewriting the Self: Histories from the Renaissance to the Present*. London: Routledge.

Pouchelle, Marie-Christine. 1990. *The Body and Surgery in the Middle Ages*. Trans. Rosemary Morris. New Brunswick, NJ: Rutgers University Press.

Pozzi, Mario, and Enrico Mattioda. 2006. *Giorgio Vasari: Storico e critico*. Florence: Olschki.

Princeton Dante Project. http://etcweb.princeton.edu/dante/pdp/.

Proctor, Robert E. 1998. *Defining the Humanities: How Rediscovering a Tradition Can Improve Our Schools, with a Curriculum for Today's Students*. Bloomington: Indiana University Press.

Puma, Richard Daniel De. 1988. *Roman Portraits*. Iowa City: The Museum.

Quarta, Daniela. 1985. "Sul *Candelaio* di Giordano Bruno." In *Il mago, il cosmo, il teatro degli astri: Saggi sulla letteratura esoterica del Rinascimento*, ed. Gianfranco Formichetti, 179–97. Rome: Bulzoni.

Quint, David. 1983. *Origin and Originality in Renaissance Literature: Versions of the Source*. New Haven, CT: Yale University Press.

———. 2000. "Courtier, Prince, Lady: The Design of the *Book of the Courtier*." *Italian Quarterly* 37: 185–95.

Quintilian. 1922. *The Institutio Oratoria of Quintilian*. Trans. H. E. Butler. 4 vols. London: W. Heinemann.

Quondam, Amedeo. 1981. "Dal 'formulario' al 'formulario': Cento anni di 'libri di lettere.'" In *Le "carte messaggiere": Retorica e modelli di comunicazione epistolare*, ed. A. Quondam, 13–156. Rome: Bulzoni.

———. 1983. "Varianti di Proteo: l'Accademico, il Segretario." In *Il segno barocco: Testo e metafora di una civiltà*, ed. Gigliola Nocera, 163–92. Rome: Bulzoni.

———. 1991. *Il naso di Laura: Lingua e poesia lirica nella tradizione del classicismo*. Modena: Franco Cosimo Panini.

———. 2000. *"Questo povero Cortegiano": Castiglione, il libro, la storia*. Rome: Bulzoni.

———. 2003. *Cavallo e cavaliere: L'armatura come secondo pelle del gentiluomo moderno*. Rome: Donzelli.

———. 2007a. *La conversazione: Un modello italiano*. Rome: Donzelli.

———. 2007b. *Tutti i colori del nero: Moda e cultura del gentiluomo nel Rinascimento*. Costabissara, Vicenza: A. Colla.

Rabil, Albert, Jr., ed. 1988. *Renaissance Humanism: Foundations, Forms, and Legacy*. 3 vols. Philadelphia: University of Pennsylvania Press.

Rajna, Pio. 1975. *Le fonti dell' "Orlando furioso."* Florence: Sansoni.

Ramat, Raffaello. 1953. *Il Guicciardini e la tragedia d'Italia*. Florence: Olschki.

Ranft, Patricia. 2006. *The Theology of Work: Peter Damian and the Medieval Religious Renewal Movement*. New York: Palgrave Macmillan.

Ray, Meredith. 2009. *Writing Gender in Women's Letter Collections of the Italian Renaissance*. Toronto: University of Toronto Press.

Rebhorn, Wayne A. 1978. *Courtly Performances: Masking and Festivity in Castiglione's "Book of the Courtier."* Detroit: Wayne State University Press.

———. 1988. *Foxes and Lions: Machiavelli's Confidence Men*. Ithaca, NY: Cornell University Press.

———. 1995. *The Emperor of Men's Minds: Literature and the Renaissance Discourse of Rhetoric*. Ithaca, NY: Cornell University Press.

———. 2000. *Renaissance Debates on Rhetoric*. Ithaca, NY: Cornell University Press.

Reiss, Timothy. 2003. *Mirages of the Selve: Patterns of Personhood in Ancient and Early Modern Europe*. Stanford, CA: Stanford University Press.

Renaut, Alain. 1997. *The Era of the Individual: A Contribution to a History of Subjectivity.* Trans. M. B. DeBevoise and Franklin Philip. Foreword by Alexander Nehamas. Princeton, NJ: Princeton University Press.

Reynolds, Reginald. 1950. *Beards: An Omnium Gatherum.* London: Allen and Unwin.

Richard, Andrew. 1993. *Scripts and Scenarios: The Performance of Comedy in Renaissance Italy.* Cambridge: Cambridge University Press.

Richardson, Brian. 1998. "The Debates on Printing in Renaissance Italy." *La bibliofilìa* 100: 135–55.

———. 2004. "Print or Pen? Modes of Written Publication in Sixteenth-Century Italy." *Italian Studies* 59: 39–64.

Ridolfi, Carlo. 1984. *The Life of Tintoretto and of His Children Domenico and Marietta.* Trans. and intro. Catherine Enggass and Robert Enggass. University Park: Penn State University Press.

Ridolfi, Roberto. 1963. *The Life of Niccolò Machiavelli.* Trans. Cecil Grayson. Chicago: University of Chicago Press.

———. 1968. *The Life of Francesco Guicciardini.* Trans. Cecil Grayson. New York: Knopf.

Robin, Diana Maury. 2007. *Publishing Women: Salons, the Presses, and the Counter-Reformation in Sixteenth-Century Italy.* Chicago: University of Chicago Press.

Rocke, Michael. 1996. *Forbidden Friendships: Homosexuality and Male Culture in Renaissance Florence.* New York: Oxford University Press.

Romano, Dennis. 1996. *Housecraft and Statecraft: Domestic Service in Renaissance Venice, 1400–1600.* Baltimore: Johns Hopkins University Press.

Roochnik, David. 1994. "Is Rhetoric an Art?" *Rhetorica* 12: 127–54.

———. 1996. *Of Art and Wisdom: Plato's Understanding of Techne.* University Park: Penn State University Press.

Rosand, David. 1997. *Painting in Sixteenth-Century Venice: Titian, Veronese, Tintoretto.* Rev. ed. Cambridge: Cambridge University Press.

Rosenthal, Margaret. 1992. *The Honest Courtesan: Veronica Franco, Citizen and Writer in Sixteenth-Century Venice.* Chicago: University of Chicago Press.

Roskill, Mark W. 1968. *Dolce's Aretino and Venetian Art Theory of the Cinquecento.* New York: New York University Press.

Ross, Sarah Gwyneth. 2009. *The Birth of Feminism: Woman as Intellect in Renaissance Italy and England.* Cambridge, MA: Harvard University Press.

Rossi, Paolo. 1970. *Philosophy, Technology, and the Arts in the Early Modern Era.* Ed. Benjamin Nelson. Trans. Salvator Attanasio. New York: Harper & Row.

Rossi, Paolo L. 1994. "The Writer and the Man: Real Crimes and Mitigating Circumstances—il caso Cellini." In *Crime, Society, and the Law in Renaissance Italy*, ed. K. Lowe and T. Dean, 157–83. Cambridge: Cambridge University Press.

———. 1998. "*Sprezzatura*, Patronage and Fate: Benvenuto Cellini and the World of Words." In *Vasari's Florence*, ed. P. Jacks, 55–69. Cambridge: Cambridge University Press.

———. 2004. "Parrem uno, e pur saremo dua: The Genesis and Fate of Benvenuto Cellini's *Trattati*." In *Benvenuto Cellini: Sculptor, Goldsmith, Writer,* ed. Margaret A. Gallucci and Paolo L. Rossi, 171–98. Cambridge: Cambridge University Press.

Rota, Arianna Arisi, ed. 2009. *Formare alle professioni: Diplomatici e politici.* Milan: FrancoAngeli.

Rowe, Katherine. 1997. "'God's handy worke': Divine Complicity and the Anatomist's Touch." In *The Body in Parts: Fantasies of Corporeality in Early Modern Europe*, ed. David Hillman and Carla Mazzio, 285–309. London: Routledge.

Rubenstein, Nicolai. 1956. "The Beginnings of Niccolò Machiavelli's Career in the Florentine Chancery." *Italian Studies* 11: 72–91.

Rubin, Patricia Lee. 1995. *Giorgio Vasari: Art and History*. New Haven, CT: Yale University Press.

Ruffini, Marco. 2011. *Art Without an Author: Vasari's "Lives" and Michelangelo's Death*. New York: Fordham University Press.

Ruggiero, Guido. 1985. *The Boundaries of Eros: Sex, Crime, and Sexuality in Renaissance Venice*. New York: Oxford University Press.

———. 2006. "Mean Streets, Familiar Streets, or the Fat Woodcarver and the Masculine Spaces of Renaissance Florence." In *Renaissance Florence: A Social History*, ed. Roger J. Crum and John T. Paoletti, 295–310. Cambridge: Cambridge University Press.

———. 2007. *Machiavelli in Love: Sex, Self, and Society in the Italian Renaissance*. Baltimore: Johns Hopkins University Press.

Rushin, Steve. 2013. "The Hirsute of Happiness." *Sports Illustrated*, September 30, pp. 42–48.

Ryan, Lawrence V. 1972. "Book IV of Castiglione's *Courtier*: Climax or Afterthought." *Studies in the Renaissance* 19: 156–79.

Sabellico, Marc'Antonio. 1985. *Del sito di Venezia città (1502)*. Ed. G. Meneghetti. Venice: Libreria Filippi.

Saccone, Eduardo. 1978. "Trattato e ritratto: L'introduzione del *Cortegiano*." *Modern Language Notes* 93: 1–21.

———. 1983. "Grazia, Sprezzatura, and Affettazione in the *Courtier*." In *Castiglione: The Ideal and the Real in Renaissance Culture*, ed. Robert W. Hanning and David Rosand, 45–67. New Haven, CT: Yale University Press.

———. 1987. "The Portrait of the Courtier in Castiglione." *Italica* 64: 1–18.

Saiber, Arielle. 2005. *Giordano Bruno and the Geometry of Language*. Aldershot, UK: Ashgate.

Saint Benedict's Rule for Monasteries. 1948. Trans. Leonard J. Doyle. Collegeville, MN: Liturgical Press.

Sansovino, Francesco. 1564. *Del secretario*. Venice: Francesco Rampazetto.

———. 1581. *Venetia, citta nobilissima et singolare, descritta in XIIII. libri da M. Francesco Sansovino. Nella quale si contengono tutte le guerre passate, con l'attioni illustri di molti senatori. Le vite de i principi, & gli scrittori veneti del tempo loro. Le chiese, fabriche, edifici, & palazzi publichi, & privati. Le leggi, gli ordini, & gli usi antichi & moderni, con altre cose appresso notabili, & degne di memoria*. Venice: Appresso Iacopo Sansovino.

———. 1942. *L'avvocato e il segretario*. Ed. Piero Calamandrei. Florence: Le Monnier.

Sasso, Gennaro. 1984. *Per Francesco Guicciardini: Quattro studi*. Rome: Istituto Storico Italiano per il Medio Evo.

Satkowski, Leon George. 1993. *Giorgio Vasari: Architect and Courtier*. Princeton, NJ: Princeton University Press.

Sawday, Jonathan. 1995. *The Body Emblazoned: Dissection and the Human Body in Renaissance Culture*. London: Routledge.

Scapecchi, Piero. 2011. "Chi scrisse *Le vite* del Vasari: Riflessioni sulla *editio princeps* del 1550." *Letteratura e arte* 9: 153–59.

Scarano, Emanuella Lugnani. 1970. "Le redazioni dei *Ricordi* e la storia del pensiero guicciardiniano dal 1512 al 1530." *Giornale storico della letteratura italiana* 147: 183–259.

Schadewaldt, Wolfgang. 1979. "The Concepts of *Nature* and *Technique* According to the Greeks." *Research in Philosophy & Technology* 2: 159–71.

Schama, Simon. 1988. *The Embarrassment of Riches: An Interpretation of Dutch Culture in the Golden Age*. Berkeley: University of California Press.

Schiefsky, Mark J. 2007. "Art and Nature in Ancient Mechanics." In *The Artificial and the Natural: An Evolving Polarity*, ed. Bernadette Bensaude-Vincent and William R. Newman, 67–108. Cambridge, MA: MIT Press.

Seigel, Jerrold E. 1968. *Rhetoric and Philosophy in Renaissance Humanism: The Union of Eloquence and Wisdom, Petrarch to Valla*. Princeton, NJ: Princeton University Press.

———. 2005. *The Idea of the Self: Thought and Experience in Western Europe Since the Seventeenth Century*. Cambridge: Cambridge University Press.

Shearman, John. 1967. *Mannerism*. Harmondsworth: Penguin.

———. 1992. *Only Connect: Art and the Spectator in the Italian Renaissance*. Princeton, NJ: Princeton University Press.

Shemek, Deanna. 1998. *Ladies Errant: Wayward Women and Social Order in Early Modern Italy*. Durham, NC: Duke University Press.

———. Forthcoming. *"In Continuous Expectation": Isabella d'Este's Epistolary Dominion*.

Shiner, Larry E. 2001. *The Invention of Art: A Cultural History*. Chicago: University of Chicago Press.

Siegel, Rudolph E. 1970. *Galen on Sense Perception: His Doctrines, Observations and Experiments on Vision, Hearing, Smell, Taste, Touch and Pain, and Their Historical Sources*. Basel: Karger.

Simon, Robert B. 1983. "Bronzino's Portrait of Cosimo I in Armour." *Burlington Magazine* 125: 527–39.

———. 1985. "Bronzino's *Cosimo I de' Medici as Orpheus*." *Philadelphia Museum of Art Bulletin* 81: 16–27.

Simonetta, Marcello. 2004. *Rinascimento segreto: Il mondo del segretario da Petrarca a Machiavelli*. Milan: FrancoAngeli.

Simons, Patricia. 1994. "Alert and Erect: Masculinity in Some Italian Renaissance Portraits of Fathers and Sons." In *Gender Rhetorics: Postures of Dominance and Submission in History*, ed. Richard C. Trexler, 162–86. Binghamton, NY: Medieval & Renaissance Texts & Studies.

———. 1995. "Portraiture, Portrayal and Idealization: Ambiguous Individualism in Representations of Renaissance Women." In *Language and Images of Renaissance Italy*, ed. Alison Brown, 263–311. Oxford: Clarendon Press.

———. 1997. "Homosociality and Erotics in Italian Renaissance Portraiture." In *Portraiture: Facing the Subject*, ed. Joanna Woodall, 29–51. Manchester: Manchester University Press.

———. 2008. "Hercules in Italian Renaissance Art: Masculine Labour and Homoerotic Libido." *Art History* 31: 632–64.

———. 2009. "Manliness and the Visual Semiotics of Bodily Fluids in Early Modern Culture." *Journal of Medieval and Early Modern Studies* 39: 331–73.

———. 2011. *The Sex of Men in Premodern Europe: A Cultural History*. Cambridge: Cambridge University Press.

Siraisi, Nancy G. 1990. *Medieval & Early Renaissance Medicine: An Introduction to Knowledge and Practice*. Chicago: University of Chicago Press.

———. 1994a. "How to Write a Latin Book on Surgery: Organizing Principles and Authorial Devices in Guglielmo da Saliceto and Dino del Garbo." In *Practical Medicine from Salerno to the Black Death*, ed. Luis García-Ballester, Roger French, Jon Arrizabalaga, and Andrew Cunningham, 88–109. Cambridge: Cambridge University Press.

———. 1994b. "Vesalius and Human Diversity in *De humani corporis fabrica*." *Journal of the Warburg and Courtauld Institutes* 57: 60–88.

Skinner, Quentin. 1981. *Machiavelli*. New York: Hill and Wang.

Smith, Pamela H. 2009. "Science on the Move: Recent Trends in the History of Early Modern Science." *Renaissance Quarterly* 62: 345–75.

Smith, Virginia. 2006. *Clean: A History of Personal Hygiene and Purity.* Oxford: Oxford University Press.

Snyder, Jon R. 2009. *Dissimulation and the Culture of Secrecy in Early Modern Europe.* Berkeley: University of California Press.

Solerti, Angelo. 1895. *Vita di Torquato Tasso.* 2 vols. Turin: Loescher.

Solmsen, Friedrich. 1963. "Nature as Craftsman in Greek Thought." *Journal of the History of Ideas* 24: 473–96.

Sottong, Heather R. 2011. "Excess and Antagonism in Giordano Bruno's *Il candelaio.*" *Carte italiane* 7: 1–13.

Sowell, Madison U. 1991. "Dante's Nose and Publius Ovidius Naso: A Gloss on *Inferno* 25.45." In *Dante and Ovid: Essays in Intertextuality*, ed. M. U. Sowell, 35–49. Binghamton, NY: Medieval & Renaissance Texts & Studies.

Springer, Carolyn. 2010. *Armour and Masculinity in the Italian Renaissance.* Toronto: University of Toronto Press.

Squarotti, Giorgio Bàrberi. 1958. "L'esperienza stilistica del Bruno fra Rinascimento e Barocco." In *La critica stilistica e il barocco letterario: Atti del secondo congresso internazionale di studi italiani*, ed. Ettore Caccia, 154–69. Florence: Le Monnier.

———. 1960. "Per una descrizione e interpretazione della poetica di Giordano Bruno." *Studi secenteschi* 1: 39–59.

Stack, Joan. 2000. "Artists into Heroes: The Commemoration of Artists in the Art of Vasari." In *Fashioning Identities in Renaissance Art*, ed. Mary Rogers, 163–75. Aldershot, UK: Ashgate.

Stahl, William Harris, and Richard Johnson. 1971. *Martianus Capella and the Seven Liberal Arts.* Vol. 1. New York: Columbia University Press.

Stallybrass, Peter. 1992. "Shakespeare, the Individual, and the Text." In *Cultural Studies*, ed. Lawrence Grossberg, Cary Nelson, and Paula A. Treichler, 593–609. New York: Routledge.

Starn, Randolph. 2002. "The Early Modern Muddle." *Journal of Early Modern History* 6: 296–307.

Sternagel, Peter. 1966. *Die artes mechanicae im Mittelalter.* Kallmunz: Lassleben.

Stewart, Peter. 2008. *The Social History of Roman Art.* Cambridge: Cambridge University Press.

Struever, Nancy. 1970. *The Language of History in the Renaissance: Rhetoric and Historical Consciousness in Florentine Humanism.* Princeton, NJ: Princeton University Press.

———. 1992. *Theory as Practice: Ethical Inquiry in the Renaissance.* Chicago: University of Chicago Press.

Summers, David. 1981. *Michelangelo and the Language of Art.* Princeton, NJ: Princeton University Press.

Swoboda, Karl M. 1982. *Tintoretto: Ikonographische und Stilistiche Untersuchungen.* Vienna: Schroll.

Tafur, Pero. 1926. *Pero Tafur: Travels and Adventures, 1435–1439.* Ed., trans., and intro. Malcolm Letts. London: Routledge.

Tasso, Torquato. 1587. *Il secretario del S. Torquato Tasso. Diviso in due parti. Con alcune rime nove del medesimo.* Ferrara: Vittorio Baldini.

———. 1875. *Le prose diverse.* Ed. Cesare Guasti. Vol. 2. Florence: Le Monnier.

Taylor, Charles. 1989. *Sources of the Self: The Making of Modern Identity.* Cambridge, MA: Harvard University Press.

Theophilus. 1961. *De diversis artibus*. Ed. and trans. C. R. Dodwel. New York: Oxford University Press.

Thomas, Anabel. 1995. *The Painter's Practice in Renaissance Tuscany*. Cambridge: Cambridge University Press.

———. 2006. "The Workshop as the Space of Collaborative Artistic Production." In *Renaissance Florence: A Social History*, ed. Roger J. Crum and John T. Paoletti, 415–30. Cambridge: Cambridge University Press.

Thomas, Keith. 2009. *The Ends of Life: Roads to Fulfilment in Early Modern England*. Oxford: Oxford University Press.

Thornton, Dora. 1997. *The Scholar in His Study: Ownership and Experience in Renaissance Italy*. New Haven, CT: Yale University Press.

Traina, Giusto. 1994. *La tecnica in Grecia e a Roma*. Rome: Laterza.

Tribby, Jay. 1991. "Cooking (with) Clio and Cleo: Eloquence and Experiment in Seventeenth-Century Florence." *Journal of the History of Ideas* 52: 417–39.

———. 1992a. "Body/Building: Living the Museum Life in Early Modern Europe." *Rhetorica* 10: 139–63.

———. 1992b. "Of Conversational Dispositions and the Saggi's Proem." In *Documentary Culture: Florence and Rome from Grand-Duke Ferdinand I to Pope Alexander VII*, ed. Elizabeth Cropper, Giovanna Perini, and Francesco Solinas, 379–90. Bologna: Nuova Alfa Editoriale.

Trinkaus, Charles Edward. 1970. *In Our Image and Likeness: Humanity and Divinity in Italian Humanist Thought*. 2 vols. Chicago: University of Chicago Press.

The Trotula: A Medieval Compendium of Women's Medicine. 2001. Ed. and trans. Monica H. Green. Philadelphia: University of Pennsylvania Press.

Tucci, Ugo. 1968. "Biringuccio, Vannoccio." In *Dizionario biografico degli italiani*, 10: 625–31. Rome: Istituto della Enciclopedia Italiana.

Tylus, Jane. 1993. *Writing and Vulnerability in the Late Renaissance*. Stanford, CA: Stanford University Press.

———. 2004. "Cellini, Michelangelo, and the Myth of Inimitability." In *Benvenuto Cellini: Sculptor, Goldsmith, Writer*, ed. Margaret A. Gallucci and Paolo L. Rossi, 7–25. Cambridge: Cambridge University Press.

Ullmann, Walter. 1966. *The Individual and Society in the Middle Ages*. Baltimore: Johns Hopkins University Press.

Valerius Maximus. 2000. *Memorable Doings and Sayings*. Ed. and trans. D. R. Shackleton Bailey. 2 vols. Cambridge, MA: Harvard University Press.

van Bavel, Bas, and Oscar Gelderblom. 2009. "The Economic Origins of Cleanliness in the Dutch Golden Age." *Past and Present* 205: 41–69.

Van Den Hoven, Birgit. 1996. *Work in Ancient and Medieval Thought: Ancient Philosophers, Medieval Monks and Theologians and Their Concept of Work, Occupations and Technology*. Amsterdam: J. C. Gieben.

Van Engen, John. 1980. "Theophilus Presbyter and Rupert of Deutz: The Manual Arts and Benedictine Theology in the Early Twelfth Century." *Viator* 11: 147–63.

Vannozzi, Bonifatio. 1613. *Della supellettile degli avvertimenti politici, morali, et christiani*. Vol. 3. Bologna: Heredi di Giovanni Rossi

Vasari, Giorgio. 1991. *Le vite dei più eccellenti pittori, scultori, e architetti*. Florence: Newton.

———. 1996. *Lives of the Painters, Sculptors and Architects*. Trans. Gaston Du C. De Vere. Intro. David Ekserdjia. New York: Knopf.

Vasoli, Cesare. 1990. "Le discipline e il sistema del sapere." In *Sapere e/è potere: Discipline, dispute e professioni nell'università medievale e moderna, il caso bolognese a confronto*, ed. Andrea Cristiani, vol. 2, 11–36. Bologna: Istituto per la Storia di Bologna.

Vegetti, Mario. 2010. "Le origini dell'insegnamento medico." In *Formare alle professioni: Figure di sanità*, ed. Monica Ferrari and Paolo Mazzarello, 23–35. Milan: FrancoAngeli.

Vernant, Jean-Pierre. 1983. *Myth and Thought Among the Greeks*. London: Routledge and Kegan Paul.

Vickers, Brian. 1988. *In Defence of Rhetoric*. Oxford: Clarendon Press.

———. 1990. "Leisure and Idleness in the Renaissance: The Ambivalence of Otium." *Renaissance Studies* 4: 1–37, 107–54.

Vickers, Nancy J. 1982. "Diana Described." In *Writing and Sexual Difference*, ed. Elizabeth Abel, 95–109. Chicago: University of Chicago Press.

Vigarello, Georges. 1985. *Le propre et le sale: L'hygiène du corps depuis le Moyen Age*. Paris: Seuil.

Vivo, Filippo de. 2007. *Information and Communication in Venice: Rethinking Early Modern Politics*. Oxford: Oxford University Press.

Vocabolario degli Accademici della Crusca. http://www.lessicografia.it/index.jsp.

von Staden, Heinrich. 2007. "Physis and Technē in Greek Medicine." In *The Artificial and the Natural: An Evolving Polarity*, ed. Bernadette Bensaude-Vincent and William R. Newman, 21–50. Cambridge, MA: MIT Press.

Vout, Caroline. 2006. "Rethinking Hadrian's Hellenism." In *Rethinking Revolutions Through Ancient Greece*, ed. Simon Goldhill and Robin Osborne, 96–123. Cambridge: Cambridge University Press.

Waddington, Raymond B. 2004. *Aretino's Satyr: Sexuality, Satire, and Self-Projection in Sixteenth-Century Literature and Art*. Toronto: University of Toronto Press.

Waldman, Louis A. 1999. "Puglio and Jacopo di Filippo 'Fornaccio': Two Unrecorded Paintings of 1524." *Notes in the History of Art* 18: 25–27.

Ward, John O. 1978. "From Antiquity to the Renaissance: Glosses and Commentaries on Cicero's *Rhetorica*." In *Medieval Eloquence: Studies in the Theory and Practice of Medieval Rhetoric*, ed. James J. Murphy, 25–67. Berkeley: University of California Press.

———. 1983. "Renaissance Commentaries on Ciceronian Rhetoric." In *Renaissance Eloquence: Studies in the Theory and Practice of Renaissance Rhetoric*, ed. James J. Murphy, 126–73. Berkeley: University of California Press.

———. 1995. *Ciceronian Rhetoric in Treatise, Scholion, and Commentary*. Turnhout: Brepols.

Warnke, Martin. 1993. *The Court Artist: On the Ancestry of the Modern Artist*. Trans. David McLintock. Cambridge: Cambridge University Press.

Weaver, Elissa B. 2002. *Convent Theatre in Early Modern Italy: Spiritual Fun and Learning for Women*. Cambridge: Cambridge University Press.

Weinberg, Bernard. 1963. *A History of Literary Criticism in the Italian Renaissance*. 2 vols. Chicago: University of Chicago Press.

Weinstein, Donald. 2000. *The Captain's Concubine: Love, Honor, and Violence in Renaissance Tuscany*. Baltimore: Johns Hopkins University Press.

Weintraub, Karl Joachim. 1978. *The Value of the Individual: Self and Circumstance in Autobiography*. Chicago: University of Chicago Press.

Weisheipl, James A. 1965. "Classification of the Sciences in Medieval Thought." *Mediaeval Studies* 27: 54–90.

Weissman, Ronald F. E. 1989. "The Importance of Being Ambiguous: Social Relations, Individualism, and Identity in Renaissance Florence." In *Urban Life in the Renaissance*, ed. Susan Zimmerman and Ronald F. E. Weissman, 269–80. Newark, NJ: University of Delaware Press.

Welch, Evelyn. 2005. *Shopping in the Renaissance: Consumer Cultures in Italy, 1400–1600*. New Haven, CT: Yale University Press.

———. 2008. "Art on the Edge: Hair and Hands in Renaissance Italy." *Renaissance Studies* 23: 241–68.

———. 2009. "Signs of Faith: The Political and Social Identity of Hair in Renaissance Italy." In *La fiducia secondo i linguaggi del potere,* ed. Paolo Prodi, 371–86. Bologna: Il Mulino.

Welles, C. Bradford. 1967. "Hesiod's Attitude Toward Labor." *Greek, Roman, and Byzantine Studies* 8: 5–23.

Whigham, Frank. 1984. *Ambition and Privilege: The Social Tropes of Elizabethan Courtesy Theory.* Berkeley: University of California Press.

White, Hayden. 1978. *Tropics of Discourse: Essays in Cultural Criticism.* Baltimore: Johns Hopkins University Press.

———. 1987. *The Content of the Form: Narrative Discourse and Historical Representation.* Baltimore: Johns Hopkins University Press.

White, Lynn, Jr. 1962. *Medieval Technology and Social Change.* Oxford: Clarendon Press.

———. 1963. "What Accelerated Technological Progress in the Western Middle Ages?" In *Scientific Change: Historical Studies in the Intellectual, Social, and Technical Conditions for Scientific Discovery and Technical Invention, from Antiquity to the Present,* ed. A. C. Crombie, 272– 314. New York: Basic Books.

———. 1968. *Dynamo and Virgin Reconsidered: Essays in the Dynamism of Western Culture.* Cambridge, MA: MIT Press.

———. 1969. *The Expansion of Technology, 500–1500.* London: Fontana Books.

———. 1978. *Medieval Religion and Technology: Collected Essays.* Berkeley: University of California Press.

Whitney, Elspeth. 1990. *Paradise Restored: The Mechanical Arts from Antiquity Through the Thirteenth Century.* Philadelphia: Transactions of the American Philosophical Society.

Williams, Raymond. 1983. *Keywords: A Vocabulary of Culture and Society.* London: Fontana Press.

Williams, Robert. 1997. *Art, Theory, and Culture in Sixteenth-Century Italy: From Techne to Metatechne.* Cambridge: Cambridge University Press.

Witt, Ronald G. 2000. *"In the Footsteps of the Ancients": The Origins of Humanism from Lovato to Bruni.* Leiden: Brill.

Wittkower, Rudolf. 1961. "Individualism in Art and Artists: A Renaissance Problem." *Journal of the History of Ideas* 22: 291–302.

Wittkower, Rudolf, and Margot Wittkower. 1963. *Born Under Saturn: The Character and Conduct of Artists: A Documented History from Antiquity to the French Revolution.* New York: Random House.

Wojciehowski, Hannah. 2011. *Group Identity in the Renaissance World.* Cambridge: Cambridge University Press.

Woodhouse, John Robert. 1978. *Baldesar Castiglione: A Reassessment of "The Courtier."* Edinburgh: Edinburgh University Press.

Woodruff, Paul. 1990. "Plato's Early Theory of Knowledge." In *Epistemology,* ed. Stephen Everson, 60–84. Cambridge: Cambridge University Press.

Woods-Marsden, Joanna. 1987. " 'Ritratto al Naturale': Questions of Realism and Idealism in Early Renaissance Portraits." *Art Journal* 46: 209–16.

———. 1998. *Renaissance Self-Portraiture: The Visual Construction of Identity and the Social Status of the Artist.* New Haven, CT: Yale University Press.

Wright, Lawrence. 1960. *Clean and Decent: The Fascinating History of the Bathroom and the Water Closet, and of Sundry Habits.* New York: Viking Press.

Xenophon. 1965. *Memorabilia and Oeconomicus.* Trans. E. C. Marchant. Cambridge, MA: Harvard University Press.

———. 1994. *Oeconomicus: A Social and Historical Commentary*. Trans. and commentary by Sarah B. Pomeroy. Oxford: Clarendon Press.

Zatti, Sergio. 1983. *L'uniforme cristiano e il multiforme pagano: Saggio sulla "Gerusalmme liberata."* Milan: Il Saggiatore.

———. 2013. "Lo scorpione e la salamandra: Sulla *Vita* di Benvenuto Cellini." In *Encyclopaedia Mundi: Studi di letteratura italiana in onore di Giuseppe Mazzotta*, ed. Stefano Ugo Baldassarri and Alessandro Polcri, 173–94. Florence: Le Lettere.

Zinano, Gabriele. 1625. *Il segretario*. Venice: Giovanni Guerigli.

Zucchi, Bartolomeo. 1600. *L'idea del segretario*. Venice: Compagnia Minima.

Zuccolin, Gabriella. 2010. "I chirurghi del Trecento: Formazione dottrinale e professionale." In *Formare alle professioni: Figure di sanità*, ed. Monica Ferrari and Paolo Mazzarello, 58–77. Milan: FrancoAngeli.

Zucker, Mark J. 1977. "Raphael and the Beard of Pope Julius II." *Art Bulletin* 59: 524–33.

INDEX

❧

Page numbers in italics indicate images.

ACKNOWLEDGMENTS

In the process of examining the notion of the individual in Renaissance Italy, this book reflects on a variety of other topics that I have been thinking about for some time now: the marvelous, wonder, professionalism, work, humanism, cleanliness, propriety, personalities, and masculinities. As a result it owes a great deal to many people—too many to recognize adequately in two acknowledgments paragraphs—since it effectively retraces passages of my own career as I became interested in those topics over time, beginning in one or two instances as far back as graduate school, which strikes me as a very long time ago, especially as I advance all the more grudgingly into middle age but serenely enough, I suppose, into grandfatherhood (Hi, Annabelle!). But in writing this book, which has taken me roughly a dozen years off and on to put together into final form, I am especially grateful to Alison Frazier, Tom Pangle, Wayne A. Rebhorn, Andrew Riggsby, and Louis Waldman, whose comments have sometimes found themselves incorporated directly into my text, although, to be sure, all errors contained within it should always be considered my own. I also owe a great debt to Stefano U. Baldassarri, Evan Carton, John Clarke, Janet Cox-Rearick, Bill Eamon, Michael Gagarin, Brian Levack, and Jorie Woods, who at different stages in the writing of this book helped me refine my argument in crucial places. My thanks as well to the following people for their help and support along the way: Katie Arens, Kit Belgum, Daniela Bini, Carl Blyth, Erwin Cook, Sally Dickson, Andrew dell'Antonio, Ingrid Edlund-Berry, Ann Johns, Julia Hairston, Charlotte Harris, Neil Kamil, David Lines, Roberto Muratore, Wendy Nesmith, Martha Newman, Antonella Olson, Guy Raffa, Massimo Scalabrini, Deanna Shemek, Lin Shivers, Nancy Struever, Eva Struhal, Paul Sullivan, Katherine Swaller, and Paul Woodruff. I'd also feel remiss if I didn't express my gratitude belatedly toward a remarkable person who long ago drew me into literature and literary studies: the late poet, dramatist, journal writer, printer, and polyglot Claude Fredericks, whose unusual and voluminous writings are only now beginning to appear in print and have recently been acquired, at least in part, by the Getty Research Institute. Lastly, I owe a great deal to the recently departed Adriano Pignotti, who taught me much about what it means to be a Florentine, even though I knew I would never be able to be one, much less authentically sound like one.

Much of Chapters 2, 5, and 6 appeared, respectively, in *Rinascimento* 43 (2003): 333–53; *The Body in Early Modern Italy*, ed. Julia L. Hairston and Walter Stephens (Baltimore: Johns Hopkins University Press, 2010), 176–94, 347–49; and the *Journal of Medieval and Early Modern Studies* 40 (2010): 325–46. A short version of Chapter 1 was presented at Indiana University, Renaissance Studies Program, First Symposium of the Series "*Techné*: Intersections of Theory and Practice in Renaissance Culture" in 2012. A version of Chapter 2 was presented at the conference "Negotiated Aesthetics: Work, Art, and Identity in the Long Fifteenth Century" at the University of Chicago in 2003. A tiny portion of Chapter 3, now so revised as to be barely recognizable from its original form, was presented at the conference "Interpreters of Culture" in Koper, Slovenia, in 2007 and then in a completely reconstituted format at the Renaissance Society of America conference in 2010. A small portion of Chapter 5 was presented at the Renaissance Society of America conference in 2007 and then at a conference honoring Eduardo Saccone at the University of Cork, Ireland, in 2008. Chapters 5 and 6 benefited from the lively discussions of the members of the Humanities Institute 2008 faculty seminar devoted to the capacious topic of "the human and its others." My thanks as well to the Gladys Krieble Delmas Foundation, which provided me with the opportunity to work in the Marciana Library in Venice for a month, during which time I also found myself tracking down, with my daughter Simone, all of Tintoretto's paintings in the city, or at least all that we were permitted to see. I am especially grateful to The University of Texas at Austin for furnishing me with relief from my teaching duties for an entire academic year in order to complete the researching and writing of the book, as well as the time needed to prepare the final manuscript for publication. And I thank Randy Diehl and Richard Flores, the Dean and the Senior Associate Dean of the College of Liberal Arts, for generously providing me with accumulated, excess funds in my professorship to help defray the cost of paying for the images and the rights to reproduce them, along with Jamie Southerland for devising a way to make this somehow work out financially. This book has been published, I am only too happy to acknowledge, with generous assistance from the Gladys Krieble Delmas Foundation and The President's Office at The University of Texas at Austin. I also thank two remarkable readers and historians, James R. Farr and John Jeffries Martin, for their incisive and encouraging reports and for allowing me, a trained literary scholar, to poach on their field, without finding myself banished from their midst for trespassing upon it. Finally, I thank Jerry Singerman for taking an immediate and sustaining interest in this book, for shepherding it through the press (with the assistance of Caroline Hayes, Erica Ginsburg, Jennifer Backer, and Holly Knowles), and for including it in his medieval and Renaissance list at the University of Pennsylvania Press.